Suiting Themselves

Dr Sharon Beder has written 6 previous books and around 140 articles, book chapters and conference papers, as well as educational monographs, consultancy reports and teaching resources. Her research has focused on how power relationships are maintained and challenged, particularly by corporations and professions. Her earlier books, some of which have been translated into other languages, are:

Power Play: The Fight for Control of the World's Electricity
Scribe, Melbourne and the New Press, New York (2003)

Selling the Work Ethic: From Puritan Pulpit to Corporate PR
Zed Books, London and Scribe, Melbourne (2000)

Global Spin: The Corporate Assault on Environmentalism
Green Books, Devon, UK and Scribe, Melbourne (1997 and 2002)

The New Engineer
Macmillan, Melbourne (1998)

The Nature of Sustainable Development
Scribe, Melbourne (1996)

Toxic Fish and Sewer Surfing
Allen & Unwin, Sydney (1989)

Dr Beder is a qualified professional engineer and worked in this field until a career shift into researching and teaching environmental politics. She has held a number of appointments at Australian universities over the past two decades – most recently as professor in the School of Social Sciences, Media and Communication at the University of Wollongong in Australia.

Her website is http://homepage.mac.com/herinst/sbeder/home.html

Suiting Themselves

How Corporations Drive the Global Agenda

Sharon Beder

from Routledge

First published by Earthscan in the UK and USA in 2006

For a full list of publications please contact:

Earthscan
2 Park Square, Milton Park, Abingdon, Oxfordshire OX14 4RN
711 Third Avenue, New York, NY 10017

Earthscan is an imprint of the Taylor & Francis Group, an informa business

First issued in paperback 2018

Notices
Practitioners and researchers must always rely on their own experience and knowledge in evaluating and using any information, methods, compounds, or experiments described herein. In using such information or methods they should be mindful of their own safety and the safety of others, including parties for whom they have a professional responsibility.

Product or corporate names may be trademarks or registered trademarks, and are used only for identification and explanation without intent to infringe.

ISBN-13: 978-1-84407-331-3 (hbk)
ISBN-13: 978-1-138-38011-0 (pbk)

Typesetting by JS Typesetting Ltd, Porthcawl, Mid Glamorgan
Cover design by Andrew Corbett

A catalogue record for this book is available from the British Library

Library of Congress Cataloging-in-Publication Data

Beder, Sharon.
    Suiting Themselves: how corporations drive the global agenda / Sharon Beder.
        p. cm.
    Includes bibliographical references and index.
    ISBN-13: 978-1-84407-331-3
    ISBN-10: 1-84407-331-9
    1. Industrial policy. 2. Corporations—Political activity. 3. Business and politics.
I. Title.
    HD3611.B42 2005
    322'.3—dc22
2005029039

Contents

List of Boxes, Figures and Tables

BOXES

FIGURES

Tables

List of Acronyms and Abbreviations

AAFTAC   American–Australian Free Trade Agreement Coalition
ABC   Association of Builders and Contractors (US)
ACCI   Australian Chamber of Commerce and Industry
ACTPN   Advisory Committee on Trade Policy and Negotiations (US)
ACTU   Australian Council of Trade Unions
ADB   Asian Development Bank
AEI   American Enterprise Institute
AIG   American International Group
ALP   Australian Labor Party
AmEx   American Express
ANC   African National Congress
APEC   Asia-Pacific Economic Cooperation
ARC   Australian Research Council
ASEAN   Association of Southeast Asian Nations
ASI   Adam Smith Institute (UK)
AusAID   Australian Government Overseas Aid Programme
BCA   Business Council of Australia
BCC   British Chambers of Commerce
BDI   Association of German Industries
BI   British Invisibles
BIAC   Business and Industry Advisory Council (of the OECD)
BJP   Bharatiya Janata party (India)
BRT   Business Roundtable (US)
CAI   Confederation of Australian Industry
CBI   Confederation of British Industry
CCPR   International Covenant on Civil and Political Rights
CED   Committee for Economic Development (US)
CEDA   Committee for Economic Development of Australia
CEO   chief executive officer
CESCR   International Covenant on Economic, Social and Cultural Rights
CFR   Council on Foreign Relations (US)
CGA   Centre for the Global Agenda
CIA   Central Intelligence Agency (US)

CIS	Centre for Independent Studies (Australia)
COW	Committee of the Whole
CPS	Centre for Policy Studies (UK)
CPSC	Consumer Product Safety Commission (US)
CSI	Coalition of Service Industries (US)
CWT	Consumers for World Trade (US)
DFID	Department for International Development (UK)
DTI	Department of Trade and Industry (UK)
EAC	Economic Advisory Council (UK)
EC	European Commission
ECAT	Emergency Committee for American Trade
EdF	Electricité de France
EPA	Environmental Protection Agency (US)
EPC	European Policy Centre
EPG	Eminent Persons Group
ERT	European Round Table of Industrialists
ESF	European Services Forum
EU	European Union
FAO	United Nations Food and Agriculture Organization
FBI	US Federal Bureau of Investigation
FBI (UK)	Federation of British Industries
FCO	Foreign and Commonwealth Office (UK)
FDI	foreign direct investment
FLG	Financial Leaders Group (UK)
FSA	Financial Services Agreement
FSA (UK)	Financial Services Authority (UK)
FTAA	Free Trade Area of the Americas
G7	Group of 7 industrialized nations: Canada, France, Germany, Italy, Japan, the UK and the US
G8	Group of 8 industrialized nations: Canada, France, Germany, Italy, Japan, Russia, the UK and the US
G10	Group of 10 industrialized nations: India, Brazil, Argentina, Cuba, Egypt, Nicaragua, Nigeria, Peru, Tanzania and Yugoslavia
GATS	General Agreement on Trade in Services
GATT	General Agreement on Tariffs and Trade
GDP	gross domestic product
GE	General Electric (US)
GNP	gross national product
GSN	Global Services Network
IBRD	International Bank for Reconstruction and Development (part of World Bank)
ICC	International Chamber of Commerce
ICT	information and communication technology

IDB	Inter-American Development Bank
IEA	Institute of Economic Affairs (UK)
IFSL	International Financial Services, London
IIE	Institute for International Economics (US)
ILO	International Labour Organization
IMF	International Monetary Fund
IPA	Institute of Public Affairs (Australia)
IPC	Intellectual Property Committee
IPP	independent power producer
ISAC	Industry Sector Advisory Committee
ITO	International Trade Organization
LLSG	Labor Law Study Group (US)
LOTIS	Liberalisation of Trade in Services Committee (UK)
MAI	Multilateral Agreement on Investment
MDB	multilateral development bank
MP	member of parliament
MTBE	methyl tertiary-butyl ether (fuel additive)
MTN	Multilateral Trade Negotiations
MWh	megawatt hour (of electricity)
NAFTA	North American Free Trade Agreement
NAM	National Association of Manufacturers (US)
NAMA	Non-Agricultural Market Access group
NCF	National Civic Federation (US)
NEDC	National Economic Development Council (UK)
NFTC	National Foreign Trade Council (US)
NGO	non-governmental organization
NPR	national public radio
NSW	New South Wales (Australia)
NZ	New Zealand
OECD	Organisation for Economic Co-operation and Development
OPIC	Overseas Private Investment Corporation
OSHA	Occupational Safety and Health Administration (US)
PCRP	pro-competitive regulatory principle
PPA	Power Purchase Agreement
PPM	processes and production methods
PPP	public–private partnership
PR	public relations
PwC	PriceWaterhouse Coopers
R&D	research and development
SOS	Save Our Sovereignty campaign
SUNS	*South–North Development Monitor*
TABD	TransAtlantic Business Dialogue
TB	tuberculosis

TBG	The Brock Group
TDO	Trade: Discover the Opportunity (US)
TNC	transnational corporation
TNT	Thomas Nationwide Transport
TRIMS	Trade-Related Investment Measures
TRIPS	Trade-Related aspects of Intellectual Property Rights
UK	United Kingdom
UN	United Nations
UNCTAD	United Nations Conference on Trade and Development
UNDP	United Nations Development Programme
UNICE	Union of Industrial and Employers' Confederations of Europe (Union des Industries de la Communauté Européenne)
UPS	United Parcel Service
US	United States
USAID	US Agency for International Development
USCIB	US Council for International Business
USIC	US Industrial Council
USTR	US Trade Representative
US Trade	US Alliance for Trade Expansion
UWUA	Utility Workers Union of America
WBCSD	World Business Council on Sustainable Development
WDM	World Development Movement
WEF	World Economic Forum
WIPO	World Intellectual Property Organization
WMX	Waste Management, Inc (US)
WTO	World Trade Organization

Acknowledgements

I would like to thank Richard Gosden, who advised me, encouraged me and commented on draft chapters during the writing of this book. I would also like to thank Damien Cahill for his help in researching Chapter 3, Truda Gray for her help in researching Chapter 4, Darren Puscas for his help in researching Chapter 7, and Jim Green for his help in researching and writing Chapter 9. The research for this book was aided by an Australian Research Council (ARC) grant.

1

A Corporate Class

conspire, v.   Collude; act in unison or agreement and in secret towards a harmful, deceitful or illegal purpose.   WORDNET[1]

... lately, the term [conspiracy theory] *has been hijacked. A range of commentators has been using the phrase to confer instant illegitimacy on any argument with which they disagree. Want to close off the terms of the debate? Call something a conspiracy theory.*   ZACHARY ROTH[2]

Klaus Schwab, who presided over the World Economic Forum (WEF) for almost 30 years, argued in 1999 that the 'sovereign state has become obsolete' and that the preference of the chief executives of large corporations is for national governments to become subservient to corporate and financial interests.[3] The WEF is an exclusive private club for the chief executives of the world's largest corporations who meet annually at the Swiss ski resort of Davos to set the 'political, economic and business agenda' for the rest of the world. Membership is by invitation only and is restricted to corporations that have over US$1 billion in sales and banks that control over US$1 billion in capital.[4]

The WEF also has numerous other more specialized meetings during the year to network, hold private discussions, share information and ideas, foster alliances and plan strategies for achieving common corporate goals. A 'club atmosphere' is deliberately cultivated and a 'privileged, informal framework for intensive business networking' is maintained. The WEF invites top policy-makers to its meetings so that members can have high-level access to government ministers, prime ministers and presidents.[5]

The WEF is clear about its agenda-setting role: 'One of our initiatives in this respect is the Centre for the Global Agenda (CGA), which will serve as a catalyst in defining, monitoring and driving the global agenda. It will act as a hub of networks and alliances on important global issues and will play a key role in the world's international system.'[6]

The purpose of the WEF, and the many other like-minded coalitions that corporations have formed during recent decades, is to ensure that corporate interests are advanced over other interests and to undermine the democratic process for deciding government priorities and policies.

Corporations have always had a certain amount of power through their ability to make decisions concerning production and employment. As they have grown in size and number, that economic power has become significant and has been used to exert political influence. Individual corporations frequently influence the political process on matters of immediate financial interest to themselves through donations and lobbying, and the threat of transferring their activities abroad. They also play a major role in setting the political and the public agenda through their use of public relations, lobbying and funding of third parties, such as media, think tanks and business organizations.[7]

However, corporations have not been content with the degree of economic power and political influence that they can wield individually. Since the mid 20th century, they have conspired to increase their power, consolidating their political influence to pressurize governments into making decisions in their favour.

During the 1970s, faced with declining profits and a proliferation of public interest groups that challenged the authority of business and sought government controls over business activities, corporate leaders created whole networks of business groups to mobilize political support and to reassert business dominance.

Confidence in free enterprise was in decline. The first wave of modern environmentalists blamed development and the growth of industrial activities for environmental degradation. Their warnings captured popular attention, resonating, as they did, with the experiences of communities facing obvious pollution in their neighbourhoods. Worst of all, from a business point of view, governments were responding with new environmental legislation.[8]

Governments worldwide responded with new forms of comprehensive environmental legislation such as clean air acts and clean water acts, and the establishment of environmental regulatory agencies. These new environmental laws were part of a general trend in legislation aimed at regulating corporate activities and constraining unwanted business activities. In the US, for example:

> ...from 1969 through 1972, virtually the entire American business community experienced a series of political setbacks without parallel in the post-war period. In the space of only four years, Congress enacted a significant tax reform bill, four major environmental laws, an occupational safety and health act, and a series of additional consumer protection statutes. The government also created a number of important new regulatory agencies, including the Environmental Protection Agency (EPA), the Occupational Safety and Health Administration (OSHA) and the Consumer Product Safety Commission (CPSC), investing them with broad powers over a wide range of business decisions.[9]

Public respect for business was at an all time low and 'for the first time since the Great Depression, the legitimacy of big business was being called into question by large sectors of the public.'[10] A Harris poll found that between 1967 and 1977, at a time when the counter-culture movement brought with it a proliferation of public interest groups – including environmental and consumer groups – the percentage of people who had 'great confidence' in major companies fell from 55 to 16 per cent.[11]

In various business meetings, corporate executives lamented their decline in influence. For example, Carter Bales, director of McKinsey and Company, New York, stated: 'Around the world, there have been challenges to the authority of each corporate actor – a breaking down, if you will, of their legitimacy'. And the president of the National Federation of Independent Business, Wilson Johnson, claimed 'we're losing the war against government usurpation of our economic freedom.'[12]

In response to government regulations, brought on by the activities of environmentalists and public interest groups, businesses began to cooperate in a way that was unprecedented, building coalitions and alliances, and putting aside competitive rivalries.

Broad coalitions of business people sought to affect 'a reorientation of American politics'. In the US, the Chamber of Commerce and the National Association of Manufacturers (NAM) were resurrected and rejuvenated, and new organizations such as the Business Roundtable (for large corporations) and the Small Business Legislative Council (for small businesses) were formed to lobby governments.[13] Corporations and allied foundations also poured huge financial resources into a network of dozens of think tanks aimed at devising and advocating policies that would shift power from government to business (see Chapter 2).

This political mobilization of business interests could be observed in other countries, too. In Australia, for example, corporations 'substantially increased their level of resources and commitment to monitoring and influencing the political environment'. They ensured that their senior executives were effective political operatives in their dealings with politicians and bureaucrats. They hired consulting firms to help with government submissions and established government relations units within their companies with direct access to the chief executive officer (CEO). Also, as in the US, 'concerted efforts were made to improve and centralize business representation at the national level' in order to mobilize and increase their power.[14]

Since the 1970s, corporate coalitions have moved from defending their economic freedom from the demands and interventions of labour unions and governments, to being far more aggressive in their goals. They now seek to expand their freedom, destroy unions and take over key areas of government policy-making and service provision. Their progressive accomplishment of this has meant that as time goes by, democratic power is undermined and thwarted, while corporate power grows.

The political mobilization of business interests meant that corporations began to act as a class rather than a collection of competing companies with some common interests. The class consciousness of top corporate executives was facilitated by the growth of inter-corporate networks of ownership and interlocking directorates of large corporations, which gave rise to a growing number of corporate executives who occupied positions on the boards of several companies. These corporate executives became politically active on behalf of business, in general, rather than individual companies. They provided the leadership for business coalitions and associations and were employed at the top levels of the largest corporations.[15]

In his book *The Inner Circle*, written during the 1980s, Michael Useem claimed that while 'a sense of class affinity based on company stewardship can hardly be said to be new, the strength of the bond has increased and a select circle of those in corporate power are now far more willing to work towards goals that serve all large companies'. His study of the US and UK found that even at that time, large corporations were becoming more and more interrelated through shared directors and common institutional investors.[16]

Various studies have shown that interlocking directorates have grown even more in the ensuing decades and have become more global. In addition, the size of corporate boards has decreased, while the proportion of outsiders on each board has increased, with CEOs and executives from other companies therefore dominating the composition of many boards.[17] Some interlocking directorates in key corporations mentioned in this book are shown in Figure 1.1.

The inner circle of corporate executives facilitated the formation of many business associations and coalitions that sought a more general political agenda than traditional trade associations – one that was not industry or region specific. The new associations present a united front for their corporate members and assert the power of large corporations in political forums. These associations cooperate with each other and 'perform largely complementary tasks'.[18] They not only share members and even leaders; but associations and coalitions often join other associations and coalitions as members, or create new associations and coalitions for specific purposes. They have also created an array of front groups that achieve their political goals while appearing to be independent of the founding corporations or associations.

In this way, a vast network of business coalitions and groups, supported by an array of well-funded think tanks and public relations firms, proliferated during the 1980s and 1990s. Their purpose is not only to coordinate public relations campaigns as in earlier times, but to exert collective pressure on policy-makers to ensure that policies increase the power and autonomy of those corporations. And many of these coalitions are now global in their reach, reflecting the transnational nature of the modern corporation, which seeks to pressure governments worldwide to implement corporate-friendly, open-access policies.

In the past, large corporations have been more willing to accept shared power. Useem (1984) noted that until the 1970s, many large corporations had tended to take a progressive attitude towards unions, government and social reform for strategic reasons:

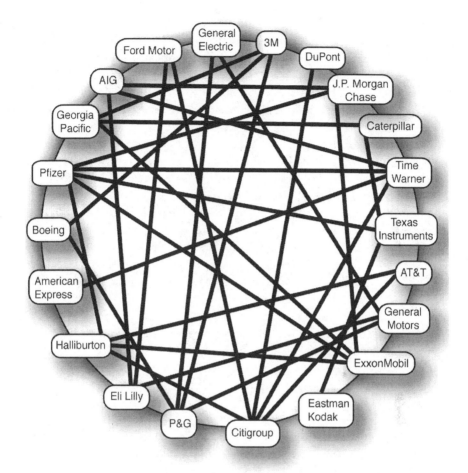

Figure 1.1 *Interlocking directorates*

Note: Corporations that are joined by a line have at least one shared person on their board of directors. So, for example, AIG has directors that are also directors of J. P. Morgan Chase, Time Warner and Eli Lilly.

Source: information from www.theyrule.net/2004/tr2.php and www.theyrule.net/2001/

> *The unalloyed exercise of raw corporate power, they recognize, can generate more problems than it is intended to solve. They are thus more prepared to accept the permanency of labour unions and government regulation, not in principle, but as a necessary compromise whose alternative could generate adversarial turmoil far more threatening to the future of free enterprise.*[19]

This is no longer the case. Although the perceived threats to business of the 1970s have long since faded into history, the political mobilization by large corporations has gained a momentum of its own. Their success has ensured the triumph of free market ideology around the world, and it seems that large corporations no longer fear that the exercise of raw power will cause them problems. They no longer accept labour unions, labour laws and government regulation as a necessary compromise. Today, they seek to destroy these institutions.

David Rockefeller, founder and chairman of the Trilateral Commission, wrote in *Newsweek* that business people favour lessening the role of government, but that this means that 'somebody has to take government's place, and business seems to me to be a logical entity to do it'.[20] The Trilateral Commission is another top-level international policy-shaping group. It is made up of people chosen from the elites of North America, Europe and Japan, including corporate heads and national leaders, past, present and future. Past members include ex-US presidents Jimmy Carter and George Bush Senior, as well as current Vice-President Dick Cheney.

The Trilateral Commission is an example of the way in which business networks can incorporate high-level government leaders and officials within their coalitions as allies against democracy. It was established in order to 'mould public policy' at a time when democracy posed a particularly vexing problem for corporations. In 1975, the Trilateral Commission published a report entitled *The Crisis of Democracy*. In it Samuel P. Huntington stated that 'some of the problems of governance today stem from an excess of democracy'. He went on to say that what was 'needed, instead, is a greater degree of moderation in democracy'. For Huntington, the 'effective operation of a democratic political system usually requires some measure of apathy and non-involvement on the part of some individuals and groups'.[21]

The degree of 'apathy and non-involvement' evident by the 1990s in the US would have pleased Huntington. Carl Boggs notes in his book, *The End of Politics*, 'by the 1990s American society had become more depoliticized, more lacking in the spirit of civic engagement and public obligation, than at any time in recent history'.[22] Citizens today, not just in the US, but in many parts of the world, feel that they cannot make a difference.

In fact, their ability to make a difference is declining as corporations increasingly determine policy decisions and governments increasingly leave social planning and decision-making about the public good, public services and infrastructure to the market.

Throughout much of the 20th century a mixed market, with strong government institutions and public provision of many essential services, brought decades of prosperity. More recently, however, business interests have been seeking to revert to some 'purer' version of capitalism where government plays a minimalist role and markets take over even those functions that Adam Smith was convinced should be the responsibility of governments.

Capitalism requires constantly expanding markets and economic growth. As existing markets become saturated, business people seek to extend their markets – in geographical scope from individual nations to the world; into areas of private life and social relationships that have not previously been commodified; and even into government activities that have traditionally been considered outside of the market – for example, the provision of essential services such as water.

Business coalitions such as the WEF, the European Business Roundtable and a range of US groups have ensured that through the World Trade Organization (WTO), the corporate goal of free trade will always have precedence over citizens' goals such as environmental protection, improved working conditions and health and safety considerations. The free trade crusade has impacted upon the ability of citizens in democratic nations to regulate in the public interest, while increasing the regulation that protects commercial interests. This book seeks to demonstrate how corporations have conspired to bring this about.

NOTES

1 *WordNet: A Lexical Database for the English Language*, Princeton University, Princeton, NJ, version 2.1, online at http://wordnet.princeton.edu/perl/webwn accessed 2 March 2006.

2 Zachary Roth, 'Those Loopy Conspiracy Theories', *Columbia Journalism Review Daily*, 7 February, 2004.

3 Quoted in Dyan Machan, 'Power Broker', *Forbes*, 15 November, 1999 and Charles Overbeck, 'Davos 98: The World Economic Forum Strikes Again', ParaScope, www.parascope.com/mx/articles/davos98.htm accessed 5 September 1998.

4 WEF, 'World Economic Forum', www.weforum.org/ 2000; 'One of the Greatest Shows on Earth', *Forbes*, 2 December, 1996, www.igc.org/ice/davos/english/greatest_show.html

5 *Ibid.*

6 *Ibid.*

7 Sharon Beder, *Global Spin: The Corporate Assault on Environmentalism*, 2nd edn, Devon, Green Books, 2002.

8 Sharon Beder, *The Nature of Sustainable Development*, 2nd edn, Melbourne, Scribe Publications, 1996, pxii.

9 David Vogel, *Fluctuating Fortunes: The Political Power of Business in America*, New York, Basic Books, 1989, p59.

10 Michael Parenti, *Inventing Reality: The Politics of the Mass Media*, New York, St Martin's Press, 1986, p67.

11 Cited in David B. Burks, 'Disenchantment with Business: A Mandate for Christian Ethics', *The Entrepreneur*, August, 1977, p1.

12 Quoted in ACC, '74th Annual Report 1977–78', Canberra, Australian Chamber of Commerce 1978, p11 and 'Why Business Finds It Tough to Polish Its Own Image', *US News & World Report*, 19 September, 1977, p64.

13 Jerome L. Himmelstein, *To the Right: The Transformation of American Conservatism*, Berkeley, California, University of California Press, 1990, p132.

14 Stephen Bell and John Warhurst, 'Political Activism among Large Firms', in Stephen Bell and John Wanna (eds) *Business–Government Relations in Australia*, Sydney,

Harcourt Brace Jovanovich, 1992, pp58–9; John Wanna, 'Furthering Business Interests: Business Associations and Political Representation', in Stephen Bell and John Wanna (eds) *Business–Government Relations in Australia*, Sydney, Harcourt Brace Jovanovich, 1992, p73.

15   Michael Useem, *The Inner Circle: Large Corporations and the Rise of Business Political Activity in the US and UK*, Oxford, Oxford University Press, 1984, p5.

16   *Ibid.*, pp6, 36.

17   See for example, Jeffrey Kentor and Yong Suk Jang, 'Yes, There Is a (Growing) Trans-national Business Community: A Study of Global Interlocking Directorates 1983–98', *International Sociology*, vol 19, no 3, 2004; William K. Carroll and Meindert Fennema, 'Is There a Transnational Business Community?' *International Sociology*, vol 17, no 3, 2002; Ernie Englander and Allen Kaufman, 'The End of Managerial Ideology: From Corporate Social Responsibility to Corporate Social Indifference', *Enterprise & Society*, vol 5, no 3, 2004, p436.

18   Useem, *The Inner Circle*, pp70-1.

19   *Ibid.*, p111.

20   Quoted in David Rockefeller, 'New Rules of the Game: Looking for New Leadership', *Newsweek*, 1 February, 1999, p41.

21   Quoted in Holly Sklar (ed) *Trilateralism: The Trilateral Commission and Elite Planning for World Management*, Cambridge, MA, South End Press, 1980, pp2, 37–8.

22   Carl Boggs, *The End of Politics: Corporate Power and the Decline of the Public Sphere*, New York, The Guildford Press, 2000, pvii.

2

National Influence

How come we can't get together and make our voices heard.
CHAIRMAN OF THE BOARD OF GENERAL FOODS[1]

The tactic by which such changes in the political agenda are secured is for corporations to search out articulate conservative economists and amenable academics, gather them together in lavishly funded tax-deductible think-tanks and pay them handsomely to inundate relevant debate with an endless stream of books and research reports.
ALEX CAREY[2]

During the early 1960s, the Kennedy administration was fighting inflation in the US and had soldiers in Vietnam. Of particular concern was the price of steel, which could affect both endeavours since it was a component of many household appliances, cars and defence equipment. The head of the Council of Economic Advisers warned that an increase in steel prices 'was the greatest single threat' to the nation's 'economic stability'.[3]

As part of his efforts to achieve price and wage restraint, Kennedy arranged a January 1962 meeting between himself, Roger Blough (chief of US Steel, which produced one quarter of all steel in the US and therefore tended to set the pay scales in the industry), Dave McDonald (head of United Steelworkers) and Arthur Goldberg (formerly counsel to United Steelworkers and, at the time, secretary of labour in the Kennedy administration). The negotiations initiated at that meeting culminated in an April agreement on a minimal wage increase in line with productivity growth. Kennedy was delighted, believing the steel industry had tacitly agreed to hold the lines on prices so long as the line on wages was held.[4]

Four days later, Blough announced a 3.5 per cent increase in his company's steel price. Kennedy was said to be 'livid with rage', realizing that the increase would make him look weak and ineffective, make the unions appear as dupes and feed inflation. He felt betrayed, accusing Blough of double-crossing him. He told his aides: 'My father told me businessmen were all pricks, but I didn't really believe he was right until now... God, I hate the bastards.'[5] This comment was deliberately leaked to the press by the White House to show how angry Kennedy was.[6]

There is some disagreement over the exact terms of abuse Kennedy used; the leak replaced 'pricks' with 'sons of bitches' and left off the reference to 'bastards'; but academic John M. Murphy notes that 'Kennedy could never remember whether he called them sons of bitches, or bastards, or pricks'.[7] One thing is certain, though: no president has since been willing to show such public disrespect to big business.

Five other steel companies made the same price increases. At a press conference the next day, Kennedy warned of the inflationary effects on the prices of homes, cars, appliances, machinery and tools that the increase would have, as well as adding an estimated US$1 billion to the cost of US defences. He stated:

> Simultaneous and identical actions of United States Steel and other leading steel corporations, increasing steel prices by some six dollars a ton, constitute a wholly unjustifiable and irresponsible defiance of the public interest.
>
> In this serious hour in our nation's history, when we are confronted with grave crises in Berlin and Southeast Asia, when we are devoting our energies to economic recovery and stability ... and asking union members to hold down their wages, the American people will find it hard, as I do, to accept a situation in which a tiny handful of steel executives, whose pursuit of private power and profit exceeds their sense of public responsibility, can show such utter contempt for the interests of 185 million Americans.[8]

The Kennedy administration retaliated against the recalcitrant steel executives with every means at its disposal: 'Blough's expense accounts were examined. And the US government said it would buy steel only from those companies that did not raise prices.' The Justice Department and the Federal Trade Commission began investigations, and executives of US Steel were served with subpoenas to appear before a grand jury the next evening while Blough was giving a televised press conference in defence of the price rise.[9] From the time of the price rise on Tuesday afternoon:

> ...the president orchestrated a ferocious public opinion campaign against the price rise. Cabinet members detailed the effects of the increase on their areas of responsibility... Attorney General Robert Kennedy spoke darkly of anti-trust actions, price collusion and grand jury investigations. The FBI [Federal Bureau of Investigation] hauled people in for questioning at three in the morning.[10]

On Friday the steel industry caved in. Firms that had not yet raised their prices kept them steady and Bethlehem Steel reversed its price increase. Realizing that US Steel could not compete if other steel companies did not raise their prices as had been secretly agreed, Blough was forced to capitulate. The remaining steel companies followed suit, rescinding their price increases.[11] It was a humiliating defeat for Blough and for the steel industry – one that they would not easily forget.

THE BUSINESS ROUNDTABLE IS BORN

Roger Blough, 'described as bookish and contemplative' and 'unassuming', a man who had grown up on a farm and started his career as a schoolteacher, was never the same again.[12] He later wrote:

> *Never before in the nation's history have so many forces of the federal government been marshalled against a single American industry ... this was the first time any president had been publicly called upon to exercise control – without authority of law – over the prices of an entire industry, and to initiate or participate in a whole series of administrative and legislative actions of a punitive nature, if that control were not accepted.*[13]

It was a turning point in Blough's life and it seems that he seethed at his humiliation at Kennedy's hands throughout the rest of the decade. He went on to be a key player in the founding of the most powerful business lobby in the country, the Business Roundtable (BRT). The BRT would make sure that such a back-down would never occur again. In future, business would stand united in its goals. Kennedy's 'Court at Camelot' had given rise to a roundtable of rebellious business knights determined to shape government policy to suit business interests and prevent government from meddling in business affairs.

The success of the BRT and other business coalitions formed during the 1970s and 1980s as part of the broader mobilization of business interests makes the events described above 'barely comprehensible' to people today. Murphy notes:

> *It comes from another world, a world in which unions swung a big stick, business executives suffered under a liberal lash, corporate heads cleared price increases with US presidents, cultural norms decreed that duty should come before profit, and, perhaps most bizarre, a world in which citizens felt confident that the government could direct the US economy ... in which government was not the problem but the solution to our problems.*[14]

It was a world in which the US president could denigrate business and put an industry in its place, and have his popular approval ratings soar as a result. It was a world that Blough and other business leaders were determined to change, and they did.

Blough retired from his position of chief executive officer (CEO) of US Steel in 1969 and founded the Construction Users Anti-Inflation Roundtable. It was made up of some 100 steel and construction companies and large corporations concerned about the rising costs of construction, which they attributed to union wage demands. The construction industry was experiencing a slump as foreign companies entered the market and a shortage of skilled workers gave unions a measure of bargaining power. The aim of the roundtable was to fight union power and wage demands. It supported an anti-union Association of Builders and Contractors (ABC), and its members used and subsidized open-shop (non-unionized) contractors for their building requirements in an effort to drive unionized contractors out of business.[15]

In 1972, 'Roger's Roundtable', as it was affectionately called by supporters, merged with two other groups to form the Business Roundtable. One of these groups was the March Group, which had overlapping membership with Roger's Roundtable. It had been formed by Fred Borch, chair of General Electric (GE), and John Harper, chair of Alcoa, together with Bryce Harlow, head of Procter & Gamble's Washington office, and consisted of a select group of CEOs of major US companies who met informally to discuss public policy issues.[16]

The March Group was the outcome of a private meeting between Borch, Harper, a member of Roger's Roundtable, and three high-level government officials. The businessmen were concerned about the increasing public resentment towards American business.[17] Present at the 1972 meeting were Arthur Burns, chair of the Federal Reserve Bank, Charles Walker, deputy treasury secretary, and John Connally, secretary of the treasury. Walker was a business economist with a background in banking and several years lobbying government on behalf of the banks as executive vice president of the American Bankers' Association (1961–1969).[18] Connally was a lawyer, who had been involved in the Texan Suite 8F Group, a group of right-wing men from politics and business who met in suite 8F of a Houston hotel, beginning during the 1930s through to the 1970s. The group's primary aim was to protect oil industry interests in Texas and included men from Brown & Root, American General Insurance Company and Kerr-McGee Oil Industries, as well as the governor of Texas. Lyndon B. Johnson was also a member. Connally became governor of Texas himself in 1963 and then a businessman before going back into politics.[19]

Connally and Walker advised the businessmen to found an organization of business CEOs who would directly lobby Congress and the White House to adopt policies that suited corporations. The March Group was formed, gathering together more than 40 CEOs from the largest corporations.

The other group in the merger was the Labor Law Study Group (LLSG). It had been set up during the mid 1960s to oppose union power and to weaken labour laws with the help of a major anti-labour public relations campaign orchestrated by Hill & Knowlton. The LLSG was made up of 12 'thought leaders', men who were top corporate labour relations executives from the largest corporations and who belonged to 'all the trade associations in every nook and cranny in the country'. They were known as 'the Twelve Apostles'. By 1968, the campaign was being described as the 'broadest united front of large and small businesses in history'.[20]

During the early 1970s, the LLSG turned its attention to government regulation and its costs to business, as well as to the need to create a more business-friendly climate of public opinion. Its merger with the March Group and with Roger's Roundtable was unsurprising given the considerable overlap in the membership of all three groups.

Thus, the BRT was born in 1972 with Borch and Blough as co-chairmen, initially, followed by John Harper as chairman from 1973–1976.[21] The BRT's agenda was to minimize government interference in economic matters, make business views known to government, 'play a larger role in formulating public policy' and generally promote the idea that everyone's welfare was dependent upon the health of US businesses.[22]

The BRT was established at a time of rising business activism in the US when political power in Congress was becoming more decentralized and fragmented, and party loyalty was weakening. Individual politicians were increasingly susceptible to pressure from a range of interest groups. Whereas previously business leaders could lobby key people in Congress, now they had to adopt a new lobbying strategy that focused on a wide number of individual Congress people.[23]

By the end of the 1970s, the BRT had 192 members, including most of the Fortune 100 companies, representing companies responsible for producing nearly half of the nation's gross national product (GNP), and was perhaps the most powerful organization in the country.[24] It has been 'credited with thwarting or watering down anti-trust, environmental, pro-labour, pro-consumer and tax-reform measures'.[25] Its power comes from its top-level membership, consisting of the CEOs of the top companies (currently employing some 10 million Americans and with combined revenue of almost US\$4 trillion – larger than the gross domestic product, or GDP, of most countries).[26] This mobilization of the most powerful business people in the country was a deliberate strategy to ensure maximum impact. As Albro Martin noted in the *Harvard Business Review*: 'The Business Roundtable almost seems a belated recognition of the frequently demonstrated historical principle that royalty always commands more attention, respect and awe than the lesser nobility.'[27]

The BRT in the US served as a model for other business roundtables in other countries, including the Business Roundtable in New Zealand and the Business Council of Australia. The European Round Table of Industrialists (ERT; see the following section) was also modeled on the BRT.

BUSINESS LOBBIES

The BRT was far from the first business lobby group in the US. The formation of business networks and coalitions to achieve political goals through a combination of public relations and political lobbying originated in the US. The National Association of Manufacturers (NAM), the leading US business organization during the earlier part of the 20th century, was one of the first general business coalitions to take advantage of the new public relations methods and to use them in order to gain political power.

NAM was formed in 1895 to promote foreign trade; but in 1903 it shifted its focus to opposing labour unions and defending the right of employers to establish work conditions, fire employees at will, and set wages without interference from unions or government. It was opposed to any government intervention in the management of business. It lobbied against government legislation that aimed to help workers, disseminated anti-union propaganda and sought to influence the outcomes of local elections to prevent pro-labour candidates from being elected.[28]

In 1913, NAM was investigated by a committee of Congress for mass dissemination of propaganda and for paying 'Congressmen to promote its legislative agenda'. The inquiry report stopped just short of accusing NAM of conspiracy:

> *The correspondence between officials and employees of the association laid before your committee and placed in evidence shows it to have been an organization having purposes and aspirations along industrial, commercial, legislative and other lines so vast and far-reaching as to excite at once admiration and fear – admiration for the genius which conceived them, and fear for the ultimate effects which the successful accomplishments of all these ambitions might have on a government such as ours.*[29]

In 1932, when public confidence in capitalism was at an all time low and Roosevelt was threatening to regulate corporations and curb their power, big business took over NAM to utilize it as a vehicle for pro-business propaganda. It restructured NAM to ensure that large corporations were well represented on the directorate. NAM claimed the right to call itself 'the voice of American industry' because it represented 35,000 manufacturers, employing some 5 million people.[30]

Wright Mills clearly described the role of NAM and associations like it that represent the top corporations as associations which unify the managerial elite and corporate rich:

> *They translate narrow economic powers into industry-wide and class-wide powers; and they use these powers, first on the economic front – for example, with reference to labour and its organizations – and, second, on the political front – for example, in their role in the political sphere. And they infuse into the ranks of smaller businessmen the views of big business.*[31]

The British Manufacturer's Association was formed in 1915 and became the National Union of Manufacturers in 1917 and the National Association of British

Manufacturers in 1961. However, this British equivalent of NAM never engaged in the extensive lobbying and propaganda campaigns that made NAM such a potent force in the US. The way in which business in the US used its power and resources to oppose unionism and government intervention was unique in scale and comprehensiveness. In Britain, unions were seen as necessary to containing radicalism and class struggle. The 1919 British Cabinet was told that 'trade union organization was the only thing between us and anarchy'.

Following World War II, when economic times were tough, UK governments – both Labour and Conservative – expected trade unions 'to play a major part in maintaining industrial discipline, curbing militancy and persuading their members to reduce their demands for higher wages'. In return, governments praised the role of trade unions and union representatives were incorporated within government processes through representation on committees, royal commissions, inquiries and boards of nationalized industries.[32] British trade union leaders tended to have narrow agendas, in terms of pay and conditions, rather than radical agendas aimed at the overthrow of the capitalist system.

In 1965, the National Association of British Manufacturers merged with the Federation of British Industries and the British Employers' Confederation to become the Confederation of British Industry (CBI), the most powerful business lobby in the UK. The CBI labels itself as 'the voice of British business'. It both formulates and promotes business-friendly government policy and opposes policies (such as environmental and labour protection policies) that are thought to interfere with business.

The CBI claims that its 'views on all business issues are regularly sought by government at the highest levels'[33] and that 'No other business organization has such an extensive network of contacts with government ministers, MPs, civil servants, opinion formers and the media.'[34] According to the UK-based Corporate Watch, few government 'policies or bills are written without extensive consultation with the CBI. It has daily contact with every level of government, with civil servants, with ministers (including the PM [prime minister]), and once a bill reaches Westminster with MPs.'[35]

In 1999, its website opened with a quote from Prime Minister Tony Blair: 'The government strongly supports business, and we work closely with the CBI as a key representative of business in Britain.'[36] When the UK took over the presidency of the European Union (EU) in 1998, the CBI noted that it would be 'working closely with the UK government to ensure that business issues are at the forefront of the agenda'.[37] Its goal of reducing business regulation has resulted in the UK being one of the least regulated nations in the world, according to the World Bank.[38]

The CBI's influence over government comes mainly from the fact that it claims to represent a broad sector of the business community, one that employs 40 per cent of the workforce (about half of these through membership of trade associations). However, the CBI also has influence because it shares the same free market ideology as key government ministers, and it claims to know what will harm business prospects and competitiveness and cause job losses. Its views on these matters are often accepted by government 'at face value'.[39]

Unlike the US BRT, the CBI's members are not limited to large corporations. More than half of its 3000 individual company members are smaller firms employing less than 200 people. Eighty of the UK's largest public companies listed in the FTSE 100 are members. Transnational companies operating in the UK are also members. Its membership includes trade associations, employer associations and professional associations. Because of the membership of these associations, the CBI claims to represent some 250,000 firms employing around half the UK workforce, giving it 'unrivalled influence with the UK government'.[40]

Despite its membership diversity, the CBI does manage to present a united business front on many issues. A Friends of the Earth report on the CBI, *Hidden Voices*, claims that this is because of the way in which policy is formulated using specially selected standing committees that are not representative of the full membership. The membership of these committees is not communicated to the wider membership. The director general and senior communications staff then have the final say on the public position of the CBI. This arrangement makes it:

> ... *convenient for a company wanting to protect its reputation to hide behind the CBI when it has a controversial view on public policy with which it does not wish to be associated. So, despite these conflicting views, the CBI continues to insist to the government that there is a unified voice from business on key policy issues when clearly there is not.*[41]

Most nations also have chambers of commerce at a local level and national level (see Chapters 7–9 for a discussion of the International Chamber of Commerce, or ICC). The US Chamber of Commerce was organized by NAM in 1916.[42] In the UK, the 100 or so local chambers are networked under the umbrella of the British Chambers of Commerce (BCC) and cover 100,000 businesses, large and small, which employ 30 per cent of the nation's workforce. The BCC claims to be 'the national voice of local business' and states that its combined membership is able 'to influence decision-makers and shape policy to ensure the best possible environment for business to succeed'.[43] Like the CBI, it opposes regulation of business, including environmental and employment regulations.[44]

The Confederation of Australian Industry (CAI) was established in 1970 and the National Farmers Federation in 1977. The Australian Business Roundtable, modelled on the US Business Roundtable and made up of chief executives of 20 of Australia's largest companies, was founded in 1980. It was established to 'enable the participation of chief executives in the public policy-making process' by identifying issues, getting them on the agenda and advocating a business position on them.[45] The Business Council of Australia took over this role when it was formed in 1983 by the chief executives of 66 large corporations, following what they perceived as a weak showing by business at the economic summit organized by the newly elected Labor government. The Business Council now represents big business in Australia.[46]

The European Round Table of Industrialists (ERT) was founded in 1983 to represent European business interests and their push for free trade. It was formed by Pehr Gyllenhammar of Volvo as 'a private circle of 17 European industrialists'. These days, it consists of around 45 European industrial leaders. ERT uses the rhetoric of competitiveness to promote deregulation, privatization and free trade.[47]

Membership is by invitation only and includes chairs and CEOs of major multinational companies headquartered in Europe. These companies include Bayer, Fiat, BP, Royal Dutch/Shell, Unilever, Hoffmann-La Roche, Total, Volvo, Renault and Siemens:

> *The ERT derives its strength from the commitment and personal in-volvement of its high-level members and from the substantial resources which ERT companies can mobilize. The combined turnover of ERT companies is over 1400 billion Euros and they employ around 4 million people worldwide.*[48]

The ERT has had privileged access to EU policy-makers and national government leaders, and that access has become institutionalized as the ERT has been integrated within EU committees such as the Competitiveness Advisory Group. Its privileged access to ministers and leaders is reinforced by personal contacts and friendships, including those between successive ERT chairs and European Commission (EC) presidents.[49] There is also some evidence of a revolving door between the European Commission and the ERT. Two commissioners who encouraged the formation of the ERT later became ERT members (representing Societé Generale de Belgique and Total).[50]

Doherty and Hoedeman, in *New Statesman and Society*, wrote:

> *... it often seems that the ERT is piping out the music, while the EU follows its policy proposals like a sedated parade of rats ... many ERT proposals and 'visions' are mysteriously regurgitated in Commission summit documents.*[51]

The Corporate Europe Observatory describes ERT's agenda-setting role as 'resulting in the prioritization by the EU of new policies benefiting corporations'.[52]

ERT was credited with being the driving force behind a single European market by former EC President Jacques Delors. A 1985 ERT paper by Wisse Dekker, 'Europe 1990: An agenda for action', was sent to heads of state and government officials throughout Europe. ERT notes: 'The arguments were convincing and the timing perfect. The single market became the most visible proposal of Jacques

Delors's new Commission.' The subsequent EC White Paper that the 1986 Single European Act was based upon closely followed ERT's plan for a single market.[53]

The ERT has various working groups, including one on the environment; however, its aims in each working group are clearly the protection of corporate profits. In its Charter for Europe's Industrial Future, entitled *Beating the Crisis*, the ERT argued that economic growth should be the goal of European policy and that 'special interests can no longer hold the global economy to ransom'. It claimed that labour costs needed to be reduced and regulations cut: 'What is needed is a standstill on new regulations... New priorities, such as the environment, should be dealt with by a cooperative approach, not by additional taxes and regulations'.[54]

The report stated that, while business people were ready to consider other objectives such as social welfare and environmental improvement, 'what industry cannot accept is that the pursuit of other objectives is used as an excuse for damaging the wealth-creating machine itself, whether by raising its costs or blocking its development'.[55] It called for a balanced approach involving 'close consultation between government, industry and science, with an end to the adversarial approach and "government by pressure groups"'.[56] The environment could be protected by consulting with industry over objectives and then allowing industry to work out how those objectives might be attained.[57]

POLICY DISCUSSION GROUPS

Business groups are also able to set agendas and influence government policy via policy discussion and advisory groups. Such groups are set up to help governments make policy and are sometimes established by or with the help of business people, and even funded by businesses.

One of the earliest policy discussion groups in the US was the National Civic Federation (NCF), which had close ties to the Republican party. It was formed in 1900 and made up of business leaders, as well as government officials, journalists, academics and union leaders who were opposed to socialism and too much government intervention. Its members included prominent business leaders, such as Andrew Carnegie, and several partners in the banking group J. P. Morgan.[58]

The NCF was utilized by the private electricity companies early in the 20th century when they decided that state regulation of private electricity monopolies was preferable to public ownership of electricity.[59] To achieve this end, Samuel Insull, who was head of the electricity association and a member of NCF, got NCF to set up a Commission on Public Ownership, which undertook a study of electricity provision (1905–1907). While seeking to appear objective, the study had particular ends in mind. Participants were carefully selected from the utilities, banks, railroads, unions, manufacturers and professions.

The study was largely funded by private utilities and their allies who were told that their contributions would be used 'to combat municipal ownership'.

Not surprisingly, the study concluded that regulated monopolies, as opposed to competing companies, were the best way to provide electricity. The NCF therefore drafted model legislation, which was promoted by the private utilities in the states where they operated. It was adopted in 13 states, including New York, Wisconsin and Massachusetts, in 1907.[60]

The NCF was soon eclipsed by other policy groups. In 1916, the National Association of Manufacturers (NAM) played a key role in creating the National Industrial Conference Board (later named the Conference Board), which would feed 'pertinent economic facts' into NAM's campaign to oppose unions and progressive legislation, such as child labour laws; organize 'joint deliberation and joint action by the manufacturers of the country'; 'command the attention of government'; and promote a better public understanding of the 'character, scope and importance of industry'.[61]

The Council on Foreign Relations (CFR) 'evolved from a monthly dinner club' in 1921. By the 1970s, when business mobilized, it was the largest of the policy organizations, and in 2000 it had just under 3900 members, many of whom were not active participants. Its links with the corporate class have been well documented. Domhoff noted: 'In a study of the directors of 201 large corporations in 1970, it was found that 125 of these companies had 293 positional interlocks with the council. Twenty-three of the largest banks and corporations had four or more directors who were members.'[62]

CFR was funded by corporations, wealthy individuals and subscriptions to its magazine, *Foreign Affairs,* and discussed policy issues at lunches and dinners, with invited speakers from governments around the world, as well as through books and other publications. In 1973, the CFR chair, David Rockefeller, founded the Trilateral Commission (described in Chapter 1).[63] Rockefeller became co-chair of the Trilateral Commission with Zbigniew Brzezinski, also a CFR member.

The Committee for Economic Development (CED) was formed in 1942. Whereas the CFR was interested in international issues, the CED focused on economic issues at home and abroad. It was primarily made up of corporate managers with a few university presidents added in to give it credibility. Its aim was to speak on behalf of business 'in the national interest', beginning with opposition to the New Deal. It received its funding from large foundations and ran a series of study groups in conjunction with selected academics. The groups produced policy recommendations that were then disseminated in pamphlet form and often converted into public policy by government.[64]

The Business Council was set up in 1933 as a governmental advisory group, and although it became independent in 1962, it was still being consulted by government officials during the 1970s. It is mainly composed of the heads of the largest corporations in the US. Its annual three-day meetings with government officials included speeches, panel discussions and report presentations, as well as social events and informal discussions in a resort atmosphere, all paid for by corporations.[65]

From the 1950s the Conference Board, the CFR and the CED worked together and had overlapping membership. These groups also had a large overlap
with the Business Council.[66] They were the more moderate of policy discussion
groups, accepting that some welfare state measures and accommodation of labour
demands were necessary to prevent social disruption. This was in contrast to NAM
and the US Chamber of Commerce, which opposed such measures. Corporations
funded both the moderate and the more extreme policy groupings and associations.
However, during the 1970s as business funds poured into the more extreme pro-
market groups, the moderate groups also became more extreme.[67]

The BRT, which was formed at this time, has become central to these corporate
policy groups, although it was only a lobby group itself. Its directors are largely
drawn from the inner circle of business leaders who are on the boards of more than
one company and are also members of other business coalitions, particularly the
Business Council, but also CED, NAM, the American Enterprise Institute (AEI),
CFR, the Conference Board and several others (see Figure 2.1).[68]

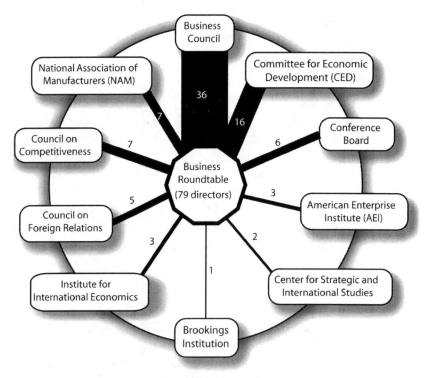

Figure 2.1 *Business Roundtable connections in 1997*

Note: Seventy-nine of the Business Roundtable directors are also members of several other policy
groups and think tanks, as shown in this figure. The spokes of the wheel depict the number of
directors shared between organizations. For example, 36 Business Roundtable (BRT) directors are
also members of the Business Council.

Source: Information from Domhoff (2002, p93)

Corporate CEOs such as Blough of US Steel, who were members of the inner circle of corporate leaders discussed in Chapter 1, played active roles in several of these groups. Besides being a director of several companies, including the Campbell Soup Company and the Chase Manhattan Bank, Blough chaired the Business Council from 1961–1962; he was an honorary trustee of the Committee for Economic Development; he was a chair and trustee for the Conference Board; he was a trustee for the US Council of International Chamber of Commerce; and he was a member of the Council on Foreign Relations.[69]

Policy discussion groups are useful to corporations because they provide a forum where corporate executives can 'familiarize themselves with general policy issues'; conflicts about the best strategies and policies can be discussed out of the public eye; and corporate leaders can observe potential members of their inner circle and select appropriate academic experts for promotion within the policy networks and into government service. The groups also confer legitimacy on corporate executives taking part as policy experts, rather than representing vested interests; provide a channel by which upcoming policy experts from academia can learn about corporate goals and expectations; and enable corporate executives to participate in the setting of government policy.[70]

Britain, too, had its policy groups, such as the Economic Advisory Council (EAC) formed during the 1930s and the Economic Planning Board established during the 1940s; but they tended to be less enduring and less influential than those in the US. One of the more long lived was the National Economic Development Council (NEDC), which was set up in 1962 to find solutions to Britain's poor post-war economic performance at the instigation of the Federation of British Industries (FBI (UK)). Unlike their US counterparts, British business people, at least those in the FBI (UK), saw a role for government in creating an economic climate for the growth of business, and this was their goal in promoting such a council. The FBI (UK) originally envisaged it as a forum for government and business.[78] In the end, it included government ministers, employer representatives and union representatives. The council was abolished in 1992 without being replaced by any other similar forum for the discussion of national economic policy.

In Australia, the Committee for Economic Development of Australia (CEDA) was formed in 1960, modelled on the US CED and to be funded by private contributions and corporate subscriptions. It was responsible for creating an Australian Business Roundtable in 1980.[79] CEDA later transformed itself into a think tank following the model of the American Enterprise Institute (see the following section).

THINK TANKS

Think tanks or research institutes utilize theoretical ideas developed by university scholars and turn them into policy ideas, which they disseminate and market.

Table 2.1 Current membership of key US policy groups: Selected corporations

	National Association of Manufacturers (NAM)[71]	US Chamber of Commerce[72]	Council on Foreign Relations (CFR)[73]	Committee for Economic Development (CED)[74]	Business Council[75]	Conference Board[76]	US Business Roundtable (BRT)[77]
Time Warner			*				
Texas Instruments				~			
Procter & Gamble	* @			+	<		
Pfizer		*		~	<		
J. P. Morgan		*		+			
General Motors	* @		#	~	<		
GE	* @		#	~	<		
Ford Motor				~			
ExxonMobil	*		#	~			
Eli Lilly				~			
E. Kodak		*	*				
DuPont	* @				<		
Dow Chemicals	*	*		~			
Citigroup			#*	+			
Caterpillar	*	*		~			
Boeing	*		*	+			
AT&T	* @	*	#				
AmEx			#	~			
AIG			*	~			
3M	* @	*					

Notes: ▨ Membership, * Board of directors, ~ Trustees, # Multiple members, + Donors, < Executive committee and officers

These policy ideas are then discussed in policy discussion groups and government advisory groups, before being taken up by government committees and turned into legislation. In most English-speaking countries, conservative think tanks have been influential in promoting a conservative pro-business reform agenda and 'widening the parameters of "respectable" opinion.'[80] As a result, free market ideas have come to dominate all policy issues.

The rise of Thatcherism in the UK can be attributed, in large part, to the endeavours of two think tanks: the Institute of Economic Affairs (IEA) and the Centre for Policy Studies (CPS). The CPS was, to some extent, an outgrowth of the older IEA. Keith Joseph, an active member of the IEA, and Margaret Thatcher, who had also been associated with the IEA, founded the CPS in 1974. While the IEA pledged itself to be 'independent of any political party' and therefore did not publish policy recommendations, the CPS was set up to formulate free market policies for the Tory party.[81]

The IEA and the CPS were small compared with the average US think tank, but were effective in the UK environment because of the 'extreme centralization of British political and public life.' This gave easy access to key people within government, the media and the financial sphere. They needed only to concentrate their persuasion on 'a strategic policy-making elite' to be effective.[82]

During the Thatcher reign, the Adam Smith Institute (ASI), established in 1981, was a driving force behind privatization. It sought to make privatization acceptable to the public by creating interests in favour of it through 'encouraging management buy-outs, cheap or free shares to employees and widespread share ownership among the public'. It organized 'right-wing talk-ins' and distributed pro-privatization literature to councillors, civil servants and the media.[83] The ASI had a reputation for getting radical ideas turned into policy:

> It is a handy sort of body for the government to have around. It can trample on taboos, shout the unthinkable, sit back and take the flack. In time, the hubbub subsides and in the still reflection that follows the idea no longer seems quite so outrageous. Whereupon, along comes a minister and polishes off the job.[84]

These think tanks, particularly the CPS, played a major role in setting the policy agenda of the Thatcher government, providing it with most of its policy initiatives, including trade union 'reforms,' privatization of public authorities, such as water and electricity, and welfare cuts. Thatcher's chief of staff, economic adviser and all four heads of the No 10 Policy Unit were former contributors to the CPS. The Policy Unit served as a conduit for ideas from the CPS and other conservative think tanks.[85]

As a result of Thatcher's free market policies, inequality increased in the UK and increased faster than any other industrialized country apart from New Zealand, where the free market formula was being applied even more zealously (see Chapter 4). The tax burden for the majority of households was increased and the poorest no longer benefited from the nation's economic growth. Between 1977 and 1990, the percentage of the population earning less than average income in the UK trebled.[86]

Union power was reduced. The combination of weakened union powers, deregulation of labour laws and the downsizing of the workforces of private and public organizations ensured that many full-time, permanent jobs disappeared for good or were replaced by part-time and/or contract positions. Even those in full-time jobs were often paid less than was needed to support a family. 'The diseases of poverty – TB [tuberculosis], rickets and others – returned.'[87]

Richard Cockett, who has charted the rise of conservative think tanks in the UK in his book, *Thinking the Unthinkable*, notes that a new consensus, which included keeping government control of industry to a minimum, has been achieved by those think tanks. The free market ideas of think tanks such as the IEA have become the new conventional wisdom, so that even the Labour party in Britain 'employs the language of economic efficiency and choice, albeit reluctantly.'[88] R. Desai, writing in *New Left Review* agrees: 'The Labour party, by the late 1980s, resigned itself to operating within the political parameters laid down by Thatcherism.'

In the US, too, conservative corporate-funded think tanks have been responsible for the transmission and promotion of free market ideas and policies: 'think tanks and foundations perform the research and advocacy functions that in many other industrial nations would be undertaken by the organized political parties'. The American political parties do not play much role in policy development and do not have policy research units. It has been suggested that American political parties are not only unable to come up with ideas, but that they lack any ideological coherence:

> *Think tanks have played a crucial role in building and supporting policy consensus and thereby replaced American parties, which tend to work rather as electoral coalitions than as places of ideological discussion and policy planning.*[89]

Ricci, in his book, *The Transformation of American Politics*, argues that politicians often lack any vision, philosophy or a coherent set of values that would enable them to deal with the mass of information at their disposal, and to distinguish between the 'good and bad, significant and insignificant, relevant and irrelevant'. Politicians and government officials therefore look to experts in the think tanks to interpret and make sense of all that information. This gives rise to a set of policy entrepreneurs based in think tanks who usually have the coherent vision that politicians lack.[90]

Corporate-funded neoconservative think tanks proliferated and expanded in the US during the 1970s, campaigning against government regulation. Their explicit political goals caused them to be referred to as advocacy think tanks.

These think tanks helped to bring Ronald Reagan to power and then influenced his policies when he was elected president in 1980. As in the UK, the relationship was two way. Reagan gave the free-market ideologues position and status; in return, they gave his ideas credibility. According to Feulner of the Heritage Foundation, 'our presence made Reaganism more acceptable'.[91]

The AEI was also 'a major source of policy advice' to Reagan. It was said to operate 'as the most sophisticated public relations system in the nation for dissemination of political ideas'.[92] It was formed in 1943 'as an adjunct to the US Chamber of Commerce' by a group of businessmen who were 'horrified' at 'talk of making wartime price and production controls permanent to prevent another depression'. One White House official told the *Atlantic* that the AEI played a large part in getting Ronald Reagan elected by making 'conservatism intellectually respectable'. Its promotion of deregulated markets found expression in Reagan policies. By 1985, it employed 176 people, boasted 90 adjunct scholars and a budget of US\$12.6 million, 45 per cent from some 600 major corporations.[93]

The Heritage Foundation was also extremely influential during the Reagan years. It provided information to members of Congress, and most of its policy recommendations, outlined in a document entitled *Mandate for Change*, were adopted by the Reagan administration. Feulner received a Presidential Citizen's Medal from Ronald Reagan for being 'a leader of the conservative movement ... who has helped shape the policy of our government'. By 1985, the foundation was almost as large as AEI. It promoted deregulation of industry, an unrestrained free market and privatization. The *Economist*'s *Good Think-Tank Guide* described the foundation's ideology as 'red-blooded, celebratory capitalism'.[94]

It was the Heritage Foundation that perfected the art of marketing ideas and forging contacts. Its policy analysts were assigned policy specialities and 'expected to develop contacts' on key congressional committees; to cultivate Congressional staff with lunches; and to keep track of the progress of bills in Congress. The foundation spends only 40 per cent of its budget on actual research. More than half of its budget goes on marketing and fundraising, including 35–40 per cent of its budget on public relations. All of this marketing enables the foundation to successfully attract mass media coverage for its publications and policy proposals. The foundation claims that it usually gets 200 or more stories nationwide from each of the position papers that it publishes.[95]

The Heritage Foundation aims its publications at government and the media, rather than the public:

> Its most avid consumers are members of the conservative congressional staffs who must brief their bosses and supply them with legislative arguments, pro or con; the conservative appointee in an executive agency who is leery of relying on the expertise of civil service employees and may want to consult with an ideologically compatible expert; and the journalist who wants to balance an article with insights drawn from an authoritative conservative source.[96]

Like the Heritage Foundation, the Cato Institute was influential during the Reagan years. The Cato Institute was another of the new generation of Washington-based think tanks established with business money in 1977. It was started with US$500,000 from Charles Koch, whose father Fred Koch, also a business man, had helped to found the John Birch Society. Koch was CEO of oil/chemical conglomerate Koch Industries.[97] Cato campaigns for reduced government and deregulation of the economy. It calls for many government functions to be turned over to the private sector. William Niskanen was acting chair of Reagan's Council of Economic Advisers in 1985 when he left to become chair of the Cato Institute. He was previously a director of economics at the Ford Motor company, a founder of the National Tax Limitation Committee and a defence analyst at the Pentagon.[98]

CORPORATE INFLUENCE

Think tanks have become essential vehicles of business propaganda and policy marketing. Rather than just react to proposed government policies, during the 1970s US corporations began to initiate policies more actively and to shepherd them through the policy-making process until they became government policy. Think tanks enabled them to do this. The more that government was attacked and its role reduced, the more freedom and opportunities were provided to business.

Oil industry money was invested through business people such as billionaire Republican Richard Mellon Scaife and Mobil Oil. Chemical industry money was invested through foundations such as the Olin Foundation. Lynde and Harry Bradley invested manufacturing money, Smith Richardson invested pharmaceutical money and the Koch family invested energy money. This influx of money meant not only that conservative think tanks proliferated, but that other think tanks moved towards the right. As Jerome Himmelstein points out in his book, *To the Right*:

> *The political mobilization of big business in the mid 1970s gave conservatives greater access to money and channels of political influence. These helped turn conservative personnel into political leaders and advisers, and conservative ideas, especially economic ones, into public policy.*[99]

The Heritage Foundation is now the wealthiest Washington-based think tank, with an annual budget of around US$35 million, thanks to direct corporate donations and indirect corporate donations through conservative foundations and individuals. Donor corporations include automobile manufacturers and coal, oil, chemical and tobacco companies.[100] Similarly, most of the Cato Institute's annual budget of around US$16 million comes from private grants and gifts from foundations, including the Sarah Scaife, Olin and Bradley Foundations;

individuals; and corporations, including Philip Morris, American Express, the American Petroleum Institute, ExxonMobil, Shell Oil, Eli Lilly and Pfizer.[101]

AEI had an annual budget of around US$18 million in 2002. Its board of directors is largely made up of the CEOs of large corporations, including American Express, Dow Chemical and ExxonMobil. Its major donors include various foundations, such as the Olin Foundation, the Scaife Foundation, the Lynde and Harry Bradley Foundation, and many corporations, including General Electric, Ford, General Motors, Eastman Kodak, the Proctor & Gamble Fund and Shell.[102]

A dozen or so foundations provide most of the funding for most conservative think tanks, including AEI, the Heritage Foundation, the Cato Institute and the Hoover Institution (see Table 2.2).[103]

Table 2.2 *Donations by selected foundations to selected think tanks, 1985–2002*

	Hoover Institution	American Enterprise Institute (AEI)	Heritage Foundation	Cato Institute
1985–2002				
Sarah Scaife Foundations[104]	$7.6 million	$4.4 million	$17 million	$1.8 million
Lynde and Harry Bradley Foundation[105]	$1.7 million	$15 million	$13 million	$560,000
John M. Olin Foundation[106]	$5 million	$7 million	$8 million	$800,000
Koch Family Foundations[107]	$5000	–	$1 million	$12.5 million
Smith Richardson Foundation[108]	$1.3 million	$4 million	–	–
1999 only				
Selected corporate foundations[109]	$128,000	$1.6 million	$341,000	$241,000

Note: All figures are in US$.

Source: Media Transparency (2005); Domhoff (2002, p83)

In order to influence government and set the agenda in a variety of policy arenas, think tanks insinuate themselves into the networks of people who are influential in particular areas of policy. They do this by organizing conferences, seminars and workshops and by publishing books, briefing papers, school kits, journals and media releases for policy-makers, journalists and people able to sway those policy-makers. They liaise with bureaucrats, consultants, interest groups, lobbyists and others. They take advantage of informal social networks – clubs, business, family, school/university. They seek to provide advice directly to the government officials in policy networks and to government agencies and committees through consultancies or through testimony at hearings. Ultimately, think-tank employees become policy-makers themselves, having established their credentials as a vital part of the relevant issue network:

> *What makes think tanks in the United States unique, besides their sheer number, is the extent to which many have become actively involved in the policy-making process. In short, what distinguishes American think tanks from their counterparts in other parts of the world is not how well financed some institutions are. Rather, it is the ability of American think tanks to participate both directly and indirectly in policy-making and the willingness of policy-makers to turn to them for policy advice that leads some scholars to conclude that US think tanks have the greatest impact on shaping public policy.[110]*

One survey published in 1982 found that most 'officials in the Department of State, the Central Intelligence Agency, the National Security Council and the Department of Defense' were more influenced in the long term by think tanks than by public opinion or special interest groups, and many were more influenced by think tanks than by the media or interaction with members of Congress. A more recent survey of Congressional staff and journalists covering government affairs found that over 90 per cent of them believed that think tanks were still influential in American politics.[111]

In their efforts to influence and become part of the policy-making process, think tanks have more in common with interest groups or pressure groups than academic institutions. Nevertheless, employees of think tanks are treated by the media as independent experts and are often preferred to experts from universities or interest groups as a source of expert opinion because they are articulate and trained to perfect the TV sound bite and give quotable quotes for newspapers. When they appear as experts on television shows or are quoted in the newspapers, they have more credibility than a company expert or a representative of a business association even though they may be pushing the same line.[112] They regularly write newspaper opinion pieces and give newspaper interviews. Many write their own newspaper columns.

An additional function that think tanks provide in the US, which is often done by the political party in other countries, is facilitation of 'elite transfer'. In countries such as the UK and Australia, cabinet ministers are chosen from the elected members of government. In the US, this is not necessarily the case. Additionally, the American system allows each new administration to appoint their own senior bureaucrats, including the staff of government departments, heads of departments and advisory councils. These are often not selected from the public service as was once the case in other countries.[113]

This means that when a new government is elected, top-level personnel in the administrative arm of government are changed for people whose ideology is more suited to the incoming government. Think tanks provide a source of such personnel. Whereas once administrations had been staffed with businessmen and party officials, presidents from Jimmy Carter through to George W. Bush have made wide use of think-tank personnel to fill high-level government positions. Reagan chose people from the think tanks and free-market policy networks to staff his administration, along with the businessmen and party officials. Some 150 of his administration came from the Heritage Foundation, the Hoover Institution and the AEI, alone.[114] Think tanks provide a fast track to a political career and a public profile in the policy arena. They also provide a place for discarded government officials to go when there is a change of government, where they can be employed until 'their' government is re-elected, while still having some influence over public policy as they wait. They form a sort of informal shadow government.[115] AEI played host to several members of the Ford administration when Ford left office, including Gerald Ford himself, who also became a resident fellow there. Describing this process as a 'carousel of power' the *Economist* said:

> *Now that Mr Reagan has left power, many of his appointees, such as Jeane Kirkpatrick and Richard Perle, are working at AEI. Every American think-tank director has a dream and a nightmare. The dream is to house the next administration; the nightmare is to house the last one. AEI seems to have managed both in the course of a decade.*[116]

The circulation of personnel suits the think tanks well. Employing ex-government officials gives a think tank access to politicians and others in government and attracts the funds of corporations who want access. When a think tank's employees are taken up by a new administration, the think tank has its best chance to have its ideas and agenda accepted by the government and to influence policy. Those employees are then able to recommend others in the think tank for government positions.

With an eye to the revolving door between think tanks and government positions, the Heritage Foundation and the Cato Institute have sought to nurture a new generation of conservative leaders within their ranks by sponsoring college students and promising junior bureaucrats, and providing them with a place to meet and socialize. The Heritage Foundation also promotes a 'talent bank' of potential candidates for official positions in government administrations on the premise that its policies will be more influential if its people are in positions of influence.[117]

> *In the past two decades, the most important function served by the network of conservative think tanks has not been the germination of new ideas, but the creation of a 'new cadre' of professionals... Not only have the dozens of conservative think tanks created a framework for disseminating ideas that exist largely outside the established*

infrastructure of academic journals, university presses and commercial publishing... they have also designed career vehicles for conservative activists and thinkers.[118]

THE POLICY PROCESS

Corporations are able to influence the process at every stage by funding university academics and research institutes, think tanks and policy discussion groups. This funding secures corporate positions on the boards of universities and think tanks, and membership of policy groups. Because of their economic power, corporations are invited onto government advisory groups. Corporations are also able to directly influence government through political donations and the offer of lucrative positions on corporate boards to politicians and government officials. Corporate influence is also enhanced by the fact that most of the top appointments to Republican and Democratic administrations are corporate executives or corporate lawyers.[119]

Corporations not only fund think tanks and policy discussion groups, but also provide free legal, accounting and other services to them and sit on their boards of directors or trustees, from where they can set their direction and select their employees. Corporate executives are also involved in the programmes and activities of these organizations. In addition, corporations identify the problems to be solved by the policies developed by these organizations.[120] Figure 2.2 shows how corporations are able to initiate and promote free market policies that will facilitate their profit-making, from conception through to implementation.

Corporate influence is bolstered by that of foundations whose wealth largely originates from corporate activity. Some foundations are funded and directed by corporations. Others are used by wealthy families, whose prosperity is derived from very successful business enterprises, to manage their money without incurring taxes. Foundations give grants to individuals and non-profit organizations, often for political ends such as propagating free-market ideology. The foundations also have extensive overlap of directors and trustees with free market policy groups and think tanks. Foundations, like corporations, initiate policy projects and programmes: 'they are extensions of the corporate community in their origins, leadership and goals'.[121]

The policy recommendations of the think tanks, policy discussion groups and advisory committees reach government through several channels. These include reports and personal representation to politicians and government officials; media reporting of news releases, speeches and conferences; and testimony at governmental committees and hearings and presidential commissions. In addition, there is an interchange of personnel – a revolving door between government and the policy community.

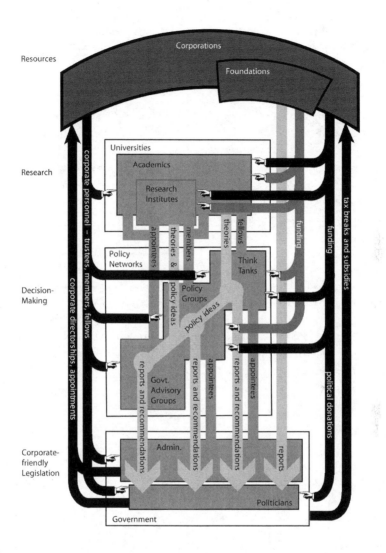

Figure 2.2 *Corporate influence on policy-making*

Note: The policy process sometimes originates with theories and ideas generated in universities. These are converted into policies – or used to justify policies – by think tanks and research institutes. They are then discussed and reshaped in policy groups and government advisory committees and transmitted to government in reports and recommendations, as well as via the transfer of personnel through political appointments. Politicians and bureaucrats then transform the policies into legislation and regulations and implement them. Corporations and foundations influence each stage of this policy process, from research through to policy and decision-making, through to legislation and enforcement. Influence is gained by funding and donations, as well as through providing personnel as members of policy and advisory groups, directors, trustees and fellows of universities and think tanks, and via the revolving door between government and business.

Source: adapted from Domhoff (2002, p72)

Politicians do not just rely on any experts, but usually prefer those who have corporate backing. Robert Bates, a professor at Duke University, suggests that politicians aren't able to independently evaluate the merit of the economic advice that they are offered:

> *In checking out whether a technocrat is 'sound,' a politician is likely to listen to major economic interests in his constituency. Politicians are likely to come to trust those technocrats whose policies enhance the economic fortunes of key constituents and thus their own political fortunes as well... Economic technocrats become powerful, and thus reform becomes politically sustainable, when they serve the interests of powerful groups: industries, sectors, or regions of the economy.*[122]

Think tanks and policy discussion groups are more useful to corporations when they are not obviously associated with business interests. Although 'their views are often indistinguishable from those of the business leaders and associations that support them financially' and make up their committees, these policy groups can claim that they are independent of 'particular' vested interests because they are funded by multiple corporations. However, while conservative think tanks and policy groups may not represent the interests of individual companies, the ideas that they promote serve the interests of big business in general.[123]

NOTES

1   Quoted in David Vogel, *Fluctuating Fortunes: The Political Power of Business in America*, New York, Basic Books, 1989, p194.
2   Alex Carey, *Taking the Risk Out of Democracy*, ed. Andrew Lohrey, Sydney, UNSW Press, 1995, p90.
3   Richard Reeves, *President Kennedy: Profile of Power*, New York, Touchstone, 1993, p294.
4   Robert Dallek, *An Unfinished Life: John F. Kennedy, 1917–1963*, New York, Little, Brown & Co., 2003, p483; John M. Murphy, 'The Language of Liberal Consensus: John F. Kennedy, Technical Reason, and the "New Economics" at Yale University', *Quarterly Journal of Speech*, vol 90, no 2, 2004, p134; Reeves, *President Kennedy*, p295.
5   Dallek, *An Unfinished Life*, p484; Brian Apelt, '100 Years of US Steel', *New Steel*, vol 17, no 4, 2001; Reeves, *President Kennedy*, p296.
6   Murphy, 'The Language of Liberal Consensus', p134.
7   *Ibid.*, p157.
8   John F. Kennedy, 'News Conference #30', John F. Kennedy Library and Museum, 11 April, 1962, www.jfklibrary.org/jfk_press_conference_620411.html.
9   Apelt, '100 Years of US Steel'; 'Roger M. Blough', *San Francisco Chronicle*, 10 October, 1985, p43; Roberta C. Yafie, 'Cerebral, Tough Exec Helped US Steel Grow', *American Metal Market*, 1 February, 1999.

10   Murphy, 'The Language of Liberal Consensus', p134.
11   Apelt, '100 Years of US Steel'; 'Roger M. Blough', p43.
12   Yafie, 'Cerebral, Tough Exec Helped US Steel Grow'; 'Management & Labor Roundtable's Blough Dies', *Engineering News-Record*, 17 October, 1985, p78.
13   Apelt, '100 Years of US Steel'.
14   Murphy, 'The Language of Liberal Consensus', pp134–5.
15   John B. Judis, *The Paradox of American Democracy: Elites, Special Interests, and the Betrayal of Public Trust*, New York, Pantheon, 2001, pp120–1; 'Labor History', United Brotherhood of Carpenters and Joiners of America, www.local157.com/history.htm accessed 16 August 2005.
16   Judis, *The Paradox of American Democracy*, p121; BRT, 'Business Roundtable History', Business Roundtable, www.businessroundtable.org/aboutUs/history accessed 16 August 2005.
17   Judis, *The Paradox of American Democracy*, p121.
18   *Ibid.*, p119; 'Charles E. Walker', LBJ School of Public Affairs, University of Texas, www.utexas.edu/lbj/faculty/view_faculty.php?fid=55 accessed 16 August 2005.
19   'John Connally', Spartacus Educational, www.spartacus.schoolnet.co.uk/JFKconnally.htm accessed 16 August 2005.
20   James A. Gross, *Broken Promise: The Subversion of US Labor Relations Policy, 1947–1994*, Philadelphia, Temple University Press, 1995, pp201–8.
21   Judis, *The Paradox of American Democracy*, p21; BRT, 'Business Roundtable History'.
22   Paul Lewis, 'Business Roundtable, in Policy Statement.' *New York Times*, 10 February, 1977, p57.
23   Vogel, *Fluctuating Fortunes*, p204.
24   Judis, *The Paradox of American Democracy*, p121; David Jacobs, 'Labor and Social Legislation in the United States: Business Obstructionism and Accommodation', *Labor Studies Journal*, vol 23, no 2, 1998.
25   Michael Parenti, *Democracy for the Few*, New York, St Martin's Press, 1995, p209.
26   Jeffrey H. Birnbaum, 'Former Powerhouse, Back at the Table', *Washington Post*, 12 July, 2004, pE01.
27   Quoted in Judis, *The Paradox of American Democracy*, p121.
28   'Violations of Free Speech and Rights of Labor', Senate Committee on Education and Labour, 14 August 1939, pp208–9.
29   Quoted in American Federation of Labor, 'National Association of Manufacturers Exposed: Revelations of Senate Lobby Investigation', Washington, DC, American Federation of Labor 1913, p18.
30   Strother Holland Walker and Paul Sklar, *Business Finds Its Voice: Management's Effort to Sell the Business Idea to the Public*, New York and London, Harper & Brothers, 1938, p53; NAM quoted in 'Violations of Free Speech', p3.
31   C. Wright Mills, *The Power Elite*, Oxford, Oxford University Press, 1956, p122.
32   Ralph Miliband, *Capitalist Democracy in Britain*, Oxford, Oxford University Press, 1982, pp57–9.
33   Archived 1999 version of CBI website, http://cbi.org.uk.
34   Quoted in Simon McRae, 'Hidden Voices: The CBI, Corporate Lobbying and Sustainability', London, Friends of the Earth, June 2005, p18.

35 'Influence/Lobbying', Corporate Watch, www.corporatewatch.org/?lid=259 accessed 18 August 2005.
36 Archived 1999 version of CBI website, http://cbi.org.uk.
37 *Ibid.*
38 Cited in McRae, 'Hidden Voices', p9.
39 *Ibid.*
40 Digby Jones, 'Transcript: British High Commission', Foreign & Commonwealth Home Office, 10 January 2005, www.fco.gov.uk/Files/kfile/TRANSCRIPT%20-%20Digby%20Jones.doc.
41 McRae, 'Hidden Voices', pp16–7.
42 'Violations of Free Speech', pp32–3.
43 BCC, 'The National Voice of Local Business', British Chambers of Commerce, www.chamberonline.co.uk/common/print.aspx?a=ba818faf accessed 18 August 2005.
44 McRae, 'Hidden Voices', p52.
45 CEDA, 'History', Committee for the Economic Development of Australia, www.ceda.com.au/New/Flash/html/body_history.html accessed 16 August 2005.
46 Wanna, 'Furthering Business Interests', p74.
47 Belén Balanyá, *et al.*, *Europe Inc. Regional and Global Restructuring and the Rise of Corporate Power*, London, Pluto Press, 2000, pp20–1; ERT, 'Achievements', European Round Table of Industrialists, 23 June, 2003, www.ert.be/pg/eng_frame.htm; ERT, 'The European Round Table of Industrialists', European Round Table of Industrialists, 8 June, 2003, www.ert.be/.
48 ERT, 'The European Round Table of Industrialists', European Round Table of Industrialists, 5 August, 2004, www.ert.be/.
49 Corporate Europe Observatory, 'Europe Inc', CEO, 8 February, 1997, www.xs4all.nl/~ceo/eurinc/ 2000; Ann Doherty and Olivier Hoedeman, 'Knights of the Road', *New Statesman & Society*, vol 7, no 327, 1994; ERT, 'ERT Highlights 1983–2003', Brussels, European Round Table of Industrialists, June 2003, pp33, 46.
50 CEO, 'Europe Inc', Corporate Europe Observatory, 8 February, 1997, www.xs4all.nl/~ceo/eurinc/ 2000; Doherty and Hoedeman, 'Knights of the Road'.
51 Doherty and Hoedeman, 'Knights of the Road'.
52 Corporate Europe Observatory, 'Europe Inc'.
53 ERT, 'ERT Highlights 1983–2003', p28; Doherty and Hoedeman, 'Knights of the Road'; Balanyá, *et al.*, *Europe Inc.*, p21.
54 ERT, 'Beating the Crisis: A Charter for Europe's Industrial Future', Brussels, European Round Table of Industrialists, December 1993, pp5–6.
55 *Ibid.*, p15.
56 *Ibid.*, p23.
57 *Ibid.*, pp23–4.
58 Patrick McGuire and Mark Granovetter, 'Business and Bias in Public Policy Formation: The National Civic Federation and Social Construction of Electric Utility Regulation, 1905-1907', *Public Power Now*, August, 1998, www.publicpowernow.org/story/2001/7/26/161517/294 ; Richard Rudolph and Scott Ridley, *Power Struggle: The Hundred-Year War Over Electricity*, New York, Harper & Row, 1986, p39.
59 Sharon Beder, *Power Play: The Fight to Control the World's Electricity*, Melbourne and New York, Scribe Publications and the New Press, 2003, pp22–6.

60 McGuire and Granovetter, 'Business and Bias in Public Policy Formation'; Thomas Hughes, *Networks of Power: Electrification in Western Society, 1880–1930*, Baltimore and London, John Hopkins University Press, 1983, p207; McGuire and Granovetter, 'Business and Bias in Public Policy Formation'.

61 'Violations of Free Speech', pp32–3.

62 Donald E. Abelson, 'Think Tanks and US Foreign Policy: An Historical Perspective', *US Foreign Policy Agenda*, vol 7, no 3, 2002; G. William Domhoff, *Who Rules America Now? A View for the '80s*, Englewood Cliffs, NJ, Prentice-Hall, 1983, p86.

63 Domhoff, *Who Rules America Now?* p87.

64 *Ibid.*, p89.

65 *Ibid.*, p134.

66 *Ibid.*, pp85, 134.

67 G. William Domhoff, *Who Rules America? Power and Politics*, 4th edn, New York, McGraw Hill, 2002, p83; Jacobs, 'Labor and Social Legislation in the United States'.

68 Domhoff, *Who Rules America?* p92.

69 William H. Hoffman Jr, 'Retired US Steel Executive, Roger M. Blough Dies at Home', *PR Newswire*, 9 October, 1985.

70 Domhoff, *Who Rules America?* p81.

71 Board of Directors (*), www.nam.org/s_nam/sec.asp?CID=201409&DID=229738; Founding Member Companies (@) www.nam.org/s_nam/doc1.asp?TrackID=&SID =1&DID=231410&CID=22&VID=2&RTID=0&CIDQS=&Taxonomy=False&s pecialSearch=False.

72 Board of Directors (*), www.uschamber.com/about/board/all.htm.

73 www.apfn.org/apfn/cfr-members.htm; Domhoff, *Who Rules America?* p86; Several members (#); Board of Directors (*), www.cfr.org/about/board_bios.php.

74 Trustees (~), www.ced.org/docs/trustees2004_05.pdf; Donors (+), www.ced.org/docs/donors_3_02.pdf.

75 Executive committee and officers (^), www.businesscouncil.com/directory/; active members www.businesscouncil.com/directory/directory.asp?ACTIVE=1.

76 Associates, www.conference-board.org/memberservices/members.cfm.

77 www.opensecrets.org/alerts/v5/alertv5_47d.asp.

78 Astrid Ringe and Neil Rollings, 'Responding to Relative Decline: The Creation of the National Economic Development Council', *Economic History Review*, vol LIII, no 2, 2000, p333–7.

79 CEDA, 'History'.

80 James A. Smith, *The Idea Brokers: Think Tanks and the Rise of the New Policy Elite*, New York, Free Press, 1991, p222.

81 Richard Cockett, *Thinking the Unthinkable: Think-Tanks and the Economic Counter-Revolution 1931–1983*, Harper Collins, 1994; R. Desai, 'Second-Hand Dealers in Ideas: Think-Tanks and Thatcherite Hegemony', *New Left Review*, vol 203, no Jan–Feb, 1994, p30; Simon James, 'The Idea Brokers: The Impact of Think Tanks on British Government', *Public Administration*, vol 71, no Winter, 1993, pp132, 182–3, 237.

82 Desai, 'Second-Hand Dealers in Ideas'.

83 Nigel Ashford, 'Politically Impossible? How Ideas Not Interests and Circumstances, Determine Public Policies', *Policy*, Autumn, 1997, p24; Dexter Whitfield, *Making It Public: Evidence and Action against Privatisation*, London, Pluto Press, 1983, p46.

84 Alan Rusbridger, 'A Thought for Tomorrow', *The Guardian*, 22 December, 1987.
85 Desai, 'Second-Hand Dealers in Ideas', p32, 34; James, 'The Idea Brokers', pp322, 497, 501.
86 John Gray, *False Dawn: The Delusions of Global Capitalism*, London, Granta Books, 2002, pp25–6, 29, 32.
87 *Ibid.*, pp25–6, 29.
88 *Ibid.*, p33; Cockett, *Thinking the Unthinkable*.
89 William Greider, *Who Will Tell the People: The Betrayal of American Democracy*, New York, Simon & Schuster, 1992, p52; Winand Gellner, 'The Politics of Policy "Political Think Tanks" and Their Markets in the US-Institutional Environment', *Presidential Studies Quarterly*, vol 25, no 3, 1995, p505.
90 David Ricci, *The Transformation of American Politics: The New Washington and the Rise of Think Tanks*, New Haven, Yale University Press, 1993, pp41–49.
91 Sidney Blumenthal, *The Rise of the Counter-Establishment: From Conservative Ideology to Political Power*, New York, Time Books, 1986, pp8, 36.
92 Mark T. Berger, *The Battle for Asia: From Decolonization to Globalization*, New York, Routledge Curzon, 2004, p150; Bette Moore and Gary Carpenter, 'Main Players', in Ken Coghill (ed) *The New Right's Australian Fantasy*, Fitzroy, Victoria, McPhee Gribble and Penguin Books, 1987, p146.
93 Domhoff, *Who Rules America?* p79; Blumenthal, *The Rise of the Counter-Establishment*, pp32–42; AEI, 'AEI's Diamond Jubilee, 1943–2003', American Enterprise Institute for Public Policy Research, 2004, www.aei.org/about/contentID.20031212154735838/default.asp.
94 Smith, *The Idea Brokers*, pp200, 286; 'The Good Think Tank Guide', *Economist*, vol 321, no 7738, 1992; Ricci, *The Transformation of American Politics*; John S. Saloma, *Ominous Politics: The New Conservative Labyrinth*, New York, Hill and Wang, 1984, p29.
95 Blumenthal, *The Rise of the Counter-Establishment*, p48; Gellner, 'The Politics of Policy "Political Think Tanks"', p502; Christopher Georges, 'Conservative Heritage Foundation Finds Recipe for Influence: Ideas Plus Marketing Equal Clout", *Wall Street Journal*, August 10, 1995; R. Kent Weaver, 'The Changing World of Think Tanks', *PS: Political Science and Politics*, vol 22, no Sept., 1989, p572; Smith, *The Idea Brokers*, p287.
96 Smith, *The Idea Brokers*.
97 People for the American Way, 'Right Wing Organizations: Cato Institute', People for the American Way, March, 2003, www.pfaw.org/pfaw/general/default.aspx?oid=9261; 'Koch Industries', Wikipedia: the Free Encyclopedia, 16 November, 2004, http://en.wikipedia.org/wiki/Koch_Industries
98 William A. Niskanen, 'Cato Institute', Cato Institute, 1995, www.cato.org/people/niskanen.html 1995; 'The Good Think-Tank Guide'.
99 Kirkpatrick Sale, *The Green Revolution: The American Environmental Movement, 1962–1992*, New York, Hill and Wang, 1993, p49; Jerry M. Landay, 'The Powell Manifesto', Mediatransparency.org, 20 August, 2002, www.mediatransparency.org/stories/powell.htm; Jerome L. Himmelstein, *To the Right: The Transformation of American Conservatism*, Berkeley, California, University of California Press, 1990, pp129, 146.

100   People for the American Way, 'Right Wing Organizations: Heritage Foundation', People for the American Way, September, 2002, www.pfaw.org/pfaw/general/default.aspx?oid=4287; Sharon Beder, *Global Spin: The Corporate Assault on Environmentalism*, 2nd edn, Devon, Green Books, 2002, p79; Heritage Foundation, 'Consolidated Financial Statements and Supplemental Schedules of Functional Expenses for the Years Ended December 31, 2003 and 2002, and Independent Auditors Report', Washington, DC, Heritage Foundation, 2004, p12.

101   People for the American Way, 'Right Wing Organizations: Cato Institute'.

102   AEI, 'Finances', American Enterprise Institute for Public Policy Research, 2004, www.aei.org/about/contentID.2002121511415722/default.asp; People for the American Way, 'Right Wing Organizations: American Enterprise Institute', People for the American Way, September, 2002, www.pfaw.org/pfaw/general/default.aspx?oid=4456

103   Domhoff, *Who Rules America?* p82.

104   www.mediatransparency.org/search_results/recipientsoffunder.php?providerID=3

105   www.mediatransparency.org/search_results/recipientsoffunder.php?providerID=1

106   www.mediatransparency.org/search_results/display_recipients_by_olin_total.htm

107   www.mediatransparency.org/search_results/kochaggregate.php

108   www.mediatransparency.org/search_results/recipientsoffunder.php?providerID=6

109   Domhoff, *Who Rules America?* p83.

110   Abelson, 'Think Tanks and US Foreign Policy'.

111   Cited in Ricci, *The Transformation of American Politics*, p2 and Strobe Talbott, 'The Brookings Institution: How a Think Tank Works', *US Foreign Policy Agenda*, vol 7, no 3, 2002.

112   Gellner, 'The Politics of Policy "Political Think Tanks"', p505; Ricci, *The Transformation of American Politics*, p162.

113   'Think Tanks: The Carousels of Power', *The Economist*, 1991; Donald E. Abelson, 'From Policy Research to Political Advocacy: The Changing Role of Think Tanks in American Politics', *Canadian Review of American Studies*, vol 25, no 1, 1995; Gellner, 'The Politics of Policy "Political Think Tanks"', p499; Smith, *The Idea Brokers*, pxv; Weaver, 'The Changing World of Think Tanks', pp570–1.

114   Blumenthal, *The Rise of the Counter-Establishment*, p33; Richard N. Haass, 'Think Tanks and US Foreign Policy: A Policy-Maker's Perspective', *US Foreign Policy Agenda*, vol 7, no 3, 2002.

115   Abelson, 'From Policy Research to Political Advocacy: The Changing Role of Think Tanks in American Politics'; Smith, *The Idea Brokers*; Weaver, 'The Changing World of Think Tanks'; Smith, *The Idea Brokers*, pp206–7; Weaver, 'The Changing World of Think Tanks', pp569, 571; Haass, 'Think Tanks and US Foreign Policy'.

116   Ricci, 'Think Tanks: The Carousels of Power'.

117   Gellner, 'The Politics of Policy "Political Think Tanks"', p500; Gellner, 'The Politics of Policy "Political Think Tanks"'; Smith, *The Idea Brokers*; David Stoesz, 'Policy Gambit: Conservative Think Tanks Take on the Welfare State', *Journal of Sociology and Social Welfare*, vol 14, no 4, 1987; Smith, *The Idea Brokers*, p207.

118   Smith, *The Idea Brokers*, p206.

119   Domhoff, *Who Rules America?* p151.

120   *Ibid.*, pp69, 71.

121   *Ibid.*, pp73–8.
122   Robert H. Bates, 'Comment', in John Williamson (ed) *The Political Economy of Policy Reform*, Washington, DC, Institute for International Economics, 1994, p32.
123   Georgina Murray and Douglas Pacheco, 'Think Tanks in the 1990s', Australian National University, www.anu.edu.au/polsci/marx/interventions/thinktanks.htm accessed 23 January 2001.

3

International Coercion

Globalization is about making every country in the world conform to neo-conservative American prescriptions in macro-economic management, taxation principles, social policy, and the laws and practices governing employment while opening their markets to American investors.
JOHN M. LEGGE[1]

The first country to fully embrace market-oriented reform was Chile, after General Pinochet ousted the democratically elected socialist government of Salvador Allende in 1973, with the support of the Central Intelligence Agency (CIA) and US-based transnational corporations.

During the 1960s, US corporations had invested billions of dollars in Chile, buying up most of their industries. This caused some concern in Chile, where leftists who believed that Chileans were being exploited organized strikes and demonstrations against US companies. Chile's main export was copper; but foreign companies – particularly US companies Anaconda and Kennecott Copper – owned 80 per cent of the copper production and made large profits out of it. In 1970, Allende campaigned for election on a platform of nationalizing Chile's major industries, including copper, and ensuring a more equitable distribution of wealth, as he had in previous elections.[2]

When it looked likely that Allende would be elected president of Chile, US corporations operating in Chile became worried that their businesses might be nationalized and put pressure on the US government to do something about it. Donald Kendall, chair of PepsiCo, telephoned President Nixon, who had once been the company's lawyer, to plead for US intervention. ITT Corporation promised US\$1 million to help the CIA stop Allende from taking power. It owned Chile's telephone company and was a major donor to the US Republican party, as well as having a former CIA director on its board. The Business Group for Latin America (later the Council of the Americas), a group of US transnational corporations – including Anaconda, ITT and PepsiCo – created by David Rockefeller in 1963, unsuccessfully offered to put up US\$500,000 for the purposes of persuading members of the Chilean Congress not to confirm Allende once he was elected. After Allende was confirmed with a large Congressional majority, it pressured the Nixon administration to impose an unofficial embargo on the Chilean economy.[3]

The CIA admits to carrying out a number of covert activities in Chile to try to prevent Allende from taking office. During the 1970 election, it funded and assisted opposition parties and candidates, as well as carrying out a number of propaganda activities, as it had done in previous elections. It then attempted to influence the Chilean Congress not to confirm Allende. Other measures taken by the US government included 'cutting off all credit, pressuring firms to curtail investment in Chile and approaching other nations to cooperate in this venture'. This 'economic offensive', according to the US Department of State, 'adversely affected the Chilean economy; a major financial panic ensued. However, US efforts to generate an economic crisis did not have the desired impact on the 24 October vote [for confirmation], nor did they stimulate a military intervention to prevent Allende's accession.'[4]

The CIA next attempted 'to instigate a coup to prevent Allende from taking office'. It supplied tear gas, submachine guns and ammunition for the coup, which had been ordered by President Nixon. An attempted coup did take place, during which a pro-democracy general was killed; but it was unsuccessful.[5] Allende became president in September 1970.

The CIA then paid US$8 million to the media, opposition political parties and private companies as part of a propaganda effort to destabilize the Allende government. It cooperated with transnational corporations at this time. A 1975 US Department of State report stated: 'In addition to providing information and cover to the CIA, transnational corporations also participated in covert attempts to influence Chilean politics.' In 1973, a second coup, which the CIA says it knew about in advance but did not instigate, succeeded.[6]

Table 3.1 *US techniques of covert action: Expenditures in Chile, 1963–1973*

Techniques	Amount
Propaganda for elections and other support for political parties	US$8 million
Producing and disseminating propaganda and supporting mass media	US$4.3 million
Influencing Chilean institutions (labour, students, peasants, women) and supporting private-sector organizations	US$900,000
Promoting military *coup d'etat*	< US$200,000

Note: Figures rounded to nearest US$100,000.

Source: Select Committee to Study Governmental Operations with Respect to Intelligence Activities (1975)

The role of the CIA in Chile was clearly to protect US business interests rather than any US national interest. Chile was not thought to pose a security risk to the US, and according to CIA advice, the US 'had no vital interests within Chile, the world military balance of power would not be significantly altered by an Allende regime, and an Allende victory in Chile would not pose any likely threat to the peace of the region.'[7] A US Department of State report noted shortly afterwards that 'The scale of CIA involvement in Chile was unusual, but by no means unprecedented.'[8]

After the coup, Pinochet was installed as dictator, and the CIA helped him to consolidate his position with the aid of, in the CIA's own words, 'ongoing propaganda projects, including support for news media committed to creating a positive image for the military Junta.'[9] The US continued to provide military assistance to the Junta while it committed its worst human rights abuses.

Pinochet put the economy into the hands of a group of economists who applied free market policies without compromise for 16 years from 1973 to 1989. These policies included drastic government spending cuts, the privatization of state-owned businesses, the lifting of all restrictions on foreign investment and the decimation of business regulations.

As a result, Chile suffered major fluctuations, oscillating between recessions and boom times while employment levels fell and bankruptcies soared. Between 1972 and 1987, Chile's per capita gross national product (GNP) fell 6.4 per cent, and unemployment averaged around 16 per cent, a performance that was worse than most other Latin American nations. Those who objected 'disappeared' or were assassinated or imprisoned.[10]

Nevertheless, the same free-market policy prescription was actively promoted by the World Bank and the International Monetary Fund (IMF), not only in Latin America, but in all parts of the world.[11] It was the driving force behind the structural adjustment programmes being imposed on all indebted developing nations. World Bank and IMF loans became conditional upon the adoption of policies such as privatization, outsourcing, downsizing of public service workforces, reducing barriers to foreign investors and redirecting government spending away from public services and publicly owned enterprises into debt servicing.

INFLUENCING DEVELOPMENT LOANS

Because corporations have so much influence on US government policy-making, as we saw in Chapter 2, the US government goes out of its way to support US-based corporations abroad. During the Clinton administration, for example, the Commerce Department built what an undersecretary called an 'economic war room' for promoting US business abroad. The *New York Times* noted that the efforts to win business often require 'arm-twisting in foreign capitals to change the way nations do business'.[12]

The arm-twisting extends to the multilateral development banks (MDBs) where the US can exert enormous influence. The World Bank, for example, is the world's largest multilateral development bank. It finances projects, makes loans to member nations and guarantees credit. It lends about US$25 billion a year, 45 per cent of which ends up in the coffers of transnational corporations (TNCs), mainly those based in Organisation for Economic Co-operation and Development (OECD) countries such as the US. It is owned by 180 member nations who provide the funds or guarantees for loans.[13] Voting power or control of the bank depends upon the amount of money each country contributes. Although the US now only has 16 to 17 per cent of the votes in the World Bank (compared with 42 per cent when the bank began), it has the right of veto over major lending decisions and it appoints the bank's president. The bank is housed in Washington, DC, and employs a high proportion of US citizens, including those at senior management level.

The IMF also lends money to low-income countries, and has become one of the few sources of such loans since Mexico threatened to default in 1982. The IMF is structured in a similar way to the World Bank: each member country contributes an amount to the pool to be loaned depending upon the size of its economy and this determines its voting power. As with the World Bank, the US has an effective veto because important decisions require an 85 per cent majority to pass.[14]

The influence of the US government and policy groups on the IMF and the World Bank (see Figure 3.1) is reinforced by the dominance of economists in the World Bank and the IMF. More than 80 per cent of the World Bank's economists, who are far more influential than the social scientists employed by the bank, were trained in either the UK or North America. There is also a well-worn revolving door between these multilateral banks and the international financial firms, such as Chase Manhattan, Deutsche Bank and J. P. Morgan – something that is encouraged by the World Bank.[15]

Despite the fact that the MDBs are supposed to make their lending decisions on the basis of economic criteria, the US habitually uses them for political purposes. A 1982 US Department of Treasury study found that 'The MDBs, by and large, have been most effective in contributing to the achievement of our global economic and financial objectives and thereby helping us in our long-term political/strategic interests.' It is no coincidence that the bank deems countries that follow a free market, low-paid labour, foreign investment-driven development model to be economically sound and credit worthy, while those that seek equity and redistribution of wealth find it difficult to get loans.[16]

When Allende's socialist government was in power in Chile, President Nixon wanted to destabilize the country by putting pressure on its economy. The administration drew up a report on 'options for the United States in the event Chile takes steps to nationalize or expropriate US business interests in Chile'. According to notes by CIA Director Richard Helms, Nixon wanted to 'make the economy scream'. One of the ways to do this was to cut off Chile's access to loans. This came to be known as the 'invisible blockade'. The American executive director of the Inter-American Development Bank (IDB) was told that he would not receive instructions from the US government on pending loans to Chile: 'this will effectively bar approval of the loans'.[17]

In order to forestall future World Bank loans to Chile, the US Department of State, with the agreement of the US executive director of the International Bank for Reconstruction and Development (IBRD) – the division of the World Bank that would make the loans – drew up a series of questions:

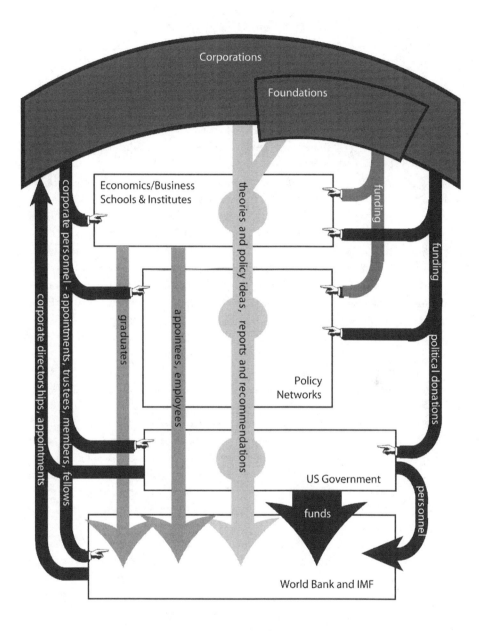

Figure 3.1 *Corporate influence on the World Bank and the International Monetary Fund (IMF)*

Note: The influence that corporations and foundations have on the US policy process through funding and interchange of personnel is similarly exerted on the World Bank and the IMF via the US policy process and as a result of personnel employed by these institutions.

Source: adapted from Domhoff (2002, p72)

> *...concerning areas where Chilean performance and policies may be most vulnerable with respect to future IBRD financing. The executive director will routinely and discreetly convey these questions to bank staff members concerned so as to insure adequate attention to them ... but without the hand of the US government showing in the process.*[18]

So, within a month of Allende's election, the US administration was already manipulating World Bank bureaucrats into making an economic case against bank loans to Chile.

Just over a year later, after Chile nationalized the US copper companies and refused to compensate them because of the excess profits that they had been taking, Nixon announced that the US would cut off all aid to Chile and 'withhold its support from loans under consideration in multilateral development banks'.[19]

Chile received nearly US$100 million in World Bank loans in the five years before Allende was elected. The bank ceased loans to Chile during the Allende term of office, despite a number of applications for well-conceived projects and Chile's loan repayments being up to date. Then, when Pinochet ousted Allende, World Bank loans began to flow again with over US$100 million in World Bank loans during the first two years and US$680 million in US government loans. MDB loans to Chile fell off again when Carter was elected US president because of Pinochet's poor human rights record; but they were reinstated by the Reagan administration. Five years after Reagan took office, MDB and US loans reached US$3 billion, including US$430 million from the World Bank.[20]

Reagan also used the World Bank to once again impose an 'invisible blockade' on Nicaragua with a view to destabilizing the economy and creating internal unrest and support for a takeover by the US-backed Contras. The Sandinista government of Nicaragua had come to power in 1979 with a socialist agenda that included nationalization of property and resources – including mines – and land reform. The Reagan administration used a variety of methods to stop MBD loans to Nicaragua going ahead, including vetoes, organized voting blocks, paper work delays and political pressure on MBD officials. From 1983, none of the MDBs made loans to Nicaragua. The reasoning given by US officials for their opposition to the loans was 'inappropriate macro-economic policies'. In addition, the Contras and CIA agents directed attacks at Nicaragua's economic infrastructure. By 1989, the Sandinista government had been forced to abandon its welfare-oriented economic policies in favour of free market reforms. It lost government in 1990.[21]

THE WASHINGTON CONSENSUS AND STRUCTURAL ADJUSTMENT

In 1990, John Williamson, an economist with experience working for the World Bank, the IMF and the UK Treasury, compiled a list of free market policies that were being pressed onto Latin American nations 'by the powers that be in Washington'.

He called this package of economic 'reforms' the 'Washington Consensus'.[22] The World Bank calls it the 'market-friendly view'. His list covered:

- *fiscal discipline*: reduced budget deficits at all levels of government (after taking account of debt);
- *public expenditure priorities*: redirecting government expenditure from areas of public demand that provide little economic return to areas with 'high economic returns and the potential to improve income distribution, such as primary health and education, and infrastructure';
- *tax reform*: broadening the tax base and cutting marginal tax rates to provide more incentive to high-income earners to invest their money;
- *financial liberalization*: aiming towards market-determined interest rates and the abolition of preferential interest rates for privileged borrowers;
- *exchange rates*: setting exchange 'to induce a rapid growth in non-traditional exports', as well as to ensure exporters remain competitive;
- *trade liberalization*: reduction of tariffs and trade restrictions;
- *foreign direct investment*: abolition of barriers to investment by foreign firms and foreign firms to be treated on the same basis as local firms;
- *privatization*: privatizing government businesses and assets;
- *deregulation*: abolition of regulations that impede investment or restrict competition, and requirement that all regulations be justified 'by such criteria as safety, environmental protection or prudential supervision of financial institutions';
- *property rights*: securing property rights without excessive costs.[23]

These were measures that would expand business opportunities, reduce the cost of doing business and minimize the regulations that business would have to abide by. They were the policies being promoted by corporate-funded think tanks in the US and the UK. The Washington Consensus was pushed by Washington policy networks supported by large corporations and international financial interests, and incorporated within an economic reform agenda for most countries in the world.

These business-friendly measures were also adopted in affluent countries by governments of many different political persuasions during the 1980s, including the conservative governments of Margaret Thatcher in the UK and Ronald Reagan in the US, and labour governments in Australia and New Zealand. By the end of the 1980s, most Western countries were moving towards smaller government and market deregulation.[24] This was not because of the power of the free market ideas themselves, or the efficacy of the policies in meeting their stated purposes. Rather, it was because of the power of those who backed these ideas: the corporations. International financial markets also played a key role, as we will see in the following section.

The Washington Consensus was a policy prescription that benefited trans-national corporations, large companies and international financial institutions, often at the expense of small local businesses, and always at the expense of the poor. It placed an 'exaggerated faith in market mechanisms' to solve economic problems and it gave economic goals priority over social goals, destroying socially beneficial traditions and desirable aspects of cultures in the process. Progressive taxation systems were destroyed and government social services decimated. In the extreme, governments were to be reduced to being responsible for little more than law and order and national defence.[25]

Imposing such conditions on nations 'undermined their national sovereignty', and the policy prescriptions of foreign bureaucrats overrode any democratic dec-isions made by elected governments.[26] Yet, they were imposed on the most vulner-able nations by the MDBs and the IMF, beginning with Mexico in 1982.

Following the onset of the debt crisis in 1982, when the Mexican government threatened to default on its US$80 billion debt, the World Bank and the IMF focused on ways to ensure that debt would and could be repaid by debtor nations, and to protect foreign investments in those countries. Multilateral banks now work with large investors to ensure that the economic systems in poor countries are conducive to profitable foreign investment. Having abandoned government stim-ulation of these economies as a development strategy, they depend upon this private investment to aid development and economic growth in poorer countries.[27]

The World Bank, for example, imposes structural adjustment programmes on countries seeking to reschedule their debts or to obtain new loans. These programmes require that borrowing countries adopt austerity measures, such as cutting welfare spending and lowering wages, as well as a number of free-market policy prescriptions aimed at opening up developing economies to foreign investors, including the removal of restrictions on foreign investment; lowering barriers to imports; devaluing the local currency; raising interest rates; cutting subsidies for local industries; and privatization of state enterprises. By the early 1990s, structural adjustment programmes had been introduced into nearly 80 developing countries at the instigation of the World Bank.[28]

Like the World Bank, the IMF imposes conditions on countries borrowing money to ensure that they are able to repay the loans; this is called 'conditionality'. In 1987, because the earlier IMF conditions were not increasing the ability of debtor nations to repay their loans, the conditions were increased 'to include structural measures – such as price and trade liberalization, privatization and a range of policies touching on economic governance'. Although nations could, in theory, say no to the IMF, it would mean not only that IMF loans were cut, but it would discourage foreign investment and other loans because so many companies and institutions looked to the IMF to give countries the stamp of approval.[29]

The IMF conditions became a standard that other aid agencies used. Countries that satisfied IMF criteria were eligible for aid from these other agencies: 'The fund therefore serves as a gatekeeper to official loans and aid and has far more power than the funds it provides directly would suggest.'[30] The acceptance of IMF policy prescriptions also gives 'the green light' to foreign investment and loans from commercial banks.

In fact, many of the nations following the World Bank/IMF prescriptions did not prosper: 'the majority of those nations that have followed the IMF's advice have experienced profound economic crises: low or even declining growth, much larger foreign debts and the stagnation that perpetuates systemic poverty'. Some countries that had declined the IMF's 'enhanced structural adjustment' loans were, in contrast, better off. Davison Budhoo, a former IMF economist who quit in disgust over IMF policies, argues that loan conditions were not imposed to meet the economic needs of the borrowing countries, but were rather aimed at satisfying the economic and social needs of developed capitalist economies. He is one of many current and former employees of the World Bank and the IMF who have publicly criticized their free market policies because they don't actually help the development of poor nations.[31]

The IMF had always argued that although the poor suffered in the short term from the austerity measures imposed by IMF structural adjustment programmes, they would ultimately benefit from the economic growth that these programmes would achieve. Asian countries had been the economic growth success stories. Therefore, the Asian crisis in 1997 opened the IMF to even more criticism. The IMF was unable to reverse the economic decline in countries such as Thailand, Indonesia and South Korea. Structural adjustment is now carried out in the name of poverty reduction, rather than economic growth. It achieves neither; but the failure to achieve economic growth is much easier to measure. The policy prescriptions remain unaltered.[32]

Like the World Bank and the IMF, other development banks have moved towards policy-based lending. The Asian Development Bank (ADB) is an example of the development banks that have moved away from 'their traditional emphasis on providing low-cost finance for public-sector projects' and 'protection of infant industries, a strong regulatory role for the state and mercantilist trade'. Instead, the ADB has aligned itself with the World Bank/IMF free market model, 'providing strategic policy advice, policy-based lending, support to the private sector and mobilizing private capital flows to developing countries'. ADB loan conditions have increased during recent years, and it is increasingly supporting private-sector projects.[33]

FINANCIAL DEREGULATION

While the IMF and the World Bank have played a large role in enforcing the Washington Consensus on poorer countries in desperate need of capital, other more affluent countries have also been forced into adopting the same formula by the world's financial markets. Their vulnerability to these markets has been facilitated by financial deregulation. Financial deregulation, in turn, has been demanded by business interests, particularly large financial firms and transnational corporations who want to be free to move their money around. The economic argument for financial deregulation has been supplied by free market think tanks and economic advisers, who have argued that the free and unregulated movement of capital is more efficient because capital can move to where it gets the best returns.[34]

Large investors have their own lobbying associations and pressure groups that pressure governments to deregulate their financial sectors and make 'the world safe for capitalism'. These include the Emerging Markets Trading Association, the Council of Institutional Investors and the Institute of International Finance. The membership of the latter, for example, is made up of 185 of the world's largest banks, funds and portfolio managers. It seeks to enable its members to engage 'with finance ministers, central bank governors, the IMF, the World Bank and other multilateral agencies designed to enhance private sector–public sector cooperation'.[35]

The US Treasury also worked hard to achieve financial deregulation. Lawrence Summers, deputy secretary of the Treasury and former chief economist at the World Bank, in a paper on 'America's role in global economic integration', stated in 1997 that 'At Treasury, our most crucial international priority remains the creation of a well-funded, truly global capital market.'[36]

Free market advocates have been aware that deregulation would enable 'private international financial markets to discipline government policy effectively'. Unfortunately, governments and citizens were not aware of this implication, and because few laypeople can understand the complexities of international financial transactions, there was little opposition to the deregulation of financial markets. This was facilitated by the fact that the relevant government departments around the world – finance and commerce – as well as the central banks, tended to be staffed by free market-oriented economists who heartily embraced deregulation. There are also close links between 'the private-sector side of international finance and the public-sector domain of national economic policies', often because of common educational backgrounds.[37]

Financial deregulation was also self-perpetuating because countries that were competing for international capital with countries that had already deregulated felt they also had to deregulate. In this way, financial deregulation created a snowball effect. The US was the first to begin deregulating its financial sector. It did so to attract investors at a time when US government deficits were high due to spending on the Vietnam War, and a weakening trade position developed as industries in Europe and Japan thrived. In addition, 'American banks and financiers who were chaffing at the bit under restrictive financial controls' lobbied hard for this deregulation, which promised more opportunities and bigger profits.[38]

In 1971, President Nixon disconnected the value of the US dollar from the gold standard. Other countries, since the Bretton Woods Conference at the end of World War II, had fixed the value of their currencies to the US dollar on the understanding that the value of the US dollar would be fixed at US$35 per ounce of gold. However, now that the value of US currency fluctuated, free of the value of gold, many countries found it very difficult to keep a fixed exchange rate between their own currency and the US dollar. This led to most adopting a floating exchange rate – that is, an exchange rate set by the market rather than the government. In 1974, Nixon deregulated the movement of capital in and out of the US. The UK followed suit in 1979, and other countries did so during the 1980s so that by the 1990s most of the world's flow of capital was deregulated.[39]

Financial deregulation involves three actions: the opening up of a nation to the free flow of capital in and out of it; the removal of regulations on financial institutions operating within a country; and the removal of political controls from the central bank.[40] In this way, the financial sector of a nation becomes part of the international financial sector, rather than a part of the domestic economy, and it serves the interests of global financial institutions rather than the interests of the local people or national governments.

Governments that follow this route are no longer able to set low interest rates, direct credit to where it is needed in the economy, or to differentiate between loans that are for productive purposes and those that are for speculative purposes. Rather than the banks being accountable to governments, governments become accountable to the international financial markets.[41] According to Indian Professor of Economics Prabhat Patnaik:

> *The essence of democracy is the pursuit of policies in the interests of the people... An economy exposed to the free flow of international finance capital, however, is obsessed with the need to appease international financiers, to retain their 'confidence': the thrust of policies in such an economy, therefore, even in principle, is not towards serving the interests of the people but towards serving the interests of the speculators, which represents an inversion of democracy.*[42]

For example, governments have to keep tax rates low to attract capital and are unable to have large budget deficits as this scares away investors. The economics editor of the *Financial Times*, Peter Norman, observed:

> *Because they process the many billions of dollars worth of investments flowing across national borders each day, the markets have become the police, judge and jury of the world economy – a worrying thought given that they tend to view events and policies through the distorting lenses of fear and greed.*[43]

Rising share prices have come to be the final arbiter of good policy. Forget opinion polls that show the public is opposed to privatization and deregulation and is fearful of massive corporate and government downsizing. The only real poll that counts is the stock market. And while such policies elicit positive market responses, politicians know them to be right.

Financial deregulation exposes 'the economy to the vortex of speculative capital movements – that is, to the flows of short-term finance in search of quick profits.' For example, only 10 per cent of transactions in currency markets represent actual trade. The rest is largely speculative. Investors today prefer to invest in mutual funds or make short-term investments in companies gambling against movements on the stock market, rather than long-term investments in the production of goods and services.[44]

During the 1990s, many investors speculated in East Asia, investing billions of dollars in real estate, the stock market, banks and corporations so that market values soared unrealistically. At the first sign of falling stock markets, there was an investor panic. Foreign capital was rapidly withdrawn from those same countries, causing a crash that involved company bankruptcies, widespread unemployment, devaluation of currencies and shortage of foreign exchange.[45] To attract foreign investment after such a rout, the IMF made the countries raise their interest rates to ridiculously high levels – up to 80 per cent – which caused havoc with property values and industrial production.

The response of speculators in markets is quick and herd like. Reactions are not well thought out nor fully informed. Speculators panic and do not want to be left behind once capital movements begin. The value of what one invests in will go up if others also want to invest in it, and down if they don't. The trick is to get out before everyone else does. Such decisions are not made on the basis of what is good for a nation's economy, but rather on the basis of trying to second guess other investors. This merely serves to create economic instability and does little to foster productive long-term investment because capital that could otherwise be used in production is used for gambling on the economies of various countries. The rapid inflow and outflow of speculative finance can cause crises in national economies.[46] David Korten, once a senior adviser to the US Agency for International Development (USAID), says of these speculators:

> *Each day, they move more than two trillion dollars around the world in search of quick profits and safe havens, sending exchange rates and stock markets into wild gyrations wholly unrelated to any underlying economic reality. With abandon, they make and break national economies, buy and sell corporations and hold politicians hostage to their interests.*[47]

Thomas Friedman uses the term the 'electronic herd' to refer to 'the faceless stock, bond and currency traders sitting behind computer screens all over the globe, moving their money around with the click of a mouse from mutual funds to pension funds to emerging market funds' and the 'big multinational corporations who now spread their factories around the world, constantly shifting them to the most efficient low-cost producers'. It is they who have become the final arbiters of 'good' government policy.[48]

Countries can still retain a veneer of democracy with choice between major parties; but because of the constraints imposed by the need to please international financial markets, the policy differences between the major parties is minimal. Whether it is a Labour party in the UK or Australia, or a Peronist president in Argentina, or the Bharatiya Janata party (BJP) in India, they all adopt the same free market policies.[49] Governments that try to deviate are punished by the markets:

> The 'soundness' of policy settings in particular countries will be judged by those bodies that control international financial capital – particularly the major international banks, large transnational corporations with major financial dealing, fund managers within key private financial institutions and the key credit-ratings agencies (such as Moody's). These judgements will be reflected in the value the 'markets' place on the currencies of the particular countries, on the attractiveness of various countries for foreign investors and on the cost and availability of credit.[50]

Credit ratings agencies, particularly Moody's and Standard and Poors, can make or break a nation's economy. For example, when these agencies downgraded the credit ratings of Brazil and Venezuela in September 1998, the financial markets of those countries collapsed. Direct investors, bond investors, pension and mutual funds all rely on credit agencies to tell them what investments are safe. The World Bank's International Financial Corporation also categorizes countries into those that are investable and those that are not. Countries are thought to be a higher political risk if their governments are likely to 'nationalize, change tax incentives or give concessions to labour unions.'[51]

Following the Asian crisis when speculators led the flight of capital out of Asia, the Malaysian government decided to introduce capital controls and fix the exchange rate of the Malaysian currency. The international financial community was incensed. Fund manager Mark Mobius, fearing it could set a precedent, called for wealthy countries to 'severely punish' Prime Minister Mohammed Mahathir. He himself subsequently withdrew some US$2 billion in investment from Malaysia. Morgan Stanley took Malaysia off its influential Capital International Index. It reinstated it when Mahathir lifted the controls.[52]

Various analysts argue that, in fact, Malaysia benefited from the capital controls. Kaplan and Rodrik from Harvard University found that 'compared to IMF programmes [which required financial deregulation], the Malaysian policies produced faster economic recovery, smaller declines in employment and real wages, and more rapid turnaround in the stock market'.[53] Similarly, Edison, from the IMF, and Reinhart, in a paper provided by the US Federal Reserve, found that the controls did help to increase interest rates, stabilize the currency and give more policy autonomy to the Malaysian government.[54]

Stiglitz, who was World Bank chief economist at the time, also admitted the success of the capital controls in Malaysia, and some thought this heralded a change in policy at the bank. Instead, Stiglitz was forced to resign from the World Bank, following pressure on the bank's president from US Treasury Secretary Lawrence Summers. The bank had not turned, nor did investors. In order to attract foreign investors, Mahathir was finally forced in 2001 to lift the last of the controls, excluding the fixed exchange rate, in order to attract foreign investors back to Malaysia.[55]

Thomas Friedman refers to the Washington Consensus prescription as the 'Golden Straitjacket'. He argues that 'As your country puts on the Golden Strait- jacket, two things tend to happen: your economy grows and your politics shrinks.' It is a straitjacket because it 'narrows the political and economic policy choices of those in power to relatively tight parameters. That is why it is increasingly difficult these days to find any real differences between ruling and opposition parties in those countries that have put on the Golden Straitjacket':[56]

> Governments – be they led by Democrats or Republicans, Conservatives or Labourites, Gaullists or Socialists, Christian Democrats or Social Democrats – which deviate too far from the core rules will see their investors stampede away, interest rates rise and market valuations fall. The only way to get more room to manoeuvre in the Golden Straitjacket is by growing it, and the only way to grow it is by keeping it on tight. That's its one virtue: the tighter you wear it, the more gold it produces and the more padding you can then put into it for your society.[57]

If a country subscribes to the free market formula, the 'Golden Straitjacket', then it is rewarded by the electronic herd with investment capital. But if they decide a country is not conforming, then they flee, taking their capital with them: 'Moody's Investors Service and Standard and Poors are the bloodhounds for the electronic herd. These credit ratings agencies prowl the world, constantly sniffing over countries' and identifying those that are slipping out of the straitjacket.[58]

Lee Hong Koo, prime minister of South Korea during the mid 1990s, sees it differently: 'We didn't realize that the victory of the Cold War was a victory for market forces above politics ... politics becomes just political engineering to implement decisions in the narrow space allowed you within this system'.[59]

OUTCOMES

However, while financial markets, banks and TNCs unequivocally benefit from the Golden Straitjacket, for ordinary people the promised increase in prosperity is illusory. In the two decades before the introduction of the Washington Consensus, when government spending and welfare schemes were looked upon with approval

(1960–1980), the income per person grew by 73 per cent in Latin America and 34 per cent in Africa. During the following two decades as the Washington consensus was implemented, incomes in Africa have declined by 23 per cent and the Latin American economies have only grown by 6 per cent.[60]

In developing countries, life expectancy has dropped. The gap between rich and poor has increased. Despite sell offs worth billions of dollars, on average people are poorer now than they were in 1998. Forty-four per cent of people in developing nations live in poverty and unemployment has doubled in the last decade. For most people in these countries, privatization means mass layoffs and high prices.[61] Even the IMF admits that 'in recent decades, nearly one fifth of the world population have regressed'.[62] This is even more evident to the populations of developing countries:

> *A popular and political ground swell is building from the Andes to Argentina against the decade-old experiment with free market capital-ism. The reforms that have shrunk the state and opened markets to foreign competition, many believe, have enriched corrupt officials and faceless multinationals, and failed to better their lives.*[63]

In countries with a tradition of strong unions, union power has been diminished through labour market deregulation, workplace restructuring and the restructuring of wage-setting systems. The state no longer intervenes to protect the weaker members of society and to ensure equity. Economic efficiency, growth and competition are now paramount. Nevertheless, despite these goals, the end result of the reforms has not been better economic performance: 'what purports to be a recipe for the revitalization of industry is more a device for redistribution from poor to rich'.[64]

Michel Chossudovsky, professor of economics at the University of Ottawa, Canada, outlines how World Bank and IMF policies have transformed low-income countries into open economic territories and 'reserves' of cheap labour and natural resources available to transnational companies and consumers in high-income nations. In the process, governments in low-income countries have handed over economic control of their countries to these organizations, which act on behalf of powerful financial and political interests in the US, Japan and Europe. Having handed over this control, they are unable to generate the sort of local development that would improve the welfare of their own people.[65]

By 2002, even economists were growing disillusioned with the Washington Consensus because of its failure to deliver on its promises: 'The "Washington Consensus" has been effectively repudiated in Washington'.[66] The Asian crisis in 1997 was followed at the end of 2001 with the economic collapse of Argentina, once the symbol of success of the Washington Consensus. Even the think tanks are having trouble justifying the consensus in the light of outcomes like this. Brink Lindsey, a scholar at the neo-conservative Cato Institute, said:

In the early '90s, there was the sense that if you just opened your markets, and stabilized prices, and privatized industries, foreign investors would come to your door and you could enjoy rapid catch-up growth rates. And what has become painfully clear is that life is much more complicated than that.[67]

As the 21st century got under way, people in Latin America, the heartland of the Washington Consensus, began voting for left-wing candidates willing to protect the national interest against the World Bank and IMF pro-market formulas. In Brazil, where incomes declined by 3 per cent despite (or because of) adherence to IMF policy prescriptions, Luiz Inacio Lula Da Silva, a candidate from the Workers party who had not even achieved 25 per cent of the vote in three previous elections, was elected as president in 2002.

In Venezuela, a leftist government led by Hugo Chavez was elected in 1998 on an anti-corruption and anti-poverty platform. Chavez has been strongly opposed by the Venezuelan business community and organized labour, but has managed to survive an attempted coup, a business strike led by oil industry management, US government opposition and a referendum to remove him. In Bolivia, which had been among the earliest to privatize in Latin America during the 1980s, indigenous leader Evo Morales came into power with the second highest vote ever for election as president, after promising to nationalize industries.[68] These governments can be expected to be put under unrelenting pressure by the international financial markets.

In Argentina, the economy has been making an unexpected recovery, growing by 8 per cent per year, attracting investors back, and lowering unemployment and poverty. And this has been achieved not by following IMF prescriptions, but 'at least in part by ignoring or even defying economic and political orthodoxy'. Rather than 'tighten its belt' as required by the IMF, it has sought to stimulate domestic consumption. And it has used government money, raised, in part, from levies on exports and financial transactions, to help the local economy rather than to pay off the banks and creditors. While European investors avoid Argentina, investors from other Latin American countries and from Asia have taken advantage of the opportunities, as have expatriate Argentines. With more money coming in than leaving, Argentina is less beholden to the IMF.[69] How long it can hold out against the IMF is an open question.

NOTES

1   John M. Legge, 'Gordon Gecko's Economics', *Dissent*, Autumn/Winter, 2003, pp26–7.
2   Seymour M. Hersh, *The Price of Power: Kissinger in the Nixon White House*, New York, Summit Books, 1983, p259.
3   Gregory Palast, 'Pepsi Demands a US Coup: Goodbye Allende. Hello Pinochet.' *The Observer*, 8 November, 1998, p9.

4   Select Committee to Study Governmental Operations with Respect to Intelligence Activities, 'Church Report: Covert Action in Chile 1963–1973', Department of State, United States Senate, 18 December 1975.

5   *Ibid.*

6   *Ibid.* ; CIA, 'CIA Activities in Chile', US Central Intelligence Agency, 18 September, 2000, www.cia.gov/cia/reports/chile

7   Cited in Select Committee to Study Governmental Operations with Respect to Intelligence Activities, 'Church Report'.

8   *Ibid.*

9   CIA, 'CIA Activities in Chile'.

10 Steve Kangas, 'Chile: The Laboratory Test', Liberalism Resurgent, www.huppi.com/kangaroo/L-chichile.htm accessed 15 August 2004; Sidney Blumenthal, *The Rise of the Counter-Establishment: From Conservative Ideology to Political Power*, New York, Time Books, 1986, pp113–114.

11 Joseph E. Stiglitz, *Globalization and Its Discontents*, New York, W. W. Norton & Co., 2002, p16.

12 David E. Sanger, 'How Washington Inc. Makes a Sale', *The New York Times*, 19 February, 1995.

13 Jeffrey Davis, *et al.*, 'Fiscal and Macroeconomic Impact of Privatization', *IMF Occasional Paper*, 22 June, 2000, www.IMF.org/external/pubs/nft/op/194/index.htm; Susan Hawley, 'Exporting Corruption: Privatisation, Multinationals and Bribery', *The Corner House Briefing*, 2000, http://cornerhouse.icaap.org/briefings/19.html.

14 Friends of the Earth, 'International Monetary Fund 101', *Multinational Monitor*, January/February, 1998.

15 Mary Ann Haley, *Freedom and Finance: Democratization and Institutional Investors in Developing Countries*, New York, Palgrave, 2001, p69; Mark T. Berger, *The Battle for Asia: From Decolonization to Globalization*, New York, Routledge Curzon, 2004, p154; Haley, *Freedom and Finance*, p108.

16 Quoted in Morris Morley, 'Behind the World Bank Loans', *Sydney Morning Herald*, 9 December, 1986, p17.

17 'Chile and the United States: Declassified Documents Relating to the Military Coup, 1970–1976', The National Security Archive, George Washington University, www2.gwu.edu/~nsarchiv/NSAEBB/NSAEBB8/nsaebb8.htm accessed 28 December 2004.

18 *Ibid.*

19 Quoted in Select Committee to Study Governmental Operations with Respect to Intelligence Activities, 'Church Report'.

20 *Ibid.* ; Morley, 'Behind the World Bank Loans', p17.

21 Peter Kornbluh, 'Washington's Secret Economic War on Nicaragua', *The San Francisco Chronicle*, 6 September, 1989.

22 John Williamson, 'In Search of a Manual for Technopols', in John Williamson (ed) *The Political Economy of Policy Reform*, Washington, DC, Institute for International Economics, 1994, p17; Institute for International Economics, 'About the Institute for International Economics', IIE, www.iie.com/ADMINIST/aboutiie.htm accessed 6 January 2001.

23 Williamson, 'In Search of a Manual for Technopols', pp26–8.

24 Peter Self, *Government by the Market? The Politics of Public Choice*, Hampshire and London, Macmillan, 1993, p70.

25   Frank Stilwell, 'Economic Rationalism: Sound Foundations for Policy?' in Stuart
     Rees, Gordon Rodley and Frank Stilwell (eds) *Beyond the Market: Alternatives to
     Economic Rationalism*, Leichhardt, NSW, Pluto Press, 1993, p36; Williamson, 'In
     Search of a Manual for Technopols', p17.
26   Stiglitz, *Globalization and Its Discontents*, p9.
27   John Weeks, 'Credit Where Discredit Is Due', *Third World Resurgence*, April, 1994,
     p32; Haley, *Freedom and Finance*, pp95–7.
28   Weeks, 'Credit Where Discredit Is Due', p33.
29   Masood Ahmed, *et al.*, 'Refocusing IMF Conditionality', *Finance & Development*,
     December, 2001, www.IMF.org/external/pubs/ft/fandd/2001/12/ahmed.htm;
     Stiglitz, *Globalization and Its Discontents*, pp42, 49.
30   Gabriel Kolko, 'Ravaging the Poor: IMF Indicted by Its Own Data', *Multinational
     Monitor*, June, 1998, p21.
31   *Ibid.*, p21; Davison Budhoo and Claude Alvares, 'Why the IMF Is a Threat to the
     South', *Third World Resurgence*, June, 1992; for a list see www.globalpolicy.org/
     socecon/bwi-wto/criticsindx.htm.
32   Kolko, 'Ravaging the Poor', p20; Chris Adams, 'Privatising Infrastructure in the
     South', *Focus on Trade*, May, 2001, www.focusweb.org/publications/2001/privatising
     %20Infrastructure%20in%20the%20South.html.
33   Asian Development Bank, 'The Bank's Policy Initiatives for the Energy Sector',
     Philippines, Asian Development Bank, May 1995; Adams, 'Privatising Infrastructure
     in the South'.
34   Eric Helleiner, 'Post-Globalization: Is the Financial Liberalization Trend Likely to
     Be Reversed?' in Robert Boyer and Daniel Drache (eds) *States Against Markets: The
     Limits of Globalization*, New York, Routledge, 1996, p194; Stephen Bell, *Ungoverning
     the Economy: The Political Economy of Australian Economic Policy*, Melbourne, Oxford
     University Press, 1997, pp103–4; Helleiner, 'Post-Globalization', p194.
35   Haley, *Freedom and Finance*, pp90–1, quote on p93.
36   Lawrence Summers, 'America's Role in Global Economic Integration', Paper presented
     at the Integrating National Economies: The Next Step, The Brookings Institution,
     Washington, DC, 9 January 1997.
37   Helleiner, 'Post-Globalization', p194; Haley, *Freedom and Finance*, p69.
38   Bell, *Ungoverning the Economy*, pp103–40.
39   *Ibid.*, pp103–40.
40   Prabhat Patnaik, 'The Real Face of Financial Liberalisation', *Frontline: India's National
     Magazine*, vol 16, no 4, 1999.
41   *Ibid.*
42   *Ibid.*
43   Peter Norman, 'Survey of World Economy and Finance', *Financial Times*, 30
     September, 1994.
44   Patnaik, 'The Real Face of Financial Liberalisation'; Eric Toussaint, *Your Money or
     Your Life! The Tyranny of Global Finance*, Translated by Raghu Krishnan, London,
     Pluto Press, 1998, p52; Maude Barlow and Tony Clarke, *Blue Gold: The Fight to Stop
     the Corporate Theft of the World's Water*, New York, The New Press, 2002, p92.
45   Patricia Ranald, 'Disciplining Governments: The MAI in the International and
     Australian Contexts', in James Goodman and Patricia Ranald (eds) *Stopping the*

Juggernaut: Public Interest Versus the Multilateral Agreement on Investment, Sydney, Pluto Press, 2000, p30.

46   Patnaik, 'The Real Face of Financial Liberalisation'.

47   David Korten quoted in Barlow and Clarke, *Blue Gold*, p93.

48   Thomas L. Friedman, *The Lexus and the Olive Tree*, New York, Farrar, Straus and Giroux, 1999, pp90–1.

49   Patnaik, 'The Real Face of Financial Liberalisation'.

50   Bell, *Ungoverning the Economy*, p105.

51   Haley, *Freedom and Finance*, pp76, 79.

52   *Ibid.*, p129.

53   Ethan Kaplan and Dani Rodrik, 'Did the Malaysian Capital Controls Work', John F. Kennedy School of Government, Harvard University, February, 2001, http://ksghome.harvard.edu/~drorik/Malaysia%20controls.PDF

54   Hali J. Edison and Carmen M. Reinhart, 'Capital Controls During Financial Crises: The Case of Malaysia and Thailand', *International Finance Discussion Papers*, no 662, 2000.

55   'World Bank Reverses Position on Financial Controls and on Malaysia', *Global Intelligence Update Weekly Analysis*, 20 September, 1999; Robert Wade, 'Showdown at the World Bank', *New Left Review*, January/February, 2001, www.globalpolicy.org/socecon/bwi-wto/wbank/2001/rwade.htm; 'Malaysia Lifts Foreign Investment Controls', *BBC News*, 2 May, 2001, http://news.bbc.co.uk/1/hi/business/130820.stm.

56   Friedman, *The Lexus and the Olive Tree*, pp86–7.

57   *Ibid.*, pp87–8.

58   *Ibid.*, pp90–1.

59   Quoted in *Ibid.*, pp88–9.

60   Greg Palast, *The Best Democracy Money Can Buy*, London, Pluto Press, 2002, p48

61   Paul Blustein, 'IMF's 'Consensus' Policies Fraying', *Washington Post*, 26 September, 2002, pE01; Richard Lapper, 'Piling on the Pressure', *Financial Times*, 5 October, 2002, p1; Juan Forero, 'Still Poor, Latin Americans Protest Push for Open Markets', *The New York Times*, 19 July, 2002, pA1.

62   Quoted in Palast, *The Best Democracy Money Can Buy*, p50.

63   Forero, 'Still Poor, Latin Americans Protest Push for Open Markets', pA1.

64   Stilwell, 'Economic Rationalism: Sound Foundations for Policy?' p35.

65   Michel Chossudovsky, 'The Global Creation of Third World Poverty', *Third World Resurgence*, January, 1992, p13.

66   John Gray, *False Dawn: The Delusions of Global Capitalism*, London, Granta Books, 2002, pxx.

67   Quoted in Blustein, 'IMF's "Consensus" Policies Fraying', pEO1.

68   Juan Forero, 'Still Poor, Latin Americans Protest Push for Open Markets', *The New York Times*, 19 July, 2002; Larry Rohter, 'In Free-Market Slump, Brazil's Voters Look for Change', *The New York Times*, 5 October, 2002; Juan Forero, 'As Bolivians Vote, Populism Is on the Rise', *The New York Times*, 30 June, 2002; Forero, 'Still Poor, Latin Americans Protest Push for Open Markets', pA1; Lapper, 'Piling on the Pressure', p1.

69   Larry Rohter, 'Argentina's Economic Rally Defies Forecasts', *New York Times*, 26 December, 2004.

4

Washington Consensus Down Under

The New Right is setting out to change the whole political agenda in Australia: it seeks to form a new 'commonsense' – that is, what people 'take for granted' and appears natural to them. BERNIE TAFT[1]

The neo-liberal experiment in New Zealand is the most ambitious attempt at constructing the free market as a social institution to be implemented anywhere this century. JOHN GRAY[2]

In 1993 an international conference was held in Washington, DC, to find ways to 'strengthen the political muscle of those politicians' who were promoting economic reforms embodied in the Washington Consensus (see Chapter 3), including free trade, limited government, deregulation of labour and financial markets, and facilitating free markets. Papers were given by key economists who had been involved in implementing economic 'reforms'. Each paper was based on country case studies so that lessons could be learned about how such reforms had been achieved in a range of countries, including Australia and New Zealand, Spain, Poland, Turkey, Chile, Mexico, Indonesia and in Eastern Europe.[3]

The conference was organized by the Institute for International Economics (IIE). The IIE is a private Washington-based think tank that focuses on international economic policy. It claims to be non-partisan, but advocates free-market economic policies which facilitate free trade and investment and minimal government intervention. It was founded in 1981 by the German Marshal Fund in the US and is funded by a number of foundations and corporations:[4]

The institute [IIE] attempts to anticipate emerging issues and to be ready with practical ideas to inform and shape public debate. Its audience includes government officials and legislators, business and labour leaders, management and staff at international organizations, university-based scholars and their students, other research institutions and non-governmental organizations, the media, and the public at large. It addresses these groups both in the United States and around the world.[5]

The IIE has 50 staff and a budget of US$5 million per annum. It is highly influential in policy circles and claims to have 'made important contributions to key trade policy decisions, including defeat of import quota legislation for steel, the Uruguay Round, NAFTA [North American Free Trade Agreement], the Free Trade Area of the Americas, APEC [Asia-Pacific Economic Cooperation], the US–Japan Framework Talks, reform of sanctions policy, and liberalization of US export controls'.[6]

As an outcome of the conference, John Williamson, senior fellow of the IIE and the person who coined the term 'Washington Consensus', put forward a tentative manual for achieving its policy prescriptions.

Step 1: Crisis

The first element needed for facilitating policy reforms was a sense of crisis, which would ensure that people were amenable to radical changes. Williamson even suggested that if such a crisis did not exist, then it might be manufactured:

> ... one will have to ask whether it could conceivably make sense to think of deliberately provoking a crisis so as to remove the political logjam to reform. For example, it has sometimes been suggested in Brazil that it would be worthwhile stoking up a hyperinflation so as to scare everyone into accepting those changes that would finally make price stabilizations attainable... Is it possible to conceive of a pseudo-crisis that could serve the same positive function without the costs of a real crisis? What is the least unpleasant type of crisis that seems able to do the trick?[7]

Without such a crisis, the advocates of change have to rely upon their power of persuasion to convince the public that 'mediocre performance is a calamity'. Alternatively, a government may be elected with a mandate for change if it publicizes its policies and campaigns on the basis of those policies before it is elected.[8]

Step 2: Change of government

The time to introduce reforms is soon after the election of a new government because the new government will enjoy a honeymoon period when the public will 'give it the benefit of the doubt and blame any sacrifices and difficulties on its predecessor'. The honeymoon period will be longer if the election follows a crisis.[9]

Step 3: Support from beneficiaries

Because the honeymoon period will not last, the reforms need to quickly generate strong support from a powerful group of beneficiaries who will oppose any repeal of the reforms and thus ensure their stability. Economic reform involves changes in the distribution of power and resources, and so it will always create opponents as well as proponents. Reform will also be easier if the opponents are disorganized, repressed or powerless. In the case of market-based reforms, the losers will include public-sector employees and 'those who derive their incomes from the un-traded sector; the employees and owners of firms that will become unprofitable when faced with market prices; the beneficiaries of government subsidies for food or housing'. But when policies are supported by powerful beneficiaries, they 'develop a vested interest in keeping the reforms in place', and even when new parties come to power it is difficult to jettison the policies that are 'highly prized by powerful interests'.[10]

Other enabling factors identified at the conference included:

- the presence of a fragmented and demoralized opposition;
- the existence in government of a team of economists ... with a common, coherent view of what needs to be done and commanding the instruments of concentrated executive authority;
- the presence at the top of a political leader with a vision of history who is not unduly concerned about being re-elected;
- the existence of a comprehensive programme for transformation of the economy and a rapid timetable for implementation;
- the will and ability to appeal directly to the public [through the media] and bypass vested interests.[11]

During the 1980s, Australia and New Zealand voters elected labour/social democratic governments to power which both set out to introduce market-oriented reforms of the type more commonly associated with the conservative governments of Margaret Thatcher in the UK and Ronald Reagan in the US. These governments focused on freeing up markets rather than planning for goals. They 'embarked on programmes of economic and social transformation arguably more comprehensive in scope and intensity than anywhere else in the Western world'. These programmes of market liberalization 'cut away many of the key mechanisms employed to achieve traditional social democratic objectives' and destroyed 'the ethos and institutional pillars upon which Labour's support had always been based'.[12]

NEW ZEALAND'S 'REFORMS'

Many of the free market strategies associated with the Washington Consensus were implemented in New Zealand beginning in 1984, when a Labour government was elected, and then by the National government when it was elected in 1990. These included:

- *Fiscal discipline*: government expenditure was reduced.
- *Public expenditure priorities*: a user-pays system was introduced for many government services; housing and industry assistance was reduced; welfare cuts occurred.
- *Tax reform*: the tax base was broadened with a goods and services tax and personal and corporate tax rates were flattened so that the top rate of tax was reduced from 66 to 33 per cent.
- *Financial liberalization*: financial institutions were deregulated.
- *Exchange rates*: the dollar was floated so that exchange rates were determined by money markets.
- *Trade liberalization*: tariffs and subsidies were reduced significantly and import licences were abolished.
- *Foreign direct investment*: foreign investment was free of restrictions.
- *Privatization*: extensive commercialization, corporatization and privatization of government enterprises and services occurred.
- *Deregulation*: price controls, and entry and operating restrictions were abolished; individual employment contracts replaced union-negotiated, industry-wide employment awards; and the power of unions was undermined.
- *Property rights*: revision of property rights laws occurred.[13]

In addition, the government goal of full employment was discarded, replaced by the goal of fighting inflation. The welfare system was reduced as spending on law enforcement and prisons increased.[14] These reforms and structural adjustments have become known as the 'New Zealand experiment' because many international policy-makers were watching with interest to see how it fared. The reforms were supported by international institutions such as the World Bank and International Monetary Fund (IMF), which was imposing such measures in debtor nations (see Chapter 3) and the Organisation for Economic Co-operation and Development (OECD), which saw New Zealand 'as an important test case for reform in a Western developed country'.[15]

New Zealand shifted from being one of the most regulated OECD countries to one of the least regulated:[16] 'Traditions of state intervention in the economy to protect social cohesion were more deeply entrenched in New Zealand than in any other Western country, with the exception of social-democratic Sweden.' The free market formula was applied in New Zealand in a more uncompromising way than in any other country before; every major social institution was 'reformed' and restructured, leaving it the closest thing there was 'to the pure neo-liberal model of lean government and a free market economy'.[17]

The business press was ecstatic. The *Economist* described the reforms as an 'exhilarating dash for economic freedom... Delighted progressive businessmen hardly dare believe that a Labour government is doing these things, while bewildered old trade union leaders loyally pretend that it isn't'. The *Economist* referred to the 'sort of socialism of which millionaires approve' and 'out-Thatchering Mrs Thatcher'.[18]

By 1995, despite the heavy social costs that the 'experiment' was exacting, international institutions and the business media were hailing the experiment as a model for the rest of the world. Moody's Investors Services described it thus: 'The reorientation of New Zealand economic policy after 1984 represented one of the most ambitious and comprehensive structural reforms undertaken by any OECD country'; but it noted: 'As it turned out, the reform process has proved somewhat tortuous and quite painful for many segments of New Zealand society'.[19]

Inequality grew in New Zealand, which had prided itself on being an egalitarian society, faster than any other industrialized country. In contrast to American commentators who were blaming a growing underclass on an overly generous welfare system, there was no underclass in New Zealand until welfare was cut and citizens were subjected to the rigours of the free market.[20]

Yet the pain suffered by the one in six New Zealanders who found themselves below the poverty line by 1993 could not be defended in the name of ensuing economic growth. According to Jane Kelsey, who analysed the New Zealand Experiment in her book, *Economic Fundamentalism*: 'Between 1985 and 1992, total growth across OECD economies averaged 20 per cent; New Zealand's economy shrank by 1 per cent over the same period' despite an increasing population. At the same time, productivity was static, unemployment skyrocketed, inflation soared (around 9 per cent per year), investment halved, overseas debt quadrupled and interest rates remained high. People left New Zealand in droves.[21]

The new government undertook reforms at a rapid rate with little consultation, not even consulting with its traditional support base of unions and lower-income earners.[22] Public consultation was replaced with 'government cultivation of the media and vast sums spent on public relations consultants and advertising'.[23] Even other members of the Cabinet, and certainly the party, were left out of decision-making and often found themselves facing a *fait accompli* when major policy changes were made.

The speed of reforms was partly a strategy to take advantage of the traditional honeymoon period enjoyed by new governments; but it was also designed to provide no opportunity for those opposed to or hurt by the reforms to organize or campaign against them before they were in place.[24] 'Critics and opponents were always on the defensive and left debating last week's reforms.' Roger Douglas, minister of finance and prime architect of the changes (referred to as Rogernomics), argued that reforms had to be quick so that interest groups did not have time 'to mobilize and drag you down' and 'the fire of opponents is much less accurate if they have to shoot at a rapidly moving target'.[25]

Parliamentary procedures and conventions were treated with contempt in order to get measures through without adequate debate. Discussion of bills was often terminated prematurely and the government frequently used 'urgency powers' to 'avoid the inconvenience of scrutiny before or by a select committee'.[26]

Kelsey notes that many potential critics amongst the activist community had been integrated within the political party structure, particularly the Labour party, and they were therefore reluctant to publicly criticize the Labour party's reforms, at least during its first term of office. Nevertheless, there were many critics of the reforms within the Labour party, and during 1985 many regional party conferences opposed the 'market-led approach'. Kelsey argues: 'The Labour government became the vehicle for a programme which neither its members nor the electorate had endorsed, and which was irreconcilable with the basic tenets of social democracy.'[27]

Early reforms included the removal of subsidies and protections and created unemployment, as well as hurt farmers and small businesses. However, such was the disgust with the previous National government that Labour had a very long honeymoon period and it gained middle-class supporters through measures such as tax cuts. The government also had strong media support and extended its honeymoon period through some fairly progressive policies in areas such as Maori rights, women's affairs and employment equity. Its popular banning of US ships with nuclear weapons from New Zealand ports fired up nationalistic feelings, and this nationalism was further fuelled by the bombing of the Greenpeace *Rainbow Warrior* in Auckland harbour by the French secret service.[28]

Labour was therefore re-elected in 1987 and began its next round of less popular reforms. The inequities of the reform programme became more obvious in the second term, aided by the report of the Royal Commission on Social Policy, and when Finance Minister Douglas pushed for a flat income tax in 1987, Prime Minister David Lange refused. Thus began the split between Lange and Douglas that ended in Douglas's resignation as minister. Two years later, in 1989, Jim Anderton, one of the Labour MPs and a former party president, formed a breakaway party, the New Labour party, which went back to traditional labour principles.[29]

The electorate expressed its disapproval of the Labour reform agenda at the next election and elected the National party to govern in 1990, only to find that the National party had, while in opposition, adopted the same free market agenda. The struggles within the National party to reach this position had been aided by international alliances and local business influence. The party had been networking with neo-conservative parties in other parts of the world, especially the Republicans in the US and the Tories in the UK, exchanging information and discussing techniques, strategies and restructuring.[30]

Ruth Richardson, the new minister for finance, agreed with Douglas's policies and was just as determined to implement them. The National government undertook the reforms that Labour had neglected, cutting back the remnants of the welfare state – including income support for the poor – and 'removing legislative protections in industrial relations'.[31]

These measures were not only driven by ideology. Falling government income as a result of tax cuts and zero economic growth meant that in order to keep budget deficits small, government services had to be cut further. Government funding of health services and education decreased, welfare benefits were reduced and more user-pay charges were introduced. However, not all National party MPs and supporters were happy with the 'Ruthanasia' programme, as it was called by detractors. A breakaway party, New Zealand First, was formed by popular MP Winston Peters.[32]

AUSTRALIA'S 'REFORMS'

Since 1983 when the Australian Labor Party (ALP) was elected in Australia, many of the free market strategies associated with the Washington Consensus have been implemented, including:

- *Fiscal discipline*: government budget deficits were replaced with surpluses at the federal level.
- *Public expenditure priorities*: federal government spending was reduced from 30 per cent of gross domestic product (GDP) to 23 per cent by 1989; entitlements to welfare and social security were cut.
- *Tax reform*: the tax base was broadened and the top rate of tax was reduced from 60 to 47 per cent.
- *Financial liberalization*: financial institutions were deregulated.
- *Exchange rates*: the dollar was floated so that exchange rates were determined by money markets.
- *Trade liberalization*: tariffs were reduced dramatically and quantitative import restrictions were removed.
- *Privatization*: government services were commercialized and government business enterprises were corporatized, subjected to competition from the private sector and, in some cases, privatized.
- *Deregulation*: many business regulations were removed; union restructuring, enterprise-based bargaining and the demise of the centralized system of wage setting or award wages also occurred.[33]

All of these reforms, termed 'restructuring', were done in the name of increased economic efficiency, productivity and industrial competitiveness. As in New Zealand, the Labor party did not signal its policies in advance and did not have a mandate to bring them in. However, the Australian Labor government used a much more consultative style and, as a result, the restructuring was much more gradual.

Vested interests affected by the changes, such as trade liberalization and tariff reduction, were bypassed and marginalized through the government's preference for dealing with the Business Council of Australia, rather than trade or industry associations, and the Australian Council of Trade Unions (ACTU), rather than individual unions.[34] Later, ALP politician John Dawkins was reported in the

Australian Financial Review as suggesting 'that in the few years after the 1983 election, the ACTU was converted to the central elements of a pro-business agenda, and through its enhanced central power, was able to engage the entire union movement in support':[35]

> *The Hawke government's formal commitment to industry policy was swept aside by a Labor 'new right' committed to economic-liberal fundamentalism in economic policy in general... The complex issues of public economic management in the late twentieth century vanished into the age-old debate between protection and free trade.*[36]

Richard Blandy, Professor of Economics at the University of Melbourne and a key figure in the new right, suggests that the restructuring of the ACTU was a key step in facilitating reform. He claims that what the government did was to accommodate 'the interests of the main potential loser – the existing trade union movement – by facilitating its restructuring to accommodate the reform while retaining a major part of its power and influence'.[37] Similarly, Greg Whitwell stresses 'the formation of peak 'encompassing' interest groups representing, in particular, employees and employers' in enabling a 'bargained consensus' to be developed in favour of market approaches.[38] Groups such as the ACTU could defend their compliance in terms of the general interest of the workers, while particular groups of workers bore the brunt of the new policies.

The Australian government introduced a more cautious set of changes than occurred in New Zealand. Whilst financial deregulation came quickly, the Australian Labor government was reluctant to deregulate the labour market because it wanted to retain union support.[39] The government's reform agenda also had support from the opposition Liberal party, which was far more supportive than the ALP of labour market deregulation, further government spending reductions and a goods and services tax.

The conversion of the Liberal party to economic rationalism – the Australian term for free market policies – was facilitated by a restructuring of the Liberal party undertaken under the leadership of businessman John Elliott during 1979–1980. Elliott, the chief executive officer (CEO) of Elders-IXL, one of Australia's largest companies, raised a substantial amount of money as federal president of the Liberal party, and was said to be 'not only the party bagman but also the Victorian party's business eyes, ears and mouth'. In reality, he was business's eyes and mouth in the Liberal party, pushing deregulation, small government and privatization.[40]

Restructuring the party gave head office more say and ensured greater 'discipline' among Liberal politicians. This made it easier for the 'dries' to win pre-selection as election candidates despite rank-and-file opposition to economic rationalist policies. Key figures of the New Right were installed with the help of Michael Kroger, who gained presidency of the party with the help of business groups such as the Small Business Association.[41] Kelly writes of the New Right: 'Its success was reflected in the fact that in 1990 there was no New Right; the 1985 extremists had become the 1990 Liberal party mainstreamers'.[42]

In a free labour market, unemployment would be solved by declining wages as a result of the automatic supply-and-demand pricing mechanism of the market. However, welfare benefits and union power, as well as minimum wage provisions, prevented the market from operating to achieve this.[43] Therefore, the process of weakening union power and dismantling central wage-fixing, begun by Labor, was undertaken with renewed vigour by the Liberals and was augmented with welfare cuts and work-for-the-dole schemes. After being returned to power for the fourth consecutive time in 2004 and winning a majority in both houses of parliament, the Howard Liberal government has greatly accelerated labour market 'reform'.

The reinvigoration of the Australian manufacturing sector that was supposed to result from economic restructuring never occurred. The extra money generated during the 1980s by lower corporate taxes, voluntary union wage restraint, higher profits and deregulation was supposed to provide the incentives to business; but it was seldom reinvested in productivity. Rather, it was squandered on 'increased executive salaries, increased luxury consumption and a mass of unproductive investment, seeking wealth through shuffling paper, takeover bids and counter-bids'.[44]

Australia's reputation for egalitarianism and equitable distribution of income was destroyed as inequities in Australia began to rival and exceed other countries. For most of Australia's history, there had been an unwritten social compact aimed at 'building a workers' paradise'. Manufacturing industries were protected so that they could pay good wages. A minimum wage was set that would be sufficient to support a family on.[45] This compact was discarded.

The free market reforms were supported heavily outside of Australia. Treasurer Paul Keating was named International Finance Minister of the Year in 1987 by the *Economist* for his reforms.[46] As in New Zealand, the major international bureaucracies, the IMF, the World Bank and the OECD encouraged the reforms. Both major political parties were converted to economic rationalism. And when the Liberals came to power, they continued and accelerated them.

CRISIS AND HONEYMOON PERIOD

Paul Kelly, in his political history of Australia during the 1980s, claims: 'The 1980s campaign to re-invent the Australian political tradition was driven by economic crisis.'[47] However, this 'crisis' that supposedly prompted the Australian reforms, or provided the excuse for them, was more rhetoric than real. High levels of unemployment and slowing economic growth (described as a recession) were attributed by policy advisers to the structure of government and the economy. Ross Garnaut, personal economic adviser to Prime Minister Bob Hawke, claimed that there was 'a structural imperative for Australia to raise productivity growth by increasing international orientation, flexibility in resource use and competition in domestic markets'.[48]

Many of the problems facing Australia were externally generated and had nothing to do with government spending or regulation. Australia and New Zealand had been two of the most prosperous countries in the world. Both subscribed to a goal of social equity and had highly regulated economies and prized social protection measures, including progressive taxation, free education and healthcare and welfare entitlements. New Zealand, in particular, had been one of the world's most comprehensive welfare states. It was only when commodity prices declined that both countries lost their economic advantage and living standards slipped to being more average for OECD countries. After 1980, agricultural products in both countries had to compete with subsidized products from Europe.[49]

An early step in the 'restructuring' process in both countries was financial de-regulation. It was taken with little public interest since people did not understand the implications, and it received little media coverage outside the financial pages of newspapers. In Australia, it followed advice from the Reserve Bank and Treasury officials, as well as the personal advisers of the prime minister and treasurer.[50] The floating of the dollar in 1983 'harnessed the Australian economy to the international marketplace – its rigours, excesses and ruthlessness'.[51]

In New Zealand, the Labour party came to government in 1984 in the midst of a currency crisis because the New Zealand dollar had come under sustained attack from foreign exchange markets and the previous government had refused to devalue it. Kelsey suggests that Roger Douglas 'deliberately precipitated the crisis when he "accidentally" released a background paper several weeks before the election saying that Labour would devalue the currency by 20 per cent' if it was elected. Additionally, a 'leaked' IMF report added to the sense of crisis. It suggested that government intervention in New Zealand had caused the economy to perform badly.[52]

The Labour government was swept to power with a large vote and the supposed crisis gave the government an excuse to start their reforms right away, despite an election campaign that failed to spell out the free market policy agenda that was to be adopted. In its first few months, the government organized an economic summit, which, according to Douglas, 'was designed to dramatize the problems of the economy to the nation and create the right climate for change'.[53]

In Australia, the Treasury promoted the idea of a crisis based on the size of the government budget deficit. In its first year of office, the Treasury predicted an AU$9.6 billion deficit and all the government's economic advisers urged them to cut that back. As a result, the Keynesian spending programme that the ALP had promised during the election campaign was abandoned.[54] According to John Langmore, who was economic adviser to the treasurer: 'The Treasury was using the tactic which the Brookings Institution survey of the Australian economy ... described as "frightening the bourgeoisie by exaggerating the deficit problem"'.[55]

In 1986, the feeling of crisis in Australia was heightened as the value of the Australian dollar declined and imports exceeded exports, causing a balance of payments deficit. The balance of payments deficit would traditionally have been simply fixed by government intervention to limit imports and control exchange rates. But government intervention was now a dirty word and debts were allowed to soar.[56]

However, it was Treasurer Paul Keating's comment that Australia might become a 'banana republic' which cemented the sense of crisis. The 'banana republic' crisis 'allowed Labor to overturn the deficit-favouring traditions of the ALP and introduce a period of fiscal rectitude which even led to budget surpluses'.[57] Kelly notes that Keating's banana republic statement 'facilitated the demise of the old order and the advance towards a new one':[58]

> It lifted community consciousness about Australia's economic predicament to an unprecedented level and it changed the limits of political tolerance... From 1986 onwards the leadership within both the Labor party and the coalition was driven, in policy terms, by the sense of economic crisis ... they both saw the economic solution as lying in a new radical market-oriented direction which involved the destruction of the old order... The banana republic episode liberated Keating from his past. He was driven by the dollar crisis to champion a series of policies that were historically anti-Labor.[59]

Belinda Probert notes that:

> Almost every unpleasant dose of medicine that Australians have been asked to swallow since the early 1980s has been prescribed to promote something called 'restructuring' – a historical process which is held out as the only cure for our economic and social ills... The process of restructuring has none the less been remorselessly promoted as vital to our survival as anything more than a 'banana republic'.[60]

BUSINESS INFLUENCE IN NEW ZEALAND

Although the National party had been the natural party for business interests, many businesses did not like the interventionist policies of the Muldoon National government and they shifted their support to Labour.[61] However, the major change in allegiances was a new and intimate alliance between the Labour government and the financial sector:

> Labour had always had strong links with the protected manufacturing sector; but in the mid 1980s it began to team up with the financial

*sector. Given the colonial structure, finance had always been an import-
ant part of the New Zealand power elite. The government was a major
owner of financial institutions, with the majority of the rest being
foreign owned.*[62]

The financial sector was the big winner from the reform process as can be seen from
Table 4.1, compiled by economist Alan Bollard, a supporter of the Washington
Consensus.

Table 4.1 *Winners and losers of free market policies*

Reform	Proponents	Opponents
Public expenditure reduction	Financial markets, employers, investors	Unions, professional providers, super-annuants, beneficiaries, unemployed, civil service
Tax reform	Financial markets, employers, investors	Low-income groups
Financial liberalization	Financial institutions, investors, shareholders, farmers	
Monetary reform	Reserve Bank, financial markets, investors	Some economists, union movement
Exchange rate liberalization	Financial markets, exporters, importers, foreign investors	Some economists
Trade liberalization	Farmers, importers, consumers, exporters	Unions, manufacturers
Foreign direct investment	Financial markets, foreign investors	Some voters
Corporatization and privatization	Financial markets, investors, some customers	Some customers, some voters, unions, Maoris, rural groups
Deregulation of industry	Some businesses	Some customers, some businesses, unions
Labour market reform	Employers, shareholders	Unions

Source: adapted from Bollard (1994, p102)

The international finance community was so pleased with the New Zealand free
market direction that it voted Roger Douglas top finance minister of the year in
1986 in *Banker* magazine. And the Labour government received NZ$3.7 million
in campaign funds from the 'newly concentrated financial sector', which enabled
it to be unconcerned with falling party membership. With the money, it was able
to run 'an American-style, capital-intensive, media-oriented electoral campaign'
at the 1987 election.[63]

According to economic analyst Brian Easton, these financial interests then went on to 'plunder' the New Zealand economy. In the wake of the 1987 financial crash which hit the New Zealand share market hard, they pressured the Labour government to privatize public assets as a way out of their troubles. The privatization of these assets involved large amounts of money flowing from the government to the financial sector. In return for their NZ$4 million election donation, financiers received hundreds of millions of dollars for advice and other services. Over NZ$100 million was paid to the private sector for help with privatizing Telecom alone. The net return to the government of the sale of the government Printery was only about one third of its asset value after expenses were paid.[64]

The government called on financiers and business leaders to head corporatized government enterprises, investigating committees and think tanks. They 'were commissioned to oversee policy reviews which prepared the ground for controversial change'. Private-sector boards of directors were also appointed to guide the new government agencies and enterprises.[65]

The most influential business group was the New Zealand Business Roundtable, which has been described as 'the most powerful [of the] driving forces of free market economic reforms transforming New Zealand'.[66] It produced reports and led 'the government through its agenda of reforms'. It was headed by a former Treasury economist and it actively pursued an agenda of market 'liberalization'. Its members were 'the direct beneficiaries of New Zealand's asset sales programme'.[67]

The roundtable's agenda was the same as the Washington Consensus, including reduced government spending 'to make room for private-sector expansion'; privatization and corporatization of government enterprises; labour market deregulation in the name of flexibility; and the avoidance of 'unjustified new regulations in areas such as the environment'.[68]

The relationship between the roundtable and the New Zealand government was so intimate that one reporter quipped that Roger Douglas and the roundtable were 'so close you couldn't slide a Treasury paper between them'. And, indeed, a member of the roundtable claimed 'that over ninety per cent of any decent policies that have come out of government in the last seven years have had a hell of a lot to do with the intellectual contribution of the roundtable'.[69]

By the time the National party was elected in 1990, it too had been converted by business interests to free market principles and minimal government intervention. National party's Ruth Richardson had done 'the rounds of the major corporates' while the party was in opposition 'and secured a foothold in the commercial community'. During the 1990 election campaign, 'business interests made it clear that they expected her to be appointed minister of finance in return for supporting National, both financially and electorally; and she was'.[70]

As mentioned earlier, National delivered more of the labour market deregulation that business wanted, including an Employment Contracts Act that the Employers' Federation and the New Zealand Business Roundtable had lobbied for. The act 'effectively de-unionized a large part of the labour force and reduced many workers' conditions'.[71] As a result, the wage bill for business declined as executive salaries and profits increased. Nevertheless, the roundtable continued to criticize the government for not moving fast enough and for slowing down its privatization programme.[72]

BUSINESS INFLUENCE IN AUSTRALIA

Kelly notes that the Labor government in Australia had three main institutional pillars of support for its market-based reforms in the wider community: the financial markets, the 'quality print media and its leading commentators' and the business community.[73]

The Business Council of Australia (BCA), the National Farmers' Federation and the Australian Mining Industry Council were vocal advocates of trade liberalization and opposed union power. The Farmers' Federation was the earliest industry group to publicly 'embrace the free market philosophy' despite the long history of government handouts to farmers, particularly in times of drought. At its 1979 conference, it advocated smaller government, reduced government expenditure, lower taxes, less protection, deregulation of the financial system, and facilitation of free trade. Later, the Farmers' Federation put together a huge AU$10 million fighting fund which it used to finance legal cases against unions. The fighting fund would also be used to challenge 'anti-business' taxes.[74]

In 1980, a study entitled *Australia at the Crossroads* by Kasper et al, commissioned by Shell Australia and written by economists, including the chief economist of Shell Australia, was published. It made the argument for economic liberalism and argued that if 'welfare state guardianism' continued Australia's economy would stagnate: 'A combination of high taxes, interventionist and large-scale government, state-endorsed restrictive trade practices, consumerism and environmentalism cripple private-sector dynamism and deter private investment.' Free market policies, such as the removal of protection, reduction of government and incentives for individual initiative were advocated as the only way to provide Australia with a dynamic future.[75]

The book, which acknowledged 'not only financial support, but much inspiration and practical help' from Shell Australia, noted that support for its free-market policy prescriptions would come from 'large-scale mining, small business and farming circles, amongst members of the liberal professions and in university economic departments' and 'parts of the media – especially newspapers and magazines'.[76]

The book became the 'inspiration of the dry movement in federal parliament after the 1980 election' and a *de facto* 'blueprint for the ideas which dominated' the 1980s.[77] It put forward a policy prescription in line with the Washington Consensus, a long time before the Labor party began to implement it.

Shell Australia also supported another book published in 1980 on Australia's future entitled *Will She Be Right?* by Kahn and Pepper. It represented the findings of a study done by the Hudson Institute, a US think tank, and Australian consultants Pak-Poy and Associates, and funded by 14 Australian corporations. Apart from Shell, funders included ANZ Bank and the Bank of New South Wales, BHP, IBM Australia, Myer Holdings, Utah Development Company, the Myer Emporium, CRA and Australian Consolidated Industries. The authors particularly acknowledged V. E. Jennings of Jennings Industries and Sir Roderick Carnegie, CEO of CRA, for their encouragement, assistance, and 'continued intellectual and moral support throughout the project'.[78]

Like *Australia at the Crossroads*, *Will She Be Right?* presented scenarios. These included 'business as usual'; a premature post-industrial society; a 'reformed' protectionist society; or 'a distinctly more dynamic economy, achieved mainly through a greatly increased emphasis on free market forces'. The business-as-usual scenario was predicted to be 'increasingly inefficient, uncompetitive and isolated'. A premature industrial society, with its focus on welfare and leisure, would stabilize at a low level of wealth, while other countries surged ahead.[79] The authors clearly preferred the dynamic free market economy, as did their business sponsors.

Prime Minister Bob Hawke and his treasurer, Paul Keating, were 'sympathetic to the ideology of the market, but, unlike the Liberals, devoid of vested interests or associations within the old business or corporate establishment... They were aggressive in seeking alliances within the business and finance "counter-establishment" ... where it was balance sheets, not class loyalties, that mattered'. The float of the dollar and the deregulation of the finance sector, in particular, secured an alliance between the government and the financial markets.[80]

When the Hawke government was elected in 1983, the Confederation of Australian Industry (CAI) was the main business umbrella group. It covered employer organizations and chambers of manufacturers. However, it was dominated by small to medium businesses and many large corporations were not part of it. When the Hawke government organized its economic summit, the CAI was invited to organize business representation; but Hawke also invited 18 CEOs of the largest companies operating in Australia – including CRA, Shell, Western Mining, BHP, Ford, Woolworths, Hookers and Boral – to represent big business.[81]

While some have suggested that business representation at the summit was fragmented and therefore weak, the truth is that the outcome of the summit was an accommodation by the trade unions of business goals and assumptions, including 'restrictions and reforms that have either been demanded by business representation or have fitted the requirements of market-driven, capital accumulation'. The summit *communiqué* 're-enforced the primacy accorded the market and private profitability and the subordinate, supportive role of state action backed by a compliant and accommodating trade union movement'.[82]

After the summit, in 1983, the large companies formed the Business Council of Australia (BCA), purportedly in response to big business's disappointment with business representation at Hawke's National Economic Summit. It was made up of the chief executives of the largest corporations operating in Australia and therefore basically represented the transnationals. It quickly eclipsed the CAI, which did not allow large corporations to be members in their own right, as 'the generator of broad business strategy on public policy questions'.[83]

The BCA played a significant role in the new agenda. It was modelled on the US Business Roundtable and sought to provide a strategy forum and voice for big business with sophisticated and well-financed research support:[84]

> *The BCA's contribution has been to help shift the terms of the debate from whether there should be change to the precise institutional form that the change should take. Early in its life, the BCA adopted a strategic approach to public policy advocacy. It committed itself to becoming involved in issue politics but not party politics; to avoid ad hoc responses to passing issues; to concentrate on winning fundamental long-term change; and to pursue long-term change on the basis of objective, research-based advocacy.*[85]

BCA members counted industrial relations as their top concern, and so the BCA funded an Employee Relations Study Commission on changing Australia's industrial relations system, chaired by Fred Hilmer, then dean of the Australian Graduate School of Management. The commission's reports, published between 1989 and 1993, recommended a system of company or enterprise-based unions rather than occupational or craft-based unions, purportedly to improve productivity and flexibility of the workforce, but in reality to reduce union power. These reports are said to 'have had a major, perhaps decisive, impact on the reform debate in the business community, and on government and the union movement'.[86] The Keating Labor government subsequently introduced enterprise-based bargaining in 1992, with the agreement of the ACTU.

The acquiescence of the ACTU can be understood, in part, from developments that had begun much earlier. From 1964, the Harvard Foundation offered leadership grants to Australian trade union leaders to enable them to travel to the US for up to six weeks to, according to Clyde Cameron, a former Labour government minister, 'brainwash them into inculcating in their thinking process, at the least, that private enterprise is the only way to go'. They were given first-class airfares and hotel accommodation and the costs of this programme were supported by multinational business interests.

Australian-based trustees of the Harvard Foundation included big businessmen such as Sir Peter Abeles, Sir Warwick Fairfax, mining CEO Hugh Morgan, the managing directors of Ford and GMX, and politicians from both sides of the political fence, including Andrew Peacock, Ian McPhee, Bob Hawke, Neville Wran, Ralph Willis and Barry Unsworth, the latter two being graduates of the programme themselves.[87] Another graduate was Michael Easson, who became Australian secretary of the Labor Committee for Public Affairs before it was discredited for having links with the Central Intelligence Agency (CIA). It had been set up and funded by the US Information Agency.[88] Easson went on to be secretary of the New South Wales Labor Council and a federal MP.

Rather than oppose unions outright as the extreme elements of the New Right were doing, the BCA chose to 'reshape the power relations between business and labour ... by redefining the very bargaining structures of the industrial relations system'. It successfully set the agenda on industrial relations policy and eclipsed the role of the ACTU in influencing the structural adjustment process.[89]

The massive influence of the BCA did not become apparent until some years later. In 1994, former Treasurer John Dawkins told a business audience that the BCA had been the dominant influence on the reform agenda during Labor's government, more dominant than Labor's traditional union supporters. His speech was reported in the *Australian Financial Review*:

> *Such was the intimacy of the relationship, Mr Dawkins claimed, that it had been useful on occasions to have the BCA appear to be a critic of the government's performance... According to Mr Dawkins, the BCA's role of policy pacesetter and critic of the government's progress had assisted the government to maintain the support of its own constituency on reform... Mr Dawkins said: 'While it was important to have the BCA as part of the cheer squad, it was useful for other reasons for the BCA to be not identified as author of the policies, and sometimes to appear as a critic of the government's performance.*[90]

Additionally, the revolving door was well oiled in Australia, and politicians from both major parties often went to work for business after their parliamentary careers were over. Relationships established between politicians and businesspeople during the 1980s 'did not withstand tests of probity' and led to prosecutions and jail sentences in some cases, particularly at the state government level.[91]

However, politicians do not have to be corrupt to form close relationships with leading businesspeople. Bob Catley in his book *Globalising Australian Capitalism* notes that social relationships are not surprising because 'there are, after all, a limited number of social outlets for the powerful and high-incomed in such moderate-sized communities'.[92] However, the relationship was more strategic than is suggested by Catley. Corporate leaders wined and dined the Labor leaders and forged close personal relationships with Bob Hawke and Paul Keating. For example, Keating stayed at businessman Robert Holmes Court's stud farm and spent New Year's Eve on board businessman Alan Bond's AU$30 million cruiser. New South Wales Premier Neville Wran spent his vacation at media mogul Kerry Packer's Palm Beach home.[93]

Hawke publicly proclaimed his friendship to Kerry Packer: 'I am pleased as prime minister of this country ... to count as a close personal friend and to measure as a very great Australian, Kerry Packer.' Hawke was also close friends with Peter Abeles, a partner of media baron Rupert Murdoch in owning Ansett Airlines and the owner of Thomas Nationwide Transport (TNT), which helped Murdoch to beat the British unions by distributing his papers in the UK. Abeles enabled Murdoch to have access to Hawke, and several meetings followed.[94]

For its part, business used this access to ensure that business views were well aired in government:

> *Each minister receives almost daily representations from business: from individual businesses, from peak business organizations, most of whom now have a professional office in Canberra, and from political lobbyists working on behalf of business.*[95]

The close relationship between Hawke and Keating and some business leaders invited some comment and controversy in labour ranks. In an article he wrote for the *Times on Sunday*, which the paper refused to publish, Brian Toohey wrote:

> *Hawke and Keating do more than enjoy the company of the new tycoons; they share their values... The stock exchange index has risen by almost 250 per cent since Hawke came to power in 1983; the number of children in poverty, by his own government's estimates, has risen to one in five. Take-home pay in real terms has fallen, while the rich have never had it so good... According to the Business Review Weekly, the Top 200 (Rich List) increased their wealth by $4700 million to $14,800 million during the first three years of this Labor government.*[96]

When the share market crash came in 1987, the Labor government was there to bail out the entrepreneurs who had invested unwisely. After all, it was these entrepreneurs who were supposed to revive the Australian economy.[97]

Business influence also extended to the media through ownership and advertising revenues. The programme of economic rationalism received the full support of the media, particularly economic journalists and columnists. The *Australian Financial Review* pushed free market ideas under the editorship of P. P. McGuinness during the early 1980s, and Murdoch's *Australian* newspaper began openly promoting free market policies in 1978 when it tried to ferment a tax revolt.[98]

A survey by Julianne Schultz and Zoltan Matolcsky found that business and economics journalists were enthusiastic supporters of free-market economic rationalism and that 65 per cent of them agreed that 'during the 1980s the media and journalists had actively pushed a Treasury line' and the majority agreed that 'the media uncritically promoted the interests of business during the 1980s'.[99] Donald Horne, well-known social commentator and historian, suggests that the appearance of a national consensus in favour of economic rationalism was 'imposed very largely by the national press gallery and the business-page pundits'.[100] Probert points out that the economy was being defined in the media as synonymous with business interests.[101] Doug McEachern, in his book on *Business Mates*, notes:

> *Often, movements in the stock market were discussed as an indicator of business confidence in the government, or the judgement of the market on various policy initiatives. For much of the 1980s, movements in the value of the currency were treated as if they were a reflex response to specific proposals and policies. Proclaiming the wisdom of the market and its policy demands were stock-in-trade of financial journalists and commentators.*[102]

The media was flooded with economic indicators and jargon that meant little to the layperson, but served to convey to people that economics was a subject that they did not know enough about to comment on or judge. Dissenting economists had trouble getting opinion pieces published in the major newspapers and regular columnists ridiculed dissenters who managed to get their ideas into the public arena in different ways.[103]

NOTES

1 Bernie Taft, 'The New Right in Practice', in Ken Coghill (ed) *The New Right's Australian Fantasy*, Fitzroy, Victoria, McPhee Gribble and Penguin Books, 1987, p27.

2 John Gray, *False Dawn: The Delusions of Global Capitalism*, London, Granta Books, 2002, p39.

3 John Willliamson (ed.), *The Political Economy of Policy Reform*, Washington, DC, Institute for International Economics, 1994.

4 Preface to *Ibid.*, px.

5 Institute for International Economics, 'About the Institute for International Economics', IIE, www.iie.com/ADMINIST/aboutiie.htm accessed 6 January 2001.

6 *Ibid.*

7 John Williamson, 'In Search of a Manual for Technopols', in John Williamson (ed) *The Political Economy of Policy Reform*, Washington, DC, Institute for International Economics, 1994, p20.

8 *Ibid.*, pp20, 25.

9 *Ibid.*, p20.

10 *Ibid.*, pp20–1; Robert H. Bates, 'Comment', in John Williamson (ed) *The Political Economy of Policy Reform*, Washington, DC, Institute for International Economics, 1994, pp31–2.

11 Williamson, 'In Search of a Manual for Technopols', p26.

12 Francis G. Castles, *et al.* (eds) *The Great Experiment: Labour Parties and Public Policy Transformation in Australia and New Zealand*, Sydney, Allen & Unwin, 1996, ppix, 18; Paul Kelly, *The End of Uncertainty: The Story of the 1980s*, St Leonards, NSW, Allen & Unwin, 1992, p15.

13   Allan Bollard, 'New Zealand', in John Williamson (ed) *The Political Economy of Policy Reform*, Washington, DC, Institute for International Economics, 1994, pp75–81; Jane Kelsey, *Economic Fundamentalism*, London, Pluto Press, 1995, pp2–4.

14   Gray, *False Dawn*, pp40–1.

15   Bollard, 'New Zealand', p92.

16   Castles, *et al.* (eds) *The Great Experiment: Labour Parties and Public Policy Transformation in Australia and New Zealand*, p16.

17   Gray, *False Dawn*, pp39–40.

18   Quoted in Kelsey, *Economic Fundamentalism*, p7.

19   Quoted in *Ibid.*, p7.

20   Gray, *False Dawn*, p42.

21   Kelsey, *Economic Fundamentalism*, p9.

22   Bollard, 'New Zealand', p94.

23   Kelsey, *Economic Fundamentalism*, p44.

24   Bollard, 'New Zealand', p97.

25   Quoted in Kelsey, *Economic Fundamentalism*, pp33–4.

26   *Ibid.*, pp42–3.

27   *Ibid.*, pp21, 35.

28   Bollard, 'New Zealand', p93; Chris Eichbaum, 'Market Liberalisation in New Zealand: Fightback! In Practice?' in Peter Vintila, John Phillimore and Peter Newman (eds) *Markets, Morals & Manifestos: Fightback! & the Politics of Economic Rationalism in the 1990s*, Murdoch, WA, Institute for Science and Technology Policy, Murdoch University, 1992, p225; Castles, *et al.* (eds) *The Great Experiment: Labour Parties and Public Policy Transformation in Australia and New Zealand*, p16; Patrick Massey, *New Zealand: Market Liberalization in a Developed Economy*, New York, St Martin's Press, 1995, p74.

29   Bollard, 'New Zealand', p101; Castles, *et al.* (eds) *The Great Experiment: Labour Parties and Public Policy Transformation in Australia and New Zealand*, p17; Kelsey, *Economic Fundamentalism*, p37.

30   Kelsey, *Economic Fundamentalism,* p39.

31   Greg Lindsay, 'Threats to Freedom Then and Now', *Policy*, Autumn, 1997, www.cis.org.au/Policy/mps.html; Massey, *New Zealand,* p74; Kelsey, *Economic Fundamentalism*, p41; Brian Easton, 'From Rogernomics to Ruthanasia: New Right Economics in New Zealand', in Stuart Rees, Gordon Rodley and Frank Stilwell (eds) *Beyond the Market: Alternatives to Economic Rationalism*, Leichhardt, NSW, Pluto Press, 1993, p150.

32   Easton, 'From Rogernomics to Ruthanasia: New Right Economics in New Zealand', p155; Kelsey, *Economic Fundamentalism,* p41.

33   Ross Garnaut, 'Australia', in John Williamson (ed) *The Political Economy of Policy Reform*, Washington, DC, Institute for International Economics, 1994, p53–4.

34   *Ibid.*, p67.

35   Pamela Williams and Stephen Ellis, 'Dawkins Kisses and Tells on BCA', *The Australian Financial Review*, 15 July, 1994, p1.

36   Winton Higgins, 'Missing the Boat', in Brian Galligan and Gwynneth Singleton (eds) *Business and Government under Labor*, Melbourne, Longman Cheshire, 1991, p108.

37 Richard Blandy, 'Labour Market Reform', in Brian Galligan, Bob Lim and Kim Lovegrove (eds) *Managing Microeconomic Reform*, Canberra, Federalism Research Centre, ANU, 1993, p29.

38 Greg Whitwell, 'Economic Ideas and Economic Policy: The Rise of Economic Rationalism in Australia', *Australian Economic History Review*, vol 33, no 2, 1993, p25.

39 Kelly, *The End of Uncertainty: The Story of the 1980s*, pp56, 77.

40 Neil Mooney, 'How Victoria Went Dry on Andrew', *The National Times*, 13–19 September, 1985, p8.

41 *Ibid.*, p8; Kelly, *The End of Uncertainty: The Story of the 1980s*, p402; Ian McLachlan, Michael Kroger, David Kemp, Peter Costello cited in Kelly, *The End of Uncertainty: The Story of the 1980s*, p403; Pamela Williams, 'New Right Exerts Its Power on Liberals', *Financial Review*, 17 December, 1987, p10.

42 Kelly, *The End of Uncertainty: The Story of the 1980s*, p253.

43 Peter Vintila, 'Markets, Morals and Manifestos', in Peter Vintila, John Phillimore and Peter Newman (eds) *Markets, Morals & Manifestos: Fightback! & the Politics of Economic Rationalism in the 1990s*, Murdoch, WA, Institute for Science and Technology Policy, Murdoch University, 1992, p10.

44 Doug McEachern, *Business Mates: The Power and Politics of the Hawke Era*, Sydney, Prentice Hall, 1991, p80.

45 Elaine Thompson, 'Where Is the Economy?' in Donald Horne (ed) *The Trouble with Economic Rationalism*, Newham, Vic, Scribe, 1992, p16; Lindy Edwards, *How to Argue with an Economist: Reopening Political Debate in Australia*, Cambridge, Cambridge University Press, 2002, p11.

46 Edwards, *How to Argue with an Economist*, p13.

47 Kelly, *The End of Uncertainty: The Story of the 1980s*, p14.

48 Garnaut, 'Australia', p57.

49 Bollard, 'New Zealand', p74; Rolf Gerritsen, 'Microeconomic Reform', in Stephen Bell and Brian Head (eds) *State, Economy and Public Policy*, Oxford University Press, Melbourne, 1994, p270; Castles, *et al.* (eds) *The Great Experiment: Labour Parties and Public Policy Transformation in Australia and New Zealand*, pp7–8.

50 Garnaut, 'Australia', p59.

51 Paul Kelly quoted in Whitwell, 'Economic Ideas and Economic Policy: The Rise of Economic Rationalism in Australia', p17.

52 Kelsey, *Economic Fundamentalism*, p29; Bollard, 'New Zealand', p99.

53 Massey, *New Zealand*, p67; Douglas quoted in Kelsey, *Economic Fundamentalism*, p32.

54 Kelly, *The End of Uncertainty: The Story of the 1980s*, p57.

55 John Langmore, 'The Labor Government in a De-Regulatory Era', in Brian Galligan and Gwynneth Singleton (eds) *Business and Government under Labor*, Melbourne, Longman Cheshire, 1991, p77.

56 Trevor Matthews, 'Employers' Associations, Corporatism and the Accord: The Politics of Industrial Relations', in Stephen Bell and Brian Head (eds) *State, Economy and Public Policy*, Oxford University Press, Melbourne, 1994, p212; John Carroll, 'Economic Rationalism and Its Consequences', in John Carroll and Robert Manne (eds) *Shutdown: The Failure of Economic Rationalism and How to Rescue Australia*, Melbourne, The Text Publishing Company, 1992, p10.

57   Castles, *et al.* (eds) *The Great Experiment: Labour Parties and Public Policy Trans-formation in Australia and New Zealand,* p15.

58   Kelly, *The End of Uncertainty: The Story of the 1980s,* p196.

59   *Ibid.,* pp196–7, 224.

60   Belinda Probert, 'Globalisation, Economic Restructuring and the State', in Stephen Bell and Brian Head (eds) *State, Economy and Public Policy,* Oxford University Press, Melbourne, 1994, p98.

61   Castles, *et al.* (eds) *The Great Experiment: Labour Parties and Public Policy Transforma-tion in Australia and New Zealand,* p16; Easton, 'From Rogernomics to Ruthanasia: New Right Economics in New Zealand', p154.

62   Easton, 'From Rogernomics to Ruthanasia: New Right Economics in New Zealand', p154.

63   Bollard, 'New Zealand', p92; Herman Schwartz quoted in Kelsey, *Economic Funda-mentalism,* p36.

64   Easton, 'From Rogernomics to Ruthanasia: New Right Economics in New Zealand', p157.

65   Bollard, 'New Zealand', p92; Kelsey, *Economic Fundamentalism,* p52.

66   G. Niness quoted in Georgina Murray and Douglas Pacheco, 'Think Tanks in the 1990s', Australian National University, www.anu.edu.au/polsci/marx/interventions/thinktanks.htm accessed 23 January 2001.

67   Bollard, 'New Zealand', p93; Eichbaum, 'Market Liberalisation in New Zealand: Fightback! In Practice?' p224.

68   Roger Kerr, 'Keeping NZ out of the Hands of the Chattering Class', *Independent Business Weekly,* 30 August, 1993, p9.

69   C. Managh and A. Gibbs quoted in Murray and Pacheco, 'Think Tanks in the 1990s'.

70   Kelsey, *Economic Fundamentalism,* p40.

71   Easton, 'From Rogernomics to Ruthanasia: New Right Economics in New Zealand', p158.

72   See, for example, Douglas Myers, CEO of Lion Nathan and chair of NZ Business Roundtable in Sam Hudson, 'Lion Chief Criticises 'Stalled' NZ Reform', *Australian Financial Reform,* 8 April, 1992, p9.

73   Kelly, *The End of Uncertainty: The Story of the 1980s,* p224.

74   Garnaut, 'Australia', p67; Kelly, *The End of Uncertainty: The Story of the 1980s,* p45; Matthews, 'Employers' Associations, Corporatism and the Accord: The Politics of Industrial Relations', p212; Nigel Austin and Deborah Hope, 'Farmers Threaten Direct Action to Smash Union Power', *The Bulletin,* 15 July, 1986, pp24–5.

75   Wolfgang Kasper, *et al., Australia at the Crossroads: Our Choices to the Year 2000,* Sydney, Harcourt Brace Jovanovich, 1980; Quoted in Marian Sawer, 'Political Man-ifestations of Australian Libertarianism', in Marian Sawer (ed) *Australia and the New Right,* North Sydney, George Allen & Unwin, 1982, p18.

76   Kasper, *et al., Australia at the Crossroads: Our Choices to the Year 2000,* pxi; Quoted in Sawer, 'Political Manifestations of Australian Libertarianism', p19.

77   Hyde quoted in Kelly, *The End of Uncertainty: The Story of the 1980s,* p41.

78   Herman Kahn and Thomas Pepper, *Will She Be Right? The Future of Australia,* St. Lucia, Qld, University of Queensland Press, 1980, pxi.

79   *Ibid.*, pp1–3, 137.
80   Kelly, *The End of Uncertainty: The Story of the 1980s,* pp56, 77.
81   McEachern, *Business Mates: The Power and Politics of the Hawke Era,* pp25–6; PA. McLaughlin, 'How Business Relates to the Hawke Government: The Captains of Industry', in Brian Galligan and Gwynneth Singleton (eds) *Business and Government under Labor,* Melbourne, Longman Cheshire, 1991, p150.
82   McEachern, *Business Mates: The Power and Politics of the Hawke Era,* pp34–5.
83   Matthews, 'Employers' Associations, Corporatism and the Accord: The Politics of Industrial Relations', p204; McEachern, *Business Mates: The Power and Politics of the Hawke Era,* p33.
84   Kelly, *The End of Uncertainty: The Story of the 1980s,* pp204–5, 276.
85   Matthews, 'Employers' Associations, Corporatism and the Accord: The Politics of Industrial Relations', p212.
86   *Ibid.*, pp212–3; Blandy, 'Labour Market Reform', p29.
87   Jane Lambrook, 'The CIA in Australia: Part 4', *Watching Brief, Public Radio News Services,* October/November, 1986, www.serendipity.li/cia/cia_oz/cia_oz4.htm.
88   *Ibid.*
89   Matthews, 'Employers' Associations, Corporatism and the Accord: The Politics of Industrial Relations', p214.
90   Williams and Ellis, 'Dawkins Kisses and Tells on BCA', p1.
91   Keith Abbott, *Pressure Groups and the Australian Federal Parliament,* Political Studies Fellow Monograph No. 3, Canberra, Australian Government Publishing Service, 1996, p34; Bob Catley, *Globalising Australian Capitalism,* Cambridge, Cambridge University Press, 1996, p88.
92   Catley, *Globalising Australian Capitalism,* p94.
93   Paul Chadwick, *Media Mates: Carving Up Australia's Media,* Melbourne, Macmillan, 1989, pp29, 32.
94   *Ibid.*, pp32–3.
95   Catley, *Globalising Australian Capitalism,* p98.
96   Quoted in Chadwick, *Media Mates: Carving Up Australia's Media,* p29.
97   *Ibid.*, p31.
98   Kelly, *The End of Uncertainty: The Story of the 1980s,* p48; Sawer, 'Political Manifestations of Australian Libertarianism', p15.
99   Julianne Schultz, 'Where Are the Alternative Views?' in Donald Horne (ed) *The Trouble with Economic Rationalism,* Newham, Vic, Scribe, 1992, pp88–9.
100 Donald Horne, 'It's Time for a Think', in Donald Horne (ed) *The Trouble with Economic Rationalism,* Newham, Vic, Scribe, 1992, p3.
101 Belinda Probert, 'Whose Economy Is It?' in Donald Horne (ed) *The Trouble with Economic Rationalism,* Newham, Vic, Scribe, 1992, pp26–7.
102 McEachern, *Business Mates: The Power and Politics of the Hawke Era,* p4.
103 Schultz, 'Where Are the Alternative Views?' p90; Evan Jones, 'Economic Language, Propaganda and Dissent', in Stuart Rees, Gordon Rodley and Frank Stilwell (eds) *Beyond the Market: Alternatives to Economic Rationalism,* Leichhardt, NSW, Pluto Press, 1993, pp263–4.

5

From Public Service to Private Profit

The Law doth punish man or woman
Who steals the goose from off the common,
But lets the greater felon loose
Who steals the common from the goose.

18TH CENTURY ANTI-ENCLOSURE SAYING[1]

Privatization is not simply a change of ownership. It is a change in the
role, responsibilities, priorities and authority of the state.

BRENDAN MARTIN[2]

Dozens of governments around the world have embarked on the road to privatization since the mid 1980s. As a result of electricity privatization and deregulation, there have been blackouts, price spikes, price manipulation, bankruptcies and electricity shortages around the world. Privatization and deregulation have seen the goal of an affordable, accessible and reliable electric service replaced by the goals of economic efficiency, competition and consumer choice.

Water privatization has also been a disaster. Rates have soared and pollution increased. Those who cannot afford the new rates have had their water supply disconnected. Diseases such as cholera have made a come back in poor nations where alternative sources of water are contaminated. Privatization has transformed water from a human right to an 'economic good' that must be paid for by those who use it.[3] And now the large European water conglomerates are preparing to buy up municipal water supplies in the US.

Yet, despite its lack of popular support and its inability to deliver on promises of better service at lower prices, privatization in its many forms has become the accepted wisdom amongst governments and opinion leaders. By the early 1990s, the term 'privatization' had become an accepted part of the language, East and West.[4] New markets were opened up all over the world as developing countries joined developed countries in allowing transnational companies to provide their essential services.

During the 1980s and 1990s, public services were reformed in various ways throughout the US, Western and Eastern Europe, Africa, Latin America, South-East Asia and in Australasia. These included the sale of government enterprises;

the introduction of new forms of management practice and incentive structures in remaining public services; the contracting out and private provision of activities within public services; the introduction of user charges; and the deregulation of essential services.[5]

Proponents of these measures argued that introducing competition and commercial concerns into public-service provision would expose the newly privatized firms and corporatized government enterprises to the disciplines of the market so that they would become more efficient and rates would be reduced. It was also supposed to raise revenue for governments, provide new sources of investment capital for expensive infrastructure and reduce the role of government in the economy.

Governments, entrusted with carrying out the will of the people and protecting public assets, were co-opted by all manner of devices, ranging from the sophisticated persuasion of corporate-funded think tanks to the less than subtle pressures exerted by international lending organizations, all combining with frequent and generous financial contributions to the campaign funds of political parties and offers of future career opportunities for retired politicians and bureaucrats.

As a result, there has been a massive *transfer* of ownership and control over government assets worldwide to private companies. The companies that have taken over these public services in most countries are transnational companies with little interest in the welfare of local citizens. Increasingly, these companies are concentrating – through mergers and acquisitions – into a small group of very large conglomerates that dominate the provision of national and international essential services.

Business groups and associations have played an active role in promoting privatization, as have individual corporations and financial institutions that see potential profit for themselves in privatization. Many businessmen were persuaded during the 1970s and 1980s that the price of government-supplied services was too high because of bureaucratic inefficiencies and because of the social goals that governments were pursuing. They believed that the uncompetitiveness of government providers made private industry uncompetitive, too.[6]

Western-based transnational corporations have sought investment in developing countries as a source of new markets because profit opportunities in affluent countries, especially in traditional areas such as primary industries and manufacturing, have declined. Privatization in developing nations offers opportunities for investment, and the corporate push for privatization policies in developing countries during the late 1980s was 'in response to a cyclical downturn in interest rates and a longer-term fall in rates of return on investment in mature industrial economies'.[7]

The United Nations Development Programme (UNDP) points out that privatization benefits transnational corporations (and some local firms) by allowing them to get access to industries in developing nations that had previously been closed to them and to buy up established enterprises, sometimes at cut-rate prices: 'In many countries the privatization process has been more of a "garage sale" to favoured individuals and groups than a part of a coherent strategy to encourage private investment.'[8]

Privatization is good for the development banks because the money raised by the asset sales helps governments to pay the interest on their loans, at least in the short term. Privatization has also been pressed by bilateral aid programmes. In addition, many bilateral and regional trade agreements incorporate some form of privatization.

The beneficiaries of privatization have been the banks, building societies, insurance companies, pension funds and other industrial and commercial companies that are able to invest in the newly privatized services and/or provide loans to those who do. In electricity, for example, the banks are major investors in power companies and their executives populate the boards of electricity companies. They have advised on privatization schemes and helped to draw up deregulation legislation around the world. They have collected fees from brokering the purchase of independent power companies worldwide and have been involved in energy trading themselves.[9]

INCREASING PRICES AND DECLINING SERVICE

Despite the rhetoric of free market advocates, the goals of governments and private companies in supplying services are quite different. Governments attempt to provide reliable services that a maximum number of people can access at a cost they can afford. Of course, they do not always succeed in this goal, particularly when they do not have access to affordable capital. Private companies, on the other hand, have a legal obligation to maximize their profit and shareholder value. Sometimes this coincides with providing a cheap, widely available, reliable service; but often it doesn't, particularly when it comes to essential services that require expensive infrastructure to distribute.

Those advocating privatization and private provision of public services claim that private ownership and competition ensure that there are incentives to minimize costs, to improve management practices and to get employees to work harder. However, there is little evidence that private or public ownership makes a difference in how efficient an organization is. For example, experience in the US and the UK, where public and private enterprises supplied electricity contemporaneously, has consistently shown that public enterprises can provide a reliable service at lower cost to ratepayers. Similarly, in England and France, municipal governments offer water services at cheaper rates than privately operated water services.[10]

In fact, the cost of essential services tends to go up rather than down after privatization. In most countries around the world where water and electricity have been privatized or deregulated, residential rates have increased, often dramatically. Water privatization caused rates to increase by 150 per cent in France and 106 per cent in England between 1989 and 1995.[11] In Manila, after privatization, water rates increased by up to 500 per cent, and when the Philippines currency was devalued and French water company Suez, which owned 40 per cent of the water company, was unable to recoup the loss through a further increase in rates, it just walked out. It is now suing the Philippine government for US$337 million for reimbursement of its losses and has left it with US$530 million in debts. Suez has also pulled out of the Buenos Aires water supply contract. Both Manila and Buenos Aires had been model privatization projects for the World Bank.[12]

In Cochabamba, Bolivia, the government was pressured by the World Bank to privatize the operating of its water supply, so in 1999 it contracted with a consortium of US-based Bechtel and UK-based United Utilities to do it. Water rates soared shortly after the consortium took over and were equivalent to one quarter of the average income in the city. People were told that their water would be cut off if they did not pay. Under the contract, they weren't even allowed to use private wells without paying the consortium.[13]

The people of Cochabamba demonstrated and protested in the streets for 8 days until martial law was declared and troops fired on the crowds, killing 2 and wounding 30 people. However, the people succeeded in getting the government to break the contract and take back control of the water supply. The consortium is suing the Bolivian government in a World Bank court for losses from the broken contract.[14]

Electricity prices around the world have risen or, at the very least, become exceedingly volatile as a result of privatization and restructuring. In the Dominican Republic, privatization of electricity, for example, led to huge price increases and frequent and lengthy blackouts. The same was true in the state of South Australia and in many states in the US. The supposed disciplines of the market have been eclipsed by price manipulation by private electricity companies seeking to boost the price of electricity and to maximize profits. In places where government-imposed price caps remain in place, retail suppliers have not been able to pass these high wholesale prices on to consumers, causing them to experience financial difficulties that have led to blackouts and government bailouts, as in California.[15]

However, electricity-generating companies around the world have generally made big profits. A World Bank study of 61 privatized electricity enterprises in 18 countries found that profitability rose an average of 45 per cent. Similarly, the private water companies have made huge profits. Between 1989 and 1995, when water rates in England were doubling, the profit margins for the private water companies increased sixfold.[16] However, this profitability of privatized companies has been achieved through price gouging rather than through the managerial expertise and increased efficiency of operations under private ownership.

The increased rates have left the poorest unable to pay and without access to these essential services, even in the wealthiest countries. In England, water disconnections of those unable to pay their rates tripled between 1991 and 1992 after privatization. Then prepayment water meters were installed in the homes of the poor so that people effectively cut themselves off if they could not pay.

Similarly, prepayment meters were installed for electricity. The problem of 'fuel poverty' affected about 16 per cent of households in the UK at the beginning of 2002. It is estimated that over 30,000 extra deaths occur each year in the UK during winter because people cannot afford to heat themselves properly.[17] Dealing with fuel poverty is considered to be an objective outside the private company goals of economic efficiency and profit.

The situation is, of course, even worse in developing countries. In South Africa, the World Bank prepared the African National Congress (ANC), even before it came to power, with 'reconnaissance missions' to promote privatization and 'full-cost recovery'. Nelson Mandela embraced privatization when he became president in 1994, saying: 'Privatization is the fundamental policy of our government. Call me a Thatcherite, if you will.' There ensued a bevy of consultants and advisers from the US, the UK, the World Bank and the International Monetary Fund (IMF) who helped the government put together a Growth, Employment and Redistribution Strategy in 1996, which was essentially a voluntary structural adjustment programme. It included a policy of full-cost recovery. Thabo Mbeki, who became president in 1999, continued with these same policies.[18] George Monbiot reported in the *Guardian*:

> *The corporations loved it. KPMG told its clients that if they went to South Africa, they'd 'find a major business opportunity about to burst forth in a country where there is a lot of good will towards UK'... The agency keeping the South African government on track is Britain's Department for International Development (DFID). This year it is giving £6.3 million to the Adam Smith Institute – the ultra-right-wing privatization lobby group – for 'public-sector reform' in South Africa. Staggeringly, the institute has been given its own budget – £5m of British aid money – to disburse as it pleases.*[19]

As a result of South Africa's privatizations, thousands have lost their jobs, increasing unemployment from 17 per cent in 1995 to 30 per cent in 2002 and deepening poverty. People who managed to hold jobs during apartheid have found that privatization has taken their jobs, increased their electricity bills and then cut them off when they couldn't pay. According to a South African government study, 'full-cost recovery' for water and electricity services, in preparation for and as a consequence of privatization, has resulted in more than 10 million people – 25 per cent of the population – having these services disconnected since 1998.[20]

Although water meters were ruled illegal in the UK in 1998 because they deprived people of their right to water, they were subsequently installed in South Africa. Even communal taps were equipped with meters that required a prepaid water card for people to get water from them. Two million people have been forced out of their homes for not paying their water or electricity bills. When 30 per cent of the state-owned telecommunications company Telkom was sold, the cost of local calls increased dramatically and phone lines in poorer households had to be disconnected.[21]

This policy of 'full-cost recovery', or user pays, was introduced under pressure from the World Bank, which maintained that there needed to be a 'credible threat of cutting service'. The idea was that the money collected from this cost recovery could be used to improve the infrastructure. Yet, full-cost recovery in essential services is not expected in many of the more affluent countries, including the US. South Africa could afford to supply everyone with water; but the imposition of market rules prevents the cross-subsidization that would be necessary to achieve this.[22]

The result in South Africa was that water bills alone came to 30 per cent of average family incomes (40 per cent with electricity). Those who were disconnected from the water supply because they could not afford it were forced to use contaminated sources of water, resulting in the spread of cholera and gastrointestinal diseases. More than 140,000 people have had cholera since 2000 and millions suffer from diarrhoea. The government ended up having to spend millions of dollars trying to control South Africa's worst outbreak of cholera, which killed hundreds of people between 2000 and 2002. Yet, the same water policies continue and prepayment meters have since been installed in Johannesburg.[23]

Opposition to privatization is becoming the focus of a new struggle for poor South Africans. At one protest march a banner read: 'We did not fight for liberation so we could sell everything we won to the highest bidder.' Similarly, the job losses and rising prices following or threatened by privatization have resulted in popular uprisings and mass protests in Argentina, Guatemala, India, Indonesia, Ghana, Peru, Ecuador, Paraguay and the Dominican Republic. Anti-privatization movements are growing in many Latin American countries. An Inter-American Development Bank (IDB) survey of 17 of these countries found that 63 per cent of people thought that privatization was not beneficial.[24]

Service and reliability have also declined after privatization and deregulation. This reduction in service provision tends to affect ordinary householders far more adversely than large industrial enterprises, which often have back-up power sources and are given cut-rate prices. The widespread electricity blackouts in the northeastern states of the US and Canada were one of the more spectacular consequences of a deregulatory process that aimed at removing government controls and letting the market decide. In a deregulated market, no one is responsible for planning or ensuring adequate generation or transmission facilities into the future. This does not matter with some commodities; but it can lead to crises in the case of electricity supply because electricity is so essential to human welfare and economic activity.

The supposed efficiency gains to be made by private competitive companies have too often occurred through short-term cost savings. These include cuts to safety, maintenance, training and research budgets. Old equipment is not regularly serviced or replaced in advance of likely failure, pipes leak and treatment plants become less effective. As a result, there are more accidents and equipment breakdowns. For electricity networks, this means an increase in equipment-related blackouts as well as blackouts related to network congestion because planning and responsibility for network maintenance and development are not a market priority.

Water quality has also declined in some parts of the world after privatization and pollution incidents have often increased, as well. For example, Compañia de Aguas, a subsidiary of Vivendi, was fined US$6.2 million for environmental violations in Puerto Rico that occurred between 1995 and 2000. A Puerto Rican government report found in 1999 that it had not maintained the aqueducts and sewers adequately. Customers were without water for months at a time, but nevertheless got charged for the water.[25]

In the Argentinean city of Tucumán, city officials took action against Vivendi for poor performance because their water was often brown. In response, Vivendi unsuccessfully sued the Government of Argentina in a World Bank court for violating its contract by not preventing the action being taken. In Buenos Aires, Suez raised rates by 20 per cent but failed to fix the sewerage system as it had been contracted to do, and 95 per cent of the sewage of the city of 10 million people went into the river.[26]

Cost savings in privatized utilities are often made by lowering rates of pay and conditions for workers or cutting the full-time workforce. Thousands of jobs are normally shed ahead of, and just after, privatization of government enterprises and services. Full-time permanent employment in privatized enterprises is increasingly replaced by part-time and temporary work. Direct employment is steadily replaced by contract employment and contract workers tend to be non-unionized and poorly paid, with little employment security and no access to benefits such as sick leave, holidays and pension contributions. There is even a trend to employ contract workers on a self-employed basis in order to avoid having to pay any statutory benefits.[27]

In the US, electricity deregulation has led to 150,000 people losing their jobs, including those who were responsible for the safety and reliability of electricity supplies, as private deregulated utilities shed staff in order to cut costs. The Utility Workers Union of America (UWUA) claims that cost-cutting has led to less frequent inspections, deferred repairs and less training, which threaten worker and public safety as well as system reliability.[28]

In the public service it was not uncommon for employees to have a strong public service ethos, particularly in the utilities where they 'traditionally took pride in their safety record, in the quality and impartiality of advice offered to consumers, and in a number of socially responsible activities such as free servicing of old age pensioners' appliances'.[29] This was lost as employees were forced to take a more commercial view of their work.

In its book on *Transforming Government Enterprises*, the Australian think tank Centre for Independent Studies (CIS) has a chapter on the need to change the culture, attitudes and beliefs of people in organizations providing public services.

It notes that these people have had 'well-developed bureaucratic and public service cultures' and sometimes 'strong professional cultures'; but this needs to be changed to a more commercial orientation.[30] To illustrate the sort of attitude that needed changing, Spicer et al quote the assistant commissioner of works:

> There were quite strong opinions expressed by people in the ministry that there were certain things that were important in the way they did business... Things like professional integrity, strong standards of professionalism, the 'one-stop shop' concept, a total life-cycle approach to doing business, a belief in certain things like plant replacement policy.[31]

The 'natural tendency of individuals' to protect things such as professional standards had, according to the authors of the CIS book, to be overcome in the shift to 'an entrepreneurial, profit-driven company'.[32]

In the case of services such as water and electricity, the conflict between commercial motives and environmental protection are also apparent as increased usage earns higher profits for private corporations but harms the environment.

Indonesia introduced legislation in 2002 to privatize and deregulate its electricity sector in return for loans from the Asian Development Bank and others, and as part of its IMF and World Bank structural adjustment programme. However, in 2004, Indonesia's newly formed Constitutional Court found that the law was unconstitutional because Indonesia's constitution states that 'economic sectors which are important to the state and crucial for the welfare of the people are controlled by the state and must be developed to give the maximum benefit to the people'. The court also found that the law unfairly required the state power company to provide electricity in less developed areas outside the main islands, while private companies could compete to supply electricity on the more populous developed islands.[33]

ATTRACTING INVESTMENT CAPITAL

A major rationale for privatization, particularly in poorer nations, has been to increase government revenue and raise capital for infrastructure development. But the increased government revenue has often turned out to be little more than a mirage. In affluent countries the loss of dividends from profitable service provision, the need to separately fund subsidies, and the cost of controlling prices tend to outweigh any financial gains from the sale of the services. For many corporations, 'economic efficiency' is actually a euphemism for keeping costs low by removing non-commercial goals from public services. The shifting of these costs to taxpayers is called making non-commercial expenditure 'transparent'.

The need for private capital has been reinforced by the new consensus of the 1980s, the Washington Consensus (see Chapter 3), which discourages governments from having balance of payment deficits. Therefore, in order to service debts, nations required 'immediate current account surpluses'. This imperative was reinforced by international organizations such as the IMF, which imposed limits on domestic credit expansion in 1976 and called for tighter budgetary controls and monetary targets.[34] This arrangement meant that governments were less able to fund capital-intensive infrastructure development, upkeep and renewal using government capital raised through loans.

Yet the private sector has been slow to invest in new infrastructure. In the case of electricity, they can charge higher prices if electricity is in short supply. Blackouts and price spikes increase as a result of lower reserve levels of generation capacity caused by the perverse incentives of the market system that give greater profits to private generating companies during times of electricity shortages. These perverse incentives not only discourage investment in new generation capacity but encourage withholding of electricity during times of peak demand to send prices higher.

In the case of water, there is little incentive to spend money on the sewage end of the water cycle. In the UK, the private water companies are among the most polluting companies in the country and although they have been successfully prosecuted many times, the fines do not deter their polluting behaviour. In Atlanta, Georgia, the government cancelled a 20-year contract with Suez because of poor water quality.[35]

Foreign investment is supposed to provide developing countries with much needed capital. However, the extent to which this foreign investment makes additional capital available for infrastructure development is questionable. Where full privatization has taken place, foreign direct investment (FDI) is increasingly going into mergers and acquisitions of existing enterprises rather than financing new investments and infrastructure. In fact, between half and two thirds of FDI worldwide consists of such mergers and acquisitions.[36] This has also occurred in Asia since the Asian crisis.

In developing countries, the money from sales of government assets usually goes towards debt repayments, while the private companies that do build new infrastructure bring little new private capital because they, too, borrow most of the funds from the development banks. If these same funds were loaned to governments they would have the funds to finance water infrastructure themselves. For example, the private consortium involved in the most expensive water privatization, that of Buenos Aires, only contributed US$30 million out of an initial investment of US$1 billion (see Figure 5.1).[37]

Governments usually find that privatized water schemes end up being more expensive for them than financing their own schemes with loans. This is because they have to pay 'cash contributions during the construction period; subsidies during the operation period – for example, in the form of non-refundable grants; and a favourable tax regime – including tax holidays, refunding of tax on construction and operation costs'.[38] The increasing demand for financial guarantees in terms

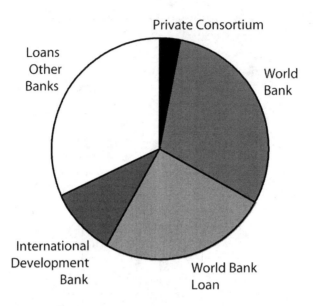

Figure 5.1 *Investment in Buenos Aires water supply during the first year*
Source: Barlow and Clarke (2002, pp161–162)

of government guarantees for the private company loans and guarantees of profits also end up being very expensive to the tax payers of poor countries.

With the many privatizations wreaking havoc, particularly in the water sector, the corporate world now prefers to promote what are called public–private partnerships (PPPs). Privatization can involve the full sell-off of government infrastructure to the private sector. Public–private partnerships, which are also a form of privatization, may involve something less than a full sale of government infrastructure. For example, in the water sector, infrastructure may be leased to the private sector, which takes over its operation and maintenance for a fixed time period – often 30 to 40 years – and collects the rates. Alternatively, the private sector may be contracted to provide the service for a fixed fee paid by the government, which collects the rates itself. Often the terms of the contract are kept secret from the public by commercial-in-confidence clauses, even in countries such as Australia that have freedom of information legislation.[39]

In the past, governments had to provide public services because private companies were unwilling to take on the costs and risks associated with constructing capital-intensive infrastructure. Now, private companies are demanding contracts that eliminate their risks and guarantee their profits. And because governments have little choice about making the investments themselves when development banks are lending money to foreign investors rather than governments, and because many governments are subject to bribes, they often agree to the most extortionate contract terms.

In Ghana, a water supply PPP involves a ten-year lease, with the government keeping control of the unprofitable aspects of water supply: the sewerage system, extension of water supply infrastructure and rural water supply. Full-cost recovery was introduced in preparation for this arrangement, meaning that rates escalated. Rates will automatically increase to offset inflation and currency devaluations. In addition, the two private companies, which will split the water system between them, will be paid a fee by the government that provides them with a guaranteed return on their investment.[40]

With electricity, governments may retain ownership of distribution and transmission infrastructure but allow new generation of electricity to be undertaken by independent power producers (IPPs). The electricity produced is then sold to the existing state utilities who distribute it to customers. IPPs are now a large market in Asia, particularly in China, Indonesia, the Philippines, India, Pakistan, Malaysia and Thailand.[41] These IPPs generally sell their electricity to a single state-owned utility according to a contract called a Power Purchase Agreement (PPA).

When private companies contract to provide services to the public they are careful to ensure that the risks of such ventures remain with the government. In this way they ensure 'the socialization of loss and the privatization of profit'. The risk that local currency might lose value against their home currency is avoided by requiring payments in foreign currency, particularly US dollars, or otherwise the payments are indexed to a hard currency such as the US dollar.[42]

Foreign investors eliminate the risk that there will not be sufficient demand for their service by ensuring that the contract guarantees a certain level of revenue or sales. For example, PPAs generally cover the first 15 to 30 years of operation of the plant and require that the state utility buy the total output of the plant.[43]

After the 1997 Asian economic crisis, the demand for power dropped in many Asian countries; but the PPAs required governments to go on paying high prices for electricity that was no longer needed. In the Philippines, power demand dropped and the country was left with an excess electricity-generating capacity of over 40 per cent. In Indonesia, there was 50 per cent overcapacity in Bali and Java as a result of IPP contracts, forcing the state-owned power authority to stop using its own power plants in favour of those of the IPPs.[44]

If a government tries to introduce competition in the generation sector, the private companies demand to be compensated for their stranded assets. And there is little incentive for new, more efficient generators to enter the market while the state utility is committed to purchasing power from established IPPs for 20 or 30 years under a PPA. Far from being more efficient forms of generation, 'the potential for inefficiencies is substantial if the IPPs meet a large share of the load'.[45]

To insulate themselves from price fluctuations in the cost of fuel, IPPs generally incorporate conditions in the PPA that compensate the investor if fuel prices rise. They may include the price of fuel in the final tariff or index the tariff to the price of oil. In the Philippines and Thailand, where the IPPs mainly use imported fuel, the price of that fuel increased by 50 per cent between 1997 and 1998. In the

Philippines, the National Power Corporation, Napacor, is responsible for supplying fuel to the IPPs.[46]

The risk that the state utility may default on its payment because of debts or inability to recoup enough from electricity consumers has also generally been transferred to the local government in the form of government guarantees. Sometimes such guarantees require money to be set aside in advance in special foreign exchange escrow accounts. Often the amount required in these accounts is in excess of PPA payments. For example, in Kenya 140 per cent of monthly payments has been demanded for a planned IPP at Kipevu, as well as a letter of credit for three months more. These tactics ensure that the IPPs have first priority in government budgeting, ahead of other needs such as health and education.[47] In other cases, governments are required to waive sovereignty and allow companies to appropriate state assets in lieu of debts.

In theory, private entrepreneurs are willing to take on risks if the return is high enough so that the greater the risks, the higher the price they charge. In reality, IPPs have often managed to ensure that the local government and credit export agencies take most of the risk, and yet they have still charged exorbitant prices. Even World Bank analysts admit 'that IPPs have often inflated supply prices for utilities'. In the Philippines, for example, the price of power from the IPPs, in 1996 – before the Asian economic crisis, was US$76 per megawatt hour (MWh) compared with US$57 for state-owned Napocor's power.[48] Electricity prices for consumers in the Philippines are now the highest in the Association of Southeast Asian Nations (ASEAN) region.

Recently, water companies have been demanding similar profit guarantees and protection against risks in their contract conditions. They argue that they cannot provide services to the very poor without government subsidies and they cannot bear the risk of currency devaluations in developing countries.[49]

DRIVING FORCES

Think tanks have played a major role in providing the intellectual rationale for privatization around the world and in setting out the policy prescriptions for it.[50] Using a range of free market economic theories and dogmas, such as private companies are more efficient, they have argued that public services should be privatized, contracted out and subject to commercial imperatives. In reality, these measures were designed to provide expanding profit opportunities for private corporations.

During the 1980s, the Thatcher government embarked on privatization in a big way, with guidance from think tanks and management consultants. Britain shifted from having the highest level of government ownership of industry of any Organisation for Economic Co-operation and Development (OECD) country during the early 1980s to being 'the fountainhead of industrial privatization, showering the alleged benefits over the rest of the world'. On the basis of the free market economic arguments and theories provided by the think tanks, the Thatcher government sought to 'move decision-making for the productive sector of the economy from public to private hands'.[51]

Privatization was not something that the public demanded. When the Conservative party came to power in the UK in 1979, it had made no mention of 'privatization' being on its policy agenda. Surveys in the following years consistently showed that the majority of people opposed the privatization of gas, telecommunications, electricity and water.[52]

The stated goal of economic efficiency was a cover for other more political and ideological goals. One such goal was to lower service costs to business by subordinating social objectives, including equity and environmental goals, to economic objectives. Furthermore, the Conservative party, through the influence of free market think tanks, was opposed to maintaining government deficits, and privatization was an easy way to do this in the short term without raising taxes.

A major aim of the corporate-funded think tanks and the Thatcher government was to reduce the role of government. Government control of industries and services such as electricity, gas, telecommunications and water was characterized as 'government interference'. Where the government protected industries for strategic reasons, this was characterized as insulating those industries from competitive pressures and allowing them to become inefficient and unable to adapt to changing circumstances.[53]

Both Chilean and British privatization were experiments driven by business interests and shaped by a mix of free market dogma and, in the case of the UK, pragmatic politics. Yet, they became models for countries that followed. And many did, to varying degrees, from Sweden and Finland in the north to Australia and New Zealand in the south. In the US, where many government services were already privately owned, although often by private monopolies, the free market push was for deregulation and the opening up of markets for competition.

Deregulation in the US was primarily driven by business interests – in particular, industries that either wanted to pay less for public services or wanted an opportunity to make profits from providing them. A series of deregulations took place during the 1980s in the airline industry, and then in natural gas, petroleum, financial services, telecommunications and railroad freight transportation. Business interests put a great deal of effort into lobbying and political donations to achieve deregulation; they 'inundated these politicos with lobbyists and contributions, and ushered a steady stream of once and future public officials through its revolving doors'.[54]

The case for deregulation could not be presented in self-interested terms to the public. It had to be presented as being in the interests of the wider public. Groups such as the large industrial energy users utilized the language of free market advocates to state their case in terms that were not too obviously self-interested.[55] The neo-conservative think tanks provided that language.

In Australia, 13 business organizations – including the Australian Chamber of Manufacturers, the BCA, the State Chamber of Commerce and Industry, the Victorian Employers Federation and the Victorian Farmers Federation – commissioned two think tanks, the Tasman Institute and the Institute of Public Affairs (IPA), in 1990 to advise on privatization of government enterprises in the state of Victoria. Project Victoria was far reaching. It covered water, ports, electricity, public transport and workers compensation.[56] The new state government, led by Jeff Kennett, implemented most of Project Victoria's recommendations after it was elected in 1991.[57]

The consequent transformation of Victoria was comprehensive and far reaching. From 1992 to 1998, the Victorian government sold AU$34 billion of assets. Most of these asset sales were in electricity and gas, but 'included trams, trains, aluminium smelter shares, forests, ports and gambling business. There was also new private investment allowed in such traditional government areas as roads, prisons, hospitals and courthouses.'[58]

While consumers, particularly residential consumers, have gained little from privatization, a whole raft of advisers, consultants, merchant bankers and stock-brokers have been enriched, as have some foreign companies and their executives. Consultants and advisers were paid about AU$160 million in the process of energy privatization in Victoria alone, and the potential of lucrative consultancies ensured an active constituency for privatization. The banks, including the Macquarie Bank, Merrill Lynch and Credit Suisse First Boston, were also major beneficiaries of privatization, making millions from advice and consultancies.[59]

This involvement of banks and financial institutions is repeated around the world. In addition, management consultants, particularly the large transnationals such as PriceWaterhouse Coopers (PwC) and KPMG, have earned large sums of money for their advice and studies on how to restructure government enterprises and privatize them. As consultants to the transnational companies that benefit from the privatizations, they have also been able to help their clients in the process.[60]

Consultants and advisers have played a dual role: first, promoting privatization as a scheme that will benefit everyone, and then reaping a good share of the benefits themselves in fees for advising on how to do it. Having been successful at this in affluent countries, some of them are now repeating their 'successes' in developing countries. For example, the Tasman Institute has been commissioned by various international agencies, including the World Bank, the Asia-Pacific Economic Cooperation (APEC), the Asian Development Bank (ADB) and AusAID, to do work on infrastructure reform in developing countries.[61]

Corporate-funded think tanks around the world ensured that by the mid 1990s there was a widely acceptable rationale for deregulation. 'Calls by large industries for utility deregulation found a ready chorus in academics, analysts and politicians who believed that competition would produce lower prices, better service and more innovation than government regulation.' By the early 1990s, 'the tide of free market hysteria reached a fever-pitch' and industry continued to lobby for deregulation.[62] Past lessons about the failings of markets in delivering public goods were conveniently forgotten.

The promoters of privatization all published reports selectively citing and describing privatization success stories in the US, UK and Europe, while neglecting to tell of the social costs of privatization. They also wrote feasibility studies on privatization and held conferences that brought together politicians, bureaucrats and private companies and consultants to discuss the wonders of privatization.[63]

From the 1980s, under pressure from the Reagan administration, the World Bank and the IMF used their growing influence over debt-laden developing nations to force them to open their public services to foreign investment. They employed the same free market economic theories to argue that private enterprises are more efficient and that the money earned from sales could be used to pay off some of their debts. Privatization is routinely prescribed for countries seeking loans. These institutions 'have overseen wholesale privatizations in economies that were previously state-sector dominated' as well as 'privatization of services that are regularly maintained in the public sector in rich countries'.[64]

Privatization was included as a core element in 70 per cent of the World Bank's structural adjustment loans in 2000. Between 1992 and 2002, 30 per cent of World Bank loans for water supply projects required privatization. In at least one case, that of the privatization of Buenos Aires water supply, the World Bank itself had a 7 per cent stake in the new Suez-controlled consortium, Aquas Argentinas.[65]

As a result of these programmes, the rate of privatization quadrupled in Latin America and tripled in Asia. During the mid 1990s, 42 African countries had undertaken some measure of privatization because of pressure from the World Bank. Between 1988 and 1998, more than 10,000 enterprises were privatized.[66]

The other international lending banks and development agencies have also promoted a policy prescription for developing countries that includes privatization of state-owned enterprises and liberalization of access for foreign investment in those enterprises. Instead of loaning money to governments, they now loan the money to foreign investors to construct and operate the infrastructure in developing countries.

Business lobbies also played a key role in promoting privatization at the global level. In the case of water, private water companies, in conjunction with the World Bank, organized a series of high-level international water coalitions to lobby for and make recommendations for privatization of water supplies and public–private partnerships. These coalitions are closely networked (see Figure 5.2). The first of these was the World Water Council – calling itself a leading water policy think tank – and the Global Water Partnership, both established in 1996. They, in turn, established the World Water Commission and an international panel of 'eminent persons' on water infrastructure financing.[67]

Figure 5.2 shows how a few senior people from the private water companies and the development banks and the IMF have played pivotal roles in putting together and running a network of closely associated water coalitions to promote

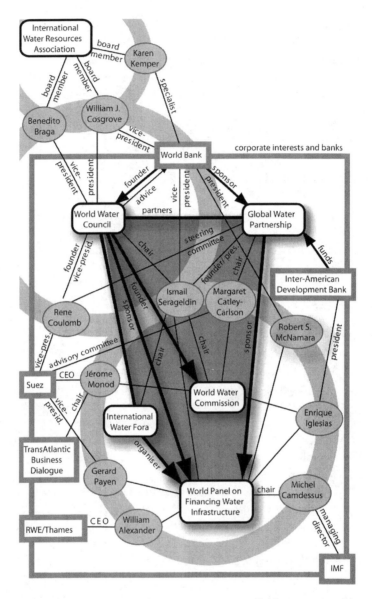

Figure 5.2 *International water privatization lobbying networks*

Note: Positions shown are not necessarily concurrent.

The international water policy-making organizations are all closely linked. For example, the World Water Council and the Global Water Partnership are partners and each sponsors the World Panel on Financing Water Infrastructure. These organizations are led by networks (overlapping circles) of key people, who are also top personnel in water companies such as Suez and RWE Thames Water, corporate coalitions such as the TransAtlantic Business Dialogue (TABD) and the development banks, which provide them with funding and sponsorship.

Source: information from Marsden (2003); Corporate Europe Observer (2005b) water privatization. These coalitions have been described as a 'kind of global high command for water'.[68] They promote privatization and private-sector involvement in water supply through advice to policy-makers, strategic reports and a series of international water fora that are held every three years.

CARTELS AND CONGLOMERATES

Privatization of services is not only transferring publicly owned assets into private hands, but also into the hands of fewer and fewer companies. The buyers of government assets and services have mainly been large transnational corporations that, over time, have bought up or squeezed out their competition. For example, three companies dominate private water provision around the world (see Table 5.1). Veolia Water, previously Vivendi Water, operates in 84 countries, employs almost 78,000 people and services 110 million people. RWE Thames Water services 70 million people. At its height in 2002, Suez serviced 115 million people in 130 countries; but during the last few years it has been withdrawing from developing countries. Between them Suez, Veolia and RWE control about 75 per cent of the world's private water supply market.[69]

Table 5.1 *The world's major water corporations*

Corporation	Water subsidiary	Country base	2003 Total revenue (Euros)	2003 Water revenue (Euros)
Veolia Environnement[70]	Veolia Water	France	28.4 billion	11.2 billion
Suez[71]	ONDEO	France	39.6 billion	6.5 billion
RWE[72]	Thames	Germany	43.9 billion	2.85 billion*
Bouygues[73]	SAUR	France	21.8 billion	2.45 billion^

Notes: * 2002   ^ Including some other services

Source: updated from Polaris Institute (2003, p4)

The growth of these companies during the 1990s was phenomenal, and most of the new customers have been in poor countries, where privatization has been forced by the World Bank and the IMF. However, they are now looking to expand into markets such as the US, where some 80 per cent of water is currently supplied by public authorities. The lobbying effort is already under way to get Congress to force municipal councils to privatize.[74]

Veolia, via its subsidiary Onyx, and Suez, via its subsidiary SITA, are also in the top three waste management corporations in the world, along with the US-based Waste Management Services (see Table 5.2).[75] Onyx, for example, services 70 million people.

Table 5.2 *The world's major waste corporations*

Corporation	Waste subsidiary	Country base	2003 Total revenue (Euros)	2003 Waste revenue (Euros)
Waste Management, Inc[76]		US		11.6 billion
Veolia Environnement[77]	Onyx	France	28.4 billion	6 billion
Suez[78]	SITA	France	39.6 billion	5.5 billion
RWE[79]	RWE Umwelt	Germany	43.9 billion	2 billion

Similarly the world of electricity supply is also becoming more concentrated. Approximately US$70 billion worth of mergers were announced worldwide between 1992 and 1996, with 83 per cent of them undertaken by US companies. They were joined in the buying frenzy by newly privatized companies in the UK and even state-owned companies such as Electricité de France (EdF). The two large British companies, PowerGen and National Power, began a spree of overseas acquisitions in 1997 in Asia, Australia, Europe and the US. 'Some analysts now suggest that by the year 2010 the world electricity scene will be dominated by eight or even fewer global companies – electricity multinationals.'[80]

Such expansion helps corporations to cut costs and spread expenses; but it is primarily done to increase profits, either by acquiring rival companies at home and so increasing their market power or by finding overseas corporations that promise high rates of return on investment. This latter prompted US companies to purchase approximately half the available power companies in the UK and Australia as soon as they were privatized.[81]

The Transnational Institute observes:

> *Despite the frequent claim about the negative impacts of public monopolies, these are often recreated by private foreign companies that manage to assume control over the whole chain of production, transmission and distribution of electricity, undermining government efforts to introduce competition and keep some authority over prices, supply and environmental standards.*[82]

In the water industry, the major water companies often work together in joint ventures. For example, Vivendi joined with RWE Thames Water to run Berlin's water system and Suez joined with RWE Thames Water to run Budapest's system. Suez also joined with RWE Thames Water and the son of Indonesian dictator General Suharto to take over Jakarta's water supply. And in France, there was a major judicial investigation into whether three of the largest water companies, Suez, Vivendi and Bouygues, had formed an illegal cartel during the early 1990s. Waste Management, Inc (WMX) has been investigated several times by US federal authorities for anti-trust activities. Anti-trust laws 'prohibit a variety of practices that restrain trade, such as price-fixing conspiracies, corporate mergers likely to reduce the competitive vigour of particular markets, and predatory acts designed to achieve or maintain monopoly power'.[83]

The Transnational Institute claims that the big energy 'corporations are already exceptionally well placed to operate jointly or to form a cartel to pressure governments, control prices and limit competition'.[84] Many energy, water and other service corporations are so large that they are often far more powerful than the local governments they contract with to supply services. This makes it very difficult for those governments to enforce terms of contracts relating to performance or to say no to rate increases without fear of retaliation. Retaliation threats are also made against more powerful governments. In the UK, when the water regulator, Ofwat, tried to get private companies to reduce their rates and improve their water quality, the giant conglomerate, Suez, threatened to slow down environmental investment and not keep to a European Union (EU) schedule to adopt environmental standards.[85]

In addition, corporations often use their power to insist on renegotiating the terms of contract after they have won a tender. Such renegotiations can involve rate increases and reductions in the scale of promised infrastructure improvements. According to the World Bank, more than half of the water contracts in Latin America were renegotiated during the 1990s.[86]

Mergers were also prompted by the convergence of services such as electricity, coal and gas. Almost half of the largest gas and electricity firms made 'convergence-related' acquisitions or 'major moves' at the end of the 1990s. Oil companies such as BP, Shell and Texaco are now acquiring power companies. The CEO of Edison International has predicted that by 2011 there will be only ten energy conglomerates worldwide.[87] Such conglomerates will have even more ability to manipulate prices and avoid competition, further negating the supposed benefits of deregulation.

Vertically and horizontally integrated companies that provide full electricity and gas service, as well as water and waste services from source to customer, are emerging. The Public Services Privatisation Research Unit noted in 1996:

> *The multinationals are now prepared to take over virtually any part of public services. Générale des Eaux is the most dramatic example of this. In the UK, it operates water companies; hospitals; refuse collection services; waste-to-energy plants; housing management; financial administration; road and bridge building; car parks; cable television; mobile phones; and is bidding for a railway franchise. In France, it operates in all these areas, plus television, catering, bus and rail transport, motorways and electricity generating – and, now, education. In the rest of the world, it is acquiring a similar range of contracts.*[88]

Générale des Eaux evolved into Vivendi, which has recently separated off some of its service business to focus on entertainment (television, film publishing, telecommunications, internet). Vivendi now only has a 20 per cent share in Veolia Environnement, which incorporates the water, waste management, energy and transport services divisions that were once part of the Vivendi empire. Similarly, Suez provides electricity, gas, water and waste management services. RWE advertises itself as 'Everything you need from one source... Electricity. Gas. Water. Recycling. Services.'[89]

The problems associated with concentration of ownership are exacerbated because of the inability of national governments to control foreign owners. First, there is the problem that foreign owners are likely to send their profits back to their home countries rather than make further investment in their facilities or spend the money in the country where they earned it, thus stimulating the local economy.[90]

Second, foreign owners can withhold services for political and economic reasons, thereby cutting off an essential part of the economic system without governments being able to do anything about it. For example, Walt Patterson relates a situation that occurred in 1998 when Quebec was experiencing an electricity crisis. A private US company shut down its plant until it could get the price it wanted for its electricity.[91] US companies also shut down supply in the Dominican Republic to force the government to pay its debt to them. Patterson observes:

> Oil multinationals with a wide portfolio of activities in different parts of the world have never hesitated to suggest that they will withdraw from a particular concession or shut down a particular oilfield if government policy appears contrary to their interest. Electricity multinationals with similarly large portfolios will have a much more potent threat at their disposal.[92]

If privatization and deregulation are taken to their logical end, which is the aim of advocates, the public will be unable to influence the development of essential services, the terms of their provision, the reliability of their supply, their accessibility or their price. These will all be decisions made by cartels of transnational corporations whose primary motivation is profit and power. These cartels will be able to exercise power over national, state and local governments.

Current trends suggest that these service transnationals will become not merely 'power centres' but 'global centres', owning systems extending across entire continents, including electricity, natural gas, water, waste management and telecommunications.[93] Given what is at stake, it is little wonder that the push for privatization and deregulation has been strong and relentless, bulldozing citizen opposition out of the way.

NOTES

1   Anti-enclosure saying, author unknown, 18th-century England.

2   Brendan Martin, 'From the Many to the Few: Privatization and Globalization', *The Ecologist*, vol 26, no 4, 1996, p147.

3   CEO, '... And Not a Drop to Drink! World Water Forum Promotes Privatisation and Deregulation of World's Water', Corporate Europe Observatory, www.corporateeurope.org/observer7/water/ accessed 3 January 2005.

4   David Parker, 'Nationalisation, Privatisation, and Agency Status within Government: Testing for the Importance of Ownership', in Peter M Jackson and Catherine M Price (eds) *Privatisation and Regulation: A Review of the Issues*, London and New York, Longman, 1994, p149.

5   Peter M. Jackson and Catherine M. Price, 'Privatisation and Regulation: A Review of the Issues', in Peter M. Jackson and Catherine M. Price (eds) *Privatisation and Regulation: A Review of the Issues*, London and New York, Longman, 1994, pp1, 5.

6   Dexter Whitfield, *Making It Public: Evidence and Action Against Privatisation*, London, Pluto Press, 1983, p44; Barry Spicer, *et al.*, *Transforming Government Enterprises: Managing Radical Organisational Change in Deregulated Environments*, St Leonards, NSW, Centre for Independent Studies, 1996, p10.

7   Chris Adams, 'Privatising Infrastructure in the South', *Focus on Trade*, May, 2001, www.focusweb.org/publications/2001/privatising%20Infrastructure%20in%20the%20South.html.

8   Quoted in Natalie Avery, 'Stealing from the State', *Multinational Monitor*, September, 1993, www.essential.org/monitor/hyper/issues/1993/09/mm0993_10.html

9   Whitfield, *Making It Public*, p49; James Walsh, *The $10 Billion Jolt*, Los Angeles, Silver Lake Publishing, 2002, pp288–9; Brian Robins, 'Banks See Big Chance in Trading Electricity', *Sydney Morning Herald*, 5–6 October, 2002, p45.

10 Jackson and Price, 'Privatisation and Regulation', p7; Sharon Beder, *Power Play: The Fight to Control the World's Electricity*, Melbourne and New York, Scribe Publications and the New Press, 2003; Maude Barlow and Tony Clarke, *Blue Gold: The Fight to Stop the Corporate Theft of the World's Water*, New York, The New Press, 2002, p90.

11 Barlow and Clarke, *Blue Gold*, p90.

12 Tom Morton, 'The Global Water Business', *Background Briefing, ABC Radio National*, 20 April, 2003, www.abc.net.au/rn/talks/bbing/stories/s833698.htm; Bill Marsden, 'Cholera and the Age of the Water Barons', The Center for Public Integrity, 4 February, 2003, www.icij.org/water/printer-friendly.aspx?aid=44 ; CEO, 'European Water TNCs: Towards Global Domination?' Corporate Europe Observatory, www.corporateeurope.org/water/infobrief1.htm accessed 3 January 2005.

13 Barlow and Clarke, *Blue Gold*, pp154–5; Morton, 'The Global Water Business'; Marsden, 'Cholera and the Age of the Water Barons'.

14 Morton, 'The Global Water Business'; Marsden, 'Cholera and the Age of the Water Barons'.

15 Beder, *Power Play*, pp122–7; 252–5, Chapter 6.

16 Cited in Anthony Hughes, 'All Charged and Ready to Go', *Sydney Morning Herald*, 11 March, 1998; Barlow and Clarke, *Blue Gold*, p90.

17   Martin, 'From the Many to the Few', p149; George Monbiot, 'Africa Exploitation on Tap', *Guardian*, 20 October, 2004; Neil Hirst, 'Consumer Protection in a Deregulated Market', Paper presented at the IEA Regulatory Forum: Competition in Energy Markets, Paris, 7–8 February, 2002, p12.

18   Mandela quoted in Jacques Pauw, 'Metered to Death: How a Water Experiment Caused Riots and a Cholera Epidemic', The Center for Public Integrity, 4 February, 2003, www.icij.org/water/printer-friendly.aspx?aid=49; Monbiot, 'Africa Exploitation on Tap'.

19   Monbiot, 'Africa Exploitation on Tap'.

20   Patrick Bond, 'The New Apartheid', *New Internationalist*, April, 2003, p24; Patrick Bond, 'ANC Privatizations Fail to Deliver in South Africa', *CorpWatch*, 18 August, 2004, www.corpwatch.org/print_article.php?&id=11500

21   Monbiot, 'Africa Exploitation on Tap'; Pauw, 'Metered to Death'; Bond, 'ANC Privatizations Fail to Deliver in South Africa'.

22   Marsden, 'Cholera and the Age of the Water Barons'; Pauw, 'Metered to Death'; Robert Weissman, 'The Anatomy of a Deal', *Multinational Monitor*, September, 2002, p19.

23   Marsden, 'Cholera and the Age of the Water Barons'; Pauw, 'Metered to Death'; Bond, 'ANC Privatizations Fail to Deliver in South Africa'; Monbiot, 'Africa Exploitation on Tap'.

24   Jon Jeter, 'For South Africa's Poor, a New Power Struggle', *The Washington Post*, 6 November, 2001, pA01; John Murphy, 'Unions in South Africa Strike over Selling of State Industries', *The Baltimore Sun*, 30 August, 2001, p18A; Juan Forero, 'Still Poor, Latin Americans Protest Push for Open Markets', *The New York Times*, 19 July, 2002.

25   Polaris Institute, 'Global Water Grab: How Corporations Are Planning to Take Control of Local Water Services', Polaris Institute, January 2003, p8; FOE, 'Dirty Water: The Environmental and Social Records of Four Multinational Water Companies', London, Friends of the Earth, December 2001, p3; Barlow and Clarke, *Blue Gold,* pp114–5.

26   Barlow and Clarke, *Blue Gold,* p115; FOE, 'Dirty Water', p6.

27   See, for example, Barlow and Clarke, *Blue Gold,* p111; Julia O'Connell Davidson, 'Metamorphosis? Privatisation and the Restructuring of Management and Labour', in Peter M. Jackson and Catherine M. Price (eds) *Privatisation and Regulation: A Review of the Issues*, London and New York, Longman, 1994, pp176–7.

28   Charlie Higley, 'Disastrous Deregulation', *Public Citizen*, December 2000, p4; Jerrold Oppenheim, 'US Electric Utilities: A Century of Successful Democratic Regulation of Private Monopolies; a Half-Decade of Failure of Experiments in Competition', Brussels, European Federation of Public Service Unions, 12 December 2001, pp19–20.

29   Davidson, 'Metamorphosis?' p173.

30   Spicer, *et al.*, *Transforming Government Enterprises: Managing Radical Organisational Change in Deregulated Environments*, p118.

31   Quoted in *Ibid.*, p119.

32   *Ibid.*, p121.

33   Quoted in Muninggar Sri Saraswati, 'Court Annuls New Electricity Law', *The Jakarta Post*, 16 December, 2004.

34 John Weeks, 'Credit Where Discredit Is Due', *Third World Resurgence*, April, 1994, p32; James Foreman-Peck, *Public and Private Ownership of British Industry 1820–1990*, Oxford, Clarendon Press, 1994, pp331, 335.

35 Polaris Institute, 'Global Water Grab', p8; CEO, 'European Water TNCs'.

36 Chakravarthi Raghavan, 'FDI Is No Panacea for South's Economic Woes', *Third World Resurgence*, October/November, 1999, www.twnside.org.sg/title/woe-cn.htm.

37 Nicholas Hildyard and Sarah Sexton, 'Cartels, "Low Balls", Backhanders and Hand-Outs', *The Ecologist*, vol 26, no 4, 1996, p148; Marsden, 'Cholera and the Age of the Water Barons'; Barlow and Clarke, *Blue Gold*, pp161–2.

38 World Bank report quoted in Barlow and Clarke, *Blue Gold*, p91.

39 *Ibid.*, p89; Marsden, 'Cholera and the Age of the Water Barons'.

40 Weissman, 'The Anatomy of a Deal'.

41 Yves Albouy and Reda Bousba, 'The Impact of IPPs in Developing Countries – out of the Crisis and into the Future', *The World Bank Group – Public Policy for the Private Sector*, December, 1998, www.worldbank.org/html/fpd/notes/162/162albou.pdf, pp1–2.

42 Navroz K. Dubash, 'The Changing Global Context for Electricity Reform', in Navroz K. Dubash (ed) *Power Politics: Equity and Environment in Electricity Reform*, Washington DC, World Resources Institute, 2002, p19; The Regulatory Assistance Project, 'Best Practices Guide: Implementing Power Sector Reform', Gardiner, Maine and Montpelier, Vermont, Energy and Environment Training Program, Office of Energy, Environment and Technology and Global Bureau, Center for the Environment, United States Agency for International Development, p12.

43 Albouy and Bousba, 'The Impact of IPPs in Developing Countries', p2; The Regulatory Assistance Project, 'Best Practices Guide', p13.

44 Mizuho Research, 'Credit Comment: National Power Corporation', Mizuho Research, 28 September 2001; Kate Bayliss and David Hall, 'Independent Power Producers: A Review of the Issues', University of Greenwich, London, Public Services International Research Unit (PSIRU), November 2000, p9.

45 Albouy and Bousba, 'The Impact of IPPs in Developing Countries', p5; Bayliss and Hall, 'Independent Power Producers', pp3, 5.

46 Albouy and Bousba, 'The Impact of IPPs in Developing Countries', p2; R. David Gray, and John Schuster, 'The East Asian Financial Crisis – Fallout for the Private Power Projects', *The World Bank Group – Public Policy for the Private Sector*, August, 1998, p3; Fernando Y. Roxas, 'The Importance and the Changing Role of the Independent Power Producers (IPPs) in the Proposed Competitive Power Market in the Philippines', Paper presented at the APEC 8th Technical Seminar & 7th Coal Flow Seminar, Bangkok, 30 October – 1 November, 2001, p2.

47 Albouy and Bousba, 'The Impact of IPPs in Developing Countries', p2; Bayliss and Hall, 'Independent Power Producers', p4.

48 The Regulatory Assistance Project, 'Best Practices Guide', p12; Albouy and Bousba, 'The Impact of IPPs in Developing Countries', p4.

49 CEO, 'European Water TNCs'; Morton, 'The Global Water Business'.

50 Parker, 'Nationalisation, Privatisation, and Agency Status within Government: Testing for the Importance of Ownership', p151; Henry Gibbon, 'Guide for Divesting Government-Owned Enterprises', Reason Public Policy Institute, www.privatization.org/Collection/Publications/htg_15--divesting_assets.htm accessed 20 July 2001.

51   Foreman-Peck, *Public and Private Ownership of British Industry,* pp319–20; Steve Thomas, 'The Privatization of the Electricity Supply Industry', in John Surrey (ed) *The British Electricity Experiment,* London, Earthscan Publications, 1996b, p40.

52   Foreman-Peck, *Public and Private Ownership of British Industry,* p333; Jackson and Price, 'Privatisation and Regulation', p15; Michael G. Pollitt, 'A Survey of Liberalisation of Public Enterprises in the UK since 1979', University of Cambridge, January 1999, p7.

53   Steve Thomas, 'Strategic Government and Corporate Issues', in John Surrey (ed) *The British Electricity Experiment,* London, Earthscan Publications, 1996a, p257.

54   Andrew Wheat, 'System Failure: Deregulation, Political Corruption, Corporate Fraud and the Enron Debacle', *Multinational Monitor,* January/February, 2002, p35.

55   Richard F. Hirsh, *Power Loss: The Origins of Deregulation and Restructuring in the American Electric Utility System,* Cambridge, Massachusetts, The MIT Press, 1999, p244.

56   Tasman Institute, 'About Us/Projects', Tasman Institute, www.tasman.com.au/main/a_nz.html accessed 20 July 2001.

57   Alan Kohler, 'The Radical Right Wing Speeds the Kennett Revolution', *The Age,* 14 February, 1997, p15.

58   Alan Moran, 'The Great Victorian Sell Off', *The Western Australian,* 23 November, 1999.

59   Robert R. Booth, *Warring Tribes: The Story of Power Development in Australia,* West Perth, The Bardak Group, 2000, pp75, 201; Rod Myer, 'Now It's Time for Stockdale Inc', *The Age,* 8 May, 1999; Luke Collins, 'Rear Window', *Australian Financial Review,* 22 October, 1999, p91.

60   Whitfield, *Making It Public,* p52.

61   Tasman Economics, 'Our Founders', Tasman Economics, www.tasman.com.au/founders/founders.htm accessed 26 June 2002.

62   Higley, 'Disastrous Deregulation', pp2–3.

63   Whitfield, *Making It Public,* p44.

64   Sustainable Energy and Economic Network, 'Enron's Pawns: How Public Institutions Bankrolled Enron's Globalization Game', Washington, DC, Institute for Policy Studies, 22 March 2002, p10; Jackson and Price, 'Privatisation and Regulation', p19; Vincent Lloyd and Robert Weissman, 'Against the Workers: How IMF and World Bank Policies Undermine Labor Power and Rights', *Multinational Monitor,* September, 2001, www.essential.org/monitor/mm2001/01september/sep01corp1.html.

65   Susan Hawley, 'Exporting Corruption: Privatisation, Multinationals and Bribery', *The Corner House Briefing,* 2000, http://cornerhouse.icaap.org/briefings/19.html; Marsden, 'Cholera and the Age of the Water Barons'.

66   *Ibid.*; Kate Bayliss, 'Privatisation and the World Bank: A Flawed Development Tool', *Global Focus,* June, 2001.

67   Marsden, 'Cholera and the Age of the Water Barons'; Karl Flecker, 'Operation Water Rights Project – Lobby Groups', The Polaris Institute, May, 2004, www.polarisinstitute.org/polaris_project/water_lords/lobby_groups/wwc_gwp_PRINT.html

68 Riccardo Petrella, water researcher quoted in Marsden, 'Cholera and the Age of the Water Barons'.

69 Polaris Institute, 'Global Water Grab'; Veolia Environnement, 'Veolia Water', Veolia Environnement, www.veoliaenvironnement.com/en/activities/water/ accessed 5 January 2004; Julio Godov, 'Water and Power: The French Connection', The Center for Public Integrity, 4 February, 2003, www.icij.org/water/printer-friendly.aspx?aid=47; CEO, 'European Water TNCs'; Morton, 'The Global Water Business'.

70 'Water', Veolia Environnement, www.veoliaenvironnement.com/en/activities/water/ accessed 5 January 2004.

71 '2003 Annual Report', Suez, 2004, www.suez.com/documents/english/docderef2003en/SUEZ_RA2003_chap4_EN.pdf.

72 '2003 Annual Report', RWE, 2004, www.rwe.com/generator.aspx/investorrelations/financial-reports/id=2324/financial-reports-page.html; 'Financial Profile', RWE Thames Water, 2004, www.rwethameswater.com/TW/division/en_gb/content/General/General_000192.jsp?SECT=General_000192.

73 'Saur', Bouygues, 2004, www.bouygues.fr/us/metiers/saur.asp.

74 Marsden, 'Cholera and the Age of the Water Barons'; Weissman, 'The Anatomy of a Deal', p18.

75 Suez, 'The 2003 Annual Report', Suez 2004, www.suez.com/documents/english/docderef2003en/SUEZ_RA2003_chap4_EN.pdf, p66.

76 'Fact Sheet', Waste Management, Inc, 2004, www.wm.com/WM/Press/MediaKit/facts.pdf.

77 'Waste Management.' Veolia Environnement, www.veoliaenvironnement.com/en/activities/Waste/ accessed on 5 January 2004.

78 '2003 Annual Report', Suez, 2004, www.suez.com/documents/english/docderef2003en/SUEZ_RA2003_chap4_EN.pdf.

79 '2003 Annual Report', RWE, 2004, www.rwe.com/generator.aspx/investorrelations/financial-reports/id=2324/financial-reports-page.html.

80 Edward B. Flowers, *U.S. Utility Mergers and the Restructuring of the New Global Power Industry*, Westport, Connecticut, Quorum Books, 1998, pp1, 175; Walt Patterson, *Transforming Electricity: The Coming Generation of Change*, London, Royal Institute of International Affairs and Earthscan, 1999, p84.

81 Flowers, *U.S. Utility Mergers,* pp1, 202.

82 Daniel Chavez, 'Lights Off! Debunking the Myths of Power Liberalisation', Amsterdam, Transnational Institute (TNI), May 2002, p3.

83 Barlow and Clarke, *Blue Gold,* pp108, 111, 126; Marsden, 'Cholera and the Age of the Water Barons'; Antitrust Division, 'Overview', US Department of Justice, www.usdoj.gov/atr/overview.html accessed 6 January 2005.

84 Chavez, 'Lights Off!', p11.

85 Barlow and Clarke, *Blue Gold,* p125.

86 CEO, 'European Water TNCs'; David Hall and Emmanuele Lobina, 'Private and Public Interests in Water and Energy', *Natural Resources Forum*, no 28, 2004, p270.

87 'Energy, the New Convergence', *The Economist*, 29 May, 1999; Patterson, *Transforming Electricity,* p84; Daniel Berman, 'The Confederate Cartel's War Against California', *San Francisco Bay Guardian*, 5 January, 2001; Merrill Goozner, 'Free

Market Shock', *The American Prospect*, 27 August, 2001, www.prospect.org/print-friendly/print/\/12/15/goozner-m.html.

88   Public Services Privatisation Research Unit, 'Public Services Privatisation Research Unit', The Privatisation Network, January, 1996, www.psiru.org/reports/96-01-TPN.doc.

89   Veolia Environnement, 'Veolia Water'; RWE, 'English Home Page', RWE, www.rwe.com/generator.aspx/homepage/templateId=renderPage/id=496/home-en.html accessed 5 January.

90   Patterson, *Transforming Electricity*, p120.

91   *Ibid.*, p121.

92   *Ibid.*

93   *Ibid.*, p121, 129–30.

6

The Trade Agenda

Free trade is one of the greatest blessings which a government can confer on a people. LORD MACAULAY, QUOTED BY GEORGE BUSH SNR[1]

One of the early US free trade proponents was William Lockhart Clayton, a successful businessman who headed the world's largest cotton brokerage firm with subsidiaries around the world. In 1936, Clayton had appeared on the cover of *Time* magazine as 'the epitome of the new American capitalist who operated on a global scale'. Clayton was a great believer in free trade because his business was based on international trade:[2]

> *To his critics, Clayton was a corporate reactionary whose brutal spec-*
> *ulative tactics and endorsement of unbridled competition helped bring*
> *ruin upon the cotton farmer. As a world trader, he came under attack*
> *for continuing to sell to Nazi Germany and Imperial Japan long after*
> *the character of those regimes became obvious.*[3]

Clayton promoted free trade as a businessman and then later as a US government representative and diplomat. Many US-based multinational companies, like Clayton's, were keen to gain access to world markets, particularly since their 'nearly exclusive access to large capital funds' gave them a competitive advantage in those markets. US administrations have therefore made free trade a top priority of international economic policy and have been keen to spread the free market message to foreign shores.[4]

Clayton argued that free trade was necessary to ensure world peace and, following World War II, he argued that economic collaboration would prevent war. While he was the US trade representative, his team managed to negotiate a tariff reduction agreement in 1947 between 18 countries. It was called the General Agreement on Tariffs and Trade (GATT).[5]

Clayton's ultimate goal was an International Trade Organization (ITO) that would remove barriers to global trade. The US government also envisaged such an organization when the World Bank and the International Monetary Fund (IMF) were set up in 1944. A charter for it was drawn up at a conference in Havana. However, there was serious business opposition to the idea, even in the US. Some business people were suspicious of an international bureaucracy that would lay down the rules of trade. Others feared the loss of tariffs and subsidies that protected their business.[6]

Many developing countries were also unconvinced of the benefits of enforced free trade, noting that the nations that had successfully industrialized had protected their own industries during development. Latin American countries saw the ITO charter as a way to 'serve the interests of the United States and damage the legitimate aspirations of the Latin American countries'.[7]

Advocates used anti-communist propaganda to promote the ITO. Secretary of State Dean Acheson told a House Committee on Foreign Affairs hearing that the US was 'engaged in a struggle between two ways of life' – free enterprise and communism – and the ITO charter could 'immeasurably strengthen us and other freedom-loving nations'.[8]

The growing compromises emerging from the negotiations angered US business advisers to the negotiations, including representatives of the National Association of Manufacturers (NAM) and the Chamber of Commerce, who began to oppose the ITO. Elvin Killheffer from the Chamber of Commerce labelled the charter 'a vast invasion of the free enterprise principle' and *Fortune* magazine claimed that the charter did nothing to promote free trade, but 'merely registers and codifies the worldwide conflict between freer trade and economic nationalism' and is 'one of the most hypocritical state documents of modern times'. It is difficult to know whether such indignation was genuine, given that one US representative suggested that 'because the charter was being attacked from the left, he would talk to some friendly delegates to see whether they might criticize it from the right, thus allowing the United States to take the middle ground'.[9]

Despite Clayton's public relations efforts, including obtaining 'the endorsement of 125 business executives, educators and other prominent individuals', the charter failed to get Congressional approval in the US and efforts to promote an ITO failed. All that was left was the GATT, and Clayton turned his efforts to getting more signatories to the GATT and broadening and deepening its scope. GATT became 'both a set of rules and a negotiating forum'.[10]

A series of *ad hoc* secret negotiating rounds followed, designed to foster free trade – that is, the removal of trade barriers such as tariffs and export bans – through setting rules for international trade and settling trade disputes. It was argued that if trade was unimpeded by trade barriers and tariffs, global economic growth would be accelerated and each country would prosper as a result.

Since 1947, there have been eight official rounds of negotiations to update the GATT rules. The last round – the Uruguay Round – began in 1986 in Uruguay, with 108 countries represented. Prior to the Uruguay Round, tariffs had been reduced by 75 per cent. Business leaders hoped that the Uruguay Round would achieve further significant reductions and also address non-tariff barriers to trade.[11] In 1989, the Australian Industries Assistance Commission noted:

As a forum for trade liberalization, the GATT's main achievement has been to reduce 'overt' quantitative restrictions and to lower average tariff levels among its (industrialized) members. Its main failures have been the exception of agriculture and textiles and clothing from much of this process, and the development of new forms of non-tariff assistance (principally, 'domestic' subsidies and 'voluntary' export restraint arrangements) against which the established GATT rules and procedures have been largely impotent.[12]

The Uruguay Round sought to address some of these failures.

LOBBYING FOR THE URUGUAY ROUND

William Brock, the US Trade Representative (USTR) under Reagan, played a key role in getting the GATT talks restarted in 1986. But he was aided in his endeavours by a range of powerful corporate lobbying groups.

Within each of the major nations that dominated the GATT negotiations, industry and business had privileged access to influence their country's negotiating position. The economic or trade ministry officials involved in the negotiations were lobbied extensively by industry at both a national level and an international level by groups such as the International Chamber of Commerce (ICC) and the Organisation for Economic Co-operation and Development's (OECD's) Business and Industry Advisory Council (BIAC).[13]

Industry Sector Advisory Committees (ISACs) had been set up in the US during the 1970s to facilitate industry input into trade policy and to 'ensure that US trade policy and trade negotiation objectives adequately reflect US commercial and economic interests'. ISACs were set up to represent 17 industry sectors and advised the president and the negotiators via the Department of Commerce and the Office of the USTR.[14]

In this way, the negotiating positions of the dominant nations reflected business interests rather than a broad spectrum of democratic interests. No other non-governmental organizations (NGOs) had the access or influence accorded to business groups. Several large and powerful business organizations campaigned for the successful completion of the Uruguay Round and the expansion of free trade. They included the World Economic Forum, the International Chamber of Commerce, the Bilderberg Club and the Trilateral Commission.

The European Round Table of Industrialists (ERT; see Chapter 2) was a leading lobbying force during the Uruguay Round and it claims some of the credit for the completion of the round. Its trade and investment working group worked closely with the US Business Roundtable 'in backing the launch of the Uruguay Round' and supporting the ongoing negotiations.[15]

ERT was vigorous in its lobbying for successful GATT negotiations. ERT Assistant Secretary General Caroline Walcot said in 1993: 'We have spoken to everybody. We have made press statements. We have written to prime ministers. We have done *everything* we can *think* of to try and press for the end of the Uruguay Round.' At the end of the round an ERT delegation of 14 chief executive officers (CEOs) met with the French prime minister 'to help resolve the European position in the talks'.[16]

The World Economic Forum (WEF) also claims it 'played a major role at the beginning of the 1980s in launching the Uruguay trade negotiations'.[17]

BOX 6.1 THE WORLD ECONOMIC FORUM (WEF)

The World Economic Forum (WEF) has 1000 foundation members who are current chief executive officers (CEOs) of the world's largest corporations. These CEOs come to WEF meetings to set the economic and political, as well as the business, agenda worldwide. The WEF claims to have 'evolved into a major force for economic integration at the corporate as well as the national economic levels'.[18]

The WEF is not a decision-making body, but one that has power through the financial clout of its members. It wields influence through bringing the world's top business people and top policy-makers together at its meetings. Government leaders are invited to WEF meetings, enabling business leaders to have high-level access to government ministers, prime ministers and presidents. The WEF produces a *Global Competitiveness Report* that ranks nations according to how business friendly their policies are. According to the WEF, competitiveness depends upon having small government, minimal government intervention in, or regulation of, the market and good incentives for investment in new technologies.[19]

The WEF claims to be the 'leading interface for business/government interaction'. In 1982, the forum invited the heads of major institutions such as the World Bank, the International Monetary Fund (IMF) and the General Agreement on Tariffs and Trade (GATT), as well as cabinet members of 'major countries', to its annual Davos meeting for the first Informal Gathering of World Economic Leaders. Various other informal groupings were subsequently established, including an Informal Gathering of Trade Ministers. The WEF also created 'CEO clubs' of the chief executive officers of the largest corporations in 13 different industry sectors.[20]

According to researcher James Goodman, 'WEF strategizing drove the neo-liberal agenda in the 1980s ... It offered a proactive forum, removed from the public gaze, and played a central role in diffusing neo-liberalism and was highly effective in extending the reign of the market.' Similarly, Kees van der Pijl, in his book, *Transnational Classes and International Relations*, states that 'Until well into the 1990s, the WEF was a pivot of neo-liberal hegemony.'[21]

Although the Uruguay Round was due to end in 1990, it foundered over a lack of agreement about reductions in protection for agriculture, particularly in Europe, and due to conflict over US efforts to extend the agreement to cover services (see Chapter 7).[22] Business from both sides of the Atlantic lobbied hard.

In 1989, William Brock set up the Eminent Persons Group (EPG) on World Trade to push for 'a successful outcome to the Uruguay Round'. The EPG was made up of 14 'influential politicians and business leaders from around the world', including Lord David Young, former UK secretary of state, trade and industry; Enrique Iglesias, president of the Inter-American Development Bank (IDB); and Paul Volcker, former US Federal Reserve Board chairman.[23] One member, Peter Sutherland, former European Commission (EC) Commissioner (1984–1988), an architect of the European single market and chair of Allied Irish Banks, later became director general of GATT in 1993 with the support of the European countries and the US. Another member, Mike Moore, New Zealand trade minister and then briefly New Zealand prime minister, became World Trade Organization (WTO) director general in 1999. The group was chaired by Otto Lambsdorff, former West German economics minister, and advised by Martin Wolf, chief economics leader writer for the London *Financial Times*, who also acted as *rapporteur* for the group.[24]

The EPG warned, at its inaugural meeting in 1990, that if the Uruguay Round failed there would be 'chaos and impoverishment' in its wake as a result of the trade stagnation and slowdown of economic growth that would ensue.[25]

The OECD ministerial meeting in 1991 stated that 'the Uruguay Round has the highest priority on the international economic agenda'. The International Chamber of Commerce (ICC) sent a delegation to Prime Minister John Major, who was hosting the 1991 London Economic Summit, to persuade him that the Uruguay Round was the 'most important and urgent issue' on the summit's agenda.[26]

The US-based Multilateral Trade Negotiations (MTN) Coalition was formed in 1990 as part of the lobbying effort to kick start the suspended negotiations: 'The potential benefits are enormous, the stakes are extremely high, and the alternative of failure catastrophic', the coalition said in a letter to Senator Lloyd Bentsen. The coalition lobbied within the US for Congressional support for the GATT negotiations and also outside the US. Coalition representatives visited London in 1991 to 'drum up British support for a wide-ranging trade agreement'.[27]

The MTN Coalition claimed to represent 14,000 US companies, including the major multinationals such as IBM, General Motors, American Express, General Electric, Citicorp and associations such as the NAM and the US Council for International Business (USCIB). It was chaired by two former US trade reps, William Brock and Robert Strauss, and its executive director was Harry Freeman, former American Express vice president (see Chapter 7).[28]

It was said to be 'the largest coalition in history'. It described itself as including 'an array of business, farm, consumer and trade associations who have joined with many leading US corporations in an education and mobilization campaign in support of comprehensive multilateral trade agreements in the current negotiating round of GATT'.[29]

However, US business was not united in promoting GATT. Some companies formed an anti-GATT coalition with labour unions – the Labor-Industry Coalition for International Trade – because of their concerns about concessions that US negotiators might make in terms of the US steel, electronics, oil, chemical and communications industries. The textile industry was particularly concerned about cuts in tariffs that protected them from imported textiles, and it led the opposition to GATT in the US. Meanwhile, other companies from the aluminium, beer, furniture, paper, semi-conductor and toy industries were concerned that tariff reductions required by GATT would not be enough, and they formed the Zero Tariff Coalition.[30]

Some senators supported a resolution to withdraw fast-track authority for the president so that the Senate could amend the deal that US GATT negotiators had agreed to. Believing this would threaten any GATT agreement that might be reached, the MTN Coalition wrote to each congressman in 1990, asking that they not condemn the GATT talks before they were completed.[31]

When the GATT negotiations were concluded and GATT's approval in Congress seemed assured, the MTN Coalition closed down, transferring its files and lobbying activities to Texas Instruments Inc. Texas Instruments CEO and Chair Jerry R. Junkins went on to play a leading role in setting up the Alliance for GATT Now, which succeeded the MTN Coalition in 1994.[32]

THE BATTLE FOR US CONGRESSIONAL APPROVAL

When the Uruguay Round was completed in 1993, with the proposed World Trade Organization (WTO) as a key outcome, most governments did not even bother to consult their citizens before approving it. In the US, approval rested with politicians who had generally not even read the agreement. Ralph Nader offered US$10,000 to any senator or member of Congress who had read the agreement and could answer 12 questions on it. The only politician to accept the challenge decided to vote against it after reading it.[33]

Congressional approval of GATT was put in doubt when the US Treasury estimated that the cuts to US tariffs involved in the GATT would cost the government US$14 billion in revenue that would have to be recouped through government spending cuts or tax increases. Under pressure, the Treasury subsequently estimated the benefits of GATT to be worth about U$100 billion in increased trade each year for US corporations.[34]

Environmental, consumer, religious, family, farm and labour groups all campaigned against GATT approval, arguing that it would have an adverse affect on jobs and undermine US environmental and safety legislation. Legislation that was threatened in this way included US car fuel-efficiency regulations; Californian requirements for warning labels on products that might cause cancer or birth defects; and legislation restricting the re-export of nuclear materials and technology.

Complaints about breaches of free trade rules were to be considered by the WTO in hearings closed to the public and the media. The WTO was therefore labelled as undemocratic.[35]

Some conservatives also joined the campaign, seeing GATT as international interference in US national sovereignty. For example, the US Business and Industrial Council began a campaign in May 1994 referred to as Save Our Sovereignty (SOS). US Trade Representative Mickey Kantor rejected their arguments, saying that the US did not have to accept WTO rulings. Ralph Nader interpreted Kantor as arguing that the 'GATT is terrific against others; but we can flout it because we're the big kid on the block'.[36]

In the face of this opposition from both right and left, Charles P. Heeter, a partner in one of the big five accountancy firms, Arthur Andersen (since discredited and bankrupt over its role in the Enron frauds), called for the business community to 'get more active to send the message to Congress that it's urgent to pass the GATT... It's a very high priority.'[37]

Following the completion of the Uruguay Round, the Business Roundtable was 'spearheading the business community's push' to get GATT approved in Congress. Its public relations (PR) consultants, the Wexler Group (see Box 6.2) 'recruited and organized' the Alliance for GATT Now, the successor to the MTN Coalition. It had a multimillion dollar budget and sought to ensure Congressional approval of the GATT agreement. The alliance served as an umbrella group for a range of free trade business coalitions and front groups, including NAM, the American Business Conference, the US Chamber of Commerce, Consumers for World Trade (CWT), the Coalition of Service Industries (CSI), the Emergency Committee for American Trade (ECAT), USCIB and the Zero Tariff Coalition (see Chapter 9 for more on USCIB).[38]

The Alliance for GATT Now campaign included Washington lobbying, grassroots campaigning, advertising and public relations, and utilized many of the same lobbyists who had helped to win the NAFTA campaign. The alliance activities were overseen by Texas Instruments chief Washington lobbyist John K. Boidock, whose Washington office became 'a GATT war room'. Chairmanship of the alliance was shared by two former congressmen who had become lobbyists. They were regular national public radio (NPR) commentators, causing Ralph Nader to accuse the alliance of indirectly buying NPR broadcasting time by doing this.[43]

The alliance membership list quickly grew to 400 companies in the first few months, and it eventually claimed that its members included more than 200,000 small and large businesses, associations and organizations. Its membership list was beefed up through membership of organizations such as the Business Roundtable, who signed up its corporate members unless they explicitly asked to be excluded. *Business Week* reported: 'It is flooding Congress with phone calls from CEOs in their districts.'[44]

One of the alliance's campaign tactics, designed by Edelman Public Relations, was to publish a deck of cards, like baseball trading cards, that were sent to each

BOX 6.2 THE WEXLER GROUP

The Wexler Group (now Wexler and Walker Public Policy Associates) is a subsidiary of PR giant Hill and Knowlton. It bills itself as 'one of the most experienced international affairs and trade advocacy-consulting firms in Washington', representing 'foreign and domestic clients'. It claims to 'have worked on every major trade bill considered by Congress since 1983', including the General Agreement on Tariffs and Trade (GATT). It specializes in grassroots coalition-building.[39]

In preparation for the North American Free Trade Agreement (NAFTA) vote, the Wexler Group 'built and activated a 50-state network of business activists' to support NAFTA, and recruited 4000 companies and associations to join USA*NAFTA. It also 'supervised paid grassroots organizers and telemarketing firms, organized weekly meetings of private-sector trade experts, senior lobbyists and heads of Washington offices of the largest US corporations, [and] participated in weekly strategy sessions with corporate, Congressional and administration leaders responsible for NAFTA'. The Wexler Group was credited with being a leading strategist for getting NAFTA passed by Congress.[40]

The Wexler group engaged in similar activities to ensure that GATT was passed by Congress in 1994. Apart from putting together the Alliance for GATT Now, it liaised between business and government, organized strategy meetings and supervised grassroots organizers:

> We are well known for our ability to build, manage and energize powerful private-sector coalitions on high-visibility and controversial issues. We have a proven track record of linking traditional and non-traditional allies into vast networks of large companies, associations, agricultural, small business, sectoral, ideological, public interest, and state and local government organizations.[41]

Wexler and Walker acts as a secretariat for these coalitions, building support, scheduling meetings, and identifying and nurturing champions for their cause in the US House and Senate. It coordinates the lobbying efforts of coalition members, and when a vote is due it sets up a 'war room' to 'coordinate logistics'. Wexler and Walker also specializes in lobbying Congress. It claims to have contacts on key Congressional committees and to have developed a computerized tracking system to record the results of meetings with politicians and their staff and their voting records, as well as the activities of supporters. This tracking system is supposed to be 'the most comprehensive privately held database' in Washington with respect to international trade legislation.[42]

congressperson, senator, state governor and others. There were seven 'all-star' cards showing individuals who championed the GATT agreement, including the three presidents in power during the Uruguay Round: Reagan, Bush and Clinton. A card for each state showed the benefits of GATT in that state; the top exports for the state; the jobs that would be gained; and the extra revenue that would be reaped. For example, the card sent to New Jersey politicians featured a picture of medicine capsules, symbolizing the state's pharmaceutical industry, and stated that GATT would hit a home run by increasing exports from and creating more jobs in the state.[45] Each card had the GATT Now logo on it.

The alliance also delivered a booklet to members of Congress entitled *Countdown to GATT* and organized corporate 'fly-ins' to bring executives to Washington to lobby Congress personally. Business Roundtable leaders each took on some of the lobbying effort. For example, Monsanto coordinated lobbying in its home state of Missouri and in the chemical industry, while Boeing did the same in Washington state and the aerospace industry. Editorial support in the newspapers was organized by Harry Freeman of American Express, who had chaired the MTN Coalition.[46]

The Wexler Group is not the only PR firm involved in the campaign for free trade. For example, the Business Roundtable hired the Dutko Group 'to win over wary senators'. The Alliance for GATT Now also employed Susan Davis International. Named by *Inside PR* magazine as one of the 'Top five public affairs agencies' in the US, Susan Davis International also specializes in grassroots coalition-building; Washington representation to 'impact [upon] the policy and decision-making process'; issues management including the 'strategic creation of large-scale public education campaigns related to public policy issues'; and government PR, including representation of clients at all levels of government.[47]

In tandem with the private industry campaign, the US administration, and particularly officials from the Department of Commerce and the Treasury, ran their own lobbying drive to get votes for GATT in Congress, hiring two high-profile Washington lobbyists for the job, Nicholas Calio and Joseph O'Neill, to coordinate lobbyists and corporate executives to 'work Capitol Hill on behalf of the agreement'. Lobbyists were given excellent access to the Clinton White House, and business groups worked with the administration to achieve approval of GATT as they had with NAFTA.[48]

The US administration also organized for big name bureaucrats to give talks to 'key groups of opinion leaders'. The Department of Commerce compiled reports on how GATT would be good for jobs and economic growth in the US, and distributed them widely to government, industry and the media. This led to accusations that the administration was directly involved in lobbying.[49]

The US government approved GATT, and in early 1995 the WTO was set up to administer GATT.

UNDERMINING DEMOCRATIC OBJECTIVES

According to Adam Smith's metaphor of the invisible hand, the whole of society benefits from private companies doing business freely in the marketplace; government regulations can only interfere with this.[50] The alternative view, not recognized by free trade proponents, is that government regulations are necessary to ensure that business activity is, indeed, in the interests of the majority. Without such regulations, transnational companies are free to accumulate market power and exercise it to avoid competition and maximize profits at the expense of consumers, small companies and developing economies.

Given the thousands of pages of rules that the WTO now presides over, 'free' trade is not about doing away with rules altogether, but rather replacing rules for companies with rules for governments, and replacing rules that protect citizens, consumers and the environment with rules that protect and facilitate traders and investors.

From the late 1960s, the GATT Secretariat, though it was unconstitutional and temporary, had become 'the most powerful, entrenched non-organization the world had seen'. Today, the WTO has greater powers than any other international institution, including powers to punish non-complying nations that are not even available to the United Nations. Over 130 nations are now members of the WTO. It has become a form of global government in its own right with judicial, legislative and executive powers:[51]

> ...the WTO has come to rival the International Monetary Fund as the most powerful, secretive and anti-democratic international body on Earth. It is rapidly assuming the mantle of a bona fide global government for the 'free trade era,' and it actively seeks to broaden its powers and reach.[52]

The WTO is able to enforce its rules through its dispute settlement mechanism. If a country complains that another is not abiding by WTO rules, the case is heard by panels of unelected lawyers and officials 'with no education or training in social or environmental issues', behind closed doors with no public scrutiny. These panels are able to find countries guilty of breaking the rules and to impose economic sanctions as punishment.[53]

Such rulings can declare legislation put in place by democratically elected governments as illegal. The WTO has fairly extensive powers to discipline nation states – as well as local, state and regional governments – for regulations and controls that are claimed to interfere with trade. WTO rules also take precedence over other international agreements, including labour and environmental agreements such as the Convention on Biological Diversity and the Montreal Protocol on Substances that Deplete the Ozone Layer.[54]

WTO regulations have important implications for environmental regulation, particularly export and import restrictions on products and practices, environmental standards and incentives to encourage environmentally sound practices.

Export/import restrictions on products

Under WTO rules, imported products may not be banned, so attempts to ban the import of environmentally damaging products would only be allowed if the environmental damage they would cause is internationally recognized (see the following section) and there is no other less trade restrictive way of preventing that damage. Bans on aluminium cans or the imposition of deposit systems, for example, would affect foreign producers and are therefore considered to be trade distorting and unnecessary since packaging can otherwise be dealt with through a waste disposal system. Countries may also wish to ban imports of hazardous materials and wastes. However, the WTO only allows this if local production or disposal of the same material is also banned.

Countries such as Indonesia and the Philippines prohibit or limit log exports to control the rate of logging and thereby protect their local forests and industry. Such bans have been opposed by Japan and Europe as being contrary to GATT and WTO rules. Environmentalists accuse the WTO of wanting 'to open up the natural resources of developing countries for exploitation by giant logging, mining and seafood companies based in the industrialized world'. For example, Mauricio Fierro, a leader of the Cascada-Chile opposition movement, argues that WTO rules 'will allow the biggest and most destructive logging companies to gain free access to vast tracts of pristine forest'.[55]

Lowering of environmental standards

The WTO encourages international standards (harmonization) and discourages countries from maintaining their own higher standards unless they are designed to protect human health or safety, the health of animals and plants, or the environment. Even in these areas, the onus is on the country wanting to implement higher standards to prove that the higher standards are necessary and that the same goals could not be achieved in a way that does not affect trade.

Therefore, where governments democratically decide to implement high standards, these have to be justified scientifically. Political and social factors shape the standards that individual countries decide upon, and often a decision has to be made despite a large amount of scientific uncertainty. That uncertainty is likely to make it very difficult for a nation to prove that its standards are necessary before a panel of hostile scientists chosen by the WTO.

An example of this is provided by the standards for pesticide residues in foods. If United Nations Food and Agriculture Organization (FAO) standards are used as the appropriate international standards, countries with more stringent standards (up to 50 times tighter in some countries) have no choice but to accept imported goods with higher levels of pesticide residues. In 1998, the WTO ruled that Japan's pesticide residue testing requirements for food imported into Japan were against WTO rules because their standards were too high.[56]

In another example, the US and Canada won a WTO challenge against a European Union (EU) ban on imported beef that had been fed with hormones. European governments believe such hormones are carcinogens.[57] In contradiction to the precautionary principle, which the WTO has labelled 'non-scientific', the WTO panel required Europe to prove that hormones caused cancer or other harm to humans eating the beef:

> *Despite a lengthy report by independent scientists showing that some hormones added to US meat are 'complete carcinogens' – capable of causing cancer by themselves – the WTO's 3-lawyer tribunal ruled that the EU did not have a 'valid' scientific case for refusing to allow the import of US beef. The losing countries are now required to pay the US $150 million each year as compensation for lost profits.*[58]

More recently, the US is using the WTO to force the EU to approve the import of genetically engineered food. US Secretary of Agriculture Ann Veneman admits that 'With this case, we are fighting for the interests of American agriculture.' The Department of Agriculture points out that WTO rules require 'sufficient scientific evidence' to support regulations to protect health and the environment, and that approvals must be granted without 'undue delay'.[59]

While countries are discouraged from enforcing higher environmental standards than those accepted internationally, countries that do not impose any standards or regulations are not penalized under the WTO. This is the case even though such a situation is like a subsidy to polluters since it allows them to keep their costs down by using the environment as a free disposal resource. It is for this reason that the Social and Economic Council in The Netherlands argues that 'it is not countries with high environmental standards that distort the trading system, but the countries with too low standards'.[60] This reasoning is recognized in the OECD's polluter pays principle; but the polluter pays principle is not recognized by the WTO.

Import/export restrictions on unsustainable practices

Even though there is provision under the WTO for countries to argue the case for environmental standards that are applied to products, there is no provision for standards to be applied to production processes and methods used in producing a product. The WTO precludes a country from acting to prevent environmental damage in another country or in the global commons. This is because placing a trade barrier on a product because of the way that it is produced in another country is seen as breaching that other country's national sovereignty. One example of this was a Dutch proposal to ban imports of tropical hardwood logged in an unsustainable way. This would not have been allowed under WTO rules.

In September 1991, when GATT was in force, Mexico complained against the US ban on tuna caught with encirclement nets. The US banned this tuna because millions of dolphins had being killed by these nets. The Mexicans argued that the US was unfairly discriminating against their tuna. The GATT panel ruled in Mexico's favour, arguing that 'regulations governing the taking of dolphins incidental to the taking of tuna could not possibly affect tuna as a product'.[61] Therefore, whether or not Mexico had regulations against this practice was not relevant to the trade in tuna.

In 1997, after the WTO had been established and sanctions could be imposed, the US lifted its embargo on tuna caught in these nets.[62] It has been argued that the primary motivation for this tuna ban on the part of the US was to protect its own tuna industry. Nevertheless, the environmental issue was a genuine one and a ban that was primarily motivated by environmental concerns would be unlikely to meet with a better reception in the WTO.

In a similar, more recent case, the WTO ruled in 1998 against US legislation that required fishers to catch shrimp using turtle-excluder devices to protect endangered sea turtles and banned imports of shrimp product from countries where such devices were not used. In another case, the US Environmental Protection Agency (EPA) voluntarily reduced its standards on the use of reformulated petrol to head off a possible challenge from Venezuela.[63]

Economic instruments to protect the environment

In the US–Canada free trade pact, which was used as a model for GATT, the government of British Columbia was prevented from planting trees because it was seen as a subsidy to the Canadian timber industry. Similarly, subsidies to stimulate cleaner production methods have been viewed as protectionist under this pact.

In addition, nations which attempt to internalize environmental costs within prices would be unable to apply tariffs to prevent similar products that have lower prices because they do not include environmental costs from coming into the country. A GATT panel, for instance, disapproved of US taxes on oil and chemical feed stocks that were levied to pay for hazardous waste clean-ups.

In February 1992, GATT released a *Document on Trade and Environment*, which stated that free trade promoted economic growth and therefore the production of resources for environmental policy. It said that where there was conflict between free trade and environmental measures taken by individual countries, free trade should be given priority.[64]

It is little wonder, then, that WTO rulings consistently favour free trade over environmental considerations. In 2001, CorpWatch noted that since 1995, when the WTO was established, 'the WTO has ruled that every environmental policy it has reviewed is an illegal trade barrier that must be eliminated or changed'. The same has been true of health and safety laws with only one exception.[65]

However, WTO rulings, and the examples given in this chapter, are only the tip of the iceberg. They send a message to nations about what is acceptable and what is not and ensure that many governments do not even try to introduce regulations that might impinge on free trade. Those that do can be headed off by threats of WTO complaints by other nations, so that the proposed legislation is killed long before a case reaches the WTO for a ruling. For example, when the EU was considering regulations to ban the import of cosmetics tested on animals, and of fur from animals caught in leg hold traps, it was enough for the US and Canada to threaten a WTO complaint to ensure that the regulations did not go ahead.[66]

Friends of the Earth in The Netherlands points out that 'policies aimed at sustainable development are much more relevant to the future of the world than the promotion of free trade', and that priority should therefore be given to sustainable development over trade. The same point was made by Dutch Minister of Housing, Physical Planning and the Environment, Hans Alders: 'Environmental policies should impose limits to trade policies rather than the other way round.'[67]

In contrast, an ERT report stated that, while businesspeople were ready to consider other objectives such as social welfare and environmental improvement, 'what industry cannot accept is that the pursuit of other objectives is used as an excuse for damaging the wealth-creating machine itself, whether by raising its costs or blocking its development'.[68]

It is not just environmental considerations that take second place to free trade, but all other social considerations. John Madeley, in his book *Hungry for Trade: How the Poor Pay for Free Trade*, notes that:

> They have elevated trade into a kind of God; nothing must interfere with it, not even food. If a country wants to pass laws that enable it to feed its people, and those laws are not consistent with so-called 'free' trade, they are disallowed. Trade is thus given a higher priority than food.[69]

In this way, the corporate goal of free trade has taken precedence over other citizen goals such as environmental protection, improved working conditions, and health and safety considerations. The WTO ensures that the interests of transnational corporations supersede those of citizens, governments and everyone else. The free trade crusade has affected the ability of citizens in democratic nations to regulate in the public interest, while increasing the regulation that protects commercial interests.[70]

Notes

1   Quoted in Steve Dryden, *Trade Warriors: USTR and the American Crusade for Free Trade*, New York, Oxford University Press, 1995, p355.
2   *Ibid.*, pp9–11.
3   *Ibid.*, p10.
4   Bob Catley, *Globalising Australian Capitalism*, Cambridge, Cambridge University Press, 1996, p12; Dryden, *Trade Warriors*, pp6, 11.

5   Dryden, *Trade Warriors,* p13.

6   Peter F. Cowhey and Jonathan D. Aronson, *Managing the World Economy: The Consequences of Corporate Alliances,* New York, Council on Foreign Relations Press, 1993, p15; Dryden, *Trade Warriors,* pp12–3.

7   Clair Wilcox quoted in Dryden, *Trade Warriors,* p17.

8   Quoted in *Ibid.,* p30.

9   Quoted in *Ibid.,* pp17, 25–7.

10 *Ibid.,* pp27–9, 31–2; Industries Assistance Commission, *International Initiatives to Liberalise Trade in Services,* Inquiry into International Trade in Services, Canberra, Australian Government Publishing Service, 1989, p3.

11 Clyde H. Farnsworth, 'Winners and Losers in Trade Talks', *The New York Times,* 29 November, 1990, pD1.

12 Industries Assistance Commission, *International Initiatives to Liberalise Trade in Services,* pp4–5.

13 Oliver Hoedeman *et. al.,* 'Maigalomania: The New Corporate Agenda', *The Ecologist,* vol 28, no 3, 1998.

14 International Trade Administration, 'Industry Consultation Program', International Trade Administration, www.ita.doc.gov/td/icp/mission.html accessed 30 June 2003.

15 ERT, 'ERT Highlights 1983–2003', Brussels, European Round Table of Industrialists, June 2003, p40; ERT, 'Achievements', European Round Table of Industrialists, 23 June, 2003, www.ert.be/pg/eng_frame.htm.

16 Walcot quoted in Belén Balanyá, *et al., Europe Inc. Regional and Global Restructuring and the Rise of Corporate Power,* London, Pluto Press, 2000, pp24–5; ERT, 'ERT Highlights 1983–2003', p53.

17 World Economic Forum, 'World Economic Forum', WEF, 2000, www.weforum. org/.

18 *Ibid.*

19 *Ibid.;* WEF, 'Global Competitiveness Report', World Economic Forum, www. weforum.org/site/homepublic.nsf/Content/Global+Competitiveness+Programme% 5CGlobal+Competitiveness+Report accessed 6 February 2005; Craig N. Murphy, 'Inequality, Turmoil and Democracy: Global Political-Economic Visions at the End of the Century', *New Political Economy,* vol 4, no 2, 1999.

20 World Economic Forum, 'World Economic Forum'.

21 Quoted in Murphy, 'Inequality, Turmoil and Democracy: Global Political-Economic Visions at the End of the Century'.

22 Peter Norman, 'London Summit Headlines Mask Main Agenda', *Financial Times,* 8 July, 1991, p13.

23 WTO, 'Mike More, WTO Director-General, 1999–2002', World Trade Organisation, www.wto.org/english/thewto_e/dg_e/mm_e.htm accessed 4 June 2003; Peter Montagnon, 'World Trade System "in Danger" Says Brock', *Financial Times,* 10 April, 1990, p6; Nancy Dunne, 'New Bid to Speed Trade Talks', *Financial Times,* 26 March, 1990a, p5.

24 Dunne, 'New Bid to Speed Trade Talks', p5; Tim Dickson and Martin Wolf, 'Sutherland Faces Toughest Brief', *Financial Times,* 28 May, 1993, p3.

25 Alan Pike, 'Trade Round Failure "Could Lead to Chaos"', *Financial Times,* 17 April, 1990, p3.

26   Norman, 'London Summit Headlines Mask Main Agenda', p13.
27   MTN Coalition quoted in Farnsworth, 'Winners and Losers in Trade Talks', pD1; Norman, 'London Summit Headlines Mask Main Agenda', p13.
28   Farnsworth, 'Winners and Losers in Trade Talks', pD1; Martin Khor Kok Peng, *The Uruguay Round and Third World Sovereignty*, Penang, Malaysia, Third World Network, 1990, p9.
29   Nancy Dunne, 'US Business Forms Trade Pressure Group', *Financial Times*, 16 May, 1990c, p4; MTN Coalition quoted in Peng, *The Uruguay Round and Third World Sovereignty*, p10.
30   Farnsworth, 'Winners and Losers in Trade Talks', pD1.
31   Nancy Dunne, 'Congress Urged to Suspend Judgement on Trade Talks', *Financial Times*, 24 October, 1990b, p3.
32   Elizabeth Newlin Carney, 'Washington Update', *The National Journal*, 12 February, 1994, p373; Texas Instruments, 'Jerry R. Junkins', Texas Instruments, 1996, www.ti.com/corp/docs/press/company/1996/jrjobit.shtml.
33   Debi Barker and Jerry Mander, 'Invisible Government. The World Trade Organization: Global Government for the New Millennium', Sausalito, CA, International Forum on Globalization (IFG), October 1999, p6.
34   Alice Lipowicz, 'No Break for Trade Lobbyists', *Crain's New York Business*, 23 May, 1994b; Alice Lipowicz, 'Pols Join NY Business Crusading for GATT', *Crain's New York Business*, 18 July, 1994a; Peter H. Stone, 'GATT-Ling Guns', *The National Journal*, vol 26, no 27, 1994b, p1571.
35   Stone, 'GATT-Ling Guns', p1571.
36   Quoted in *Ibid*, p1571.
37   Quoted in Lipowicz, 'Pols Join NY Business Crusading for GATT'.
38   'Pro-GATT Forces Play Their Face Cards', *Legal Times*, 1 August, 1994, p5; Stone, 'GATT-Ling Guns', p1571; Andrew Wheat, 'A Year in the Life of the GATT Business Lobby', *Multinational Monitor*, October, 1994, www.multinationalmonitor.org/hyper/issues/1994/10//mm1094_05.html.
39   Wexler & Walker Public Policy Associates, 'International Trade', Wexler & Walker Public Policy Associates, http://wexlergroup.com/trade_p.htm accessed 8 June 2003.
40   *Ibid.*; 'Pro-GATT Forces Play Their Face Cards', p5.
41   Wexler & Walker Public Policy Associates, 'International Trade'; Wexler & Walker Public Policy Associates, 'Coalitions and Grassroots', Wexler & Walker Public Policy Associates, http://wexlergroup.com/coal_p.htm accessed 8 June 2003.
42   *Ibid.*
43   Stone, 'GATT-Ling Guns', p1571; Wheat, 'A Year in the Life'.
44   Lipowicz, 'No Break for Trade Lobbyists'; Wheat, 'A Year in the Life'; Douglas Harbrecht, 'Dealy Would Mean the Death of GATT', *Business Week*, 5 December, 1994, p34.
45   Adam Geller, 'But How's the Bubble Gum? GATT Lobbyists Paper the Capital in Trading Cards', *The Trenton Record*, 26 July, 1994; 'Pro-GATT Forces Play Their Face Cards', p5.
46   Joan Lowy, 'GATT Lobby Turns Effort to Pivotal Senate', *Pittsburgh Post-Gazette*, 28 November, 1994; 'Pro-GATT Forces Play Their Face Cards', p5; Stone, 'GATT-Ling Guns', p1571.

47 Shawn Zeller, 'Dutko's Story, a Testament to Its Founder', *The National Journal*, vol 35, no 10, 2003; SDI, 'Recent and Present Clients', Susan Davis International, www. susandavis.com/newpage1.htm accessed 8 June 2003; SDI, 'About Us', Susan Davis International, www.susandavis.com/aboutusdi.htm accessed 8 June 2003.

48 Stone, 'GATT-Ling Guns', p1571; Peter H. Stone, 'Friends, After All', *The National Journal*, vol 26, no 43, 1994a, p2440.

49 Stone, 'GATT-Ling Guns', p1571.

50 Chakravarthi Raghavan, *Recolonization: GATT, the Uruguay Round & the Third World*, London, Zed Books, 1990, p35.

51 John Braithwaite and Peter Drahos, *Global Business Regulation*, Cambridge, Cambridge University Press, 2000, p177; Tony Clarke, *By What Authority! Unmasking and Challenging the Global Corporations' Assault on Democracy through the World Trade Organization*, Polaris Institute and International Forum on Globalization, 1999, pp4–5; Barker and Mander, 'Invisible Government', p2.

52 Barker and Mander, 'Invisible Government', p1.

53 *Ibid.*, p2.

54 *Ibid.*, p6.

55 Gustavo Gonzalez, 'Chilean Forestry Project a Symbol of Fight against WTO', in *Who Owns the WTO? Corporations and Global Trade*, www.corpwatch.org/, Corporate Watch, 1999.

56 Barker and Mander, 'Invisible Government', pp26–7.

57 *Ibid.*, pp9, 26.

58 Peter Montague, 'The WTO and Free Trade', *Rachel's Environment & Health Weekly*, 21 October, 1999.

59 USDA, 'U.S. And Cooperating Countries File WTO Case against EU Moratorium on Biotech Food and Crops', US Department of Agriculture, 13 May, 2003, www. usda.gov/news/releases/2003/05/0156.htm

60 Sander Van Bennedom and Manus Van Brakel, 'Will GATT Undermine UNCED? An Analysis of the Environmental Implications of GATT Policies', Friends of the Earth Netherlands 1992, p4.

61 Quoted in *Ibid.*, p10.

62 '"GATT-Zilla Vs Flipper" Dolphin Case Demonstrates How Trade Agreements Undermine Domestic Environmental, Public Interest Policies', Public Citizen, 11 April, 2003, www.citizen.org/print_article.cfm?ID=9298.

63 Barker and Mander, 'Invisible Government', p18; Stone, 'GATT-Ling Guns', p1571.

64 Van Bennedom and Van Brakel, 'Will GATT Undermine UNCED? An Analysis of the Environmental Implications of GATT Policies', p11.

65 'Corporate Globalization Fact Sheet', CorpWatch, 22 March, 2001, www.corpwatch. org/print_article.php?&id=378.

66 Joel Bakan, *The Corporation: The Pathological Pursuit of Profit and Power*, New York, The Free Press, 2004, p24.

67 Van Bennedom and Van Brakel, 'Will GATT Undermine UNCED? An Analysis of the Environmental Implications of GATT Policies', p14; Elders quoted in Greenpeace International, 'UNCED Undermined: Why Free Trade Won't Save the Planet', Greenpeace UNCED Report, March 1992, p15.

68   ERT, 'Beating the Crisis: A Charter for Europe's Industrial Future', Brussels, European Round Table of Industrialists, December 1993, p15.
69   John Madeley, *Hungry for Trade: How the Poor Pay for Free Trade*, Global Issues Series, London and New York, Zed Books, 2000, p1.
70   Ralph Nader, Introduction to Lori Wallach and Michelle Sforza, *The WTO: Five Years of Reasons to Resist Corporate Globalization*, (ed) Greg Ruggiero, The Open Media Pamphlet Series, New York, Seven Stories Press, 1999, pp9–10.

7

Trade in Services

The GATS [General Agreement on Trade in Services] is not just something that exists between governments. It is first and foremost an instrument for the benefit of business, and not only for business, in general, but for individual services companies wishing to export services or to invest and operate abroad. EUROPEAN COMMISSION[1]

American Express (AmEx) has been cited in *Business Week* as a prime example of the new breed of stateless corporation pioneering a borderless future in which 'open markets, deregulation and unimpeded flow of capital' is the norm.[2] Nevertheless, AmEx, the stateless corporation, found it convenient to identify its interests with the US national interests when it came to lobbying US policy-makers and negotiators.

During the 1970s, AmEx was facing saturation of its markets at home, as well as increasing competition from other companies offering credit cards, and needed to expand to new countries in order to grow. Overseas markets were turning out to be extremely lucrative, and AmEx targeted the most affluent customers in each country and was able to under-price European companies by supplying only the most profitable elites.

However, AmEx was having trouble accessing markets in some countries and it believed that the General Agreement on Tariffs and Trade (GATT) negotiations might provide a solution. In 1979, the chief executive officer (CEO) of AmEx, James D. Robinson III, asked AmEx Vice President Harry Freeman to get a new round of GATT negotiations started that would include services. When Freeman asked what budget limitations there were, Robinson responded: 'Don't worry about money. This is so important, you will have an unlimited budget.'[3]

With so much money at his disposal, Freeman was able to have dedicated staff in Brussels, Tokyo, Washington, New York and elsewhere. AmEx had clout not only because it was a 'corporate superpower', but because its board included some political heavyweights, including Henry Kissinger, Vernon Jordan and Drew Lewis, with Gerald Ford, former US president, as an 'outside adviser'. AmEx 'enlisted the aid' of Citicorp and American International Group (AIG), and the CEOs of these three financial corporations went to ministerial meetings through the early 1980s until the Uruguay Round of negotiations started in 1986.[4]

These corporations were particularly interested in having 'financial services' included in a trade agreement. Freeman described how:

> *The first thing we did in 1979 was to coin the phrase. You will not see the term 'financial services' before 1979. We did that by asking everybody in the company to talk about financial services, particularly with the media, and in about two years the term financial services was part of the lexicon… We were quite successful in the Uruguay Round in defining financial services as 'any service of a financial nature'. This allowed us to have more and more allies, and you have to take care of your allies.*[5]

Freeman also promoted the phrase 'goods and services' by getting his staff to write to journalists who used the term 'goods' to tell them they had missed out the term 'services'. In the early 1980s, he claims they wrote at least 1600 such letters and in this way succeeded in getting the phrase 'goods and services' widely adopted. Getting acceptance of the phrase 'trade in services' was more difficult because it was not immediately apparent what it meant, particularly with respect to banks.[6] Most people do not see the establishment of a foreign bank in a country as trade in the sense of export and import.

Freeman and executives from Citicorp and AIG formed a broad coalition of service-sector corporations as 'allies', including non-financial service companies, to better influence Congress. Until this point, corporate executives in fields as diverse as entertainment, engineering, transportation and finance did not identify as 'part of a coherent "services" sector with common interests'.[7]

AmEx CEO Robinson also became a leading advocate of free trade in his own right. He was appointed as chair of President Bush's influential Advisory Committee on Trade Policy and Negotiations (ACTPN) in 1987 and in that role he oversaw US GATT negotiations. This committee was comprised of up to 45 people from a range of sectors, including business, labour and agriculture, and advised the US Trade Representative (USTR) directly:[8]

> *Indicative of the company's farsightedness, Robinson even achieved acclaim as an early proponent of Third World debt relief, propounding the 'Robinson Rollover' plan… Key to its fiscal clemency is the requirement that Third World governments expose their economies and populations to market discipline according to stringent restructuring formulas.*[9]

As well as overseeing US GATT negotiations, Robinson was a corporate member of the Multilateral Trade Negotiations (MTN) Coalition, 'the leading pressure group on GATT' (see Chapter 6). MTN's executive director was none other than Harry Freeman, who left AmEx under a cloud when it was alleged that he was part of a campaign to discredit Swiss banker Edmond Safra, a rival to AmEx. Although Freeman took the fall for the smear campaign, he remained close to AmEx and continued his work on liberalizing financial services and lobbying government to support GATT.[10]

The role of multinational corporations in incorporating services within the free trade agenda is undisputed. David Hartridge, director of the World Trade Organization (WTO) Services Division until 2001, admitted that 'without the enormous pressure generated by the American financial services sector, particularly companies like American Express and Citicorp, there would have been no services agreement'.[11]

THE COALITION OF SERVICE INDUSTRIES (CSI)

The Coalition of Service Industries (CSI), a group of large US-based multinational for-profit service corporations, was formed in 1982 with Freeman as chair. Its purpose was to get services included in the GATT round of negotiations. It sought to make trade in services 'a central goal of future trade liberalization initiatives'. It claims to have 'played an aggressive role in writing' and 'shaping' the General Agreement on Trade in Services (GATS) which was included in the WTO at the end of the Uruguay Round.[12]

GATS aimed to open up the provision of all services to international 'free trade'. It prohibits governments from discriminating against foreign transnational companies that want to buy government services or compete to supply them in areas that governments agree to liberalize. As a result, CSI hoped that large sectors of government services would be privatized and opened to foreign investment.

CSI's 'foremost goal is to open foreign markets to US business and allow them to compete abroad'. To do this it seeks to reduce barriers to trade in services in foreign markets through influencing international trade negotiations. It boasts of its 'excellent access to US and foreign governments and international organizations'. According to Freeman: 'The US private sector on trade in services is probably the most powerful trade lobby, not only in the United States, but also in the world.'[13]

Darren Puscas of the Canadian Polaris Institute notes that many members of CSI are involved in privatizing public services:

> ... the direct connection between the corporations involved in the push
> for privatization of services (including many public services) and the
> push for trade agreements which will provide a legally binding lock-in
> for privatized services (through GATS and FTAA [Free Trade Area of
> the Americas]) is clear.[14]

CSI is open about being 'above all, an advocacy organization, aggressively representing the interests of its members'. Those members include General Electric,

Halliburton, Citigroup, AT&T, J. P. Morgan Chase, American Express, United Parcel Service (UPS), AOL Time Warner, Microsoft and PriceWaterhouse Coopers (PwC) – companies that provide services such as finance, telecommunications, energy, the professions, travel, entertainment, the media, transport and information technology. Enron was an active member, as was its disgraced auditor, Arthur Andersen. Enron's input was further facilitated by having former employee Robert B. Zoellick as Bush's trade representative in the negotiations.[15]

At a World Trade in Services Conference in 1995, Joan Spero described how CSI achieved its success during the Uruguay Round. Spero, AmEx treasurer and special vice president for international corporate affairs, chaired the CSI's Financial Services Group. In 1993, Spero became US undersecretary of state for economic, agricultural and business affairs.[16]

Spero explained how CSI took a three-pronged approach: targeting public opinion, the US Congress, and the US Executive. A public campaign to promote the importance of the service sector was aimed at changing public perceptions and therefore indirectly influencing Congress and the Executive. The message conveyed was that services were important to the economy; provided many good-quality jobs; and promoted technological and productivity advances; and that these services were part of US trade and should be covered by GATT negotiations.[17]

In aid of reinforcing this message, CSI persuaded *Fortune* magazine to publish a Services Industry 500 just as it did the Fortune 500 list of manufacturing companies. It also put together and publicized data and statistics to prove what a large proportion of exports, gross domestic product (GDP) and jobs could be attributed to service industries. CSI also lobbied for legislation requiring the Commerce Department to collect data on the services industry as a category. It lobbied for legislation that included trade in services as part of the US Trade Act so that countries with trade barriers against US service exports would be subject to sanctions in the same way as other exports.[18]

Making alliances with the government executive was easier than with Congress because the Office of USTR and the Department of Commerce not only saw the advancement of US business interests as part of their roles, but also embraced the idea of a multilateral trade agreement more readily than some members of Congress. US Deputy Secretary of Commerce Samuel Bodman told a conference in 2002 that 'The secretary and I see our role and the mission of the Commerce Department as being the advocate for the American business community.'[19]

The government administration therefore readily worked with business to persuade Congress. Dean O'Hare, chair of CSI and CEO of Chubb Corporation, claims that CSI has been a partner with 'succeeding US administrations, going back to the mid 1970s' in pushing for trade liberalization. 'It is really an extraordinary example of government/industry cooperation that should serve as a benchmark for the rest of the world.'[20]

According to Spero, the service industries, as part of their lobbying strategy, identified 'champions' in Congress to promote their aims. CSI put together an influential block of members of Congress who had significant service industries as part of their constituencies. These included the members 'from New York (finance), California and Tennessee (audio-visual), Hawaii and Florida (tourism), Washington and Louisiana (maritime shipping) and New Jersey (telecommunications)'. It then encouraged these members to write letters strongly supporting liberalization of trade in services to the USTR.[21]

And while key members of Congress influenced the Executive at the behest of the CSI, the Executive, in turn, influenced the Congress at Congressional hearings, 'where industry experts and administration officials "testified" side by side on the importance' of the global liberalization of services trade to the US economy. In this way, according to James P. Zumwalt, who later became economic counsellor, United States Embassy, Beijing, 'the services industry and the US trade negotiators entered into a "symbiotic relationship" that involved formal briefing sessions and "informal consultations"and "strategy sessions"... Both sides understood that services industry political support meant that services industry priorities would remain among the foremost US negotiating objectives.'[22]

The Uruguay Round was to last until 1994 and it was towards the end of the negotiations that services got included in the agreement. Freeman states: 'At the close of the Uruguay Round, we lobbied and lobbied. We had about 400 people from the US private sector.' Similarly, O'Hare, chair of CSI, stated: 'It took Herculean efforts to get services into the Uruguay Round and there was tremendous opposition... Yet, in the final analysis, we succeeded in getting the GATS agreement.'[23]

The crucial role of CSI in getting the GATS agreement included in the Uruguay Round has been widely recognized. It has also been involved in negotiations over other free trade agreements between the US and other countries.[24] By these means it seeks to increase business opportunities for its members in foreign countries.

THE GENERAL AGREEMENT ON TRADE IN SERVICES (GATS)

GATS includes a framework agreement outlining the rules under which trade in services should occur, annexes to that agreement, and schedules of commitments by individual countries as to which sectors they are opening to GATS rules. The idea is that subsequent negotiation rounds will involve nations committing to the opening of more and more of their service sectors to GATS. GATS is administered by a Council for Trade in Services within the WTO.

GATS covers the following types of services:

- *cross-border supply* – services supplied from abroad such as international postal services or e-commerce;
- *consumption abroad* – where citizens of a country travel overseas to consume the product, such as education or tourism;

- *commercial presence* – where services are provided within a nation by transnational companies through foreign investment and local branches, such as banks or insurance services; and
- *presence of natural persons* – where personnel from overseas visit a country to supply the service, such as accountancy or engineering.[25]

Under GATS rules, once a country decides to 'liberalize' its electricity or water it cannot put any limits on foreign ownership or limit how much of the industry one company can own. Furthermore, a government is not allowed to favour local businesses, so that if it subsidizes renewable sources of electricity, such as hydroelectricity, and these subsidized sources are mainly owned by local companies, then this could be interpreted as discriminating against foreign service providers who use 'dirty' sources of power, such as oil and gas.[26]

If services such as health and education are also committed to GATS, then government subsidies would be seen as giving unfair advantage to local providers. And it is likely that governments would not be able to set price caps on the fees charged for essential services such as water and electricity. Governments would therefore lose the ability to ensure that these services were affordable to their poorer citizens (unless sectors of the population are directly subsidized with taxpayer funds, which would be paid to the foreign companies).[27]

GATS also prevents national governments from putting quantitative limits on services once a service sector has been committed to opening up. So, if a government agrees to open up tourism services, for instance, it cannot then limit the number of beach resorts to protect the environment or the atmosphere of an area without being open to challenge under GATS rules.[28]

GATS restrains governments from imposing standards that might hinder free trade in these services. Article VI of the GATS agreement only allows regulations where regulatory objectives are legitimate; the regulation is necessary; and the regulation does not restrict trade more than necessary. Illegitimate regulations might include professional standards, taxation policies and other policies to achieve objectives such as preserving government services or providing employment:[29]

> *As a practical matter, this means nations will have to shape laws protecting the air you breathe, the trains you travel in and the food you chew by picking not the best or safest means for the nation, but the cheapest methods for foreign investors and merchants.*[30]

Attempts within the WTO to establish a list of legitimate objectives for regulations has proven difficult. GATS requires that domestic regulations such as environmental regulations should be developed in accordance with international standards, and this is one criteria against which necessity would be measured – that is, if regulations accord with international standards they would meet the necessity test.[31]

BOX 7.1 WORLD TRADE ORGANIZATION (WTO) TELMEX RULING

In 2004, the US won a case against Mexico over its telecommunications services GATS commitments. The WTO panel found that Mexico had failed to ensure that its major telecommunications supplier provided interconnection to US suppliers at a reasonable price in order to allow the US telecommunications companies to provide cross-border telecommunications services. It also found that Mexico had failed to provide US companies with access to private leased circuits in Mexico and to prevent anti-competitive practices.[32]

Mexico had argued that foreign firms given access to the Mexican telecommunications market should have to contribute to the cost of developing and maintaining the telecommunications infrastructure. However, the WTO panel rejected this argument. According to the WTO, Mexico's efforts to ensure universal service so that even the poor have access to telephone services is legitimate, but it must be done in a way that is 'no more burdensome that necessary' to foreign companies. Cross-subsidization, whereby the infrastructure to provide the service to the poor is paid for, in part, by companies not supplying services to the poor, is more burdensome than necessary because other countries provide universal service in other ways and therefore cross-subsidization in not 'necessary'.[33]

Ironically, in the US access to telecommunications networks is not provided at a 'reasonable price'; but the US telecommunications industry is dominated by US firms and so the US is unlikely to face a GATS complaint from another country.[34]

Defenders argue that GATS does not apply to 'government-provided' public services. However, the definition of such services is very narrow and is confined to services supplied by governmental authority 'neither on a commercial basis, nor in competition with one or more service suppliers'. The proportion of public services provided by government monopolies on a completely non-commercial basis in these days of widespread free market 'reforms' are few and far between. Government services all over the world have been opened up to competition and corporatized to operate on a commercial basis. Similar wording in the European Union (EU) Treaty has not protected government services and in eight challenges, the government services have been deemed not to be covered by the exemption for government services.[35]

The Indonesian government says that it is committed to liberalizing its education sector 'despite protests from local university rectors' whose universities would have to compete with foreign universities that would be allowed to set up in Indonesia. The rectors argue that 'Universities are not a business commodity that can be liberalized in such a way. Apart from the task of transferring and developing knowledge and the sciences, they also have the task of maintaining and developing the nation.' However, Minister of Trade Mari Elka Pangestu, who is also an economist at the Center for Strategic and International Studies and has been a WTO negotiator, argues that competition will be phased in over time.[36]

Ongoing negotiations require countries to make requests for services to be opened to competition in other countries and then to make offers of which services they themselves are willing to open up. Once commitments have been agreed, they are not reversible and any privatization and liberalization that has already occurred or does occur in the sector cannot be reversed. This ensures that the interests of foreign investors are protected.[37]

As part of the official offers and requests process, the European Commission (EC) has requested that other nations open up their water sectors, large parts of their energy sectors, including electricity, and other sectors such as transport to competition from abroad. These requests were not an outcome of democratic decision-making in Europe, but were kept secret until they were leaked.

There are ongoing efforts to keep GATS offers and requests secret and therefore to inhibit public debate and democratic input into decision-making. In January 2003, Pascal Lamy, the EC trade commissioner, advised governments that they would not be able to distribute copies of offers to their parliaments.[38]

The Corporate Europe Observatory argues that the leaked requests show that the EC intends 'to use the GATS talks to deregulate and *de facto* privatize essential services, particularly in the South'.[39] According to the World Development Movement, any developing country escaping privatization of services under World Bank or International Monetary Fund (IMF) structural adjustment packages (see Chapter 3), or seeking to reverse them, 'will feel a left hook coming in from the WTO'. It notes that if GATS negotiations are successful, 'governments will be forced to privatize services and the sale will be irreversible'.[40] Moreover, GATS will provide an excuse for governments that want to privatize against the will of the people for reasons of corruption or ideology or misconception. They can pass on responsibility for the decision to the WTO, which has required it.

Business coalitions such as the CSI, with the support of government bureaucracies, intend to ensure that success through lobbying, persuasion, influence and pressure. On its webpage, the EC calls on business to network; to provide advice to negotiators; to persuade governments in countries where they do business of the benefits of free trade in services; and to generally spread the good news at home and abroad.[41]

FINANCIAL SERVICES

When GATS was agreed to at the end of the Uruguay Round, a number of negotiations were left unfinished. These included negotiations on maritime transport, financial services, telecommunications and the movement of personnel. Negotiations on telecommunications and financial services – including banking, securities and insurance – were concluded in 1997.

To achieve the GATS and the financial services agreement that followed in 1997, multinational corporations trading in services have formed coalitions of high-level business leaders, with ready access to key government bureaucrats, to increase their power and influence over the agenda and direction of trade negotiations. These corporations hope to 'broaden and deepen the commitments made in GATS' so that eventually every WTO member will open every service sector to foreign companies without restriction.[42]

In making the case for the Financial Services Agreement (FSA), the International Chamber of Commerce (ICC) and other business groups argued that the liberalization and deregulation of financial services would benefit developing countries: it would enable foreign firms to introduce new skills and products to developing countries; facilitate investment; 'enable reliable and efficient settlement of payments'; give easier access to more diverse sources of capital; and, through competition, promote efficiency and lower costs for loans and better interest rates.[43]

Developing countries were not convinced and opposed the agreement, but were eventually pressured into accepting it. The IMF had already been enforcing many similar requirements for opening access to foreign financial services through its loan conditions to poorer countries; so the resistance to their introduction at the WTO was less strenuous than might otherwise have been expected. Nevertheless, South Korea and Malaysia managed to hold out against the pressure while other countries caved in during final hour, early morning negotiations.[44]

The US and Europe, which had most to gain from the agreement, clearly used the financial crisis in Asia as a bargaining chip to persuade many Asian countries to agree. Asian nations were told that the agreement was necessary before foreign investors would invest in their countries again. Some even blamed the financial crisis on the lack of liberalization in the past. Andrew Buxton, chair of Barclays Bank and president of the British Bankers Association, argued that 'Much of the crisis in the financial sector in Asia in 1997 was due to poor supervision of financial institutions, coupled with a lack of inward investment through restrictions on the liberalization process.'[45]

The promise of more foreign investment persuaded many countries. Egyptian Ambassador Mounir Zahran pointed out that the deal was rather one sided as it would allow US and European financial companies to compete in the South, while financial companies from the South were unlikely to be able to compete in the North: 'But we all need trade finance and foreign investment, and have agreed to this in the hope that this will help bring in finance and foreign investments.'[46]

However, as Chakravarthi Raghavan wrote in *Third World Economics*, the reason for high levels of foreign investment before the crisis was the 'high growth rates and higher returns' in Asian countries than in the investors' home countries; furthermore, even if there was better access for financial services, the attractive growth rates and returns were no longer there.[47]

The 1997 agreement was finalized with the help of various business lobby groups, such as CSI's Financial Services Group and others, described later in this chapter. The World Economic Forum (WEF) also claims that it 'made a contribution to the process and negotiation of financial services liberalization through private meetings among key players' in 1996 and 1997. The WEF Davos meeting in early 1997 came up with a 'Statement of objectives for financial services negotiations', which was 'in a sense, a "bill of rights" for world financial services trade in the 21st century'.[48]

Business lobbyists turned up in force at the final negotiating meeting in Geneva at the end of 1997. Edmund Andrews, in the *New York Times*, observed:

> *US companies were a conspicuous presence in and around the neg-*
> *otiations here in Geneva. Citibank, Goldman Sachs, Merrill Lynch*
> *and numerous insurance companies – particularly the American*
> *International Group and Aetna – established command posts at the*
> *President Wilson Hotel, about a half mile from the headquarters of the*
> *World Trade Organization.*[49]

Similarly, Ragahvan claims that the negotiations 'bordered on a farce ... as messages went back and forth from Geneva to Washington, and according to reports, between the US Treasury and the American International Group (AIG) and its backers in the US Congress'. The WTO 'Secretariat and its leadership, instead of functioning on behalf of all the membership in a multilateral negotiating process, was tacitly helping the US to bully and face down one or two countries, who were not ready to meet its demands'.[50]

The Financial Services Agreement became an annex to the GATS agreement. It included a framework for international trade in financial services, including the removal of rules and barriers to foreign banks, insurance companies and investment companies operating on equal terms with local companies.[51] Over 100 nations signed up to it, with varying individual commitments to the extent that they would do this. Many countries committed to allowing foreign firms to establish wholly owned asset management subsidiaries in their countries. Fewer agreed to open up cross-border access to foreign firms, where the services are provided from abroad.

The WTO and US and European officials all lavished praise on the agreement when it was made:

> *Representatives of US financial service industries rushed into the WTO*
> *lobby to distribute effusive statements of support to the pact and how*
> *it would enable them to serve consumers globally, but not concealing*
> *their glee that they would now be able to operate and gain in many*
> *developing country markets.*[52]

Despite the public elation, corporations regarded the agreement as just a beginning. Most countries committed themselves to little more than locking in their existing levels of market opening.[53] However, even this is significant given that it meant that no reversal or government controls can be imposed in the future even if there is a democratic decision to do so. This is so undemocratic that in some nations such agreements are thought to be unconstitutional. The Canadian Constitution, for example, states: 'Every act shall be so construed as to reserve to Parliament the power of repealing or amending it, and of revoking, restricting or modifying any power, privilege or advantage thereby vested in or granted to any person.'[54]

Despite this corporate victory over democracy, banker Andrew Buxton complained: 'There are still countries, such as India, where hardly any progress was made in the 1997 agreement and where more pressure is needed ... we cannot allow existing members of the WTO to opt out completely.'[55] Financial corporations sought to gain further commitments following the agreement, including commitments to:

- give foreign investors the right to establish wholly owned businesses, subsidiaries, branches and offices in all financial service sectors with the same rights as local businesses;
- give foreign investors the same access to domestic and international markets as local companies;
- lift restrictions on cross-border services and consumption of services abroad;
- lift limits on investments in joint ventures and domestic financial institutions;
- facilitate the entry of key business personnel without onerous restrictions and permitting procedures;
- grandfather existing investments – that is, ensure they are not subject to new rules and restrictions after they have been established; and
- lock in and improve market access to pension provision.[56]

PROLIFERATION OF BUSINESS COALITIONS

The CSI demonstrated the power of business coalitions in setting the agenda and influencing the outcomes of trade negotiations during the Uruguay Round and the subsequent Financial Services Agreement (FSA) negotiations. In fact, it inspired similar service industry coalitions in other countries that hope to profit from access to markets in foreign countries.[57] These include the Australian Services Roundtable, the Irish Coalition of Service Industries and the Hong Kong Coalition of Service Industries. In addition, research centres catering to these new lobbies have blossomed. For example, the Australian National University has established a Services Industries Research Centre to provide research and distribute information relevant to the services sector.

But CSI did more than provide a model to emulate. It also actively took part in the formation of later coalitions. As can be seen from Figure 7.1, Harry Freeman from American Express, and the CSI itself, played a major role in the formation and running of some of these business coalitions, including the MTN Coalition, the Financial Leaders Group and the Global Services Network. CSI is also one of the Associate Expert Groups for the Business and Industry Advisory Committee (BIAC) to the Organisation for Economic Co-operation and Development (OECD).[58]

On the other side of the Atlantic, British Invisibles (BI), a UK business coalition, played an active role in forming and running national and European business coalitions. BI was founded during the late 1960s to promote UK financial businesses around the world.[59] It sought liberalization of trade in services, particularly financial and related services – including legal, accountancy, consultancy and shipping – 'invisibles' being a technical term for services, investment income and transfers.

In 2001, BI changed its name to International Financial Services, London (IFSL). The group must have decided that the name British Invisibles had unfortunate connotations of secrecy, perhaps apt though, considering its behind-the-scenes lobbying and networking activities. IFSL seeks to identify and remove barriers to its members operating in overseas markets and to 'ensure that the objectives and priorities of the UK-based industry are high on the agenda during the forthcoming WTO negotiations'.[60]

Unlike CSI, British Invisibles formalized its access to key government bureaucrats through a committee structure that included sympathetic government officials from the Department of Trade and Industry (DTI), Her Majesty's Treasury, the Foreign and Commonwealth Office (FCO), the Bank of England and the Financial Services Authority (FSA (UK)). This Liberalisation of Trade in Services (LOTIS) Committee began meeting during the early 1980s with the aim of influencing the GATT negotiations. It became the main lobbying organization for the UK financial services industry.[61]

Because of the hybrid business–government nature of the LOTIS committee, financial corporations were privy to government information that was not publicly available, including internal EU papers and draft submissions to the WTO from other nations. They also had high-level access to government negotiators and WTO officials. For example, when the chair of a later LOTIS Committee gave evidence at the House of Lords European Committee, he had to explain 'why it was acceptable and right for the private sector to give its views direct to the Commission rather than through member state governments'.[62]

This 'corporate state alliance' has been criticized by Erik Wesselius of GATS Watch because 'the distinction between public and private has become completely blurred', and the LOTIS meetings where government officials and business executives discuss WTO negotiation strategies in private give the 'UK financial services industry an unjustified control over large parts of the UK trade policy agenda... Privileged cooperative arrangements between business and government as embodied in IFSL/LOTIS do not belong in a truly democratic policy-making process'.[63]

During the negotiations for the Financial Services Agreement, the CSI got together with British Invisibles to form the Financial Leaders Group (FLG) in

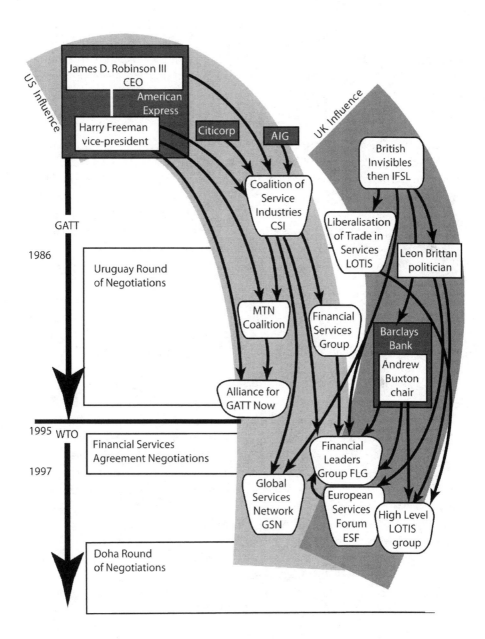

Figure 7.1 *Organizations and networks lobbying for free trade in services*

Note: The proliferation of trade in services groups and coalitions originated with American Express (AmEx) in the US and British Invisibles in the UK. Key people such as Harry Freeman from AmEx and Leon Brittan and Andrew Buxton from British Invisibles and Barclays Bank were active in forming and leading these coalitions, which had a close relationship with each other and overlapping memberships.

1996. The group includes financial leaders from Europe, North America, Japan and Hong Kong, representing such banking giants as Barclays, Chase Manhattan, Goldman Sachs and the Bank of Tokyo-Mitsubishi. FLG broadened support for financial services deregulation and 'proved a key player in securing the 1997 Financial Services Agreement'.[64]

The formation of FLG was encouraged by EU Trade Commissioner Leon Brittan. During the negotiations, Brittan, who had 'learned from the negotiations the importance of the American private sector in advising the US administration on deal-making', encouraged 'the European private sector to make contact with their counterparts across the Atlantic so as to build up a partnership in favour of a permanent deal'. He played a key role in the formation of the TransAtlantic Business Dialogue (TABD; see Chapter 8) in 1995, which enables the CEOs of US and European companies to present a unified and powerful front to trade negotiators. As EC vice president, Brittan met regularly with TABD. When the FSA agreement was made in 1997, Brittan claimed his strategy had 'paid off handsomely'.[65]

The creation of FLG was also 'spurred by the World Economic Forum, which has been the catalyst for key international meetings among US and EC negotiators, and business representatives'.[66] Banker Andrew Buxton, from BI's LOTIS Committee, became co-chair of FLG with Ken Whipple, president of Ford Financial Services and chair of the Financial Services Group of CSI. Whipple had decided that 'success in financial services negotiations would be more likely were financial leaders here [in the US] and in Europe to work together to ensure a success'.[67]

Brittan was so pleased with the job that FLG did in jump-starting the stalled talks that he invited Buxton to form a European services network to promote further progress in the more general services area. Brittan noted: 'A similar effort will be needed for the next round of service liberalization negotiations.'[68]

The European Services Forum (ESF) was formed in 1998 (originally called the European Services Network) to provide private-sector advice and information directly to the EU's WTO negotiators. Its formation was supported by CEOs of leading European corporations and federations, as well as Europe's major employer association, the Union of Industrial and Employers' Confederations of Europe (UNICE). Naturally, British Invisibles became a 'prominent member' of ESF. So, too, did companies that have benefited from privatization of services, such as the giant water companies Suez and Vivendi/Veolia.[69]

Buxton was the first chair of the ESF. He noted that CSI 'has shown us the way'. Like the CSI, the aim of ESF is to actively promote the interests of its members. According to ESF Managing Director Pascal Kerneis, 'the European industry understood that it was important to work together in order to exchange information and to defend global European service industries positions'.[70]

ESF is an official member of the EU delegation at WTO conferences, as well as being a registered non-governmental organization (NGO) at the same conferences. It produces position papers on various aspects of services liberalization that are distributed to EC officials and negotiators, and EC officials attend ESF Policy Committee meetings, where these papers are discussed. It is also apparent that the EC not only played a role in setting up the ESF, but that it has also 'actively sought ESF guidance in formulating its GATS negotiating positions' and even, according to Wesselius, 'prioritized' that advice over that of member states:[71]

> It is, of course, unjustifiable for the European Commission to treat corporate advice on an equal footing with the input from EU member states in formulating EU GATS negotiating objectives and strategies; but it has been able to do so due to the lack of effective democratic control of EU external trade policy ... privileged cooperative arrangements between business and government have no place in a democratic policy-making process.[72]

FLG's success with the Financial Services Agreement was partly attributed to its structure, and ESF was keen to emulate it. FLG consists of two tiers: a high-level group of CEOs and chairpeople of corporations, supported by a Financial Leaders Working Group with lower-level corporate executives.[73] FLG relies on the power of this coalition of corporate heavy weights in its high-level group to have influence:

> The unanimity in the Financial Leaders Group became a message to governments that the US and European financial community wanted meaningful liberalization and a substantial success, and that the negotiators should cooperate to achieve it. The strategy clearly worked.[74]

Buxton used the same structure for the ESF: a European Service Leaders Group which includes the CEOs of more than 40 companies and a Policy Committee which includes 39 service industry federations covering 20 service sectors, UNICE and representatives of the CEOs in the Leaders Group. Both were supported by a secretariat hosted by UNICE. The Leaders Group provides the high public profile and muscle: 'They give the political impetus to the ESF messages and are the ambassadors of ESF, spreading the messages of the European service industries around the world in their various business travels.' The Policy Committee formulates policy and carries out ESF activities, and the secretariat services both groups.[75]

A year later, in 1999, British Invisibles followed suit by creating a High Level LOTIS Group composed of around 15 heads of companies, including European heads of US service companies Morgan Stanley and PriceWaterhouse Coopers (PwC). Senior government officials also attend meetings of the High Level LOTIS Group.[76] The inaugural chair was none other than the ubiquitous Andrew Buxton, chair of both FLG and ESF. He was succeeded by Leon Brittan in 2001 when Brittan was no longer EU trade commissioner.

The CSI also cooperated with British Invisibles in the formation of the Global Services Network (GSN). GSN follows the LOTIS model of incorporating government officials. It is basically an online forum of business leaders, government officials and think-tank personnel from around the world who are 'committed to increased trade and investment in services'. It was set up in 1998 at an invitation-only conference in the UK with the aim of 'building support for liberalization of world services trade in the next big round for services negotiations to begin in 2000'.[77]

GSN is administered by CSI and has the same goals. To achieve these goals, GSN recognized the need to enlist regulators to their cause; increase political and public support through selling the benefits of trade liberalization; and enhance access and involvement of the private sector in multilateral trade negotiations. Its inaugural organizing committee included representatives of the CSI and service industry coalitions from the UK, Canada, Hong Kong, Ireland and Argentina, as well as the Association of British Insurers, the Canadian Bankers Association, the French Federation of Insurance Companies and the London Investment Bankers Association.[78]

The Business and Industry Advisory Committee (BIAC) to the OECD is another business coalition that ranks the liberalization of trade in services as one of its top priorities. BIAC was formed in 1962 to enable business and industry to have an official input into OECD policy-making through an independent organization. BIAC represents the 'principal industrial and employer's organizations in OECD countries', including the US Council for International Business (USCIB), the Confederation of British Industry (CBI) and the Australian Chamber of Commerce and Industry (ACCI).[79]

BIAC 'offers business and industry an excellent opportunity to participate in inter-governmental discussions on policy issues, thus giving the business community a chance to shape the development of long-term policies in OECD countries'. It has a Trade Committee which plays an active role in the WTO negotiations, 'identifying areas for further liberalization by governments'. The committee is chaired by Nancie S. Johnson, vice president of DuPont Government Affairs (US) (who also chairs USCIB's Trade Policy Committee).[80]

ONGOING LOBBYING

Minutes of the LOTIS meetings from 1999 and 2000, leaked to the Corporate Europe Observatory, give an idea of the extensive international networking that the service industry coalitions were part of; the alliance of government officials and corporate executives; and the high-level privileged access to which members were privy.[81]

The minutes also give an idea of the strategies that were being employed by the more powerful nations to achieve their objectives. To cover the fact that the liberalization agenda was being pushed by the EU and the US, committee members suggested a third country could promote their agenda:

> *Some felt that a small WTO member, such as Hong Kong or Singapore, might be encouraged to take the initiative... The US shared this view that the industrialized world should not be perceived to be pushing its own agenda at this juncture.*[82]

A similar strategy had been proposed by the CSI with respect to free movement of skilled personnel between countries. The idea was 'to encourage a country like India to be a *demandeur*, enabling the EU and US to respond sympathetically'. Tony Simms, a member of the UK Mission to the WTO and chair of the WTO Working Party on GATS rules, suggested the LOTIS Committee approach the Confederation of Indian Industry for this purpose. Over the next couple of months PwC facilitated a paper by the Indians on the topic.[83]

The minutes also made it clear that there were differences between the US and European business over the strategies to be employed in attaining liberalization of trade in services. US trade barriers posed a particularly delicate problem for European business. The EC was reluctant to push the US on their barriers in case it would 'undermine the important alliance between the private sector in the EU and the US *vis à vis* third countries'. However, the LOTIS Committee agreed that US barriers should be confronted.[84]

Business coalitions also became impatient with the slow process of individual nation commitments. BIAC urged the OECD Trade Committee to get the WTO Secretariat to investigate ways in which GATS negotiations could bypass the process by which each nation makes offers to commit particular service sectors to GATS because this was very slow and painstaking. It suggested a 'top-down' structure where, instead of offering sectors for market opening, all sectors would be considered open unless a nation asked for an exception. It also sought ways to have cross-sector issues taken out of the GATS negotiations and made part of the WTO general agreements. An example would be movement of skilled personnel across borders.[85]

Robert Vastine, president of CSI since 1996, also argued that the 'request-offer' negotiations should be supplemented with 'bold and innovative' negotiating methods, such as pressing for commitments that applied across all sectors; 'the negotiation of model schedules for each sector'; and pro-competitive regulatory commitments. Such regulatory commitments 'mean abandoning forms of regulation by which governments limit the introduction of new products, restrict use of market-based pricing, and in other ways constrain competition'.[86]

In the area of express delivery services, the CSI wants there to be WTO rules against profits derived from national postal services being used to cross-subsidize other postal services that US companies want to compete with. It also wants rules to prevent taxes from private companies being used to subsidize national postal services. In terms of financial services, CSI wants nations to commit to pensions policies that would 'encourage private savings for retirement' and thus provide opportunities for foreign investment companies to profit from people's retirement, which would be precluded by a government pension scheme.[87] The Bush administration is currently pushing for this approach to aged pensions in the US.

Healthcare services are another CSI target. The CSI makes the doubtful claim that competition in the US healthcare field has enabled cost reductions to occur while quality has improved. The companies involved stand to gain from the opportunities that the rapid growth of healthcare expenditures in some other countries might offer. This requires that nations open up their healthcare markets to competition and allow majority foreign ownership of their healthcare facilities.[88]

US companies have been excluded from this profit opportunity by the fact that healthcare has traditionally been a government responsibility in most countries. In OECD countries, barriers such as restrictive licensing of healthcare professionals and 'excessive privacy and confidentiality regulations' continue to be an obstacle to US companies. In developing countries, while barriers are fewer, the danger for US healthcare companies is that more will be put in place as the countries develop.[89]

The CSI also wants to facilitate the flow of US professionals and business people to foreign countries by getting US negotiators to press for an agreement on business mobility that would enable business people and qualified professionals to enter a country without a visa to work on specific assignments. In furtherance of this aim, it wants the negotiators to champion 'freedom of association' for these professionals and the elimination of requirements or prohibitions that national professional societies might have in place.[90]

The task of convincing developing nations that the foreign provision of services is essential for their development is an ongoing task. BIAC recommended that the OECD undertake a study of the economic benefits of liberalization in key service sectors in order to 'build a broader constituency for liberalization'. It also recommended that it improve its collection of service-related statistics to show to the public how important services are to the economy.[91]

ESF also plans to put together case studies of how liberalization in the service sector has helped developing countries and to use them to persuade the governments of developing countries. Buxton told the 1999 World Services Congress that European negotiators 'need to have good news stories – examples of where liberalization has shown clear benefits'. He recognized that there would be some losers in the liberalization process and it was the threatened institutions that would 'lobby hardest against the liberalization process'.[92]

Examples of beneficial liberalization were somewhat contentious. Buxton, for example, cited Enron's controversial Dabhol power plant, which he said 'will bring much needed reliable electricity power to the country'. In fact, it ended up producing electricity that was far too expensive for the locals to buy.[93]

Service industries are particularly keen to open up government procurement markets because procurement by government and public authorities and agencies represents such a large share of government expenditure. They claim, without any real evidence, that this opening up in developing countries will enable better-quality services to be available at lower prices and facilitate technological and knowledge transfer, which would promote sustainable development.[94]

The task of persuading local politicians of the need for services deregulation, at home and abroad, also continues. CSI President Vastine told a Senate Finance Committee hearing that because 'foreigners have a high propensity to consume US services' and because US service companies tended to be competitive in most service sectors, reducing trade barriers would stimulate US trade and reduce the US current account deficit. Vastine argued that US domestic policies should be formulated to enhance the competitiveness of service companies – for example, 'permitting US-based financial services companies to reinvest earnings overseas without first being taxed by the US'.[95] This would be an advantage that local companies would not have.

A key role which the business coalitions play in the ongoing negotiations is to provide access to key politicians and bureaucrats involved in the negotiations. Members of CSI are assured that their membership 'provides a cost-effective, leveraged way to ensure' that their interests are represented and their voices heard in all the important places. For fees of up to US$25,000 per year (2003), they are promised access to key people in US Congress, US government agencies, international organizations such as the WTO, and foreign governments including the European Commission. They are promised that they will be able to 'help shape US government positions on key issues of concern through frequent interaction with US government officials' and expand their business opportunities abroad by taking part in 'missions to key foreign markets', such as China and India.[96]

CSI, through its Research and Education Foundation, runs a World Services Congress to bring together business people, government officials and academics from around the world in support of liberalization of trade in services. In addition, CSI runs conferences in the US in conjunction with the US Department of Commerce to facilitate business–government dialogue, with the aim of enabling its members to make recommendations to US negotiators regarding shaping the US negotiating agenda and expanding US trade objectives.[97] Such conferences attract the highest level bureaucrats and officials, including the WTO director general designate and the deputy USTR in 2002.

The CSI also has good relations with the media: 'One of the things that distinguish the American private sector from the rest of the world is its relationship to the media, which is very good.'[98] It helps that various media organizations, such as Reuters, are members and have their own interest in free trade in services. Reuters is also a member of the LOTIS Committee.

All these business coalitions work closely together for similar goals, which is perfectly understandable given their common origins and overlapping membership and leadership. For example, FLG press releases include contacts from CSI, British Invisibles and ESF. CSI and IFSL continue to jointly administer the group. In fact, CSI has a hand in all but the European-based LOTIS groups and the ESF. The ESF, nevertheless, works closely with the CSI and has a similar, if less strident, agenda.[99]

The prominence of business coalitions in the UK and the US in promoting services and creating business networks, global and regional, to augment their efforts reflects the fact that these are the two largest exporters of services in the world. Christopher Roberts, formerly UK director general of trade policy and chair of LOTIS, recognizes that 'The greatest pressure for liberalizing financial services comes, as one would expect, from the EU and US. The views of both reflect substantial input from the private sector.'[100]

Service industry coalitions are supported in their efforts to gain unrestricted access to global markets by think tanks and organizations such as the OECD. For example, in 1999 the American Enterprise Institute (AEI), the Brookings Institution, the Center for Business and Government of Harvard University and the CSI's Education and Research Foundation organized a conference on GATS in Washington, DC. The papers given at the conference were published as a book, and funding came from the CSI Foundation, the European Commission, the Mark Twain Institute (founded by Freeman), and government bodies in Canada, France and Japan.[101]

NOTES

1   European Commission, 'Opening World Markets for Services: Towards GATS 2000', European Commission, http://gats-info.eu.int/gats-info/g2000.pl?NEWS=bbb accessed 10 May 2003.
2   Cited in Brian Ahlberg, 'American Express: The Stateless Corporation', *Multinational Monitor*, November, 1990, http://multinationalmonitor.org/hyper/issues/1990/11/mm1190_11.html.
3   Quoted in Harry Freeman, 'Comments and Discussion', *Brookings-Wharton Papers on Financial Services 2000*, 2000, p456.
4   Ahlberg, 'American Express'; Freeman, 'Comments and Discussion', p456.
5   Freeman, 'Comments and Discussion', p457.
6   *Ibid.*, p457.
7   James P. Zumwalt, 'Pressure Politics and Free Trade: Influence of the Services Industry on the Uruguay Round', National Defense University, 16 December 1996, pp3–4.
8   Ahlberg, 'American Express'; Peter Drahos and John Braithwaite, 'Who Owns the Knowledge Economy? Political Organising Behind TRIPS', *The Corner House Briefing*, no 32, 2004, p11.
9   Ahlberg, 'American Express'.
10 *Ibid.*
11 Quoted in Darren Puscas, 'Enron-Style Corporate Crime and Privatization', Ottawa, Polaris Institute, 19 June 2003, p3.

12 USCSI, 'About CSI', Coalition of Service Industries, www.uscsi.org/about/ accessed 2 May 2003; R. Vastine, 'Statement of Robert Vastine, President, Coalition of Service Industries', Senate Finance Committee Subcommittee on International Trade, 21 October 1999.

13 USCSI, 'Membership', Coalition of Service Industries, www.uscsi.org/members/ accessed 2 May 2003; Robert Vastine, 'Trade Remedy System under the WTO Frame-work: Functions and Mechanism, the Role of Trade Associations', Paper presented at the 2002 Annual Conference of the Advisory Committee of the Shanghai WTO Affairs Consultation Center and 2002 WTO Forum, Shanghai, 5–7 November, 2002, p1; Freeman, 'Comments and Discussion', p458.

14 Puscas, 'Enron-Style Corporate Crime and Privatization', p2.

15 USCSI, 'About CSI'; USCSI, 'Membership'; Pratap Chatterjee, 'Enron: Pulling the Plug on the Global Power Broker', *CorpWatch*, 13 December, 2001, http://corpwatch. org/issues/PRT.jsp?articleid-1016; Tony Clarke, 'Enron: Washington's Number One Behind-the-Scenes GATS Negotiator', *CorpWatch*, 25 October, 2001, http:// corpwatch.org/issues/wto/featured/2001/tclarke.html; Darrem Puscas, 'A Guide to the Enron Collapse: A Few Points for a Clearer Understanding', Canada, Polaris Institute, 12 February 2002, pp11–12.

16 Ahlberg, 'American Express'; Zumwalt, 'Pressure Politics and Free Trade', p4.

17 Spero cited in Zumwalt, 'Pressure Politics and Free Trade', p5.

18 *Ibid.*, pp5–8.

19 Samuel Bodman, 'Remarks', Paper presented at the Services 2002 Conference, Washington DC, 5 February, 2002.

20 Zumwalt, 'Pressure Politics and Free Trade', p6; Dean R. O'Hare, 'Introductory Remarks', Paper presented at the Services 2002 Conference, Washington DC, 5 February, 2002, p3.

21 Cited in Zumwalt, 'Pressure Politics and Free Trade', pp4, 8.

22 *Ibid.*, pp8–11.

23 Freeman, 'Comments and Discussion', p458; O'Hare, 'Introductory Remarks', p3.

24 USCSI, 'About CSI'.

25 Erik Wesselius, 'Behind GATS 2000: Corporate Power at Work', Amsterdam, Transnational Institute, May 2002, p5.

26 Marjorie Griffin Cohen, 'From Public Good to Private Exploitation: Electricity Deregulaton, Privatization and Continental Integration', Nova Scotia, Canadian Centre for Policy Alternatives, July 2002, pp10–11.

27 CEO, 'WTO and Water: The EU's Crusade for Corporate Expansion', Corporate Europe Observatory, www.corporateeurope.org/water/infobrief3.htm accessed 3 January 2005.

28 Wesselius, 'Behind GATS 2000', p5.

29 ESF, 'ESF Second Position Paper on Public Procurement in Services', European Services Forum, 25 November, 2002, p5; Wesselius, 'Behind GATS 2000', p4.

30 Gregory Palast, 'Necessity Is Mother of Gats Intervention', *The Observer*, 15 April, 2001.

31 ESF, 'ESF Second Position Paper', pp5–6.

32 WTO Panel, 'Mexico – Measures Affecting Telecommunications Services', World Trade Organization, 2 April, 2004, www.internationaltraderelations.com/WTO. Mexico%20Telecom%20Case%20(Panel%202004).htm.

33   Ellen Gould, 'Panel Strips WTO of Another Fig Leaf', *WTOWatch*, 16 July, 2004.
34   *Ibid.*
35   CEO, 'GATS: Undermining Public Services', *Corporate Europe Observer*, June, 2001, www.corporateeurope.org/observer9/gats.html.
36   Zakki P. Hakim and Sri Wahyuni, 'Govt Committed to Liberalizing Education Sector', *The Jakarta Post*, 27 October, 2004.
37   Wesselius, 'Behind GATS 2000', p3.
38   'Europe Forbids Sell-Off Debate', *The Ecologist*, March, 2003, p7.
39   CEO, 'Leaked Confidential Documents Reveal EC's Neoliberal GATS Agenda', *Corporate Europe Observer*, May, 2002, www.corporateeurope.org/observer11/gats.html.
40   World Development Movement, 'The Missing Link: Debt and Trade', World Development Movement, 3 February, 2001, www.wdm.org.uk/cambriefs/Debt/misslink.pdf 2002, p3.
41   European Commission, 'Opening World Markets for Services'.
42   USCSI, 'Services 2000 Submission', 1999.
43   Institute for International Economics, 'Financial Services Liberalized Little in Recent WTO Agreement', IIE, 22 June, 1998, www.iie.com/publications/cases/dobsjqpr.htm; Victor L. L. Chu, 'The Case for Open Markets in Financial Services', International Chamber of Commerce, 2002, www.iccwbo.org/home/news_archives/2003/stories/financial.asp ; Alistair Abercrombie, 'Seminar on GATS and Financial Services', International Financial Services, London, 11 May, 2004, www.ifsl.org.uk/tradepolicy/viewpoint.cfm.
44   Public Citizen, 'MAI Shell Game – IMF', Public Citizen, www.citizen.org/print_article.cfm?ID=1098 accessed 3 July 2003; Edmund L. Andrews, 'Agreement to Open Up World Financial Markets Is Reached', *New York Times*, 13 December, 1997.
45   Chakravarthi Raghavan, 'Close Encounters at the WTO', *Third World Economics*, 16–31 December, 1997, www.twnside.org.sg/title/coun-cn.htm; Andrew Buxton, 'The European Services Network: Keynote Speech', Paper presented at the Preparatory Conference for the World Services Congress, The University Club, Washington DC, 2 June, 1999, p3.
46   Quoted in Raghavan, 'Close Encounters at the WTO'.
47   *Ibid.*
48   Vastine, 'Hearing on World Trade Organization Singapore Ministerial Meeting', in *Subcommittee on Trade of the House Committee on Ways and Means*, House Committee on Ways and Means, waysandmeans.house.gov/legacy/trade/105cong/2-26-97/2-26vast.htm.
49   Andrews, 'Agreement to Open Up World Financial Markets Is Reached'.
50   Raghavan, 'Close Encounters at the WTO'.
51   Leon Brittan, *A Diet of Brussels: The Changing Face of Europe*, London, Little, Brown and Company, 2000, p132.
52   Raghavan, 'Close Encounters at the WTO'.
53   Institute for International Economics, 'Financial Services Liberalized Little in Recent WTO Agreement'; Chu, 'The Case for Open Markets in Financial Services'; Abercrombie, 'Seminar on GATS and Financial Services'.
54   Interpretation Act, R.S.C. 1985, c, 1-21, quoted at www.gwb.com.au/gwb/news/mai/uncons.html.

55 Buxton, 'The European Services Network', p4.
56 Abercrombie, 'Seminar on GATS and Financial Services'; FLG, 'Commentary on Proposals for Liberalisation in Financial Services', Financial Leaders Group, 21 September 2001.
57 O'Hare, 'Introductory Remarks', p2.
58 BIAC, 'eBIAC: The Voice of the Business Community at the OECD', Business and Industry Advisory Committee to the OECD, 28 May, 2003, www.biac.org/.
59 Abercrombie, 'Seminar on GATS and Financial Services'.
60 IFSL, 'Trade Policy', International Financial Services, London, www.ifsl.org.uk/tradepolicy/home_left.cfm accessed 2 May 2003.
61 IFSL, 'What We Do', International Financial Services, London, www.ifsl.org.uk/tradepolicy/whatwedo.cfm accessed 2 May 2003.
62 Erik Wesselius, 'Liberalisation of Trade in Services: Corporate Power at Work', GATSwatch 2001; Liberalization of Trade in Services (LOTIS) Committee, 'Minutes of Meeting, Tuesday, 21 March 2000', Department of Trade and Industry 2000.
63 Wesselius, 'Liberalisation of Trade in Services'.
64 V. Sridhar, 'Big Business at Work', Frontline, 11–24 December, 1999, www.frontlineonnet.com/fl1626/1626180.htm; USCSI, 'The Financial Leaders Group/Financial Leaders Working Group', Coalition of Service Industries, www.uscsi.org/groups/finLeader.htm accessed 30 October 2004; FLG, 'Commentary on Proposals for Liberalisation in Financial Services', p1; Abercrombie, 'Seminar on GATS and Financial Services'.
65 Brittan, A Diet of Brussels, p131; TABD, 'TABD History: 1995–2002', TransAtlantic Business Dialogue, 2002, http://tabd.com/history.html; CEO, 'TransAtlantic Business Dialogue (TABD)', Amsterdam, Corporate Europe Observatory, 25 October 1999.
66 Vastine, 'Hearing on World Trade Organization Singapore Ministerial Meeting'.
67 Ibid.; IFSL, 'What We Do'.
68 Ibid.; Leon Brittan, 'Europe's Prescriptions for the Global Trade Agenda', European Union, 24 September, 1998, www.eurunion.org/news/speeches/1998/9809241b.htm.
69 'European Services Industry Unites in Favour of Ambitious World-Wide Trade Liberalisation', Global Services Network, www.globalservicesnetwork.com/esn_announcement.htm accessed 2 May 2003; Abercrombie, 'Seminar on GATS and Financial Services'; IFSL, 'What We Do'.
70 Buxton, 'The European Services Network', p5; ESF, 'About ESF', European Services Forum, www.esf.be/e_pages/about.htm accessed 2 May 2003; Pascal Kerneis, 'The Perspective of the European Private Sector in the GATS Negotiations', Paper presented at the Regional Seminar on Services: ASEAN, Bangkok, Thailand, 27 June, 2000, p4.
71 ESF, 'About ESF'; Wesselius, 'Behind GATS 2000', pp9–10; Buxton, 'The European Services Network', p1.
72 Wesselius, 'Behind GATS 2000', pp9–10.
73 Ibid., p7.
74 Vastine quoted in Ibid., p7.
75 Kerneis, 'The Perspective of the European Private Sector', p3; 'European Services Industry Unites'.

76   IFSL, 'What We Do'; Gregory Palast, 'The WTO's Hidden Agenda', *CorpWatch*, 9 November, 2001, www.corpwatch.org/issues/PRT.jsp?articleid=722.

77   Vastine, 'Trade Remedy System', p1; W. K. Chan, 'Preparing for Services 2000', Global Services Network, June, 1998, www.globalservicesnetwork.com/preparing_for_services_200.htm; IFSL, 'What We Do'; GSN, 'Global Services Network', www.globalservicesnetwork.com/ accessed 2 May 2003; GSN, 'Global Services Network Formed; Services 2000 Issues Agreed', Global Services Network, 26 April, 1998, www.globalservicesnetwork.com/ditchley_park_declaration.htm.

78   GSN, 'Global Services Network Formed; Services 2000 Issues Agreed'.

79   BIAC, 'eBIAC'.

80   *Ibid.*; BIAC, 'BIAC Priorities for the WTO Doha Negotiations and Recommendations to the OECD', Paris, Business and Industry Advisory Committee to the OECD, 20 February 2003, p3; BIAC, 'Priorities for OECD and WTO Work: BIAC Submission on Trade-Related Issues to the OECD', Paris, Business and Industry Advisory Committee to the OECD, June 1998b, p2.

81   www.gatswatch.org/LOTIS/.

82   Liberalization of Trade in Services (LOTIS) Committee, 'Minutes of Meeting, Tuesday, 25 January 2000', HM Treasury, London 2000.

83   Liberalization of Trade in Services (LOTIS) Committee, 'Minutes of Meeting, Friday, 22 September 2000', Bank of England 2000; Liberalisation of Trade in Services (LOTIS) Committee, 'Minutes of Meeting, Friday, 8 December 2000', Institute of Chartered Accountants in England and Wales 2000.

84   Liberalization of Trade in Services (LOTIS) Committee, 'Minutes 25 Jan 2000'.

85   BIAC, 'Revised BIAC Statement on OECD Work on Trade in Services', Paris, Business and Industry Advisory Committee to the OECD, June 1998a, pp2–3.

86   Vastine, 'Statement'.

87   USCSI, 'Services 2000 Submission', 1999.

88   *Ibid.*

89   *Ibid.*

90   *Ibid.*

91   BIAC, 'Revised BIAC Statement', p1.

92   Kerneis, 'The Perspective of the European Private Sector', p6; Buxton, 'The European Services Network', p3.

93   Buxton quoted in Kerneis, 'The Perspective of the European Private Sector', p7; Sharon Beder, *Power Play: The Fight for Control of the World's Electricity*, New York, New Press, 2003, Chapter 18.

94   ESF, 'ESF Second Position Paper', p1.

95   Vastine, 'Statement'.

96   USCSI, 'Membership'.

97   USCSI, 'CSI Foundation', Coalition of Service Industries, www.uscsi.org/csifoundation/ accessed 2 May 2003; USCSI, 'Services 2000', Coalition of Service Industries, www.uscsi.org/events/services2000conf.html accessed 2 May 2003; USCSI, 'Services 2002', Coalition of Service Industries, www.uscsi.org/meetings/services2002/flyer.pdf accessed 2 May 2003.

98   Freeman, 'Comments and Discussion', p459.

99   ESF, 'About ESF'; Wesselius, 'Behind GATS 2000', p9.

100 Abercrombie, 'Seminar on GATS and Financial Services'; Christopher Roberts, 'Lotis Chairman Stresses Importance of Services Liberalisation', International Financial Services London, 24 October, 2002, www.ifsl.org.uk/pressreleases/detail.cfm?Id=79.

101 Pierre Sauvé and Robert M. Stern (eds) *GATS 2000: New Directions in Services Trade Liberalization*, Washington DC, Brookings Institution Press, 2000, ppvii–viii.

8

Coercing Trade Agreements

Trade rules play a crucial role in the capacity of a company or corporation to gain or lose in the market, and to serve its aim of achieving higher profits. For TNCs [transnational corporations], trade and investment rules determine their freedom to move freely around the globe, making use of the cheapest labour and production, playing suppliers off against each other, achieving economies of scale, and locating in the largest and most lucrative markets. THE TRANSNATIONAL INSTITUTE[1]

During the 1970s, Edmund Pratt, chief executive officer (CEO) of Pfizer, noticed that his company was losing significant market share in developing countries 'because our intellectual property rights were not being respected in these countries'.[2] Pfizer is a transnational pharmaceutical company that set up operations in developing countries ahead of many other US pharmaceutical companies.

Some developing countries did not have patent laws at this time because there was no economic incentive to do so. Others had patent laws but did not enforce them properly. Some required the patent owner to license local firms to produce the drugs if they weren't being produced by the patent owner in their country at a reasonable price. In India and Argentina, the processes and methods of manufacturing pharmaceutical drugs could be patented, but not the final products. This allowed competitors to make the same drugs using different methods and sell them at a much lower price.[3]

Although Pfizer's overall profitability did not depend upon developing country markets since they represented such a small proportion of its overall sales, the fact that generic versions of Pfizer drugs could be manufactured and sold so cheaply in these countries 'raised embarrassing questions about the connections between patents and drug prices'. Pfizer also viewed these countries as potential growth markets.[4]

Through the 1970s and early 1980s, Pfizer together with IBM – another 'globally ambitious, intellectual property-intensive' company where Pratt had spent his early career – unsuccessfully tried to persuade government officials in the US and in developing countries that intellectual property rights needed to be protected.[5] Nor were they successful at persuading the World Intellectual Property Organization (WIPO), which administered a Convention on Intellectual

Properties, of the need for high standards of protection for patents. Being a United Nations (UN) agency, each member nation of WIPO had a single vote and the majority voted against tougher international patent protections.

For Lou Clemente, Pfizer's general counsel, the 'experience with WIPO was the last straw in our attempt to operate by persuasion'. Instead, Pfizer decided to organize and mobilize business interests to pressure governments for change. It was already a well-connected company (see Figure 8.1) and well placed to do this. For example, during this time Pratt was head of the US Business Roundtable (see Chapter 2).[6]

Pfizer decided first that the GATT negotiations might be a more conducive atmosphere to make rules about intellectual property, one where the US could exercise its muscle to overcome developing country opposition. Pratt put himself forward for the influential Advisory Committee on Trade Policy and Negotiations (ACTPN) and by 1981 had been appointed as its chair by Ronald Reagan. He held this position for six years until after the Uruguay Round had started and James Robinson from American Express replaced him as chair (see Chapter 7).[7]

Under Pratt's leadership the advisory committee formed a task force on intellectual property with John Opel, chair of IBM – also a leading member of the

Figure 8.1 *Some of Pfizer's business association connections*

Source: adapted from Santoro and Paine (1995, pp7–8)

advisory committee – at its head. In this way, the committee became a key source of advice to the US Trade Representative (USTR) on the importance of including intellectual property rights in the forthcoming Uruguay Round of GATT. In addition, on ACTPN advice, the position of assistant USTR for international investment and intellectual property was created in 1981.[8]

The task that Pfizer set itself was to link intellectual property with free trade. This was not so easy, given that intellectual property rights had traditionally been associated with monopoly privileges that prevented competition and inhibited free trade. In fact, patents are so readily granted in the US these days that companies are patenting obvious ideas, such as the use of a shopping cart symbol on internet sites, merely to obstruct competition.[9]

Moreover, GATT had been about trade barriers and it was not clear how intellectual property rights fitted in with this, particularly if a nation applied its patent laws without discriminating against foreign firms. The term Trade-Related aspects of Intellectual Property Rights (TRIPS) was therefore employed to ensure that opponents could not argue that GATT was not the appropriate forum for intellectual property rights discussions.[10]

Pfizer conducted an international and domestic campaign to associate intellectual property protection with trade issues. Pratt made a series of speeches to business audiences linking intellectual property with trade and investment, and other Pfizer executives made the same case to national and international trade associations. The Chemical Manufacturers Association and the Pharmaceutical Manufacturers of America were amongst those that joined the campaign.[11] Peter Drahos and John Braithwaite outline this campaign in their book *Information Feudalism*:

> *Like the beat of a tom-tom, the message about intellectual property went out along the business networks to chambers of commerce, business councils, business committees, trade associations and business bodies. Progressively, Pfizer executives who occupied key positions in strategic business organizations were able to enrol their support for a trade-based approach to intellectual property. With every such enrolment, the business power behind the case for such an approach became harder and harder for governments to resist.*[12]

The campaign popularized the term 'piracy' to denigrate countries that had weak intellectual property laws and particularly to smear Asian countries, whose booming economies were making inroads into US markets:

> *Japanese manufacturing triumphs began to be seen as a portent of US deindustrialization. Public myths began to be constructed in the US about this success. American ideas, American know-how were being stolen by the Japanese, it was widely believed.*[13]

Although pharmaceutical companies readily appropriated the labour of indigenous peoples, the story disseminated by Pfizer was one of innovative companies in the US risking large sums of money and effort on research into new drugs and then having their rightful rewards unfairly stolen from them when they finally discovered a successful drug, by countries who ignored the rules.[14]

The story told by developing nations was a different one – one that claimed that a weaker intellectual property rights regime is necessary to aid development. They argued that not having tough rules enabled local companies to manufacture pharmaceutical drugs at a price that their citizens could afford, and similarly local manufacture of herbicides and fertilizers enabled farmers to grow much needed food. India was able to develop its own pharmaceutical industry, under its own patent regime, so that it was self-sufficient and the price of drugs was much more affordable to its poverty stricken population.[15]

In order to get the think tanks on side, Pfizer framed intellectual property as an issue of liberal values, individual property rights, fair reward for labour, pride in US achievements and national interest. Pfizer also donated funds to think tanks such as the American Enterprise Institute, the Hoover Institution, the Heritage Foundation and the Brookings Institution. It funded specific projects and conferences that produced reports that reinforced Pfizer's version of the intellectual property story.[16]

Once the Uruguay Round began, Pfizer and its allies had to persuade the US government negotiators that not only was intellectual property a key element in free trade, but that it was so important to the US economy that no GATT deal should be agreed upon which did not include intellectual property protections. Pratt, from Pfizer, and Opel, from IBM, formed the Intellectual Property Committee (IPC) in 1983 to aid in this effort. Its membership of 12 large US transnational corporations (TNCs) included General Electric, DuPont, General Motors, Johnson and Johnson, and Monsanto, and the CEOs of these companies had direct access to both the US president and the USTR because of the size of their companies.[17] Pratt later claimed:

> *The committee helped convince US officials that we should take a tough stance on intellectual property issues and that led to trade-related intellectual property rights being included on the GATT agenda when negotiations began in Punta del Este, Uruguay, in 1986.*[18]

TRADE DECISION-MAKING

The GATT was a favoured forum for business interests to achieve international rule changes because it was dominated by trade ministries and officials who were sympathetic to business concerns. Pratt preferred GATT as a forum to make intellectual property rules because the developed nations, and particularly the US, held so much sway there:

Unlike in WIPO [the World Intellectual Property Organization], we thought we could achieve real leverage through GATT. Many of the countries lacking intellectual property protection at least had important trading relations with the United States and the rest of the developed world. Moreover, through GATT we could forge intellectual property standards that were supported by dispute resolution and enforcement mechanisms, both of which were lacking in WIPO.[19]

The undemocratic nature of decision-making in both the GATT negotiations, and later in the World Trade Organization (WTO), has ensured that the trade rules agreed to are skewed in favour of the more affluent nations that are pushing for free trade. Of the estimated US$200 billion plus in benefits expected to be reaped from the Uruguay Round by 2005, less than 30 per cent is likely to go to developing nations and most of that to a few nations in Asia and Latin America.[20]

According to the UK charity Panos, most developing nations are likely to be 'worse off than before. Sub-Saharan Africa is expected to lose around US$1.2 billion a year from freer trade.' This skewing of benefits is not only because poorer countries export less, but also because 'the most dynamic exports of developing countries' remain the most protected products in developed countries.[21]

Although the GATT holds free trade to be the ideal, it does allow many exceptions to the rules, particularly those preferred by the more powerful nations who are calling the shots. As a result, many subsidies, tariffs and 'voluntary export restraints' remain in place. Developing world nations have not only been disadvantaged by such protectionism, but also by the opening of markets in industrial goods in their own countries because they have not had a sustained opportunity to develop under a protective regime, as have more affluent countries. Panos notes:

Despite successive trade rounds, products in those sectors where developing countries have a comparative advantage still face high barriers in industrialized countries. These include textiles and clothing, vegetables and fish, processed foods, leather and rubber goods, cars and electronics. According to UNDP [United Nations Development Programme]:

- *Average tariffs on industrial country imports from developing countries are 10 per cent higher and for the least developed countries 30 per cent higher than the global average.*
- *Developing countries lose about US$60 billion a year from agricultural subsidies in the industrial nations and from the barriers they face on exports of textiles and clothing.*[22]

Activists from low-income countries have argued that free trade might be fair and mutually beneficial between equal partners – but not where there are large differences in economic power and stages of economic development. The analogy of a race between a poorly fed African child and a world champion sprinter has been used. Applying the same rules to each of them so that they both start at the same time and run the same distance would hardly be considered a 'fair' race. Similarly, free trade between high-income nations and nations with much less development that have been exploited by developed nations in the past is not fair. It results in multinational corporations taking control of industries in low-income countries, and local companies being unable to develop and compete.[23]

It is generally the nations that are economically dominant that push for free trade because they are able to ensure that they will reap the benefits. During the 19th century, when Britain was a leading industrial power, it was also 'the most vigorous proponent of free trade', utilizing the arguments of Adam Smith and his followers to make their case. During the late 1940s, following the war, half of the world's production was being produced in the US and it was the US that dominated the push for free trade. Throughout the following decades the US government pressured US allies to allow free trade and made its loans to other nations dependent upon facilitating policies that would suit the needs of US companies. These policies included the dismantling of European colonial empires and trade barriers, all with a view to establishing an international regime of free trade.[24]

By the 1990s, Europe was also a major driver of free trade. Leon Brittan, a European Union (EU) trade commissioner at the time (see Chapter 7), has since argued that 'The reality, as opposed to the myth, is that Europe has evolved, and is increasingly evolving, in the direction of free markets and free trade.'[25] However, the concept of 'evolution' as a natural and inevitable process disguises the lobbying and public relations (PR) efforts and power exercised to achieve that 'evolution'.

In fact, Brittan says of his own role: 'I like to think that my work bulldozing through reforms which levered open markets, intensified competition and put public-sector monopolists on the back foot contributed to changing the terms of the debate.' He is particularly proud of being able to head off 'social regulatory burdens' – that is, regulations that sought to achieve social goals.[26]

When GATT was first formed in 1947, decisions were passed by majority vote, with each country having one vote. Major amendments required a two-thirds majority to pass and those countries that voted against them were not bound by them. From 1959, after many developing nations had joined GATT, decisions required a consensus rather than a majority vote in order to prevent any block of nations, particularly developing nations, from taking control of GATT decision-making.[27]

Although the US had originally preferred some form of weighted voting where countries with larger economies had more votes, it soon recognized that this would have deterred many countries from joining GATT. As US economic power grew, it saw that it could 'influence' voting without a formal and obvious weighting mechanism. Countries that did not accept the wishes of the major economic powers could lose access to International Monetary Fund (IMF) and other loans and suffer from trade sanctions.[28]

The WTO also uses consensus decision-making, although its constitution allows for voting. As with GATT, a consensus is deemed to have been reached if no individual member country formally objects to a decision. This is certainly very different from full agreement on the part of all members. 'This system makes it easier for powerful countries to overcome opposition through threats and pressures, since critical delegates need only remain silent for the "consensus" decision to go through.'[29]

Many people infer that, because a consensus is required, no agreements can be made within the WTO that would disadvantage individual countries or result in an unfair distribution of benefits, since those who are disadvantaged would oppose them. Consensus decision-making therefore carries with it a certain legitimacy that is exploited by those who should know better. For example, Brittan argues that the conspiracy theorists might claim that the purpose of the WTO is to 'open the markets of the world to the domination of Anglo-Saxon multinationals and their business practices. On the contrary, whatever its imperfections, the enormous strength of the WTO is that its rules can only be agreed by consensus on a global basis and are then just as enforceable by the poor against the rich as the other way round.' Similarly, former WTO Director General Mike Moore presented the WTO as 'built on democratic values' that give it legitimacy: 'No country is forced to sign our agreements. Each and every one of the WTO's rules is negotiated by member governments and agreed by consensus.'[30]

However, in practice, some countries exert much more power and influence than others in such agreements and small countries do not feel that they can object. A Caribbean delegate claimed: 'It requires superhuman conviction of one of the members to oppose what the major countries want.'[31] Larger countries are able to threaten to prevent imports from or reduce investment in a dissenting nation if they do not go along with an agreement.

The US and the European Commission (EC) have not only dominated GATT/WTO negotiations, but set the agenda:

> *Most initiatives, proposals and alternative packages that evolve into documents presented for formal approval have usually been developed first in Brussels and Washington, discussed informally by the trans-atlantic powers, then in increasingly larger caucuses (for example, Quad countries [US, EU, Japan and Canada], G7 [Canada, France, Germany, Italy, Japan, the UK and the US], OECD [Organisation for Economic Co-operation and Development]).*[32]

In other words, a consensus is formed amongst the most powerful nations first and then presented to other countries as a *fait accompli* – a done deal. The formal WTO sessions are merely a time for speech-making when ministers get the opportunity to express themselves; but the real decisions are made in back rooms where many smaller, poorer countries are excluded. When developing countries object to the proposed agreements, they are listened to and then ignored. They have the option of objecting to the final consensus; but as a former Indian ambassador to GATT, B. L. Das, says: 'The immediate political cost of withholding consensus appears to them to be much heavier than the burden of these obligations in the future.'[33]

Pressure applied to the developing country delegations include attempts to discredit negotiators back in their home capitals, threats to withdraw tariff preferences and other retaliatory measures, and promises of rewards for acceding. Developing countries that export to the EU or the US 'fear that bilateral trade relations will be affected' or that aid will be cut.[34]

Time frames are also too short to allow delegations to consult with their own citizens, stakeholders or other government ministers. Having been presented with a final text, agreed upon in back rooms by selected powerful countries, national delegates are lucky to have more than a day to consider it before the final decision is taken. They are told that there is no time to make changes and that they either have to take the text or leave it.[35]

Aileen Kwa notes in her study of *Power Politics in the WTO* that:

> When efficiency is prioritized before democracy, special interests can prevail over the interests of the majority. This may be the rich countries over the poor or an elite in rich countries over the rest of their population.[36]

The same process is used for proposal development. This is facilitated by the fact that the higher levels of the secretariat are staffed with Europeans and North Americans. The secretariat's bias becomes significant in its tabling of proposals and negotiating texts, the setting and promotion of meetings and agendas, the presentation of consensus views, and their selection of dispute settlement panels.[37]

The strong countries also tend to benefit most from the disputes procedure. In its first two and a half years, the WTO received 100 complaints. Of these, 34 were lodged by the US and 21 by the EC.[38]

Trade issues have traditionally been considered to be an area that should be handled by specialist experts in trade who make technocratic decisions, rather than elected officials accountable to the public. WTO papers are not published and trade negotiators do not discuss the likely trade-offs that they will have to make with citizens of their countries before they embark on the negotiations, nor are the citizens informed of the content of the negotiations and the positions taken by their negotiators:[39]

> ... the trade regime was operated as a tight-knit 'club'... For a long period of time, the trade regime's clubbishness, low profile and obscure workings were seen as a virtue. A clique of committed economists and diplomats and a small secretariat in Geneva toiled quietly in pursuit of

a vision of open markets... The closed and secretive nature of the regime isolated – and insulated – the trade policy-making process from day-to-day politics, keeping at bay the protectionist interests that are active in many countries.[40]

However, the political nature of trade rules is now very evident, even though the process of making the rules continues to be undemocratic, and the bullying tactics of the large economic powers acting on behalf of transnational corporations have increased.

Chakravarthi Raghaven in his book *Recolonization* describes how the solidarity of developing world countries was broken down by pressure early in the Uruguay Round. This pressure from the US, Europe and Japan involved offering political 'support to beleaguered regimes against their domestic opponents or externally against neighbours'; financial pressure 'in terms of debt negotiations'; and using their 'vast panoply of powers to reward or punish – capacity to maintain or deny [preferential] benefits, threat of harassing actions like anti-dumping and countervailing proceedings, quotas'.[41]

URUGUAY ROUND NEGOTIATIONS

Originally, GATT merely aimed to reduce tariffs on manufactured goods. In doing so it recognized that developing countries still needed to retain some tariff protection while they developed and some preferential treatment for entry into the markets of industrialized nations.[42] However, the Uruguay Round went far beyond, in both power and scope, the limited objectives of lowering tariffs on manufactured goods. Pressured by transnational corporations, negotiators from the US and the EU sought to include services, intellectual property rights and investment rights as part of GATT despite the opposition of developing nations.

Since the end of the Cold War, US negotiators have been free to overtly exercise their power, and they did this during the Uruguay Round when developing nations were refusing to agree to Trade-Related Intellectual Property Rights (TRIPS), Trade-Related Investment Measures (TRIMS) and a General Agreement on Trade in Services (GATS; see Chapter 6). Developing countries had little to gain from these expansions of the free trade agenda and much to lose. For example, because around 96 per cent of all patents are held by corporations based in affluent countries, a TRIPS agreement was of no benefit to poor nations and would only cost them money and inhibit their development.[43]

The Uruguay Round was supposed to start during the early 1980s; but developing countries, particularly the Group of 10 industrialized nations (G10) – India, Brazil, Argentina, Cuba, Egypt, Nicaragua, Nigeria, Peru, Tanzania and Yugoslavia – opposed the broadening of the GATT agenda to include these services, intellectual property and investment rules.[44]

To get recalcitrant countries to submit, the US exercised its economic muscle by taking retaliatory trade actions against South Korea and Brazil. According to Michael Ryan in his Brookings Institution book, *Knowledge Diplomacy*, this was a bullying strategy: 'The action was intended to signal that negotiations would go on one by one under threat of bilateral trade sanctions or they could take place within the GATT round; but negotiations would take place. The gambit worked' and the Uruguay Round got under way in 1986.[45]

However the developing nation opposition to these issues continued through-out the negotiations, as did US trade sanctions aimed at pressuring these countries to comply. Countries such as Mexico, Thailand and India suffered losses of millions of dollars during the Uruguay Round from US retaliatory trade measures because they refused to reform their intellectual property laws. The US made aid to Brazil conditional upon its cooperation on patent reforms.[46]

At the start of the Uruguay Round, only the US was pushing for TRIPS. The US Trade Representative told US business leaders: 'I'm convinced on intellectual property and trade; but when I go to Quad meetings, they are under no pressure from their industry. Can you get it?' Pfizer and the newly formed Intellectual Property Committee (IPC) therefore went to work at the international level to persuade corporations in Europe and Japan that it was in their interests to get intellectual property rules into the GATT agreement.[47]

IPC set up a tripartite coalition with the Union of Industrial and Employers' Confederations of Europe (UNICE) and the Japanese federation of economic organizations (Keidanren), which has more than 1000 corporate members in Japan, including Toyota, Mitsubishi, Nissan and Sony. Each member organization persuaded its own government of the need for intellectual property protection to be included in GATT. The coalition produced a 100-page blueprint for negotiators entitled *Basic Framework of GATT Provisions on Intellectual Property: Statement of Views of the European, Japanese and United States Business Communities.* Such a consensus report from powerful businesses in the three most powerful sectors of the world was clearly influential and difficult to ignore. IPC also put direct pressure on the EC and the Japanese government, threatening to oppose US Congressional ratification of GATT if a strong TRIPS agreement was not included.[48]

According to Richard Steinberg, professor of law at the University of California:

> In late spring of 1990, US negotiators decided to try to build a US government consensus on what some at the office of the US Trade Repres-entative (USTR) referred to internally as 'the power play,' a tactic that would force the developing countries to accept the obligations of the Uruguay Round agreements. The State Department supported the approach and, in October 1990, it was presented to EC negotiators, who agreed to back it.[49]

The 'power play' was an all or nothing approach that involved incorporating GATT, GATS, TRIPs and TRIMs and various other agreements as integral parts of the WTO, 'binding on all members'. After joining the WTO, the EC and the US would withdraw from earlier GATT commitments and be free to erect tariffs and barriers to imports from countries that did not join the WTO. This provided a powerful incentive for countries to join the WTO despite disliking many of the rules it embodied. From 1991, the unpopular agreements were integrated within all negotiating drafts.[50]

Ryan has referred to this sort of strategy as linkage bargaining. The idea is that various issues are linked together, whether or not they have anything to do with each other, so that unpopular rules can be linked with those that opposing countries want and the whole package is agreed to. In the case of GATT, developing countries wanted better access to textile, apparel and agricultural markets; but they had to agree to GATS and TRIMS and TRIPS to get that improved access.[51]

The draft text, which included all the various agreements, was named the Dunkel draft text, after GATT Director General Arthur Dunkel:

> *In India, the Dunkel draft text was labelled 'DDT' and thought to be just as dangerous for the health of the country as the chemical of that name. For those who had seen the Indian-designed patent system produce a flourishing pharmaceuticals sector capable of competing in global markets, DDT was very hard to swallow... Hundreds of thousands of Indian farmers protested in the streets about the patenting of seeds; but there were no negotiations in which the mass unrest could have been utilized to support a position.*[52]

The GATT Secretariat, and particularly the director general, had control of the negotiating drafts, and after Dunkel was replaced by Peter Sutherland as director general, a senior US trade official told Braithwaite and Drahos that Sutherland was 'conspiring with us' so that it was virtually impossible for most countries to change the texts. Countries wanting to change the text had to get consensus support to do so: 'That meant effectively that only [we] and possibly the EU could do it.'[53] Other nations had neither the staff resources nor the economic power to build such a consensus in a short time.

The final TRIPS agreement ensured that patents last for at least 20 years and copyright for 50 years – very generous given that most companies would have recouped their research and development (R&D) costs in a much shorter time than this.[54]

Millennium Round negotiations

Following the successful outcome of the Uruguay Round and the establishment of the WTO in 1995, various business lobbies worked to get a new round of WTO negotiations started that would include issues such as investment and the opening of government procurement to tender from foreign companies. The US Council for International Business (USCIB) claims to have 'helped secure the launch of the new round of WTO trade negotiations' using the networks of the International Chamber of Commerce (ICC) and the Business and Industry Advisory Council of the OECD (BIAC) 'to build overseas support for US business objectives' in the new round. It states:

> American business stands to be a major winner from the new round of trade liberalization talks, launched in November 2001 under the World Trade Organization. USCIB worked diligently to help set the table for a new round, laying out benchmarks for US negotiators in a variety of areas and exploring the possible inclusion of new issues like competition policy, environment and investment.[55]

The Europeans have also played an active role in promoting the new round. The European Round Table of Industrialists (ERT; see Chapter 2) established a working group on foreign economic relations in 1998, chaired by Peter Sutherland, now an ERT member but formerly director general of GATT. It led a delegation to meet with the director general of the WTO, Renato Ruggiero, to discuss the launch of a new round of negotiations and continued to make the case when Mike Moore took over from Ruggiero. The ERT continues to work with the US Business Roundtable (BRT) to ensure the success of this Millennium Round of negotiations.[56]

Similarly, the European employers' association, UNICE, has 7 working groups and more than 20 lobbyists on WTO issues. It worked with the EC to gather support for a new, comprehensive round that would include issues such as investment and government procurement. It was 'by far the most visible European lobby group' at the 1999 Seattle WTO ministerial meeting.[57]

The BRT claimed that any delay in the Millennium Round negotiations would 'result in slower world economic growth... Trade liberalization of goods and services could create annual global income gains of up to US$2.8 trillion by 2015' – gains that would be made primarily by BRT members. For BRT, the round offered 'unrivalled opportunities' to 'increase US access to international markets throughout the world'. BRT joined with ERT, the ICC and the Canadian Council of Chief Executives in 2003 to launch a multimillion dollar advertising campaign to support the Millennium Round. The aim was to persuade the public that further free trade will create billions of dollars' worth of wealth for all concerned.[58]

Business groups had hoped that a new round would begin at the WTO ministerial meeting in Seattle in December 1999 and spent millions lobbying to that end. President Clinton had even promised to cancel the debts owed to the US by the poorest countries, particularly in Africa.[62]

The Seattle host committee was chaired by Bill Gates, CEO of Microsoft, and Philip Condit, CEO of Boeing and chair of BRT's Taskforce on International

BOX 8.1 US ALLIANCE FOR TRADE EXPANSION (US TRADE)

The newly formed US Alliance for Trade Expansion (US Trade) ran a series of 'education' events across the US in the lead up to the Seattle WTO ministerial meeting. It also organized a 'war room' in Seattle in the week before the WTO ministerial meeting 'to provide rapid response from the pro-trade business community to the many allegations expected to be raised by protestors'.[59]

US Trade was chaired by executives from Boeing, Caterpillar and Procter & Gamble. Its steering committee included members of the American Chemistry Council; the National Association of Manufacturers (NAM); the Coalition of Service Industries (CSI; see Chapter 7); the Emergency Committee for American Trade (ECAT); the National Foreign Trade Council (NFTC; see Chapter 10); Ford Motor Company; Texas Instruments; the Business Roundtable (BRT); the US Council for International Business (USCIB), which proclaimed itself a leading member; and the US Chamber of Commerce. It was housed at NAM.[60]

As with other coalitions, its members featured a who's who of American corporations and trade associations, including the American Petroleum Institute, Bayer, Chubb, Consumers for World Trade, DaimlerChrysler, DuPont, Federal Express, Hewlett-Packard, the National Mining Association, Nestlé and Pfizer. It aimed to:

> ...promote the benefits of economic growth, job expansion and higher living standards in the United States as a result of free trade, with a special emphasis on the advantages the US receives by its participation in the rules-based multilateral trade liberalization through the World Trade Organization (WTO).[61]

Trade and Investment. The host committee offered corporations various levels of access to negotiators and ministers according to their level of donation: 'All emerald corporate donors, for example, which gave over a quarter of a million dollars, would receive special access to private events with top government and trade officials at the WTO meetings in Seattle.'[63]

However, at the meeting the US and the EU could not agree on agricultural trade concessions, and developing countries claimed that while they were having to open up their markets, the affluent countries were not making similar concessions. Developing countries, sick and tired of being marginalized in the decision-making process and encouraged by the vigorous street protests going on outside (see Chapter 10), refused to passively go along with any negotiated deal that they had not participated in.[64]

As a result of the developing countries' demands for greater participation, new guidelines were formulated for WTO negotiations that included the need to inform all countries of informal consultations; giving those with an interest an opportunity to be heard; not assuming that one country represents other countries;

and informing all countries of the outcome of informal consultations. However, in practice the only real change in subsequent negotiations was the inclusion of several less developed countries in some consultations. At the next ministerial meeting in Doha in 2001, developing countries again found themselves marginalized. However, this time the US and the EU were more united. This was partly because of the efforts of the TransAtlantic Business Dialogue (TABD).[65]

BOX 8.2 TRANSATLANTIC BUSINESS DIALOGUE (TABD)

The TransAtlantic Business Dialogue (TABD) is a coalition of over 100 European and US top corporate executives, which was formed in 1995. Because its membership consists of corporate chief executive officers (CEOs) of large transnational corporations, TABD has high-level daily access to governments and uses it to pressure them to remove trade barriers, 'including costly inefficiencies caused by excessive regulation'. TABD is jointly convened by the US administration and the European Commission, but 'managed and driven' and funded by industry. The Clinton administration 'established an entire inter-agency working group just to work on the TABD's demands'.[66]

The Corporate Europe Observatory notes that:

> Over the past few years, the TABD has presented its demands in the form of a 'scorecard', setting 'priorities' for governments to focus on, and even going as far as to set 'deadlines' for completion. The audacity of this 'scorecard' approach reflects the cosy relationship the TABD enjoys with government, and its conviction that its recommendations will be carried out.[67]

TABD develops policies that suit big business. The US and the EU then present them to the World Trade Organization (WTO) as 'done deals'. *Public Citizen* notes:

> The TABD has been labelled the 'new paradigm for trade liberalization' by its proponents because it eliminates the 'middle man' from trade policy-making. That middle man is the US and EU governments, and by extension, US and EU citizens and consumer, labour and environmental NGOs [non-governmental organizations].[68]

The TABD gives the US–EU block strategic direction in the WTO negotiations, and this provides a formidable power block to bully and marginalize smaller countries. This was evident at the WTO ministerial meeting in Doha in 2001. An African delegate claimed: 'We made so many suggestions before Doha but they were ignored… We gave texts. We didn't know where they went; but they didn't find their way to the draft declaration.' Similarly, a South Asian delegate pointed out: 'We would object to a text; but it would still appear. We would state we wanted a text added in, and still it would not appear.'[69] Ambassador Chidyausiku of Zimbabwe noted:

*In Doha, the spin-doctors had realized that in Seattle, ministers felt
ignored, and developing countries were prepared to bite the bullet. In
Doha, they created a process, where ministers could go to the Committee
of the Whole (COW) and discuss and raise issues; but nobody was taking
into account what they said. They were just venting their frustration.
That feeling of being part of the process dented their anger of being
uninvolved. But, in fact, there was a smaller group taking the decisions
of the whole.*[70]

Developing nations were denied access to 'green room' discussions. This is a
system of private, informal negotiations between self-selected nations, typically
the US, EU, Canada, Japan, Australia, New Zealand, Switzerland and Norway,
and a few others including a few trusted developing countries. Excluded nations
have to 'hang around in the corridor' waiting to find out what has been decided.
Negotiations continued day and night and small delegations from poorer nations
were worn out from lack of sleep. In addition, the US and the EU put pressure on
the presidents and prime ministers of various African and Asian countries to reign
in their delegates at Doha.[71]

US Trade Representative Robert Zoellick, WTO Director General Mike
Moore and EU Trade Commissioner Pascal Lamy were all promoting the message
that free trade, and, in particular, the proposed new trade round, was part of the
war against terrorism. 'Launching new trade talks and security issues, before only
remotely connected, became one and the same cause... The US and EU WTO
trade agendas, though starkly self-interested, became a small concession in return
for continued good political relations and being part of the new coalition against
terrorism.' In particular, Pakistan and Malaysia, both of which had initially been
very opposed to the new round, became less strident after 11 September 2001.
Both also received some sort of US aid package at this time.[72]

A supposed link between terrorists and those who were opposed to free trade
was also made by various business lobby groups. The ICC stated on its website that
if the Doha talks failed it would 'be acclaimed by all enemies of freer world trade
and investment, including those behind the attacks at the World Trade Center
and the Pentagon.' O'Hare, chair of USCIB, also lumped 'the forces of terror and
anti-globalization' into the same anti-trade category.[73] It was a theme taken up by
US negotiators. Mokhiber and Weissman noted in *Alternet*: 'No one has been more
shameless in linking their agenda to the terror attack than US Trade Representative
Robert Zoellick.'[74]

On the last day the assembly was presented with a document that was even
worse, from the perspective of developing nations, than the previous versions that
they had been negotiating. At this late stage the only choice that countries had was
to acquiesce or object to the text and be blamed for the failure of the talks. In the
post-September 11 atmosphere, where the US was on the lookout for enemies to
blame, no country was willing to do this.[75] Thus, the new round was launched.

Following Doha, a coalition of developing nations presented the WTO with a set of reform measures to ensure that future negotiations would be more fair, open and democratic. However, the powerful players continued to meet in secret to set the agenda of the forthcoming ministerial meeting at Cancún, Mexico, in 2003, and the 'arm-twisting and blackmailing practices', to use EU Trade Commissioner Lamy's words, also continued.[76]

The draft text presented to the Cancún meeting was put together by the WTO without consultation with the full WTO membership and reflected the position of the US and the EU, rather than the developing nations. After days of 'negotiations', a revised draft was presented to the meeting, a day before it was due to end, that still ignored the views of the developing countries, still contained the issues that they had rejected, including investment and government procurement, and failed to make any progress on the issue of free trade in agriculture.[77]

A major reason for the intransigence of the US and the EU in the negotiations was the pressure put on them by business. Not only were various powerful business coalitions pushing for free trade to be expanded in order to incorporate free investment (see Chapter 9), but the agribusiness lobby was well represented at Cancún. The US delegation alone included some 70 corporate advisers, including those representing the interests of agricultural corporations. These interests were also well represented in the EC delegation. In addition, some high-level officials had backgrounds in agribusiness, including the US secretary of agriculture and the chief US agricultural trade negotiator.[78]

While corporate advisers were included in many delegations and had access to negotiating documents, non-governmental organizations (NGOs) and civil society representatives were excluded. Those developing nations that tried to include them were pressured not to, according to an ActionAid report that cited Uganda and Kenya as examples. Similarly, the UK criticized some EU countries for sharing too much information with civil society representatives.[79]

For this round, developing countries had formed coalitions and negotiating blocks to counter the power of the developed nation coalitions, and US and EU attempts to break down these developing nation coalitions were unsuccessful. Although George Bush personally telephoned the heads of state of individual countries, and other countries were offered expanded export quotas and bilateral free trade agreements with the US, most nations stuck to their groupings.[80]

The betrayal felt by the developing nations at seeing the revised draft, the obstinacy of the EU and the US in refusing to give any ground, and the ability of developing countries to maintain a united front and not give in this time led to the failure of the negotiations. The brinkmanship of the powerful countries, which had worked so well in the past, in insisting on agreement to a total package that would include investment and government procurement backfired this time.[81]

Efforts to break down developing nation unity continued after the meeting. The ActionAid report on the negotiations notes:

The central strand to this strategy is to turn developing countries against each other, breaking off individual countries from broader coalitions and offering preferential treatment to favoured groupings if they distance themselves from more critical voices at the WTO. This divide-and-rule strategy is particularly dangerous at a time when WTO negotiations have again become increasingly secretive.[82]

Chakravarthi Raghavan, editor of the *South–North Development Monitor* (SUNS), says that in talks during 2004, the chair of the WTO's Non-Agricultural Market Access (NAMA) negotiating group met with individual and small groups of countries, during which he showed them proposals to get their comments but would not give them the documents so they were unable to take them back to their governments to discuss them.[83]

Further negotiations in 2004 resulted in the dropping of investment, government procurement and competition policy from the agenda of the current round of negotiations; but in return 'developing nations will have to open up their economies to imports of manufactured goods and to large service companies in return for vague promises on agricultural reform'. According to Peter Hardstaff from the World Development Movement (WDM), speaking in August 2004 after a framework agreement had been reached for ensuing WTO negotiations:

...the negotiating process has once again been characterized by secrecy, power politics and the exclusion of the poorest countries. The past week of talks has seen Africa sidelined, while the group of 'five interested parties' – USA, EU, Brazil, Australia and India – has negotiated on the rest of the world's behalf.[84]

NOTES

1 Quoted in Maria Elena Hurtado, 'More Power to the World Trade Organization? The International Trade Controversy', London, Panos, November 1999, p10.
2 Pratt quoted in Michael A. Santoro and Lynn Sharp Paine, 'Pfizer: Global Protection of Intellectual Property', Harvard Business School 1995, p6.
3 Peter Drahos and John Braithwaite, 'Who Owns the Knowledge Economy? Political Organising Behind TRIPS', *The Corner House Briefing*, no 32, 2004, p5; Santoro and Paine, 'Pfizer', pp6, 15–16.
4 Drahos and Braithwaite, 'Who Owns the Knowledge Economy?', p5; Santoro and Paine, 'Pfizer', p2.
5 Michael P. Ryan, *Knowledge Diplomacy: Global Competition and the Politics of Intellectual Property*, Washington, DC, Brookings Institution Press, 1998, pp67–8.
6 Santoro and Paine, 'Pfizer', p7.
7 Drahos and Braithwaite, 'Who Owns the Knowledge Economy?', p7; Ryan, *Knowledge Diplomacy*, p105.

8   Drahos and Braithwaite, 'Who Owns the Knowledge Economy?', p11; Ryan, *Knowledge Diplomacy*, p68.

9   Barry Fox, 'Europe Fights Tide of Absurd Patents', *New Scientist*, 8 January, 2005, p22; Drahos and Braithwaite, 'Who Owns the Knowledge Economy?', p8.

10 Santoro and Paine, 'Pfizer', p9.

11 Drahos and Braithwaite, 'Who Owns the Knowledge Economy?', p8; Ryan, *Knowledge Diplomacy*, p69.

12 Drahos and Braithwaite, 'Who Owns the Knowledge Economy?', p8.

13 *Ibid.*, p10.

14 *Ibid.*, p9.

15 Ryan, *Knowledge Diplomacy*, p108; Drahos and Braithwaite, 'Who Owns the Knowledge Economy?', p5; Santoro and Paine, 'Pfizer', pp6, 15–16.

16 Drahos and Braithwaite, 'Who Owns the Knowledge Economy?', p9.

17 Ryan, *Knowledge Diplomacy*, p69; John Braithwaite and Peter Drahos, *Global Business Regulation*, Cambridge, Cambridge University Press, 2000, p204.

18 Edmund J. Pratt, 'Intellectual Property', Pfizer, 1995, www.pfizer.com/are/about_public/mn_about_intellectualpropfrm.html.

19 Quoted in Santoro and Paine, 'Pfizer', p9.

20 Hurtado, 'More Power to the World Trade Organisation?', p1.

21 *Ibid.*, pp1, 5.

22 *Ibid.*, p9.

23 'Titanic Battle for the World's Future', *Third World Resurgence*, November, 1990.

24 Steve Dryden, *Trade Warriors: USTR and the American Crusade for Free Trade*, New York, Oxford University Press, 1995, p5; Bob Catley, *Globalising Australian Capitalism*, Cambridge, Cambridge University Press, 1996, p12; Peter F. Cowhey and Jonathan D. Aronson, *Managing the World Economy: The Consequences of Corporate Alliances*, New York, Council on Foreign Relations Press, 1993, p13.

25 Leon Brittan, *A Diet of Brussels: The Changing Face of Europe*, London, Little, Brown and Company, 2000, p2.

26 *Ibid.*, pp49–50.

27 Richard H. Steinberg, 'In the Shadow of Law or Power? Consensus-Based Bargaining and Outcomes in the GATT/WTO', *International Organization*, vol 56, no 2, 2002, p343.

28 *Ibid.*, p345; Debi Barker and Jerry Mander, 'Invisible Government. The World Trade Organization: Global Government for the New Millennium', Sausalito, CA, International Forum on Globalization (IFG), October 1999, p5.

29 John Hilary, 'Divide and Rule: The EU and US Response to Developing Country Alliances at the WTO', ActionAid International, July 2004, p4.

30 Steinberg, 'In the Shadow of Law or Power?', pp345, 360–1; Brittan, *A Diet of Brussels*, p44; Moore quoted in Kwa, 'Power Politics in the WTO', Bangkok, Focus on the Global South, January 2003, p18.

31 Quoted in Kwa, 'Power Politics in the WTO', p36.

32 Steinberg, 'In the Shadow of Law or Power?', pp354–5.

33 Quoted in Walden Bello in Preface to Kwa, 'Power Politics in the WTO', p8.

34 *Ibid.*, pp12, 44.

35 *Ibid.*, pp40–41.

36 *Ibid.,* p40.
37 Steinberg, 'In the Shadow of Law or Power?', p355.
38 Braithwaite and Drahos, *Global Business Regulation,* p184.
39 Daniel C. Esty, 'The World Trade Organization's Legitimacy Crisis', *World Trade Review,* vol 1, no 1, 2002, p10; Braithwaite and Drahos, *Global Business Regulation,* pp209–11.
40 Esty, 'The World Trade Organization's Legitimacy Crisis', p11.
41 Chakravarthi Raghavan, *Recolonization: GATT, the Uruguay Round & the Third World,* London, Zed Books, 1990, p76.
42 James Goodman, 'Stopping a Juggernaut: The Anti-MAI Campaign', in James Goodman and Patricia Ranald (eds) *Stopping the Juggernaut: Public Interest Versus the Multilateral Agreement on Investment,* Sydney, Pluto Press, 2000, p20.
43 Hurtado, 'More Power to the World Trade Organization?', p4.
44 Ryan, *Knowledge Diplomacy,* p108.
45 *Ibid.,* p108.
46 Drahos and Braithwaite, 'Who Owns the Knowledge Economy?', p13; Santoro and Paine, 'Pfizer', p16.
47 Drahos and Braithwaite, 'Who Owns the Knowledge Economy?', p17.
48 *Ibid.,* p22; Santoro and Paine, 'Pfizer', pp10, 18; IPC, Keidanren and UNICE, *Basic Framework of GATT Provisions on Intellectual Property: Statement of Views of the European, Japanese and United States Business Communities,* The Intellectual Property Committee, Keidanren and UNICE, 1988.
49 Steinberg, 'In the Shadow of Law or Power?', p360.
50 *Ibid.,* p360.
51 Ryan, *Knowledge Diplomacy,* pp92–4.
52 Drahos and Braithwaite, 'Who Owns the Knowledge Economy?',p28.
53 Quoted in Braithwaite and Drahos, *Global Business Regulation,* p196.
54 Hurtado, 'More Power to the World Trade Organization?', p18.
55 USCIB, 'Policy Advocacy', US Council for International Business, www.uscib.org/index.asp?documentID=824 accessed 18 May 2003.
56 ERT, 'ERT Highlights 1983–2003', Brussels, European Round Table of Industrialists, June 2003, pp68, 97.
57 CEO, 'Business Responses to Seattle', *Corporate Europe Observer,* April, 2000, www.corporateeurope.org/observer6/businessresponse.html; CEO, 'European Industry in Seattle', *Corporate Europe Observer,* April, 2000, www.corporateeurope.org/observer6/europeanindustry.html.
58 BRT, 'The Business Roundtable Urges WTO Members to Complete Bold Market Access Agreement to Energize World Economic Growth', The Business Roundtable, 16 May, 2003, www.brtable.org/press.cfm/929; 'Business Leaders See Coming Year as Pivotal for Enhancing America's Competitiveness', *PR Newswire,* 12 January, 2005; National Journal cited in InvestmentWatch, 'US Business Round Table (BRT)', Coporate Europe Observatory, www.investmentwatch.org/tncdb/BRT.html accessed 30 June 2003.
59 USTrade, 'Unique Coalition Formed to Support Trade: Alliance to Promote Benefits of Trade, Importance of WTO Ministerial', USCIB, 15 April, 1999, www.uscib.org/index.asp?documentID=1376; Michael Paulson, 'Business Leaders Fight Back

against Anti-WTO Forces', in *Who Owns the WTO? Corporations and Global Trade*, www.corpwatch.org/, Corporate Watch, 1999.

60 USTrade, 'Unique Coalition Formed to Support Trade'; USCIB, 'Adoption of Trade Promotion Authority – A Big Step Forward', *USCIB E-Newsletter*, August/ September, 2002, www.envoynews.com/uscib/e_article000092118.cfm

61 USTrade, 'USTrade', IDFA, 10 May, 2002, www.idfa.org/intl/ustrade.cfm; USTrade, 'Unique Coalition Formed to Support Trade'.

62 John Madeley, *Hungry for Trade: How the Poor Pay for Free Trade*, Global Issues Series, London and New York, Zed Books, 2000, pp11, 16.

63 Tony Clarke, *By What Authority! Unmasking and Challenging the Global Corporations' Assault on Democracy through the World Trade Organization*, Polaris Institute and International Forum on Globalization, 1999, p1.

64 Madeley, *Hungry for Trade*, pp13–14; Kwa, 'Power Politics in the WTO', p19.

65 Kwa, 'Power Politics in the WTO', p19; CEO, 'TABD Back on Track?' *Corporate Europe Observer*, December, 2001, www.corporateeurope.org/observer10/tabd.html; Public Citizen, 'MAI Shell Game – the Transatlantic Economic Partnership (TEP)', Public Citizen, www.citizen.org/print_article.cfm?ID=1050 accessed 3 July 2003.

66 TABD, 'The TABD in 2002', TransAtlantic Business Dialogue, 2002, http://tabd. com/about/about.html; TABD, 'About the TABD', TransAtlantic Business Dialogue, www.tabd.com/about accessed 6 November 2004; Public Citizen, 'MAI Shell Game – the Transatlantic Economic Partnership (TEP)'.

67 Belén Balanyá, *et al.*, *Europe Inc. Regional and Global Restructuring and the Rise of Corporate Power*, London, Pluto Press, 2000, p107.

68 Public Citizen, 'MAI Shell Game – The Transatlantic Economic Partnership (TEP)'.

69 Quoted in Kwa, 'Power Politics in the WTO', p23.

70 Quoted in *Ibid.*, p26.

71 Jeffrey J. Schott and Jayashree Watal, 'Decision-Making in the WTO', Institute for International Economics, March, 2000, www.iie.com/publications/pb/pb00-2.htm; Kwa, 'Power Politics in the WTO', pp26–29.

72 Kwa, 'Power Politics in the WTO', pp32–3.

73 Quoted in Oliver Hoedeman and Ann Doherty, 'Joining Forces: Big Business Rallies after Seattle', in Eveline Lubbers (ed) *Battling Big Business: Countering Greenwash, Infiltration and Other Forms of Bullying*, Devon, UK, Green Books, 2002, p77.

74 Russell Mokhiber and Robert Weissman, 'The Wartime Opportunists', *Alternet*, 3 October, 2001, www.alternet.org/print.html?StoryID=11638.

75 Kwa, 'Power Politics in the WTO', pp29–31.

76 Hilary, 'Divide and Rule', p5.

77 *Ibid.*, pp6, 10.

78 *Ibid.*, p22.

79 *Ibid.*, p23.

80 *Ibid.*

81 *Ibid.*, pp11–12.

82 *Ibid.*, p24.

83 Kanaga Raja, 'North Attempts to Split Developing-Country Alliances', *South–North Development Monitor*, 27 July, 2004.

84 WDM, 'New Deal Exposes Flaws of Trade (Offs) System', World Development Movement, 1 August 2004.

9

Deregulating Investment

...the primary objective of the corporate 'investment' agenda is to ensure the ability of speculators and multinational corporations to move capital in and out of countries without governmental involvement or public interest rules.   PUBLIC CITIZEN[1]

This [Multilateral Agreement on Investment] could well be the most anti-democratic, anti-people, anti-community international agreement ever conceived by supposedly democratic governments.   DAVID KORTEN[2]

In 1991, while the Uruguay Round of the General Agreement on Tariffs and Trade (GATT) negotiations was still under way, the US Council for International Business (USCIB) began working on the idea of a 'free investment' agreement that would enable US corporations to unconditionally invest their money in any sector of any country, and for those investments to be protected. 'For US multinationals, the new world trading order was being increasingly conceptualized in terms of investment flows rather than movement of goods.'[3]

The USCIB was founded in 1945 to promote free trade and to represent US businesses in the United Nations (UN). Today, its membership includes over 300 transnational companies, law firms and business associations and it remains committed to 'promoting open markets and freer trade around the world'. Its executive committee includes executives of 3M, ExxonMobil, General Electric, AT&T, Du Pont, Nike, Dow Chemical and Chubb Corporation.[4]

The USCIB works through a number of committees and working groups made up of corporate executives. 'Members are frequently invited to join US government or business observer delegations to major international summits, conferences and meetings.' The USCIB claims to give 'business a seat at the table', enabling it to influence regulatory decisions around the world through the organization's 'unparalleled global network of industry affiliations', its access to domestic and international policy-makers, and its 'reputation for reliable policy advice'.[5]

USCIB's Investment Committee sought 'the establishment and maintenance of an international environment conducive to foreign investment'.[6] Some elements of investment deregulation had been included in the existing World Trade Organization (WTO) agreements. The Trade-Related Investment Measures

---

BOX 9.1 THE ORGANISATION FOR ECONOMIC CO-OPERATION AND DEVELOPMENT (OECD)

Formed in the 1960s, the Paris-based Organisation for Economic Co-operation and Development (OECD) brings together representatives of the 30 wealthiest countries. The OECD operates as an economic think tank for its member countries, providing research and analysis. Its agenda is neo-liberal reform – trade and investment deregulation, privatization, workplace 'reform' and so on. These countries get together to make agreements and set policies and 'to promote rules of the game in areas where multilateral agreement is necessary for individual countries to make progress in a globalized economy'.[10]

(TRIMS) agreement prevents member nations from discriminating in favour of companies based in their own country, even if it is for the purpose of developing national productive capability, local skills or helping national industries to mature. Nor can member nations impose conditions on foreign investment, or provide incentives to encourage foreign companies to use local labour or local materials or to sell their product to local consumers. Such policies, usually put in place to ensure that foreign investment will benefit local people, were to be phased out over two to seven years depending upon a nation's level of development.[8]

The General Agreement on Trade in Services (GATS) also included elements of an open investment agreement, allowing foreign investment in agreed service sectors without discrimination. However, transnational corporations want foreign investment to be deregulated in all areas of trade and services. Similarly, the 1997 Financial Services Agreement contains elements of financial investment deregulation, but not enough to satisfy major corporations.

A comprehensive multilateral agreement on investment became a 'top priority for lobby groups such as the European Round Table of Industrialists (ERT), the European employers' federation [Union of Industrial and Employers' Confederations of Europe] (UNICE) and the International Chamber of Commerce (ICC)', as well as for US-based lobby groups. The 1000 largest transnational corporations (TNCs) headquartered in OECD countries – particularly the US, the European Union (EU) and Japan – are responsible for most of the foreign investment around the world.[9]

Yet, the Uruguay Round negotiations showed that an international investment treaty would meet strong resistance from developing countries. In order to bypass this opposition, it was decided to secretly negotiate a comprehensive treaty in the OECD, and then to pressure developing countries to sign up.

To this end, the USCIB worked with the Business and Industry Advisory Committee (BIAC), which has consultative status with the OECD. The USCIB represents US business on BIAC. BIAC became an enthusiastic supporter of an OECD agreement on investment and worked on it from 1991. In March 1995, the USCIB put together a statement of US business objectives which it submitted to BIAC, and this 'formed the basis of the formal BIAC submission to the OECD'.[10]

In May 1995, formal negotiations began within the OECD for a Multilateral Agreement on Investment (MAI). This was applauded by the USCIB, which stated: 'Over the past four years, the USCIB and its counterparts in BIAC have provided business views on pre-negotiation work on the MAI and have urged the OECD to move toward negotiation of a wider investment instrument.'[11]

BIAC was involved in the formal negotiations with the OECD's MAI Negotiating Group, as well as informal consultations and lobbying:

> *BIAC reiterates its strong urging to all OECD member governments to conclude an MAI embodying high standards of liberalization and protection of investors in the shortest possible time. In our view, this continues to be the most important OECD work.*[12]

In Australia, the MAI was supported by the Australian Chamber of Commerce and Industry (ACCI) and the Business Council of Australia (BCA) – both members of BIAC – as well as the Centre for Independent Studies (CIS) think tank and the Treasury, which argued that it 'would help Australian companies gain greater access to foreign markets'. In fact, the ACCI, BCA and the CIS criticized the draft agreement for being too weak.[13]

The International Chamber of Commerce (ICC) has been credited with designing the first draft of the MAI. The ICC includes members such as USCIB and the ACCI. The MAI negotiators relied heavily upon the ICC so that 'almost all of the proposals in the ICC's April 1996 *Multilateral Rules for Investment* report can be found in the first MAI draft, completed nine months later'. What is more, 'the draft MAI proposed the ICC's own court of arbitration as one of the three possible bodies to be used by corporations to resolve disputes'.[14]

The ICC was able to use its ready access to government leaders and its consultative status at major international summits to lobby for the MAI at the highest levels. It argued that governments should have to guarantee the security of investments made in their countries but should not be able to impose performance requirements on foreign investors.[15]

The USCIB had various other points of access to the MAI negotiations (see Figure 9.1). It arranged direct access for its members to the chair of the OECD's MAI Negotiating Group, Frans Engering. It had its own working group on MAI, which claimed to have 'helped shape US negotiating positions by providing business views and technical advice on specific policy issues at regular meetings with US negotiators before and after each MAI negotiating session'.[16] It lobbied other business groups such as Keidanren in Japan, which became an active supporter of the MAI.

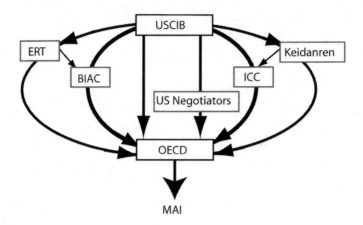

MAI

Figure 9.1 *Business lobbying for the Multilateral Agreement on Investment (MAI)*

Note: The US Council for International Business (USCIB) was able to influence the Organisation for Economic Co-operation and Development (OECD) on the MAI both directly and through its influence with US negotiators and various lobby groups. The USCIB was the US representative on the Business and Industry Advisory Council (BIAC) and the International Chamber of Commerce (ICC). It was also influential with like-minded business organizations such as the European Round Table of Industrialists (ERT) and Keidanren in Japan.

The European Round Table of Industrialists (ERT; see Chapter 2) had also been pushing for a 'GATT for investment' since the early 1990s. The European Commission (EC) played a key role, led by Commissioner Leon Brittan, in co-ordinating the positions of member states in the negotiations. Brittan stated:

> *We need to tear down the existing obstacles to investment and stop new hurdles being thrown up in its way. Nothing short of a comprehensive set of binding international rules will create the level playing field which is so vital for the European economy.*[17]

Transnational corporations (TNCs) lobbied national governments and the OECD individually, and through sectoral industry associations and lobby groups. Business coalitions in various other countries also actively lobbied for the MAI. In Canada, for example, MAI proponents included the Canadian Business Council on National Issues (a BIAC member and the Canadian equivalent of the US and European business round tables), the Canadian Chamber of Commerce and the Canadian Council for International Business.[18]

The Corporate Europe Observatory noted that the 'cosy consultations between governments and corporate lobby groups throughout the MAI drafting process' were evidence of the way in which 'the business agenda is wholeheartedly embraced by several of the most influential negotiating delegations'.[19]

Foreign investment

Until the 1980s, developing nations got most of their foreign capital through loans from banks, governmental and international institutions, and from aid. These sources of capital declined during the 1980s, to be partly replaced by direct investment by private investors. At the same time, interest rates increased and commodity prices fell, further depleting the capital that poorer countries had access to. A Corporate Europe Observatory briefing reported in early 1998 that 'since 1995, governments all over the world have made some 600 changes in national investment legislation, 95 per cent of which have resulted in greater liberalization'.[20]

There are two main forms of foreign investment: foreign direct investment (FDI), in which the owner has a controlling share, and portfolio investment, such as the purchase of stocks, bonds or other financial assets. FDI has been growing rapidly around the world, 'outstripping growth in international trade'. The figures have fluctuated over the years; but during the late 1990s about 85 per cent of FDI came from OECD-based corporations.[21]

The difference between loans and foreign investment as a source of capital is primarily in who decides where the investment will go. With loans, a government can borrow money for projects it wishes to see completed, including public services. In contrast, foreign investors decide which projects they will invest in on the basis of likely financial returns. With a loan, the outflows, in terms of interest payments, are scheduled and regular, whereas foreign investment, particularly portfolio investment, can be withdrawn at the discretion of the investor. Furthermore, the rates of interest on loans, even from commercial banks, are often far less than the rates of return expected by foreign investors. The actual rates of return on FDI in developing countries during the late 1990s were around 16–18 per cent annually, according to the World Bank, and even higher in sub-Saharan Africa, where they were 24–30 per cent per year.[22]

Increasingly, corporations based in OECD countries have invested in developing countries to take advantage of cheap labour, weak environmental standards and access to cheap raw materials. Some developing countries have also become increasingly attractive because of their growing markets, or their proximity to growing markets. As markets in affluent Western countries become more saturated and opportunities are reduced, the attractiveness of developing countries to TNCs has increased.[23]

Free market advocates argue that a deregulated investment regime is good for developing countries because it attracts foreign investors and provides those countries with much needed capital for jobs, infrastructure and technological advancement. However, the extent to which this foreign investment makes additional capital available for such development is questionable. Between one half and two thirds of FDI worldwide consists of mergers and acquisitions of existing companies.[24]

Developing countries have tried to impose conditions on foreign investment to ensure that it is compatible with development needs and that outflows of capital are controlled.[25] Conditions include requirements and regulations:

- to prevent the practices of TNCs and cartels that 'distort trade through allocation of global markets and by restraining or blocking exports from a given country';[26]
- for investors to purchase some local products and materials;
- to prevent transfer pricing and 'predatory pricing to eliminate competitors';[27]
- for technology transfer and technology licensing on reasonable terms;
- to ensure that foreign companies operate for a minimum time after they are set up so that they will reinvest some of their profits within the country.[28]

It is just such requirements and regulations that an investment agreement would prevent. The South Commission argued that:

> ... it is a travesty of the facts to describe as trade distortions measures adopted by the host countries to minimize the harmful and maximize the favourable impact of foreign investments on the national economy. In a world of monopolies, transfer pricing and internationalization of economic processes represented by the TNCs, investment regulatory measures are not trade distorting.[29]

Critics of deregulated foreign investment have also argued that investment deregulation would give foreign companies the same logging or mining rights as local companies, and that this would inevitably lead to more rapid environmental degradation.[30] Oxfam International points out:

> The economies of many developing countries are often dominated by sectors, such as mining or agriculture, which require careful management if they are to generate long-term benefits for local people and not be overexploited for short-term gain. Oxfam research shows that investment in the extractive sector can have adverse consequences for the environment and long-term development, locking countries into patterns of export activity that are prone to boom-and-bust cycles, which generate weak gains for human development. Many governments consequently restrict foreign ownership of these key industries, require approval for such acquisitions or insist that they be carried out as joint ventures.[31]

William Witherell, director of finance, fiscal and enterprise affairs at the OECD, noted: 'Although investment regimes have become much more open and welcoming in the recent past, there is no assurance that they will remain so in the years to come.'[32] The aim of any investment agreement is not only to further deregulate investment, but to lock in any deregulation that has already occurred. However, as the Corporate Europe Observer has recognized:

> *The events now unfolding in Argentina and other Latin American countries, for example, where there is growing demand for more socially just policies following the failure of the neo-liberal economic model, demonstrate how crucial it is that economies refrain from permanently binding investment liberalization with the WTO.*[33]

Investors have pushed for deregulation of investment in various fora, including the WTO, the International Monetary Fund (IMF), the World Bank and the OECD, as well as through bilateral and regional agreements. This 'forum-hopping' avoids the risks of putting all of the deregulation eggs into one basket. Another tactic associated with forum-hopping is 'leap-frogging' – that is, establishing greater promotion and protection of foreign investment in one forum (for example, a bilateral or regional agreement) and then attempting to match, or exceed, those standards in other fora.[34]

THE MULTILATERAL AGREEMENT ON INVESTMENT (MAI)

Speaking at an informal OECD conference in 1994, Jonathan Startup, head of multilateral trade negotiations in the UK Department of Trade and Industry (DTI), noted the difficulties in reaching agreement on investment deregulation. He suggested: 'It may be that the best way forward is to start by developing a set of rules in the OECD before trying to widen the debate into the WTO.'[35]

Proponents believed that confining the negotiations to the OECD would enable a 'high standard' agreement to be reached fairly quickly – that is, a comprehensive, binding agreement with high levels of investment protection.[36] Pressure could then be put on developing countries who wanted to attract foreign investment to sign up to it. According to Witherell at the OECD: 'Signing up to the MAI will indicate loudly and clearly to investors that the country concerned subscribes to the highest standards in market access, legal protection and equitable treatment.' Such countries would not be able to renegotiate the MAI as it would be a done deal, but would be able to lodge temporary reservations to some of its provisions.[37]

The ICC recognized that 'most of the problems addressed under the agreement occur outside the OECD membership. It is thus crucial that as many non-OECD countries as possible accede to the agreement.'[38] Witherell admitted that many WTO members were unlikely to sign up to the MAI; but when negotiations for a WTO investment agreement were undertaken in the future, 'it is reasonable to expect that the MAI would serve as a reference, as would other recent investment agreements such as the North American Free Trade Agreement (NAFTA)'.[39]

Another advantage of using the OECD as a negotiating forum was that it was easier to keep negotiations secret. Although the commencement of the negotiations was announced, early drafts of the MAI were not publicly available until a confidential draft of the MAI was leaked to the Council of Canadians, who posted it on the internet in 1997 (later drafts were put on the internet by the OECD itself). There was so little media coverage of the progress of MAI negotiations before this that the MAI was voted the number one under-reported story in the US mainstream media in 1998 by Project Censored, based at Sonoma University.[40]

Knowledge of the MAI negotiations was even limited in certain business and government circles. A few government ministries and departments (for example, commerce and trade) were heavily involved, while others were excluded. Even the US Congress was not kept informed of the negotiations. A *Business Week* report in February 1998 noted that 'most law-makers have never even heard of the Multilateral Agreement on Investment because secretive talks by the Clinton administration have been carried out beneath congressional radar'. It described the MAI as 'the explosive trade deal you've never heard of'.[41]

The details of governmental negotiating positions were also kept secret to a large degree, especially in the early phases of the negotiations. By contrast, many corporations and their lobby groups had considerable involvement in developing national positions on the MAI. The MAI was, in fact, driven by OECD-based TNCs and their political allies.

The MAI would have enabled corporations 'to move capital in and out of countries without governmental involvement or public interest rules'; to compete with local companies in every sector of the economy; and to buy any business or property, from natural resources to defence industries. On top of this, corporations wanted 'the right to sue governments for cash damages (paid from public funds) for restitution' if investor rights were violated.[42]

The MAI would have reduced the ability of national governments to put restrictions on foreign investment in their countries or to favour local companies over TNCs. Such restrictions were called 'disciplines'. The agreement was to cover all forms of investment in all sectors and at every level of government, including health, education, cultural, banking and essential public services. As a result, a nation would not be able to favour national firms as owners of a privatized water or electricity company. Nor could it restrict foreign investment in fishing, agriculture or forestry in order to restrict exploitation of natural resources.[43]

Sanctions against companies on the basis of their environmental or human rights records would not have been allowed. Government policies, including those that gave preferences to small businesses, minorities or women and those in developing countries that sought to keep farmland under peasant control, could all have been challenged. Countries that wanted to foster local development through conditions on investment, such as use of local suppliers, materials or labour or technology transfer, would have been prohibited, as would restrictions on capital flows out of a country.[44]

The MAI would have prevented environmental legislation that could be argued to impose barriers to free investment in the same way that the WTO prevents environmental legislation that provides barriers to free trade (see Chapter 6). And environmental regulations that imposed costs on foreign investors or reduced their profits may have been cited as 'uncompensated expropriations'. Similarly, the MAI cited boycotts, public protests and strikes as actions that might be considered expropriations because of their impact on profits, for which taxpayers might have to compensate investors.[45]

The MAI was intended to be binding, and non-compliance would have resulted in corporations suing governments for millions of dollars, perhaps hundreds of millions, in compensation. Corporations would have no obligations placed on them in return for the added protections, and any attempt by governments to impose such obligations would be banned by the MAI. According to one commentator:

> The treaty, in effect, subordinates the right of elected governments to set national economic policy to the right of national corporations and investors to conduct business – investing and divesting – however they see fit.[46]

MAI negotiations bog down

In February 1997, OECD governments each submitted a list of exceptions – that is, sectors that they wanted to be exempt from MAI coverage. These exceptions turned out to be numerous and, in some cases, open ended. This generated considerable conflict amongst member governments and their business lobbies. Disputed exceptions included the EU's intention to retain positive discrimination for investment within regional economic integration organizations (such as the EU itself); the French-led push for cultural industries to be entirely exempt from MAI provisions; the US intention to apply MAI disciplines to the federal level only; and the determination of the US government to maintain sanctions on foreign companies that invest in or trade with Cuba, Libya or Iran.

After the MAI draft text was leaked, public debate escalated. What the international community found 'was so serious and shocking, that the MAI has now emerged as a top or high priority campaign issue for many citizen organizations'.[47] National governments came under increasing pressure to reveal details about their negotiating positions and to modify those positions.

In October 1997, non-governmental organizations (NGOs) from over 70 countries presented their concerns to the OECD secretary general and MAI negotiators from various countries:

The NGOs included Friends of the Earth International, the World Wide Fund for Nature International, the Third World Network, Public Citizen ... the World Development Movement (UK), as well as groups based in Canada, Germany, France, Holland, Central Europe, Mexico, Ghana, India, Bangladesh and Nepal.[48]

A joint statement presented to the OECD, endorsed by over 565 NGOs based in 68 countries, said: 'The draft MAI is completely unbalanced. It elevates the rights of investors far above those of governments, local communities, citizens, workers and the environment.' It went on:

There is an obvious need for multilateral regulation of investments in view of the scale of social and environmental disruption created by the increasing mobility of capital. However, the intention of the MAI is not to regulate investments but to regulate governments. As such, the MAI is unacceptable.[49]

Critics noted that the MAI would undermine international environmental agreements, such as the Kyoto Protocol on Climate Change, the Basel Convention on Hazardous Waste and the Convention of Biological Diversity. The World Business Council on Sustainable Development (WBCSD) lent its support to the MAI in an attempt to give it green credentials. WBCSD's agenda of 'promoting global market liberalization and self-regulation by business instead of government intervention as a recipe for sustainable development' accorded with MAI goals. Its membership also overlapped with BIAC.[50]

There were moves to belatedly include some token environmental and labour clauses in the MAI in order to assuage critics and to help national governments ratify the agreement; but this was very much opposed by business groups.[51] BIAC threatened to withdraw its support if this happened and the USCIB argued vociferously against the proposed clauses. Australia and New Zealand were amongst the countries that most strongly opposed the inclusion of labour or environmental standards in the MAI.[52]

ICC President Helmut Maucher proclaimed that he had lost his enthusiasm for the MAI as a result of the proposed extra 'social wording'. The ICC argued that the 'MAI is not the right place in which to set specific levels of environmental protection' and that 'any attempt by OECD governments to use the MAI as a basis for defining and promulgating core labour standards would pre-empt ongoing discussion on these issues at the International Labour Organization'.[53]

In effect, attempts to water down the MAI to mute the growing opposition were out of the question from the corporate point of view because that would defeat the whole goal of a 'high standard' agreement.[54] This meant that elements of the opposition could not be co-opted with promises of compromises, as so often happens with other agreements.

The anti-MAI campaign picked up pace in early 1998. Because of the wide scope of the proposed agreement, opposition was broad. It included unions, environmental and consumer groups, human and indigenous rights groups, local and regional governments, and church groups. Opposition to the MAI in developing countries also grew, and links were forged between anti-MAI campaigners in those countries and those in OECD countries.[55]

The MAI negotiations were suspended for six months in April 1998 to allow time for proponents to build up popular support for it. An OECD Ministerial Statement argued that investment was 'an engine of growth, employment, sustainable development and rising living standards in both developed and developing countries'. The USCIB wrote in the *Washington Times* that the MAI would benefit the US and increase 'the economic pie' globally.[56]

The OECD embarked on a 'strategy of information, communication and explication' and belated consultations. These consultations did not aim at true participation, but persuasion. *Public Citizen* described the 'MAI charm offensive' as aiming 'to lull with false satisfaction and pacify by presentation of seats near the "table" the MAI's critics who have been effectively demanding major substantive changes in trade and investment policies'. However, *Public Citizen* pointed out that there was no intention to significantly change the text of the MAI and the seats near the table would merely allow NGOs 'to observe already done deals', while distracting them from making 'meaningful substantive demands'.[57]

The *Financial Times* lamented that the OECD had been 'ambushed by a horde of vigilantes'. The *Economist* described the 'sinking of the MAI' and speculated that an expected extension of MAI negotiations 'will most likely be a stalling tactic until the MAI can be transferred to the WTO'.[58]

In September 1998, the USCIB defended the collusion between business and OECD governments, and the exclusion of other interested parties from deliberations on the MAI, by asserting that 'civil society has become a mantra' and, in any case, the corporate sector has a 'vital – and unique – role in civil society'. Governments needed the 'technical expertise' of the business sector, the USCIB argued, whereas 'one-issue groups cannot possibly provide the same breadth of advice needed by governments in any sophisticated trade negotiation'. The USCIB also claimed that corporations often provide governments with proprietary information to help in formulating negotiating positions, and that it would be inappropriate to share this information with NGOs and unions.[59]

Timothy Deal, senior vice president of the USCIB, characterized MAI opposition as 'Flat Earth Society meets the black helicopter crowd'. Deal asserted that the media often acted as the unwitting tool of activists determined to stop the MAI. In line with the free market dogma that what is good for business is good for everyone, Deal asserted that 'We in the American business community believe that MAI is good not only for business but for the United States, generally.'[60]

The exclusion of developing countries from the negotiations was particularly difficult to justify since they were expected to sign on later. A March 1998 article in the *Economist* neatly summarized a number of developing country objections:

> Few developing countries seem prepared to sign something they did not help to shape. Instead, the governments of developing countries increasingly see MAI as an exercise in neo-colonialism, designed to give rich-world investors the upper hand. This unease has been handled badly. The OECD's constant reference to MAI's 'high standards' has given the impression that standards in non-OECD countries are decidedly low. Developing countries also object that MAI would offer them little because they cannot trade concessions on foreign investment for advantages in other areas, such as freer access to rich countries for their farm products.[61]

In April 1998, OECD ministers welcomed the 'full participation as observers' of eight non-OECD countries to the MAI negotiations 'with a view to their becoming founding members of the MAI'. The eight countries were Argentina, Brazil, Chile, Estonia, Hong Kong, China, Latvia, Lithuania and the Slovak Republic.[62] However, 'consultation' with developing country governments, or even their 'full participation as observers', was clearly no substitute for their inclusion in negotiations.

Support for trade and investment deregulation was further undermined by the 1997 East Asian financial crises. It is generally believed that the crisis was caused by the unregulated flow of foreign investment capital into and then out of Asia (see Chapter 3). For example, Professor Jagdish Bhagwati, a former adviser to the director general of GATT and world authority on trade liberalization, blamed excessive capital mobility for the financial crises in Mexico in 1994 and in Asia in 1997.[63]

Significant unilateral financial deregulation had occurred during the 1990s, even without any multilateral agreement. Developing countries were sometimes coerced into unilateral deregulation in fulfilment of their loan conditions. Financial deregulation, like privatization and trade liberalization, were common elements of World Bank and IMF structural adjustment programmes (see Chapter 3).[64]

Developing countries now try to regulate the flow of speculative capital in order to avoid the sort of crisis that hit Asia in 1997. They put restrictions on how much money can come into their countries so that domestic economies are not swamped by it and they try to favour long-term over short-term investment. Some countries, such as Chile, even tried to limit the outflow of capital by having rules requiring investment finance to be in the country for at least one year, although returns on that investment could still leave the country. It is just such restrictions that financial 'liberalization' seeks to prevent. Nevertheless, business coalitions blatantly cite the Asian crisis in support of their liberalization efforts.[65]

In October 1998, French Prime Minister Lionel Jospin announced that France would not participate in the upcoming MAI Negotiating Group meeting, announcing that it would prefer discussions on investment deregulation to take place in the WTO. He referred to the Asian financial crisis: 'in light of recent turmoil – the hasty and sometimes unreasonable movements that have gripped markets – it does not seem wise to us to see, to an excessive degree, private interests encroaching on the state's sphere of influence'. Other countries withdrew soon after, including Canada, Australia and the UK.[66]

The MAI corpse was buried in early December 1998 when senior officials from OECD countries met informally, agreeing only to carry out 'analytical' work and for OECD members and interested non-member countries to cooperate on investment deregulation. The OECD released a statement after the meeting confirming that 'negotiations on the MAI are no longer taking place'.[67]

ONGOING EFFORTS

The combination of internal dissent and public opposition meant that efforts to achieve an MAI within the OECD were abandoned. However, the objective was not withdrawn. Both the USCIB and Keidanren continue to promote investment liberalization as a top priority in other fora, including the WTO.[68] Together with these business coalitions, the OECD pushed for an investment agreement to be included in the Millennium Round of WTO negotiations.

In the meantime, cash-strapped developing countries have continued to loosen regulations on foreign investment. By 2002, there were over 2000 bilateral investment agreements that protect foreign investments, but contain no social and environmental protections for the citizens of the countries involved. Even regional free trade agreements such as NAFTA tend to aim at protecting investments as much as freeing up trade. A WTO investment treaty would not replace these agreements but reinforce and augment them.[69]

The IMF not only plays a major role in opening up markets in developing countries for foreign investors, but it bails those investors out in times of crisis. After the 1997 Asian crisis the IMF 'recovery packages' for South Korea, Thailand and Indonesia 'included a number of provisions that might have been taken straight from the text of the MAI'.[70] *Public Citizen* explains:

> *Prior to the Asian financial crisis, for example, the IMF pressured South Korea to remove restrictions on foreign capital flows. South Korean law required companies seeking to borrow more than a certain amount on international markets to obtain government approval. These rules were removed after IMF pressure. Subsequently, South Korean firms piled up a heavy burden of short-term, dollar-denominated debt, a key factor in the Asian financial crisis. When the South Korean currency*

crashed, these companies could no longer meet their debt obligations. Yet, in the wake of the crisis, the IMF insisted that the South Korean government remove the few remaining restrictions on foreign speculators and multinational corporations. South Korea was forced to comply while its currency remained crushed. The second wave of IMF-fuelled liberalizations has now led to [the] buy-up, often at fire sale prices, of many Korean government and private assets by multinational corporations.[71]

Nobel winning economist James Tobin has said: 'It is hard to escape the conclusion that the countries' currency distress is serving as the opportunity for an unrelated agenda – including the obtaining of trade concessions for US corporations and expansion of investment possibilities.'[72]

The IMF's role after the Asian crisis was reinforced by the US government, which set up a monitoring system to make sure that countries receiving IMF loans undertook the liberalization required of them by the IMF. Those countries found to be not complying would be faced with termination of IMF loan payments.[73]

After the failure of the MAI, the IMF, with the backing of some of the wealthier countries, sought to expand its official articles of agreement so that it would have official power to require member countries, and not just those receiving emergency loans, to remove capital flow and investment regulations. This would cover money invested in a nation's stock market and not just loans related to trade and direct investment.[74] According to the *Washington Times*: 'The IMF is moving on a plan that could override national and even local limits on how and where corporations can spend their money.' The IMF has taken up where MAI negotiators left off.[75]

The dream of an international agreement to protect the right of investors to invest in any country, not just those beholden to the IMF and the World Bank, with minimal conditions and maximum guarantees, lives on despite the failure of the MAI. Transnational corporations and their lobby groups continue to lobby for it in the WTO although it has been dropped from the current round of negotiations.

NOTES

1 *Public Citizen*, 'Multilateral Agreement on Investment (MAI)', www.citizen.org/trade/issues/mai/ accessed 3 July 2003.

2 David Korten (author of *When Corporations Rule the World*) quoted in Ad Hoc Working Group on the MAI, *MAI Multilateral Agreement on Investment: Democracy for Sale?* New York, Apex Press, 1998.

3 John Braithwaite and Peter Drahos, *Global Business Regulation*, Cambridge, Cambridge University Press, 2000, p182.

4 USCIB, 'About USCIB', US Council for International Business, www.uscib.org/index.asp?documentID=697 accessed 18 May 2003.

5   USCIB, 'Policy Advocacy', US Council for International Business, www.uscib.org/index.asp?documentID=824 accessed 18 May 2003; USCIB, 'About USCIB'.

6   USCIB, 'Policy Advocacy'.

7   OECD, 'About OECD', Organisation for Economic Co-operation and Development, www.oecd.org/about/0,2337,en_2649_201185_1_1_1_1_1,00.html accessed 5 February 2005.

8   Jonathan Startup, 'An Agenda for International Investment', in *OECD Documents: The New World Trading System: Readings*, Paris, OECD, 1995, p189.

9   Oliver Hoedeman, 'Corporate Lobbying for a 'MAI' in the WTO', in *Investment and Competition Negotiations in the WTO – What's Wrong with It and What Are the Alternatives*, Brussels/Berlin, Seattle to Brussels Network, 2002, p12; Patricia Ranald, 'Disciplining Governments: The MAI in the International and Australian Contexts', in James Goodman and Patricia Ranald (eds) *Stopping the Juggernaut: Public Interest Versus the Multilateral Agreement on Investment*, Sydney, Pluto Press, 2000, p22.

10 Belén Balanyá, *et al.*, *Europe Inc. Regional and Global Restructuring and the Rise of Corporate Power*, London, Pluto Press, 2000, p112.

11 USCIB, 'USCIB Applauds Launch of OECD Negotiations on Multilateral Investment Agreement', US Council for International Business, 24 May, 1995, www.uscib.org/dboecdnego.asp.

12 BIAC, 'Priorities for OECD and WTO Work: BIAC Submission on Trade-Related Issues to the OECD', Paris, Business and Industry Advisory Committee to the OECD, June 1998, p3.

13 Quoted in James Goodman, 'Stopping a Juggernaut: The Anti-MAI Campaign', in James Goodman and Patricia Ranald (eds) *Stopping the Juggernaut: Public Interest Versus the Multilateral Agreement on Investment*, Sydney, Pluto Press, 2000, p37.

14 Tony Clarke, *By What Authority! Unmasking and Challenging the Global Corporations' Assault on Democracy through the World Trade Organization*, Polaris Institute and International Forum on Globalization c. 1999, p11; Balanyá, *et al.*, *Europe Inc.*, pp112–3.

15 InvestmentWatch, 'Letter to WTO Delegates Warning of the High-Standard Agreement WTO-Investment Agreement Demanded by the ICC', Coporate Europe Observatory, 25 April, 2003, www.investmentwatch.org/articles/shefali25april.html; Debi Barker and Jerry Mander, 'Invisible Government. The World Trade Organization: Global Government for the New Millennium', Sausalito, CA, International Forum on Globalization (IFG), October 1999, p38.

16 Quoted in Joel Bleifuss, 'Building the Global Economy', *In These Times*, 11 January, 1998, p13.

17 Balanyá, *et al.*, *Europe Inc.*, p110.

18 Belén Balanyá, *et al.*, 'MAIgalomania! Citizens and the Environment Sacrificed to Corporate Investment Agenda', Corporate Europe Observatory, February, 1998, www.xs4all.nl/~ceo/mai/mmania07.html.

19 *Ibid.*

20 David Woodward, 'Financial Effects of Foreign Direct Investment in the Context of a Possible WTO Agreement on Investment', Paper presented at the NGO Workshop on WTO Negotiations on Investment and New Issues, Geneva, 18–19 March, 2003, p1; Balanyá, *et al.*, 'MAIgalomania!'.

21 OECD, 'MAI: The Multilateral Agreement on Investment', *Policy Brief*, vol 2, 1997a; OECD, 'Open Markets Matter: The Benefits of Trade and Investment Liberalisation', *Policy Brief*, vol 6, 1998b.
22 Woodward, 'Financial Effects of Foreign Direct Investment', p5.
23 'The Need to Regulate Foreign Investment', *Third World Resurgence*, vol 90/91, 1998, p17.
24 Chakravarthi Raghavan, 'FDI Is No Panacea for South's Economic Woes', *Third World Resurgence*, October/November, 1999, www.twnside.org.sg/title/woe-cn.htm.
25 Chakravarthi Raghavan, *Recolonization: GATT, the Uruguay Round & the Third World*, London, Zed Books, 1990, p148.
26 *Ibid.*, p148.
27 *Ibid.*, pp149–50.
28 OXFAM International, 'The Danger of an Investment Agreement under the WTO', in *Investment and Competition Negotiations in the WTO – What's Wrong with It and What Are the Alternatives*, Brussels/Berlin, Seattle to Brussels Network, 2002, p5.
29 Quoted in Raghavan, *Recolonization*, p157.
30 Balanyá, *et al.*, *Europe Inc.*, pp 115–6.
31 OXFAM International, 'The Danger of an Investment Agreement', p5.
32 William H. Witherell, 'An Agreement on Investment', *The OECD Observer*, vol 202, 1996, p6.
33 Corporate Europe Observatory, 'Corporate Conquistadors in Cancun: The EU Offensive for WTO-Investment Negotiations', InvestmentWatch, July 2003.
34 These terms are used by Patricia Ranald, 'Global Institutions, Democracy and Accountability: The WTO after the MAI and Seattle', The World In Context, 2000, www.context.co.nz:8080/stories/storyReader$601 accessed 3 July 2003.
35 Startup, 'An Agenda for International Investment', p191.
36 Goodman, 'Disciplining Governments', p36; Witherell, 'An Agreement on Investment', p7.
37 Witherell, 'An Agreement on Investment', p7.
38 ICC, 'Business States Its Views on OECD Investment Agreement', International Chamber of Commerce, 16 January, 1998, www.iccwbo.org/home/news_archives/1998/business_states_its_views.asp.
39 Witherell, 'An Agreement on Investment', pp7–8.
40 Noam Chomsky, 'Domestic Constituencies', *Z Magazine*, May, 1998, www.zmag.org/ZMag/articles/chomskymay98.htm; Project Censored, 'Censored 1999: The Top 25 Censored Media Stories of 1998', Project Censored, 1999, www.projectcensored.org/c1999.htm.
41 Balanyá, *et al.*, 'MAIgalomania!'; Paul Magnusson and Stephen Baker, 'The Explosive Trade Deal You've Never Heard Of', *Business Week*, 9 February, 1998.
42 Public Citizen, 'Multilateral Agreement on Investment (MAI): Background Information on the MAI', Public Citizen, 2003, www.citizen.org/trade/issues/mai/ accessed 3 July 2003.
43 Oliver Hoedeman *et al.*, 'MAIgalomania: The New Corporate Agenda', *The Ecologist*, vol 28, no 3, 1998; OECD, 'Progress Report on Multilateral Agreement on Investment', OECD MAI Negotiating Group, May, 1997b, www.oecd.org//daf/investment/fdi/mai/mairap97.htm.

44 International Forum on Globalisation, 'Should Corporations Govern the World?' *Third World Resurgence*, vol 90/91, 1998, p9; Bleifuss, 'Building the Global Economy', p13; Hoedeman *et al.*, 'MAIgalomania'; International Forum on Globalization, 'Should Corporations Govern the World?' *Third World Resurgence*, 1998; Bleifuss, 'Building the Global Economy', p13; Tony Clarke, 'The Corporate Rule Treaty', *Third World Resurgence*, vol 90/91, 1998, p11.

45 International Forum on Globalisation, 'Should Corporations Govern the World?', p10.

46 Martin Khor, 'What Is MAI?' *Third World Resurgence*, vol 90/91, 1998a, p7; Bleifuss, 'Building the Global Economy', p13.

47 Khor, 'What Is MAI?', p6.

48 *Ibid.*, p6.

49 '565 Groups Say 'No' to MAI', *Third World Resurgence*, vol 90/91, 1998, pp23–4.

50 Balanyá, *et al.*, 'MAIgalomania!'.

51 Balanyá, *et al.*, *Europe Inc.*, p115.

52 Goodman, 'Disciplining Governments', p38; Balanyá, *et al.*, 'MAIgalomania!'.

53 Balanyá, *et al.*, *Europe Inc.*, p119; ICC, 'Business States Its Views on OECD Investment Agreement'.

54 Goodman, 'Disciplining Governments', p36.

55 Khor, 'What Is MAI?', pp5–8; Goodman, 'Disciplining Governments'.

56 OECD, 'Ministerial Statement on the Multilateral Agreement on Investment (MAI),' Organisation for Economic Co-operation and Development, 27–28 April, 1998, www.oecd.org/media/release/nw98-50a.htm; *Washington Times* cited in Balanyá, *et al.*, 'MAIgalomania!'.

57 Goodman, 'Disciplining Governments', p42; Balanyá, *et al.*, *Europe Inc.*, p120; Public Citizen, 'OECD & Governments Launch 'MAI Charm-Offensive'', Public Citizen, May, 1998, www.citizen.org/print_article.cfm?ID=1095.

58 Guy de Jonquieres, 'Network Guerillas', *Financial Times*, 30 April, 1998; 'The Sinking of the MAI', *The Economist*, 14 March, 1998, pp85–6.

59 USCIB, 'Civil Society and Trade Negotiations: A Business Perspective', US Council for International Business, September, 1998, www.uscib.org/civsocst.asp.

60 Timothy Deal, 'Investment E-Paranoia', *Journal of Commerce*, 7 January, 1998, p7A.

61 'The Sinking of the MAI', pp85–6.

62 OECD, 'Communique: Ministerial Statement on the Multilateral Agreement on Investment (MAI),' Organisation for Economic Co-operation and Development, 27–28 April, 1998a, www.oecd.org/media/release/nw98-50a.htm.

63 Goodman, 'Disciplining Governments', p31.

64 Razeen Sally, 'Developing Country Trade Policy Reform and the WTO', *Cato Journal*, vol 19, no 3, 2000, p405; Gregory Palast, 'IMF's Four Steps to Damnation', *Observer*, 29 April, 2001, p7.

65 Martin Khor, 'US and IMF Putting More Squeeze on the South?' *MAI discussion list/Third World Network Features*, 14 April, 1998b; Dean R. O'Hare, 'The Future of the Global Trading System: Where to from Here?' Paper presented at the APEC CEO Summit 2001, Shanghai, 20 October, 2001.

66 'French Government Announces Withdrawal from MAI Negotiations', *Reuters*, 14 October, 1998; Balanyá, *et al.*, *Europe Inc.*, p109.

67   OECD, 'Informal Consultations on International Investment', Organisation for Economic Co-operation and Development, 3 December, 1998.

68   Balanyá, *et al.*, 'MAIgalomania!'.

69   Marrianne Hochuli, 'Investment Agreements as One-Sided Enforcement of Investor Rights I', in *Investment and Competition Negotiations in the WTO – What's Wrong with It and What Are the Alternatives*, Brussels/Berlin, Seattle to Brussels Network, 2002, p1.

70   Balanyá, *et al.*, 'MAIgalomania!'.

71   Public Citizen, 'MAI Shell Game – IMF', Public Citizen, www.citizen.org/print_article.cfm?ID=1098 accessed 3 July 2003.

72   Quoted in Balanyá, *et al.*, 'MAIgalomania!'.

73   Khor, 'US and IMF Putting More Squeeze on the South?'.

74   Public Citizen, 'MAI Shell Game – IMF'; Khor, 'US and IMF Putting More Squeeze on the South?'.

75   Quoted in Khor, 'US and IMF Putting More Squeeze on the South?'.

10

Globalization Versus Democracy

We should put the business 'horse' before the government 'cart'.
TIMOTHY J. HAUSER (FORMER ACTING US UNDER
SECRETARY FOR INTERNATIONAL TRADE)[1]

Business coalitions feared that the collapse of the Multilateral Agreement on Investment (MAI), and the controversy surrounding it, might stall or reverse precariously balanced moves to progress investment deregulation in the World Trade Organization (WTO). These fears were realized at the WTO ministerial meeting in Seattle in 1999. Developing nation opposition to a new round of negotiations was supported by over 1000 non-governmental organizations (NGOs) – environmental, labour, consumer and development. Their petition, 'Stop the WTO Round', which was circulated before the Seattle meeting, claimed that the international trading system was unfair and was shaped 'around the offensive interests of large transnational corporations'. More than 50,000 people from all over the world protested at the meeting itself. At that time, they were the 'largest demonstrations witnessed in the US since the Vietnam War'.[2]

The failure to reach an agreement on a new round of negotiations at the Seattle meeting was due to conflict between WTO nations (between the US and Europe and between developed and developing countries). Developing nation governments were strengthened in their resistance by public opposition all over the world and mass protests in the immediate vicinity. The MAI controversy had instilled greater public scepticism about the claimed benefits of trade and investment deregulation, and the failure of the MAI negotiations instilled a belief in opponents that it was possible to slow – perhaps even reverse – the corporate agenda.

Fred Bergsten, director of the Institute for International Economics (IIE) and former US assistant secretary of the Treasury for International Affairs, told the 2000 meeting of the Trilateral Commission (see Chapter 1) that the backlash against globalization was threatening 'the prosperity and stability of the world economy':

> *All this occurs after two decades when a market-oriented philosophy, the so-called 'Washington Consensus,' seemed to gain near-universal approval and provided a guiding ideology and underlying intellectual consensus for the world economy, which was quite new in history.*[3]

De Jonquieres noted in the *Financial Times* that 'the unexpected success of the MAI's detractors in winning the public relations battle … has set alarm bells ringing'. From now on, it would be 'harder for negotiators to do deals behind closed doors and submit them for rubber-stamping by parliaments. Instead, they face pressure to gain wider popular legitimacy for their actions by explaining and defending them in public.'[4]

Similarly, Dan Esty wrote in the World Economic Forum's bimonthly magazine *World Link* that, following Seattle:

> *While the received wisdom within the trade community has been that the best trade policy outcomes arise from quiet diplomacy and decisions made outside the glare of publicity (and the scrutiny of self-serving special interests), this approach to governance has resulted in deep suspicion that multinational corporations dominate the trade regime.*[5]

Also writing in *World Link*, Walter Mead, a senior fellow from the US Council on Foreign Relations, noted that public concern ranged from people in Europe who are concerned that free trade 'will eviscerate the European social system and impose an unwanted alien dog-eat-dog capitalist model', to people in Asia who are bitter about the impacts of a financial crisis which they blame on the workings of the financial markets, to people in Latin America who believe that market economic systems concentrate wealth but do nothing for mass poverty, to people in the developing world generally who are disappointed that free trade promised by the WTO has not helped their situation.[6]

As Mead recognized, it was becoming clear that free trade was not benefiting the majority of people. Hundreds of millions of people in the world went hungry while food was exported to countries where people were more likely to suffer from being overweight. A decade of trade and investment liberalization had left 54 countries worse off than they had been at the start of the decade. Only those developing nations that had maintained some protection for their economies, China and India, made gains.[7]

It was also clear that prioritizing free trade rules over national legislation was very unpopular. A survey conducted by MORI for *The Ecologist* found that the vast majority of people in the UK (around 90 per cent) felt that governments should be able to protect the environment, employment conditions and human health – and restrict the imports of goods to do so – even if the interests of transnational companies were damaged in the process.[8]

To counter the growing public opposition to free trade negotiations, particularly with regard to services and investment, business launched a new public relations campaign. Opposition to the expansion of free trade rules was labelled 'globophobia', and business groups sought to portray free trade in a more favourable light.

Hoedeman and Doherty from the Corporate Europe Observatory describe how: 'Since Seattle, US business has engaged in a multifaceted, multimillion dollar counter-campaign involving individual corporations, lobby groups like the Business Roundtable and the US Chamber of Commerce, corporate-sponsored think tanks and, of course, the ever-faithful PR [public relations] industry'. Similarly, Phillip Babish from the National Radio Project noted how 'corporations are showering the US Congress with well-funded lobbying campaigns and pro-free trade think tanks are engaging in an information war for public opinion'.[9]

The US Business Roundtable (BRT), for example, has a Taskforce on International Trade and Investment whose priorities included implementing 'a trade education programme to increase general awareness and understanding of the importance of trade to US economic growth'.[10] One of BRT's goals was to reinstate 'fast-track' or Trade Promotion Authority for the president that would enable him (or his representatives) to negotiate international trade agreements without referring the details to Congress. Congress would only have the power to approve or reject the final agreement. This was a way of bypassing democratic and non-business input into the negotiation process and, of course, it was opposed by many sectors of society, including labour, environmental and consumer groups.

BRT spent millions on lobbying, public relations and advertising to support 'fast-track' authority. Its reported lobbying expenditure went from US$8.3 million in 1999 to US$21.5 million in 2000. It utilized a front group, goTrade, to make the running on the issue: 'to pay office visits to members of Congress, generate letters and phone calls, and work with local media outlets to generate stories about the value of trade'.[11] Fast-track authority was restored in August 2002.

The European business response was more indirect, according to the Corporate Europe Observatory: 'While the US corporate world has engaged in an all-out confrontational counter-offensive, EU-based transnationals have generally tried to steer clear of direct confrontation with their critics.' European business coalitions such as the European Round Table of Industrialists (ERT) and the European Services Forum (ESF) 'intensified their behind-the-scenes lobbying and left the public' campaigning to Trade Commissioner Pascal Lamy and industry-funded think tanks such as the European Policy Centre (EPC) and the Centre for European Policy Studies. Exceptions included an information campaign by Swedish employer organization Svenskt Nringsliv, targeting high school students and a campaign by the Association of German Industries (BDI).[12]

Not all business coalitions were willing to leave the campaign to others. The Union of Industrial and Employers' Confederations of Europe (UNICE) called for business to be more proactive in its lobbying efforts in order to 'counteract' the activists' 'impressive media campaign'. Similarly, in the UK, Leon Brittan (see Chapter 7) argued that 'the business voice must make itself heard above the noise being generated from other sources threatening the ongoing health of the system'. Brittan argued that business could not afford to ignore the protesters, particularly since 'there are worrying signs that political resolve is weakening in some parts of the globe'. The business community had to 'strengthen the resolve of governments' by presenting a strong, united front.[13]

It was generally recognized that the internet had played a major role in mobilizing opposition to the MAI and the WTO at Seattle and PR firms advised that business interests also utilize the internet to promote the pro-free trade message and attack anti-WTO NGOs.[14] A host of new websites emerged, including the BRT's goTrade site, www.gotrade.org/. goTrade included:

> ... [the] establishment of locally organized pro-trade networks, each complete with a comprehensive local trade story, and a pro-trade advertising campaign for those districts where such a campaign would be effective... Other elements of the programme include a schedule of special community events and forums; educational outreach to local high schools and other educational institutions; timelines for meetings with officials from the Congress and Executive Branch; as well as introductory outreach to local and regional news media. The programme is reviewed annually, with success measured through Congressional voting records, polling, 'learned' media coverage and public feedback.[15]

In its counter-offensive, corporate interests had three goals: to present globalization in the form of free trade and investment as in everyone's interests; to undermine opponents; and to prevent non-trade issues, such as labour or the environment, from taking priority over trade concerns.

IN EVERYONE'S INTEREST

For two decades the issue of whether free trade was a good thing had not been on the public agenda. Politicians who favoured unrestricted free trade presented globalization as an inevitable fact of life, an unstoppable force of progress. Bill Clinton had clearly spelled it out as US president by saying that 'globalization is not a policy choice; it is a fact'. Similarly, UK Prime Minister Tony Blair emphasized that the process was 'irreversible and irresistible'.[16]

Transnational corporations (TNCs) had focused their efforts on lobbying government officials and politicians. Now the business community was faced with the stark reality that they had taken their free trade agenda beyond the point where the public would meekly accept it. It was necessary to regain public confidence in the business agenda. IIE's Bergsten argued that public 'education' was required 'first and foremost' to show how globalization was beneficial to all countries and most groups, although clearly there would be costs and losers.[17]

The US Council for International Business (USCIB) took part in PR efforts, including 'business community outreach efforts to inform the American public and US Congress on the benefits of trade' and international 'outreach activities' to 'civil society'. USCIB Chair Dean O'Hare argued that since World War II, peace had been 'built to a large extent by the growth of international trade that has woven this world together'. He urged business to 'constantly advance the arguments in support of trade liberalization in all our communications with our customers, our employees and with our government representatives'.[18]

The habit of associating free trade with world peace was a long one. The US administration had used the slogan 'If goods can't cross the borders, soldiers will' when it was pushing for free trade during the 1940s. The International Chamber of Commerce (ICC) claims to have been founded, after World War I in 1919, on the idea of 'world peace through world trade'.[19] This phrase was also a campaign slogan of Thomas J. Watson, one-time president of ICC and founder of IBM, which later did business with Nazi Germany. Now, ICC not only claims that world trade brings world peace, but also that it eradicates poverty and represents the poor people of the world, as well as world business. In a statement to G8 heads of state in 2002, it said:

> *Business is concerned that the anti-globalization groups are pressuring governments to hinder progress in the very areas that can eradicate poverty and narrow the gap between rich and poor. Opening export markets, expanding foreign direct investment … ICC calls upon the G8 governments, with the authority they derive from mass democratic elections, to stand firm in the face of groups that are mostly unaccountable and represent small minority views or narrow vested interests. We cannot curb the chances of poor people to profit from participation in a thriving global economy.*[20]

World Economic Forum (WEF) members and associates also claim that they are only thinking of what is best for the poor. Bill Gates, at the WEF's Asia-Pacific Summit in September 2000, dismissed the thousands of protesters outside the meeting, arguing that globalization was good for the poor. This was a theme that the WEF was promoting.

The protests against the WTO at Seattle provided one of the main focuses for WEF discussions at Davos in 2000, which were also beset by protesters outside the meeting venue. Those attending, from business people to presidents and prime ministers, agreed that free trade was good and should be promoted; but 'nearly everyone in Davos agreed that globalization has an image problem'.[21] There was much discussion on how to present globalization as more than just a market or economic force.

WEF members recognized that free trade leads to winners and losers, and often results in greater inequalities in developed and developing nations; but this was not their concern. Their problem was how to strengthen 'public faith in a market economy' and show ordinary people that they, too, can benefit from it. Mead pointed out that for the first time there is a 'broad degree of consensus among economists and policy-makers about what ought to be done… The trick, as always, is winning public support for good policies.'[22]

While continuing to promote free trade and globalization, the WEF now stresses the need for economic development 'with a human face'. It wants to ensure that 'the concerns and questions of an anxious public' are answered convincingly. WEF President Klaus Schwab declared the 1999 Davos meeting as 'a kind of landmark in reintroducing the notion of social responsibility to the corporate sector'. He coined the term 'responsible globality' to use in place of 'globalization'. The meeting literature for the 2000 Davos meeting announced: 'Among the many facets of the globalization process is the realization that the process cannot have only an economic and business face. It also needs to acquire a full social and ethical dimension to be sustainable.'[23]

This concern with development 'with a human face' is not because members are concerned about the plight of the poor and dispossessed, but because the political instability that might arise from opposition to globalization and free trade is bad for business. Schwab claimed that the lack of social cohesion produced by community opposition to globalization and to corporate activities creates vulnerabilities for the corporate sector. 'Globalization is seen as a heartless economic process that destroys jobs and cultures. It has become a scapegoat for everything which is bad.'[24]

International Financial Services, London (IFSL) also embarked on a communications campaign in 2000 to promote the benefits of free trade, particularly the General Agreement on Trade in Services (GATS): 'We thought this required a very wide-ranging campaign and a combined effort between government and the private sector.' The Global Services Network (GSN) was preparing 'cuff-notes' to enable businesspeople to respond to anti-GATS claims.[25]

At a meeting of the Liberalisation of Trade in Services Committee (LOTIS), Malcolm McKinnon, from the UK Department of Trade and Industry (DTI), pointed out 'that the pro-GATS case was vulnerable when the NGOs asked for proof of where the economic benefits of liberalization lay'. Peter Maydon, from the UK Treasury, suggested 'that developing countries should be encouraged to refute the arguments put forward by the NGOs'. Another strategy, recommended by David Wood of the Confederation of British Industry (CBI), was to build 'an industrial voice in those countries'. Henry Manisty from *Reuters* offered his company's help in publicizing the business view.[26]

The problem of gaining acceptance for services liberalization in developing countries was repeatedly discussed at LOTIS meetings. Members noted that the Koreans and Thais who had opened up their markets had done so under pressure from the International Monetary Fund (IMF), rather than out of a 'genuine conviction' about the benefits of liberalization. It was recommended that more effort be put into 'selling' free trade ideas to the developing world, and this would require that papers prepared for LOTIS that 'expressed a unified UK, EU and US industry view' be modified with this objective in mind. The papers would then be 'forwarded to government officials in advance of the WTO ministerial meeting'.[27]

Various other reports on the benefits to developing nations were compiled. The European Commission (EC) 'had worked up a research report on the benefits of [market] opening which they hoped would lead to a more liberal approach on the part of developing countries'. IFSL also initiated a research project by Professor John Dunning of the Economists Advisory Group on the economic benefits of services liberalization for developing countries in order to persuade developing countries and to counter hostile NGOs. The project would feature case studies and be funded to the tune of UK£50,000–£70,000 by IFSL and corporate sponsors.[28]

The Business and Industry Advisory Committee (BIAC) also argued that free trade and open markets provide the essential ingredients for economic growth and poverty reduction in developing countries. It claimed: 'What matters most is to ensure that the mechanics, dynamics and benefits of further trade liberalization are positively perceived and understood by all.' It argued that the special treatment available for developing countries as a result of the Uruguay Round impeded their 'access to the benefits of trade and competitive markets' and therefore should be phased out.[29]

The Emergency Committee for American Trade (ECAT) ran public information programmes, including a web-based 'employee outreach' programme entitled Trade: Discover the Opportunity (TDO), which teaches 'how trade is helping employees achieve a better life and offers real life examples of ordinary Americans who are achieving their dreams because of expanding trade opportunities'. Member companies receive 'educational materials', such as posters and newsletter templates, to adapt for their own employees.[30]

BOX 10.1 EMERGENCY COMMITTEE FOR AMERICAN TRADE (ECAT)

The Emergency Committee for American Trade (ECAT) was formed in 1967 by executives of large American companies who were concerned that a global trade war would eventuate as a result of import restrictions that the US government was bringing in and that other nations would retaliate. Today, ECAT supports expansion of the World Trade Organization (WTO) agreements through lobbying US Congress and US administration officials; testifying at government hearings; networking with like-minded organizations; and 'public information programmes'.[31]

Although ECAT is not forthcoming about who its members are, it claims that its membership:

> . . . is comprised of the heads of major American companies with international operations, representing all major sectors of the US economy. The annual sales of ECAT member companies total over 1 trillion dollars, and the ECAT companies employ approximately 4 million people.[32]

ECAT also commissioned various studies to show how important free trade and investment are to economic growth. Its fourth study in 2002, subtitled *The Public Opinion Disconnect*, addressed the growing public opposition to free trade and investment. It recognized that 'the majority of Americans think trade and FDI [foreign direct investment] hurt the US economy, on balance, with large majorities also worrying that trade and investment generate labour-market costs in terms of job destruction and lower wages'. However at the same time, most Americans see information and communication technologies (ICTs) as a 'main driver of economic growth' and will even tolerate job losses in the name of technological progress. The study therefore sought to show that free trade and investment were necessary to the development of innovation in ICT. It urged 'policy-makers and business leaders' to 'articulate the essential role that trade and investment play in the creation and use of ICT goods and services – and thereby play in the improvement of US living standards'.[33]

UNDERMINING OPPONENTS

Various tactics were used to undermine opponents, ranging from attacking them as selfish and ill informed to attempting to co-opt and placate them. In an example of the first tactic, Mexican President Ernesto Zedillo referred to opposition to unconstrained globalism as 'globaphobia' and characterized protesters as 'a peculiar alliance' of 'forces from the extreme left, the extreme right, environmentalist groups, trade unions of developed countries and some self-appointed representatives of civil society' whose primary aim was to stop developing countries from developing. Similarly, former USCIB President Abraham Katz labelled the anti-globalization movement as enemies of an open market system, business and free enterprise.[34]

Public relations firms prepared information for the business world about anti-globalization protesters and how to deal with them. The PR firm Hill and Knowlton prepared a background briefing for corporations in the lead up to the September 2000 Asia-Pacific World Economic Forum Summit, warning of the planned protests. The briefing included information on the protest organizers, the s11 group (named after the date of the summit on 11 September). Hill and Knowlton offered corporations assistance in dealing with protests and a strategy from Hill and Knowlton's crisis and issues management team.[35]

Burson-Marsteller subsidiary, Black, Kelly, Scruggs and Heally, distributed a *Guide to the Seattle Meltdown* to its corporate clients, describing the various NGOs who protested in Seattle against the WTO. The accompanying memo said: 'We wanted to share this *Guide* with you, not so much as a retrospective on the past, but as an alarming window on the future.'[36]

In Europe, as in the US, public relations firms eagerly offered their services in bridging what the International Chamber of Commerce (ICC) secretary general sees as the 'communications deficit' that has contributed to the 'backlash

against globalization'. For example, Edelman, one of the PR giants, offered corporate clients help with 'EU and WTO public affairs, media relations and crisis
preparedness'.[37]

Free trade advocates in the UK, following the Seattle meeting and subsequent
mass protests at high-level business and trade meetings, demanded that NGOs be
better 'controlled' through codes of conduct and certification processes requiring
'appropriate' standards of behaviour. Those NGOs that complied would be offered
a seat at the negotiation table. Those that did not would be marginalized.[38] Leon
Brittan urged business to 'take up the cudgels', attract media attention and show
that NGOs were advocating solutions that would 'harm growth and employment
here [in Europe] and overseas'.[39]

At LOTIS meetings, government officials and corporate executives discussed
strategies for countering the anti-globalization movement. The possibility that the
World Development Movement, which had initiated an anti-GATS campaign, was
'open to persuasion' was raised but dismissed as doubtful by a DTI representative
attending the meeting. Members speculated that 'Not all NGOs would be turnable
and this was enabling certain governments with protectionist tendencies to hide
behind them.'[40]

The European Commission established 'dialogues with civil society' to enable
NGOs, both business and non-profit, to discuss their concerns about trade policy
with EC bureaucrats. However, activists were cynical of the process: 'On the
premise of taking into account the concerns of civil society, the EC would present
its position, listen to the supportive comments of the business lobbyists and the
fierce critiques of the campaigners ... and keep its WTO policies unchanged'.[41]

These dialogues were also a way of removing the debate from the public arena
to a forum behind closed doors and separating the moderate NGOs who were
willing to work with the EC from the more radical NGOs that would see this as an
attempt at co-option. While NGO personnel wasted their time trying to persuade
the bureaucrats rather than the public, business would have the opportunity to
hear the best arguments of their opposition and adjust their 'own lobbying strategy
and public rhetoric' accordingly.[42]

Token consultation has also been adopted by the WTO. In answer to allegations of secrecy, the WTO 'equipped its new council chamber with a public
gallery and invited representatives of more than 150 NGOs' to its next ministerial
meeting.[43]

The need to appear to be more open and avoid the appearance of backroom
dealings was not lost on WEF organizers, either. They sought to present a more
open, humane persona and to raise WEF's public profile. Its meetings now have
sessions that are open to carefully screened journalists and are reported on its web
pages. These sessions are sometimes addressed by invited representatives of NGOs,
some of whom are critics of unrestrained economic globalization. However, the key
part of the WEF meetings are the many private discussions that take place during
these meetings and the WEF's web pages have sections that are only accessible by

members. One journalist described how the 'working press' at Davos (as opposed to the WEF club of Media Leaders) are kept in a 'dungeon-like basement' and fed 'reams of handouts, session summaries and snatches of the proceedings watched on live, closed-circuit TV'.[44]

REGULATIONS AND SANCTIONS

Business coalitions are opposed to any efforts to incorporate labour, environmental or social issues within WTO rules unless they facilitate free trade. ECAT is typical in its argument that 'these issues are, for the most part, best addressed in alternative fora and through alternative policy approaches'. Business coalitions are also opposed to national regulations that seek to protect the environment or workers at the expense of free trade and investment. Additionally, they generally oppose sanctions imposed on trading partners for political reasons. ECAT refers to these as 'ineffective and counterproductive'.[45]

The USCIB opposes any policies that might impede free trade, including regulations based on precaution; use of trade sanctions for non-commercial policy purposes; and approaches to sustainable development that do not emphasize the importance of open markets, free trade and economic growth. The US Coalition of Service Industries (CSI) would like national regulations to be 'more market oriented' and 'pro-competitive' in their interpretation and application. CSI's regulatory prescription is aligned with that put forward by Claude Barfield from the American Enterprise Institute (AEI). He promotes 'minimally intrusive' regulations. Consumer protection laws should merely allow consumers 'to have adequate information to make informed and independent judgements'.[46]

Leaked documents indicate that LOTIS was influential in getting EC negotiators to push for a strict 'necessity test' within GATS that would require governments wanting to regulate services to prove that such regulations were not 'more burdensome than necessary' to companies involved. A WTO secretariat memo states that trade ministers had agreed that if such regulations were challenged in the WTO, a defence of 'safeguarding the public interest' would be rejected. The memo suggests that if the WTO adopted 'efficiency' as a criterion rather than public interest, then government leaders would have more excuse to eliminate unwanted regulations even if their citizens wanted them. If regulatory authorities or citizen groups demand regulation of a particular hazard, politicians could avoid it by saying that WTO rules would not allow this as it was too burdensome to industry.[47]

In this way, WTO rules favour trade over public welfare even more than those in the North American Free Trade Agreement (NAFTA), which require regulatory measures to be 'least trade restrictive'. For example, NAFTA administrators had ruled – after appeal from the Canadian maker of the petrol additive MTBE – that California could not ban MTBE from petrol to prevent groundwater pollution. This was because banning MTBE was not the 'least trade restrictive' way of dealing with the problem of polluted groundwater. The alternative of digging up and repairing petrol-holding tanks all over the state to stop them from leaking into groundwater, although expensive, was considered to be preferable because it was less trade restrictive.[48] This 'least trade restrictive rule' is also part of WTO rules.

USCIB and BIAC both oppose attempts to include environmental and social provisions in trade agreements. The USCIB is particularly concerned about uniform standards, sanctions and any trade-related measures to achieve social and environmental ends. BIAC also opposes labelling schemes used by individual countries to differentiate between goods on the basis of environmental and other criteria: 'Non-product related processes and production methods (PPM) labelling discriminates unfairly against identical like products and influences consumer spending and, consequently, market access.' It hopes this issue of 'discriminatory labelling' will be dealt with in the WTO.[49]

Although the USCIB is a participant in the International Labour Organization (ILO), it is loath to see ILO recommendations made mandatory in any trade or other multilateral agreement. USCIB President Thomas Niles told a US House Sub-Committee that USCIB opposed the inclusion of labour issues in the WTO. He argued that any trade sanctions based on non-compliance with labour standards would be 'the first step toward a new protectionism' and that imposing trade barriers based on labour standards would not promote better compliance. Rather, 'the key to better labour standards is economic development, which can be achieved through increased trade and investment flows, not sanctions'.[50]

Similarly:

> *BIAC has long held the view that the ILO, not the WTO, is the competent body to deal with conditions of work... We continue to believe it would be damaging to trade and investment, and counterproductive to the improvement of labour conditions, to introduce trade sanctions for violations of any agreed labour standards or to include binding social clauses in trade agreements or investment treaties.*[51]

BIAC is also concerned about corporate codes of conduct which, it argues, raise the costs of doing business and can undermine the competitiveness of corporations based in countries that introduce them. International codes such as the *OECD Guidelines for Multinational Enterprises* and the *ILO Tripartite Declaration of Principles Concerning Multinational Enterprises and Social Policy* are okay so long as governments do not make them binding. Government-enforced or third-party labelling schemes and external auditing of companies for compliance to codes of conduct would also be unacceptable.[52]

Government and business members of LOTIS wrestled with how to publicly differentiate between the regulations that corporations wanted to outlaw and those that they wanted to keep or establish. The use of the term 'pro-competitive regulation' or 'pro-competitive regulatory principles' (PCRPs) was repeatedly discussed. Michael Foot from the Financial Services Authority (FSA) said that the term '"pro-competitive" gave the wrong impression' and others thought it was not a term that could be sold to developing countries. The US had proposed using 'trade-related regulatory principles'. Matthew Goodman from Goldman Sachs International suggested 'getting rid of the term "pro-competitive" but holding on to the concept' and Steve Robson from Her Majesty's Treasury suggested 'using a code on the lines of "transparent, fair and effective"'.[53] Indeed, the terms 'transparent, fair and effective' have become common in the free trade literature on regulation.

The National Foreign Trade Council (NFTC) is the leading business coalition in the campaign against sanctions. It has taken legal action to prevent state and local governments from discriminating against companies who do business in countries where governments abuse human rights. For example, it won a precedent-setting case in 1999 against Massachusetts legislation that added 10 per cent to government tenders from companies that did business with Burma (Myanmar).[54]

Box 10.2 National Foreign Trade Council (NFTC)

The National Foreign Trade Council (NFTC) is one of the oldest business coalitions lobbying for free trade and open markets. It was formed in 1914 and currently has over 300 US companies as members.[55] Its board of directors includes the American International Group (AIG); Bechtel; Boeing; BP America; Caterpillar; Citigroup; ExxonMobil; Ford Motor Company; General Electric; Halliburton; Hill and Knowlton; Pfizer; and Procter & Gamble.

On its website, the current US Trade Representative (USTR) thanks the NFTC for 'all your efforts to help us prepare for the WTO ministerial in Doha' and for its 'tremendous amount of work to promote the launch' of a new round of WTO negotiations. And US Vice-President Richard Cheney, former chief executive officer (CEO) of Halliburton, says: 'From the point of view of Halliburton, one of the most valuable organizations we are a part of is the NFTC.'[56]

The NFTC offers its members influence, access to the US Congress and the Executive, information and expertise. It claims to shape and support free trade agreements such as the North American Free Trade Agreement (NAFTA) and the WTO through providing 'a broad-based US business voice and leadership' in negotiations and engagement 'at the highest levels with key decision-makers'. The NFTC's contribution to portraying regulations as trade barriers include presentations to embassies of developing countries and a White Paper on the economic harm that regulations do when they seek to reduce risks but are not fully based on science.[57]

The NFTC's interest in free trade is based on the financial interests of its members rather than free market ideology; therefore, it is also a big supporter of export credit agencies such as Overseas Private Investment Corporation (OPIC) and Ex-Im Bank, which basically subsidize companies operating overseas. It spends well over US$1.5million each year on government lobbying.[58]

It is common in many US states and cities for locals to express their disfavour of foreign regimes through 'selective purchasing' laws. For example, during the 1980s such laws had succeeded in getting some large US companies to withdraw from South Africa, and in the late 1990s companies such as Apple computer, Levi Strauss, Eastman Kodak and PepsiCo were withdrawing from Burma to ensure that their US business continued.[59]

NFTC President Frank Kittredge stated in relation to the court case that NFTC won against the Massachusetts law: 'This ruling has broad, nationwide significance, and should help to put an end to local efforts to make foreign policy.' In other words, he opposed local democratic efforts to influence local government purchasing decisions. The NFTC had also lobbied in Washington to have the law overturned by the federal government.[60]

USA*Engage is a corporate front group that was formed in 1997 by the NFTC to promote the business case against sanctions. The NFTC continues to play a leading role in its activities and maintains its website. As a front group, USA*Engage enables corporations to push for trade with dictators and regimes who abuse human rights without fronting up themselves and suffering a loss of corporate reputation. According to Frank Kittredge, president of NFTC and vice chairman of USA*Engage, 'USA*Engage was formed because a lot of companies are not anxious to be spotlighted as supporters of countries like Iran or Burma... The way to avoid that is to band together in a coalition.'[61]

USA*Engage succeeded in getting dozens of supportive newspaper editorials following its formation. The results seemed to be paying off in 2000 when 'the House Republican leadership agreed to ease the trade embargo against Cuba ... the House voted to make permanent China's normal trading rights in the United States ... the Clinton administration announced it would lift economic sanctions against North Korea' and a House bill proposed lifting sanctions on food and medicine to Libya, Iran and Sudan.[62]

The Institute for International Economics (IIE) conducted a study on the cost of sanctions, which was partly funded by the NFTC and released at USA*Engage's first press conference. USA*Engage has also made good use of reports and studies funded by NAM, the Cato Institute, the Center for Strategic and International Studies and the Center for the Study of American Business. These think tanks all receive funding from USA*Engage members.[63]

USA*Engage managed to get its allies in Congress to sponsor a bill in 1997: the Enhancement of Trade, Security and Human Rights through Sanctions Reform Act. The act would make sanctions very difficult to impose unless they were to remedy unfair trading practices. It would require a comprehensive assessment of the 'likely impact on US foreign policy, economic and humanitarian interests' of any proposed sanctions, as well as a cost-benefit analysis of the economic impact on private companies. It would exempt companies with pre-existing contracts from sanctions imposed, and would require sanctions to be reauthorized every two years.

BOX 10.3 USA*ENGAGE

USA*Engage has more than 600 corporate members from all sectors of the economy, as well as 40 national and state associations and organizations. It campaigns against selective purchasing laws and sanctions by persuading 'policy-makers, opinion leaders and the public' of the economic costs and ineffectiveness of sanctions.[64]

It seems that the National Foreign Trade Council (NFTC) hired public relations (PR) consultants and coalition builders, the Wexler Group (see Chapter 6), to set up and maintain USA*Engage. Members include the National Association of Manufacturers (NAM); Unocol and Caterpillar, which do business in Burma; Mobil and Texaco, which do business in Nigeria; and Boeing, Westinghouse and ABB, which are all keen to do business in China.[65]

USA*Engage argues that 'American values are best advanced by engagement of American business and agriculture' – hence its name. It claims that this engagement inevitably improves the lives of people worldwide and therefore advances democracy and human rights. In contrast, unilateral economic sanctions impose costs on the US by spoiling relationships with allies; increasing costs of imported goods; and compromising the competitiveness and investment opportunities of US companies by giving competing foreign companies the opportunity to access markets that the US is boycotting.[66]

USA*Engage claims direct access to US Congressional, administration, state and local officials. It particularly targets members of Congress by estimating the cost of sanctions to their constituents. It also recruits 'respected foreign policy and economic experts to speak out against sanctions, actively engage the media and provide outreach' in key states. In this way, USA*Engage claims to have 'effectively recast the political debate on sanctions'.[67]

USA*Engage is chaired by Caterpillar Inc's director of government affairs, William Lane, who also played an active role in lobbying for the General Agreement on Tariffs and Trade (GATT). Lane detailed USA*Engage's strategy:

> We engaged the academic community and think tanks. We engaged non-traditional business allies ranging from religious and humanitarian organizations to human rights groups. We engaged Congress and the Clinton administration.[68]

An internal memo obtained by *Mother Jones* magazine suggests that the bill was initially drafted by the Wexler Group.[69]

As part of the lobbying for this bill, USA*Engage wrote to its members in 1998 asking for their help in 'mounting a grassroots letter writing campaign' in favour of the bill. Such a campaign would involve 'senior executives, suppliers, facility managers and, wherever possible, employees', and would support 'our Congressional champions' who were asking for help to make the bill a top priority: 'if we are going to prevail we must act now... In their view and ours, a successful legislative strategy hinges on our ability to rapidly assemble large, bipartisan cosponsor lists.'[70]

The Trade Sanctions Reform and Export Enhancement Act was passed in 2000 but lacked some of the teeth that USA*Engage would have liked, and it continued to lobby for further legislative reform until the issue was sidetracked by the events of 11 September 2001.[71]

CORPORATE COALITIONS

Business coalitions and networks work on the principle that a 'combined voice is more powerful than one that is fragmented'.[72] Companies that are theoretically competitors in the market cooperate with each other to protect business interests against democratic regulations and restrictions. Individual firms network with national sectoral associations, national sectoral associations network within national peak associations such as the US Chamber of Commerce or the US Council for International Business (USCIB), and national peak associations network with international peak associations such as the ICC.[73]

The USCIB notes that:

> Leading American companies increasingly recognize that to succeed abroad, they must join together with like-minded firms to influence laws, rules and policies that may undermine US competitiveness, wherever they may be... By helping shape international regulation and expand market access for US products and services, USCIB members can lower the costs of doing business abroad and enhance their long-term profitability.[74]

The European Services Forum (ESF) similarly recognized that 'By tabling a coordinated document, the industry will be stronger within the European Union and vis-à-vis the other WTO member states, and will give to their sectoral requests a political dimension that individual sectors will not be able to achieve.'[75] The Intellectual Property Committee (IPC) used the same strategy in putting together the *Basic Framework* document on intellectual property with UNICE and Keidanren (see Chapter 8).

A great number of trade coalitions have been formed for this purpose of presenting a combined and powerful voice for business. These coalitions are tightly networked, as shown in Figure 10.1. They are also closely interrelated through their common corporate membership, as depicted in Table 10.1. This multiplicity of coalitions with heavily overlapping membership and leadership enables corporations to multiply their power and influence.

Corporations are interconnected through overlapping board memberships, and in the US those with the most extensive connections – American Express, Sara Lee, Chase Manhattan Bank, General Motors, Procter & Gamble – tend to play

Table 10.1 *Membership of some key US trade coalitions (past and present)*

	National Foreign Trade Council (NFTC)[76]	US Council for International Business (USCIB)[77]	US Coalition of Service Industries (CSI)[78]	Intellectual Property Committee (IPC)[79]	USA* Engage[80]	US Alliance for Trade Expansion (US Trade)[81]	TransAtlantic Business Dialogue (TABD)[82]	Council of the Americas[83]	US Business Roundtable (BRT)[84]
P&G	■	■		■	■	■	■	■	■
Pfizer	■	■		■		■	■	■	■
Halliburton	■	■		■		■		■	
GE	■	■		■	■	■	■	■	■
Ford Motor	■	■			■	■	■	■	■
ExxonMobil	■	■			■	■		■	■
E Kodak	■	■			■	■	■		■
DuPont	■	■			■	■	■	■	■
Dow Chemicals		■			■	■	■	■	■
Citigroup	■	■	■			■	■	■	■
Caterpillar	■				■	■	■	■	■
Boeing	■	■			■	■		■	■
AmEx		■	■			■	■	■	■
AIG	■	■	■		■	■	■	■	■
ABB	■				■	■	■	■	■
3M	■	■			■	■		■	■

Notes: ■ Membership

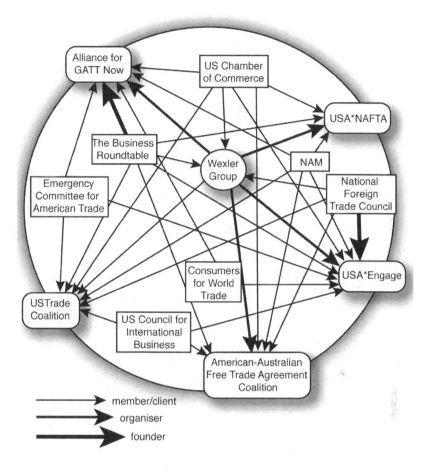

Figure 10.1 *The interlinking of some US trade groups*

Note: In this figure, the overlapping US trade groups and business coalitions are shown. Each arrow represents a relationship between two groups, ranging from membership to leadership.

a central role in the network. Their directors are 90 to 95 per cent male, 95 per cent white, usually business executives, bankers or corporate lawyers, and tend to vote Republican. The few business leaders who don't fit this profile, nevertheless, adhere to corporate values.[85] These directors, along with the leaders of supporting think tanks and policy groups, constitute a corporate class with common interests in fostering a pro-business political climate that has minimal scope for democratic intervention.

The inner circle, people who are directors of more than one company, provide the leadership for the corporate class: organizing and running the business coalitions where common goals and strategies are worked out; coordinating the public relations specialists, think tanks and media outlets that manipulate public opinion;

Table 10.2 *Some key business leaders*

	Corporations	Free trade coalitions	Other
Harry Freeman	Vice president, American Express	Executive director, Multilateral Trade Negotiations (MTN) Coalition Founder and chair, Coalition of Service Industries (CSI) Media liaison, Alliance for GATT Now	Chair, Mark Twain Institute
Andrew Buxton	CEO (1992–1999) and chair (1993–1999), Barclays Bank Director, Bank of England, CapitaLand UK Holdings Ltd, Xansa UK Ltd, United Bank of Kuwait PLC, among others	Founder and chair, European Services Forum (ESF) Founder and co-chair, Financial Leaders Group (FLG) Founder and chair, High Level LOTIS Group	President, British Bankers' Association
Donald V. Fites	Chairman and CEO, Caterpillar Inc. (1990–1999) Director, Mobil, A. K. Steel, AT&T Wireless, Georgia-Pacific, Oshkosh Truck Corporation, among others	Chair, US Business Roundtable (BRT) Chair, National Foreign Trade Council (NFTC) Member, Business Council	Chair US–Japan Business Council Director, National Association of Manufacturers (NAM) President's Advisory Committee on Trade Policy and Negotiations 1998 Consumers for World Trade (CWT) award
William C. Lane	Director, Government Affairs, Caterpillar Inc	Chair, USA*Engage Co-chair, US Trade Co-chair, US–Chile Free Trade Coalition Founder, Zero Tariff Coalition Founder, Illinois North American Free Trade Agreement (NAFTA) Coalition Vice president, Alliance for GATT Now Co-chair, American–Australian Free Trade Agreement Coalition (AAFTAC)	Member, US Industry Advisory Committee for Trade Policy
Jerry R. Junkins	Chair (1988–1996) and CEO (1985–1996), Texas Instruments Director of Caterpillar Inc., Proctor & Gamble Company and 3M	Chair, Alliance for GATT Now Chair, BRTs International Trade and Investment Task Force International Leadership Award from US Council for International Business (USCIB) Member, Business Council	President's Advisory Committee on Trade Policy and Negotiations

Table 10.2 (*continued*)

	Corporations	Free trade coalitions	Other
Dean O'Hare	CEO and chair, Chubb Corporation (1988–2002) Director of Fluor Corporation and H. J. Heinz Company	Chair, CSI Chair, USCIB Co-chair, FLG	President's Advisory Committee on Trade Policy and Negotiations Past chair, American Insurance Association Chair, Services Working Committee, Pacific Basin Economic Council
Edmond T. Pratt Jnr	CEO and chair, Pfizer Director of General Motors, International Paper, Chase Manhattan, among others	Chair, BRT Co-founder, Intellectual Property Committee (IPC) Member, Business Council	Chair, Advisory Committee on Trade Policy and Negotiations Assistant secretary of the army for Kennedy administration
Frank Kittredge	Vice president of General Electric's Asia-Pacific Division Director, Crane and Company, Inc.	President, NFTC Vice chair, USA*Engage	Committee member, US State Department Advisory Committee on International Economic Policy Advisory board member, Trade Law Study Group Board director, Singapore Trade Development Board, National US–Arab Chamber of Commerce Chairman, US – Association of Southeast Asian Nations (ASEAN) Center for Technology Exchange
Philip M. Condit	Chair (1997–present) and CEO (1996–present), Boeing Director, Hewlett-Packard Company	Board of Trustees, USCIB Co-chair, TransAtlantic Business Dialogue (TABD) Chair, BRT and chair, BRT's International Trade and Investment Task Force	Chair, US–China Business Council Member, Council on Foreign Relations, World Economic Forum (WEF), President's Export Advisory Council, Council on Competitiveness, US–Japan Business Council, Board of Hewlett-Packard
Anne Wexler	Chair of Executive Committee, Wexler and Walker	Clients include NFTC, USA*Engage, USA*NAFTA, Alliance for GATT Now	Top policy aide to President Carter Deputy under secretary of Commerce Member, Council on Foreign Relations

setting the agendas for policy groups; guiding their policy recommendations onto government agendas; filling positions in successive government administrations and as government advisers; and thereby ensuring conducive public policy outcomes. In this way, government is intimately connected with the corporate power elite, or inner circle, and this is increasingly the case in other nations around the world.

The key leadership role of a few corporate executives in mobilizing and organizing free trade coalitions confirms Useem's theory about the 'inner circle' of corporate power (see Figure 10.2 and Table 10.2).

The inner circle are powerful within the corporate community because of their top-level management positions within large corporations, their board membership of other large corporations and their leadership positions in business associations. Because of these multiple positions, they are able to network with others in similar positions and mobilize resources and express support for political goals shared by others in the circle. Their views tend to 'reflect the broader thinking of the business community' rather than the concerns of an individual company.[86]

The enlistment of regulators, bureaucrats and politicians in their cause has been a key achievement of those lobbying for various agreements within the GATT and the WTO. This is made easier by the phenomenon of the revolving door. Large financial corporations are able to offer lucrative positions, including directorships, to those who are supportive of their aims. Some government officials have also gone on to play key roles in business coalitions (see Table 10.3).

Leon Brittan, former UK minister and EU trade commissioner (now Lord Brittan of Spennithorne), went on to be vice chair of UBS-Warburg, a key lobbyist for liberalization of financial services, and chair of the High Level LOTIS Group. Christopher Roberts was director general of Trade Policy at UK's Department of Trade and Industry (DTI) until 1997 and the UK's chief trade negotiator during the Uruguay Round before becoming chair of the LOTIS Committee and vice chair of its High Level Group. Some do not even wait until they leave their government jobs. For example, Alistair Abercrombie, one of the DTI's 'lead services negotiators', took a 'two-year secondment' to British Invisibles where he was director of trade policy and secretary to its LOTIS Committee.[87]

The 'unprecedented levels of strategic alliances and global networks' created by transnational corporations (TNCs) have been referred to as a new form of capitalism: 'alliance capitalism'. In this new form of capitalism, TNCs have more in common with and show more loyalty to TNCs from around the world than with the countries they are headquartered in.[88] Despite this shift in allegiance, national governments still go out of their way to facilitate the business activities of these TNCs and to ensure that their policies do not unduly impede those activities.

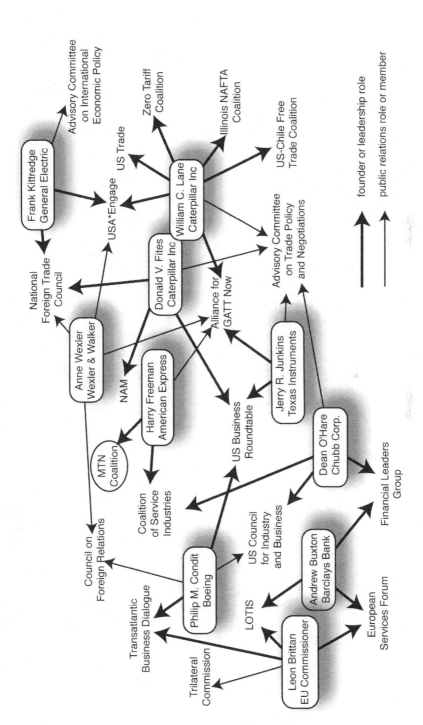

Figure 10.2 *Key people linking trade coalitions*

Advisory Committee on International Economic Policy

Frank Kittredge General Electric

National Foreign Trade Council

USA*Engage US Trade

Zero Tariff Coalition

William C. Lane Caterpillar Inc

Illinois NAFTA Coalition

US-Chile Free Trade Coalition

Donald V. Fites Caterpillar Inc

Advisory Committee on Trade Policy and Negotiations

Anne Wexler Wexler & Walker

Alliance for GATT Now

NAM

Harry Freeman American Express

Jerry R. Junkins Texas Instruments

MTN Coalition

US Business Roundtable

Council on Foreign Relations

Coalition of Service Industries

Dean O'Hare Chubb Corp.

Financial Leaders Group

Philip M. Condit Boeing

US Council for Industry and Business

Transatlantic Business Dialogue

LOTIS

Andrew Buxton Barclays Bank

European Services Forum

Trilateral Commission

Leon Brittan EU Commissioner

founder or leadership role

public relations role or member

Table 10.3 *Some key government officials*

	Government positions	Free trade coalitions	Think tanks and other coalitions	Corporation positions
Leon Brittan	Minister – UK Parliament (1979–1986) European Union (EU) trade commissioner Vice president, European Commission (EC) (1989–1993, 1995–2000) House of Lords	Initiator, European Services Forum (ESF) Chair, High Level LOTIS Group	Fellow, Policy Studies Institute (1988) Trilateral Commission Chair, Conservative Group for Europe	Advisory director, Unilever Vice chair, UBS Warburg
William E. Brock	US Congress (1963–1970) US senator (1971–1976) US Trade Representative (USTR) (1981–1985) US secretary of labor (1985–1987)	Chair, Multilateral Trade Negotiations (MTN) Coalition Founder, Eminent Persons Group	Trustee, Center for Strategic and International Studies Board, Committee for Economic Development Co-chair, US–Canada Partnership for Growth	Chair, The Brock Group (TBG) (1988–1995)
Robert S. Strauss	USTR (1977–1979) Ambassador to Soviet Union (1991–1992)	Chair, MTN Coalition	Trustee, Center for Strategic and International Studies Council on Foreign Affairs Chair, US–Russia Business Council	Partner at Akin, Gump, Strauss, Hauer and Feld, L.L.P.
Peter Sutherland	EC commissioner Director general, General Agreement on Tariffs and Trade (GATT)	Eminent Persons Group (EPG) on World Trade	Member of European Round Table of Industrialists (ERT)	Chair, Allied Irish Bank Chair, Goldman Sachs, British Petroleum (BP)
Robert Vastine	Deputy assistant secretary, Treasury Legislative director in Senate Staff director of Senate Republican Conference	President, Coalition of Service Industries (CSI)	President, Congressional Economic Leadership Institute Founder, Alliance for American Innovation	

NOTES

1   Timothy J. Hauser quoted in V. Sridhar, 'Big Business at Work', *Frontline*, 11–24 December, 1999, www.frontlineonnet.com/fl1626/1626180.htm.

2   USCIB, 'Summary of US Council Recommendations for the May WTO Ministerial', US Council for International Business, May, 1998, www.uscib.org/wtost.asp; John Madeley, *Hungry for Trade: How the Poor Pay for Free Trade*, Global Issues Series, London and New York, Zed Books, 2000, p12; Oliver Hoedeman and Ann Doherty, 'Joining Forces: Big Business Rallies after Seattle', in Eveline Lubbers (ed) *Battling Big Business: Countering Greenwash, Infiltration and Other Forms of Bullying*, Devon, UK, Green Books, 2002, p65.

3   C. Fred Bergsten, 'The Backlash against Globalization', The Trilateral Commission, 2000, www.trilateral.org/annmtgs/trialog/trlgtxts/t54/ber.htm.

4   Guy de Jonquieres, 'Network Guerillas', *Financial Times*, 30 April, 1998.

5   Dan Esty, 'Trade Storms', *World Link*, May/June, 2000.

6   Walter Mead, 'The Case for Capitalism', *World Link*, September/October, 2000.

7   Madeley, *Hungry for Trade*, pp1–2; Mark Engler, 'Globalization's Lost Decade', *Z Magazine*, 5 August, 2003, www.zmag.org/content/print_article.cfm?itemID=40 1&sectionID=13.

8   Editorial, 'Who Cares About Global Trade?' *The Ecologist*, May, 2000, p17.

9   Hoedeman and Doherty, 'Joining Forces', pp67, 71; Phillip Babich, 'Spinning Free Trade: The Battle for Public Opinion', *Making Contact, National Radio Project*, 5 July, 2000.

10 BRT, 'International Trade and Investment', The Business Roundtable, 2001, www.brtable.org/issue.cfm/9/yes/0.

11 opensecrets.org, 'Business Associations', The Center for Responsive Politics, www.opensecrets.org/pubs/lobby00/topind08.asp and www.opensecrets.org/lobbyists/indusclient.asp?code=N00&year=2000&txtSort=A accessed 2 August 2003; BRT, 'The Business Roundtable Launches Multifaceted TPA Campaign', The Business Roundtable, 29 October, 2001, www.brtable.org/press.cfm/611.

12 Hoedeman and Doherty, 'Joining Forces', pp67, 71, 72.

13 CEO, 'European Industry in Seattle', *Corporate Europe Observer*, April, 2000, www.corporateeurope.org/observer6/europeanindustry.html; Leon Brittan, 'Liberalising World Trade: Why Business Must Make Its Voice Heard', Service Industries Trends, 23 March, 2001, www.sitrends.org/ideas/expert.asp?EXPERT_ID=27.

14 Hoedeman and Doherty, 'Joining Forces', pp64–5, 70–71.

15 goTrade, 'The Go Trade Initiative', Business Roundtable, www.gotrade.org/tradeducation.html accessed 24 December 1999.

16 Quoted in Editorial, 'Who Cares About Global Trade?', p16.

17 Bergsten, 'The Backlash Against Globalization'.

18 USCIB, 'Policy Advocacy', US Council for International Business, www.uscib.org/index.asp?documentID=824 accessed 18 May 2003; Dean R. O'Hare, 'The Future of the Global Trading System: Where to from Here?' Paper presented at the APEC CEO Summit 2001, Shanghai, 20 October, 2001; O'Hare quoted in Hoedeman and Doherty, 'Joining Forces', p77.

19   John Braithwaite and Peter Drahos, *Global Business Regulation*, Cambridge, Cambridge University Press, 2000, p177; ICC, 'Business and the Global Economy', International Chamber of Commerce, 8 May, 2002, www.iccwbo.org/home/statements_rules/statements/2002/G8kananskis.asp.

20   ICC, 'Business and the Global Economy'.

21   James Graff and Thomas Sancton, 'Davos Listens to the World', *Time International*, 14 February, 2000.

22   Mead, 'The Case for Capitalism'.

23   WEF managing director, Claude Smadja, quoted in Peter Costigan, 'Why S11 Should Welcome the WEF', *The Age*, 30 August, 2000; Schwab quoted in 'Economics and Social Cohesion', *Time International*, 15 February, 1999 and Costigan, 'Why S11 Should Welcome the WEF'.

24   Ethan Kapstein, 'Directions to Democracy', *World Link*, May/June, 2000; Schwab quoted in 'Economics and Social Cohesion'.

25   Liberalisation of Trade in Services (LOTIS) Committee, 'Minutes of Meeting, Tuesday, 25 January 2000', HM Treasury, London 2000; Liberalisation of Trade in Services (LOTIS) Committee, 'Minutes of Meeting, Friday, 8 December 2000', Institute of Chartered Accountants in England and Wales 2000.

26   Liberalisation of Trade in Services (LOTIS) Committee, 'Minutes of Meeting, Tuesday, 21 March 2000', Department of Trade and Industry 2000; Liberalisation of Trade in Services (LOTIS) Committee, 'Minutes of Meeting, Thursday, 22 Feburary 2001', Lloyd's, London 2001.

27   Liberalisation of Trade in Services (LOTIS) Committee, 'Minutes 25 Jan 2000'; High Level LOTIS Group, 'Minutes of Meeting, Monday 15 November', Barclays Bank PLC 1999.

28   Liberalisation of Trade in Services (LOTIS) Committee, 'Minutes 25 Jan 2000'; Liberalisation of Trade in Services (LOTIS) Committee, 'Minutes 22 Feb 2001'.

29   BIAC, 'BIAC Priorities for the WTO Doha Negotiations and Recommendations to the OECD', Paris, Business and Industry Advisory Committee to the OECD, 20 February 2003, pp1–2.

30   ECAT, 'Trade Resources', Emergency Committee for American Trade, www.ecattrade.com/resources/subsection.asp?id=17 accessed 8 June 2003.

31   ECAT, 'About ECAT', Emergency Committee for American Trade, 2002, www.ecattrade.com/about/.

32   Calman J. Cohen, 'Testimony before the Subcommittee on Trade', House Committee on Ways and Means, 30 September, 1997, http://waysandmeans.house.gov/legacy/trade/105cong/9-30-97/9-30cohe.htm.

33   Matthew J. Slaughter, 'Technology, Trade and Investment: The Public Opinion Disconnect', Emergency Committee for American Trade 2002, pp4–5.

34   Ernesto Zedillo, 'Globaphobia', *World Link*, March/April, 2000; Abraham Katz, 'Remarks by Abraham Katz', US Council for International Business, 8 December, 1998, www.uscib.org/index.asp?documentID=2239; 'Prepared Statement by Abraham Katz, President, United States Council for International Business', US Senate Finance Committee, 28 January 1999.

35   Hill & Knowlton, '"S11" Protest Brief', Melbourne, Hill and Knowlton 2000.

36 Black Kelly Scruggs & Healy, 'Guide to the Seattle Meltdown', Common Dreams News Center, 10 March, 2000, www.commondreams.org/headlines/031000-03.htm.

37 Quoted in Hoedeman and Doherty, 'Joining Forces', p75 and CEO, 'Business Responses to Seattle', *Corporate Europe Observer*, April, 2000, www.corporateeurope. org/observer6/businessresponse.html.

38 Hoedeman and Doherty, 'Joining Forces', p73.

39 Brittan, 'Liberalising World Trade'.

40 Liberalisation of Trade in Services (LOTIS) Committee, 'Minutes 8 Dec 2000'; Liberalisation of Trade in Services (LOTIS) Committee, 'Minutes 25 Jan 2000'.

41 Hoedeman and Doherty, 'Joining Forces', p74.

42 *Ibid.*, pp74–5.

43 de Jonquieres, 'Network Guerillas'.

44 James Goodman, 'The WEF: Capital's First International?' S11, www.s11.org/wef_1sti.html accessed 5 September 2000; Sean Healy, 'Corporate Club "Shapes Global Agenda"', Wollongong, S11 Resource Kit 2000.

45 ECAT, 'Summary of ECAT Positions on Issues', Emergency Committee for American Trade, www.ecattrade.com/statements/content.asp?ID=127 accessed 8 June 2003.

46 USCIB, 'Policy Advocacy'; 'Services 2000 USTR Federal Register Submission', Federal Register Notice [FR Doc. 98-22279]: Solicitation of Public Comment Regarding US preparations for the World Trade Organization's Ministerial Meeting, Fourth Quarter 1999, 21 October 1999; Claude Barfield, 'Comments and Discussion', *Brookings-Wharton Papers on Financial Services 2000*, 2000, p455.

47 Gregory Palast, 'The WTO's Hidden Agenda', *CorpWatch*, 9 November, 2001, www. corpwatch.org/issues/PRT.jsp?articleid=722.

48 *Ibid.*

49 BIAC, 'BIAC Priorities', pp3, 6; USCIB, 'Policy Advocacy'.

50 'Prepared Statement by Thomas M. T. Niles, President, United States Council for International Business', US House US House Committee on Ways and Means Trade Subcommittee, 8 February 2000.

51 BIAC, 'Priorities for OECD and WTO Work: BIAC Submission on Trade-Related Issues to the OECD', Paris, Business and Industry Advisory Committee to the OECD, June 1998, p6.

52 *Ibid.*, p6.

53 Liberalisation of Trade in Services (LOTIS) Committee, 'Minutes of Meeting, Monday, 8 November 1999', Lloyd's, London 1999; Liberalisation of Trade in Services (LOTIS) Committee, 'Minutes of Meeting', Corporation of London's Marketing Suite, 23 September 1999; High Level LOTIS Group, 'Minutes 15 Nov 1999'; Liberalisation of Trade in Services (LOTIS) Committee, 'Minutes 25 Jan 2000'.

54 Jim Lobe, 'Rights-Trade: Multinationals Win US Court Victory over Activists', *Inter Press Service*, 24 June, 1999.

55 NFTC, 'Welcome to NFTC', National Foreign Trade Council, www.nftc.org accessed 8 June 2003.

56 *Ibid.*

57   NFTC, 'Membership Benefits', National Foreign Trade Council, www.nftc.org/ default.asp?Mode=DirectoryDisplay&id=121 accessed 8 June 2003; NFTC, 'NFTC Policy Activities', National Foreign Trade Council, www.nftc.org/default.asp?Mod e=DirectoryDisplay&id=94 accessed 8 June 2003; NFTC, 'NFTC's 2003 Goals', National Foreign Trade Council, www.nftc.org/default.asp?Mode=DirectoryDisplay &id=117 accessed 8 June 2003.

58   NFTC, 'NFTC Policy Activities'; opensecrets.org, 'Business Associations'.

59   Lobe, 'Rights-Trade'; Belén Balanyá, *et al.*, *Europe Inc. Regional and Global Restructuring and the Rise of Corporate Power*, London, Pluto Press, 2000, pp126–7.

60   Kittredge quoted in Lobe, 'Rights-Trade'; Deirdre Shesgreen, 'Can States Set Trade Policy?' *Legal Times*, 17 August, 1998.

61   NFTC, 'NFTC Policy Activities'; Kittredge quoted in Ken Silverstein, 'So You Want to Trade with a Dictator', *Mother Jones*, May/June, 1998, http://bsd.mojones.com/ mother_jones/MJ98/silverstein.html

62   Silverstein, 'So You Want to Trade with a Dictator'; Mann, 'A Corporate Coup D'etat'.

63   Silverstein, 'So You Want to Trade with a Dictator'.

64   USA*Engage, 'About Us', USA*Engage, www.usaengage.org/about_us/index.html accessed 29 May 2003.

65   Silverstein, 'So You Want to Trade with a Dictator'.

66   USA*Engage, 'About Us'.

67   *Ibid*.

68   'Pro-GATT Forces Play Their Face Cards', *Legal Times*, 1 August, 1994, p5; Lane quoted in Jim Mann, 'A Corporate Coup D'etat', *Los Angeles Times*, 5 July, 2000.

69   Doug Bereuter *et al.*, 'Co-Sponsor H.R. 2708, the Sanctions Reform Act', 18 February, 1998; Silverstein, 'So You Want to Trade with a Dictator'.

70   Memo included in online version of Silverstein, 'So You Want to Trade with a Dictator'.

71   William R. Hawkins, 'Sanctions "Reform" Hits a Dead End', Trade Alert, 21 March, 2002, www.tradealert.org/view_art.asp?Prod_ID=402

72   Andrew Buxton, 'The European Services Network: Keynote Speech', Paper presented at the Preparatory Conference for the World Services Congress, The University Club, Washington DC, 2 June, 1999, p2.

73   Braithwaite and Drahos, *Global Business Regulation,* p491.

74   USCIB, 'About USCIB', US Council for International Business, www.uscib.org/ index.asp?documentID=697 accessed 18 May 2003.

75   Pascal Kerneis, 'The Perspective of the European Private Sector in the GATS Negotiations', Paper presented at the Regional Seminar on Services: ASEAN, Bangkok, Thailand, 27 June, 2000, p5.

76   Board of Directors – www.nftc.org/default.asp?Mode=DirectoryDisplay&id=134

77   www.uscib.org/index.asp?documentID=1846

78   www.uscsi.org/members/current.htm.

79   Michael A. Santoro and Lynn Sharp Paine, 'Pfizer: Global Protection of Intellectual Property', Harvard Business School 1995, p9; Michael P. Ryan, *Knowledge Diplomacy: Global Competition and the Politics of Intellectual Property*, Washington, DC, Brookings Institution Press, 1998, p88.

80 www.usaengage.org/about_us/members/index.html
81 www.idfa.org/intl/ustrade.cfm; Michael Paulson, 'Business Leaders Fight Back Against Anti-WTO Forces', in *Who Owns the WTO? Corporations and Global Trade*, www.corpwatch.org/, Corporate Watch, 1999.
82 http://tabd.com/
83 www.counciloftheamericas.org/coa/membersnetwork/members1.html
84 www.opensecrets.org/alerts/v5/alertv5_47d.asp
85 G. William Domhoff, *Who Rules America? Power and Politics*, 4th edn, New York, McGraw Hill, 2002, pp21–4.
86 Michael Useem, *The Inner Circle: Large Corporations and the Rise of Business Political Activity in the US And UK*, Oxford, Oxford University Press, 1984, pp61–2, 108.
87 Erik Wesselius, 'Liberalisation of Trade in Services: Corporate Power at Work', GATSwatch 2001.
88 Leslie Sklair, *Globalization: Capitalism and Its Alternatives*, Oxford, Oxford University Press, 2002, p65.

11

Conclusion: The Triumph of Corporate Rights

The most effective way to restrict democracy is to transfer decision-making from the public arena to unaccountable institutions: kings and princes, priestly castes, military juntas, party dictatorships, or modern corporations.   NOAM CHOMSKY[1]

Towards the end of the 1970s we witnessed a turning point in history. The rise of Thatcherism in the UK and Reaganism in the US, as well as the conversion of labour and social democratic governments in countries such as Australia and New Zealand to free market policies, marked a shift in government priorities. Corporate interest began to take priority over national interests and the nation state began to fade as the pre-eminent organizing principle for human societies.

This was no natural or inevitable evolution but an outcome fostered and nurtured by the transnational corporations (TNCs) who have most to gain from it. They have used their power and influence over governments to promote free trade and deregulated business enterprise as the highest goal of government policy. They have augmented their economic power by creating and supporting vast and far-reaching corporate networks dedicated to political persuasion. These corporate power blocks are able to manipulate and coerce elected and appointed members of governments and international institutions around the world to adopt policies that suit TNCs.

The rise of corporate power and the increasing importance accorded to markets mean that TNCs are eclipsing the nation state as the driving force behind policy-making. So-called 'free' markets are becoming the new organizing principle for the global order. The idea that governments should protect citizens against the excesses of free enterprise has been replaced with the idea that government should protect business activities against the excesses of democratic regulation. As a consequence, the ideals of the nation state have been diluted and distorted.

After several centuries of development, these ideals were ultimately expressed in the Universal Declaration of Human Rights, adopted by the United Nations General Assembly in 1948, after World War II. It was a significant statement of moral and political principles that formed the basis of subsequent human rights treaties and national constitutions and has become part of international customary law, which binds all nations.

Human rights include the right to life, liberty, health and well-being. They apply to every human being throughout their lives, no matter where they live or what their religion, occupation, race, colour, gender or age. They are regarded as essential to human dignity and as inalienable, which means that they cannot be taken away, sold or given away. Governments have a duty to 'respect, protect and promote them'. Human rights are supposed to have absolute priority over any political lobbying or economic trade-offs.[2]

The Universal Declaration was later reinforced by the International Covenant on Economic, Social and Cultural Rights and the International Covenant on Civil and Political Rights. These covenants, adopted by the UN in 1966, elaborate the rights in the Universal Declaration and are binding on the 130 or more nation states that have signed them. The Universal Declaration of Human Rights, together with the two international covenants, make up the International Bill of Human Rights.

The International Covenant on Civil and Political Rights (CCPR) includes the right to freedom of thought, conscience and religion; freedom of association and peaceful assembly; the assumption of innocence until proven guilty at a fair trial; freedom from arbitrary arrest or detention; freedom from torture and cruel, inhuman and degrading treatment; and freedom from slavery or forced labour. Most significantly, it protects the right of citizens to participate in the governance of their nations.

The International Covenant on Economic, Social and Cultural Rights (CESCR) includes rights to an adequate standard of living, health, education, social security, work in proper working conditions for fair wages, participation in cultural life, and the benefits of social progress. These are rights that place an obligation on governments to adopt policies to ensure that individuals and groups are equally able to develop to their full potential.[3]

However, with the eclipse of the nation state and the mobilization of corporate power, corporate rights and the priority of free trade are progressively trumping human rights and undermining democratic efforts to protect those rights. The World Trade Organization (WTO) and its rules represent the culmination of years of corporate political mobilization, much of it carried out before civil society became aware of what was being accomplished. The WTO is today an instrument of business interests. It represents the triumph of corporate coalitions over democratic regulations that are intended to protect the human rights of workers, consumers and communities, as well as the environments in which they live and work or which they value.

An early indicator of the shape of things to come occurred in 2004, with a victory of transnational gambling corporations over democratic governance. A WTO panel ruled that the US government could not ban internet gambling. The panel conceded 'that the measures at issue were indeed designed so as to protect public morals or to maintain public order', but decided that the measures were not allowable because:

> ...the United States had failed to demonstrate that they were 'necessary' since it had not shown that there was no WTO-consistent alternative measure reasonably available that would provide the United States with the same level of protection against the risks it had identified.[4]

In answer to the issue of whether a nation had the right to regulate in response to democratically formulated policy, the panel of three trade experts that made the gambling ruling stated: 'Members' regulatory sovereignty is an essential pillar of the progressive liberalization of trade in services; but this sovereignty ends whenever rights of other members under the GATS [General Agreement on Trade in Services] are impaired.'[5]

In other words, the ban on internet gambling was ruled to be a trade restriction that interfered with the rights of another member of GATS – in this specific case, the complainant state, Antigua – where at least one transnational gambling corporation had its nominal base of operations. According to the ruling, if the US wants to protect public morals, it has to find a way to do it which does not restrict corporate rights to trade – otherwise the onus is on the US government to prove that no such alternative exists.

The WTO ruling requires US regulations to be changed at both the state and federal levels of government. Gambling is subject to a variety of restrictions that may now be challenged under this ruling. These include 'state monopolies on lotteries, exclusive rights granted to native tribes to operate casinos, and local bans on certain forms of gambling [such as] slot machines'.[6]

The ruling is significant because it shows that the WTO can overrule the right of democracies to decide to legislate in order to protect public morals and to maintain public order when such legislation interferes with the rights of other nations – and, by implication, TNCs – to trade globally without impediment. Yet, even if free trade is more economically efficient, markets are supposed to serve society, rather than societies serving the imperatives of free markets.

Some people may argue that an original commitment to opening sectors of a nation's economy to liberalization was made democratically; therefore, the WTO is merely enforcing an earlier democratic decision. However, this book has shown clearly that such decisions are far from democratic. In the case of developing nations, such decisions are coerced, and in the case of more powerful nations such as the US, they result from the exercise of corporate power and manipulation. However, what is significant about the WTO is that it locks such decisions in place so that democracies are unable to subsequently respond to changing circumstances or public pressure.

At the time that the US government made its GATS commitments to opening up its recreation services in 1993, it was unable to foresee the technological changes that would lead to internet gambling being such a major problem, and so it did not specify gambling as an exception. Now that internet gambling has turned out to be such a major issue, the government is no longer able to ban it, even if this is what a majority of citizens want to do. Instead, it must find a way to protect public morals that does not interfere with the rights of TNCs to exploit gamblers via the internet.

The implications of the judgement are far reaching. It has been suggested that the ruling would mean that under Europe's unlimited GATS commitments for solid and hazardous waste disposal services, 'no European jurisdiction – be it local, regional or national – can prohibit foreign-owned operations from disposing of hazardous waste by "incineration or other means", even if these means are totally illegal for domestic firms under local laws'.[7] As with the gambling case, governments will have to find alternative ways of protecting public health that do not interfere with the rights of TNCs to dispose of hazardous waste as they see fit.

The protection of public health and morals has traditionally been given priority in democracies, and even human rights are subject to limits that enable governments to protect them. In other words, individual human rights may be democratically limited by governments in order to protect public health and morality. The International Covenant on Civil and Political Rights, which came into force in 1976, states that:

> The above-mentioned rights shall not be subject to any restrictions except those which are provided by law, are necessary to protect national security, public order (ordre public), public health or morals or the rights and freedoms of others. (Article 12)

Even in these exceptional circumstances, human rights can only be limited by governments if they can 'demonstrate that the limitations do not impair the democratic functioning of the society'.[8]

The WTO, however, places the corporate right to free trade above these democratic priorities. In the process, corporate rights have become even more important than individual human rights. Governments may protect public health and morals only in so far as this does not interfere with corporate rights to free trade and investment. In addition, as we saw in Chapter 3, any backtracking on free market policies will be punished by international financial institutions and foreign investors.

According to Article 25 of the Universal Declaration of Human Rights (1948):

> Everyone has the right to a standard of living adequate for the health and well-being of himself and of his family, including food, clothing, housing and medical care and necessary social services, and the right to security in the event of unemployment, sickness, disability, widowhood, old age or other lack of livelihood in circumstances beyond his control.[9]

The world has never achieved this worthy goal; but it was once a democratic ideal. However, this ideal conflicts with corporate goals, and corporations have ensured that such rights have become mere privileges that must be paid for. In a corporate-dominated world, the right to an adequate standard of living is subordinate to the right of corporations to make profits out of providing every human service. Essential services such as water and electricity that are crucial to the fulfilment of this human right are increasingly denied to poor people when these services are turned into tradeable commodities that TNCs can make profits from.

The right of every member of society to 'take part in the conduct of public affairs' has been usurped by corporations who have avoided and bypassed democratic decision-making and rendered it meaningless. The right to work in proper conditions for fair wages and to benefit from social progress has been whittled away as corporations and their executives appropriate an ever larger share of national income and encourage governments to remove worker protections and welfare entitlements in the name of economic growth and competitiveness in a global market.

The right to life and health are neglected as millions die each year from contaminated air and water, and millions more suffer the health impacts of industrial and agricultural chemicals that are used to boost industrial production and profits. Efforts to regulate pollution and environmental degradation are resisted by corporations and, according to the WTO, must be proven to be necessary and the least trade-restrictive option or otherwise must give way to the greater right of corporations to trade.

Democratic ideals such as an adequate level of health and education for all have been sacrificed to provide business opportunities for corporations. The tragedy is that by the time the world's citizens realize the consequences of this loss, their ability to regain power and to reorder priorities democratically will be obstructed by the WTO. The collective corporate ambition to rise above the reach of democratic controls will have attained its ultimate success.

NOTES

1   Noam Chomsky, 'Domestic Constituencies', *Z Magazine*, May 1998, www.chomsky. info/articles/199805--.htm.

2   J. G. Merrills, 'Environmental Protection and Human Rights: Conceptual Aspects', in Alan E. Boyle and Michael R. Anderson (eds) *Human Rights Approaches to Environmental Protection*, Oxford, Clarendon Press, 1996, pp25–7; Moira Rayner, 'History of Universal Human Rights – up to WW2', Universal Rights Network, http://www. universalrights.net/main/histof.htm accessed 25 April 2005; Michael R. Anderson, 'Human Rights Approaches to Environmental Protection: An Overview', in Alan E. Boyle and Michael R. Anderson (eds) *Human Rights Approaches to Environmental Protection*, Oxford, Clarendon Press, 1996, p21.

3 Alan Boyle, 'The Role of International Human Rights Law in the Protection of the Environment', in Alan E. Boyle and Michael R. Anderson (eds) *Human Rights Approaches to Environmental Protection*, Oxford, Clarendon Press, 1996, p46.

4 WTO Panel, 'United States – Measures Affecting the Cross-Border Supply of Gambling and Betting Services', World Trade Organization, 10 November 2004, p135.

5 *Ibid.,* p209.

6 'Highlights of the US – Gambling Decision', *WTOWatch*, 2 December, 2004.

7 *Ibid.*

8 International Commission of Jurists, 'Siracusa Principles on the Limitations and Derogation Provisions in the International Covenant on Civil and Political Rights', Washington, DC, American Association for the International Commission of Jurists 1985.

9 UN, 'Universal Declaration of Human Rights', United Nations, 1948, http://www.un.org/Overview/rights.html.

Bibliography

Abbott, K. (1996) *Pressure Groups and the Australian Federal Parliament*, Political Studies Fellow Monograph No 3, Australian Government Publishing Service, Canberra

Abelson, D. E. (1995) 'From Policy Research to Political Advocacy: The Changing Role of Think Tanks in American Politics', *Canadian Review of American Studies*, vol 25, no 1, pp93–126

Abelson, D. E. (2002) 'Think Tanks and US Foreign Policy: An Historical Perspective', *US Foreign Policy Agenda*, vol 7, no 3, http://usinfo.state.gov/journals/itps/1102/ijpe/pj73toc.htm

Abercrombie, A. (2004) 'Seminar on GATS and Financial Services', International Financial Services, London, 11 May, www.ifsl.org.uk/tradepolicy/viewpoint.cfm

ACC (Australian Chamber of Commerce) (1978) *74th Annual Report 1977–1978*, ACC, Canberra

Ad Hoc Working Group on the MAI (Multilateral Agreement on Investment) (1998) *MAI Multilateral Agreement on Investment: Democracy for Sale?* Apex Press, New York

Adams, C. (2001) 'Privatising Infrastructure in the South', *Focus on Trade*, May, www.focusweb.org/publications/2001/privatising%20Infrastructure%20in%20the%20South.html

AEI (American Enterprise Institute for Public Policy Research) (2004a) *AEI's Diamond Jubilee, 1943–2003*, www.aei.org/about/contentID.20031212154735838/default.asp

AEI (2004b) *Finances*, AEI, www.aei.org/about/contentID.2002121511415722/default.asp

Ahlberg, B. (1990) 'American Express: The Stateless Corporation', *Multinational Monitor*, November, www.multinationalmonitor.org/hyper/issues/1990/11/mm1190_11.html

Ahmed, M., Lane, T. and Schulze-Ghattas, M. (2001) 'Refocusing IMF Conditionality', *Finance and Development*, December, www.IMF.org/external/pubs/ft/fandd/2001/12/ahmed.htm

Albouy, Y. and Bousba, R. (1998) 'The Impact of IPPs in Developing Countries – Out of the Crisis and Into the Future', *The World Bank Group – Public Policy for the Private Sector*, December, www.worldbank.org/html/fpd/notes/162/162albou.pdf

American Federation of Labor (1913) *National Association of Manufacturers Exposed: Revelations of Senate Lobby Investigation*, American Federation of Labor, Washington, DC

Anderson, M. R. (1996) 'Human Rights Approaches to Environmental Protection: An Overview', in Boyle, A. E. and Anderson, M. R. (eds) *Human Rights Approaches to Environmental Protection*, Clarendon Press, Oxford

Andrews, E. L. (1997) 'Agreement to Open Up World Financial Markets is Reached', *New York Times*, 13 December

Antitrust Division (2005) *Overview*, US Department of Justice, www.usdoj.gov/atr/overview.html accessed 6 January 2005

Apelt, B. (1985) 'Roger M. Blough', *San Francisco Chronicle*, 10 October, p43

Apelt, B. (2001) '100 Years of US Steel', *New Steel*, vol 17, no 4, pp26–28

Ashford, N. (1997) 'Politically Impossible? How Ideas, Not Interests and Circumstances, Determine Public Policies', *Policy*, autumn, pp21–25

Asian Development Bank (1995) *The Bank's Policy Initiatives for the Energy Sector*, Asian Development Bank, the Philippines, May, www.adb.org/Documents/Policies/Energy_Initiatives/default.asp?p=policies

Austin, N. and Hope, D. (1986) 'Farmers Threaten Direct Action to Smash Union Power', *The Bulletin*, 15 July, pp24–26

Avery, N. (1993) 'Stealing from the State', *Multinational Monitor*, September, www.essential.org/monitor/hyper/issues/1993/09/mm0993_10.html

Babich, P. (2000) 'Spinning Free Trade: The Battle for Public Opinion', *Making Contact, National Radio Project*, 5 July

Bakan, J. (2004) *The Corporation: The Pathological Pursuit of Profit and Power*, The Free Press, New York

Balanyá, B., Doherty, A., Hoedeman, O., Ma'anit, A. and Wesselius, E. (1998) *MAIgalomania! Citizens and the Environment Sacrificed to Corporate Investment Agenda*, Corporate Europe Observatory, February, www.xs4all.nl/~ceo/mai/mmania07.html

Balanyá, B., Doherty, A., Hoedeman, O., Ma'anit, A. and Wesselius, E. (2000) *Europe Inc. Regional and Global Restructuring and the Rise of Corporate Power*, Pluto Press, London

Barfield, C. (2000) 'Comments and Discussion', *Brookings-Wharton Papers on Financial Services 2000*, pp453–463

Barker, D. and Mander, J. (1999) *Invisible Government – The World Trade Organization: Global Government for the New Millennium*, International Forum on Globalization (IFG), Sausalito, CA, October

Barlow, M. and Clarke, T. (2002) *Blue Gold: The Fight to Stop the Corporate Theft of the World's Water*, The New Press, New York

Bates, R. H. (1994) 'Comment', in Williamson, J. (ed) *The Political Economy of Policy Reform*, Institute for International Economics, Washington, DC

Bayliss, K. (2001) 'Privatisation and the World Bank: A Flawed Development Tool', *Global Focus*, June, www.psiru.org/reports/2000-11-U-WB.doc

Bayliss, K. and Hall, D. (2000) *Independent Power Producers: A Review of the Issues*, University of Greenwich, Public Services International Research Unit (PSIRU), London, November, www.psiru.org/reports/2000-11-E-IPPs.doc

BBC (British Broadcasting Corporation) News (2001) 'Malaysia Lifts Foreign Investment Controls', *BBC News*, 2 May, www.news.bbc.co.uk/1/hi/business/130820.stm

BCC (British Chambers of Commerce) (2005) 'The National Voice of Local Business', BCC, www.chamberonline.co.uk/common/print.aspx?a=ba818faf, accessed 18 August 2005

Beder, S. (1996) *The Nature of Sustainable Development*, 2nd edition, Scribe Publications, Melbourne

Beder, S. (2002) *Global Spin: The Corporate Assault on Environmentalism*, 2nd edition, Green Books, Devon

Beder, S. (2003) *Power Play: The Fight to Control the World's Electricity*, Scribe Publications and The New Press, Melbourne and New York

Bell, S. (1997) *Ungoverning the Economy: The Political Economy of Australian Economic Policy*, Oxford University Press, Melbourne

Bell, S. and Warhurst, J. (1992) 'Political Activism Among Large Firms', in Bell, S. and Wanna, J. (eds) *Business–Government Relations in Australia*, Harcourt Brace Jovanovich, Sydney

Bereuter, D., Hamilton, L. H., Crane, P. M., Blumenauer, E., Ewing, T. W., Kolbe, J. and Manzullo, D. A. (1998) *Co-Sponsor H.R. 2708: The Sanctions Reform Act*, letter reproduced by USA*Engage, 18 February, www.usaengage.org/archives/legislative/dearhouse.html

Berger, M. T. (2004) *The Battle for Asia: From Decolonization to Globalization*, RoutledgeCurzon, New York

Bergsten, C. F. (2000) *The Backlash against Globalization*, The Trilateral Commission, www.trilateral.org/annmtgs/trialog/trlgtxts/t54/ber.htm

Berman, D. (2001) 'The Confederate Cartel's War Against California', *San Francisco Bay Guardian*, 5 January

BIAC (Business and Industry Advisory Committee to the OECD) (1998a) *Revised BIAC Statement on OECD Work on Trade in Services*, BIAC, Paris, June 1998, pp2–3

BIAC (1998b) *Priorities for OECD and WTO Work: BIAC Submission on Trade-Related Issues to the OECD*, BIAC, Paris, June 1998, p2

BIAC (2003a) *BIAC Priorities for the WTO Doha Negotiations and Recommendations to the OECD*, BIAC, Paris, 20 February 2003, p3

BIAC (2003b) *eBIAC: The Voice of the Business Community at the OECD*, BIAC, Paris, 28 May 2003, www.biac.org/

Birnbaum, J. H. (2004) 'Former Powerhouse, Back at the Table', *Washington Post*, 12 July, pE01

Black Kelly Scruggs and Healy (2000) *Guide to the Seattle Meltdown*, Common Dreams News Center, 10 March 2000, www.commondreams.org/headlines/031000–03.htm

Blandy, R. (1993) 'Labour Market Reform', in Galligan, B., Lim, B. and Lovegrove, K. (eds) *Managing Microeconomic Reform*, Federalism Research Centre, ANU, Canberra

Bleifuss, J. (1998) 'Building the Global Economy', *In These Times*, 11 January, p13

Blumenthal, S. (1986) *The Rise of the Counter-Establishment: From Conservative Ideology to Political Power*, Time Books, New York

Blustein, P. (2002) 'IMF's "Consensus" Policies Fraying', *Washington Post*, 26 September, pE01

Bodman, S. (2002) 'Remarks', Paper presented at the Services 2002 Conference, Washington, DC, 5 February

Boggs, C. (2000) *The End of Politics: Corporate Power and the Decline of the Public Sphere*, The Guildford Press, New York

Bollard, A. (1994) 'New Zealand', in Williamson, J. (ed) *The Political Economy of Policy Reform*, Institute for International Economics, Washington, DC

Bond, P. (2003) 'The New Apartheid', *New Internationalist*, April, p24

Bond, P. (2004) 'ANC Privatizations Fail to Deliver in South Africa', *CorpWatch*, 18 August, www.corpwatch.org/print_article.php?&id=11500

Booth, R. R. (2000) *Warring Tribes: The Story of Power Development in Australia*, The Bardak Group, West Perth

Bouygues (2004) 'Saur', Bouygues, www.bouygues.fr/us/metiers/saur.asp

Boyle, A. (1996) 'The Role of International Human Rights Law in the Protection of the Environment', in Boyle, A. E. and Anderson, M. R. (eds) *Human Rights Approaches to Environmental Protection*, Clarendon Press, Oxford

Braithwaite, J. and Drahos, P. (2000) *Global Business Regulation*, Cambridge University Press, Cambridge

Brittan, L. (1998) *Europe's Prescriptions for the Global Trade Agenda*, European Union, 24 September, www.eurunion.org/news/speeches/1998/9809241b.htm

Brittan, L. (2000) *A Diet of Brussels: The Changing Face of Europe*, Little, Brown and Company, London

Brittan, L. (2001) 'Liberalising World Trade: Why Business Must Make Its Voice Heard', *Service Industries Trends*, 23 March

BRT (US Business Roundtable) (2001a) *International Trade and Investment*, BRT, www.brtable.org/issue.cfm/9/yes/0

BRT (2001b) *The Business Roundtable Launches Multifaceted TPA Campaign*, BRT, 29 October 2001, www.brtable.org/press.cfm/611

BRT (2003) *The Business Roundtable Urges WTO Members to Complete Bold Market Access Agreement to Energize World Economic Growth*, BRT, 16 May 2003, www.brtable.org/press.cfm/929

BRT (2005) *Business Roundtable History*, BRT, www.businessroundtable.org/aboutUs/history, accessed 16 August 2005

Budhoo, D. and Alvares, C. (1992) 'Why the IMF is a Threat to the South', *Third World Resurgence*, June, pp14–17

Burks, D. B. (1977) 'Disenchantment with Business: A Mandate for Christian Ethics', *The Entrepreneur*, August, pp1–4

Buxton, A. (1999) 'The European Services Network: Keynote speech', Paper presented at the Preparatory Conference for the World Services Congress, The University Club, Washington, DC, 2 June

Carey, A. (1995) *Taking the Risk Out of Democracy*, Lohrey, A. (ed) UNSW Press, Sydney

Carroll, J. (1992) 'Economic Rationalism and its Consequences', in Carroll, J. and Manne, R. (eds) *Shutdown: The Failure of Economic Rationalism and How to Rescue Australia*, The Text Publishing Company, Melbourne

Carroll, W. K. and Fennema, M. (2002) 'Is There a Transnational Business Community?', *International Sociology*, vol 17, no 3, pp393–419

Castles, F. G., Gerritsen, R. and Vowles, J. (eds) (1996) *The Great Experiment: Labour Parties and Public Policy Transformation in Australia and New Zealand*, Allen & Unwin, Sydney

Catley, B. (1996) *Globalising Australian Capitalism*, Cambridge University Press, Cambridge

CEDA (Committee for the Economic Development of Australia) (2005) *History*, CEDA, www.ceda.com.au/New/Flash/html/body_history.html, accessed 16 August

Chadwick, P. (1989) *Media Mates: Carving up Australia's Media*, Macmillan, Melbourne

Chan, W. K. (1998) *Preparing for Services 2000*, Global Services Network, June, www.globalservicesnetwork.com/preparing_for_services_200.htm

Chatterjee, P. (2001) 'Enron: Pulling the Plug on the Global Power Broker', *Corp Watch*, 13 December, www.corpwatch.org/issues/PRT.jsp?articleid–1016

Chavez, D. (2002) *Lights Off! Debunking the Myths of Power Liberalisation*, Transnational Institute (TNI), Amsterdam, May, www.tni.org/reports/energy/lightsoff.pdf

Chomsky, N. (1998) 'Domestic Constituencies', *Z Magazine*, May, www.zmag.org/ZMag/articles/chomskymay98.htm

Chossudovsky, M. (1992) 'The Global Creation of Third World Poverty', *Third World Resurgence*, January, pp13–20

Chu, V. L. L. (2002) *The Case for Open Markets in Financial Services*, International Chamber of www.iccwbo.org/home/news_archives/2003/stories/financial.asp

CIA (US Central Intelligence Agency) (2000) *CIA Activities in Chile*, CIA, 18 September, www.cia.gov/cia/reports/chile

Clarke, T. (1998) 'The Corporate Rule Treaty', *Third World Resurgence*, vol 90/91, pp11–4

Clarke, T. (circa 1999) *By What Authority! Unmasking and Challenging the Global Corporations' Assault on Democracy through the World Trade Organization*, Polaris Institute and International Forum on Globalization, www.polarisinstitute.org/pubs/pubs_pdfs/bywhatauthority.pdf

Clarke, T. (2001) 'Enron: Washington's Number One Behind-the-Scenes GATS Negotiator', *Corp Watch*, 25 October, www.corpwatch.org/issues/wto/featured/2001/tclarke.html

Cockett, R. (1994) *Thinking the Unthinkable: Think-Tanks and the Economic Counter-Revolution 1931–1983*, Harper Collins, London

Cohen, C. J. (1997) *Testimony before the Subcommittee on Trade*, House Committee on Ways and Means, 30 September, www.waysandmeans.house.gov/legacy/trade/105cong/9–30–97/9–30cohe.htm

Cohen, M. G. (2002) *From Public Good to Private Exploitation: Electricity Deregulation, Privatization and Continental Integration*, Canadian Centre for Policy Alternatives, Nova Scotia, July

Collins, L. (1999) 'Rear Window', *Australian Financial Review*, 22 October, p91

Committee on Education and Labour (1939) 'Violations of Free Speech and Rights of Labor', Report no. 6, part 6, US Senate, Washington DC

Corporate Europe Observatory (1997) *Europe Inc.*, Corporate Europe Observatory, 8 February 1997, www.xs4all.nl/~ceo/eurinc/ 2000

Corporate Europe Observatory (1999) *TransAtlantic Business Dialogue (TABD)*, Corporate Europe Observatory, Amsterdam, 25 October

Corporate Europe Observatory (2000a) 'Business Responses to Seattle', *Corporate Europe Observer*, April, www.corporateeurope.org/observer6/businessresponse.html

Corporate Europe Observatory (2000b) 'European Industry in Seattle', *Corporate Europe Observer*, April, www.corporateeurope.org/observer6/europeanindustry.html

Corporate Europe Observatory (2001a) 'GATS: Undermining Public Services', *Corporate Europe Observer*, June, www.corporateeurope.org/observer9/gats.html

Corporate Europe Observatory (2001b) 'TABD Back on Track?' *Corporate Europe Observer*, December, www.corporateeurope.org/observer10/tabd.html

Corporate Europe Observatory (2002) 'Leaked Confidential Documents Reveal EC's Neoliberal GATS Agenda', *Corporate Europe Observer*, May, www.corporateeurope.org/observer11/gats.html

Corporate Europe Observatory (2003) *Corporate Conquistadors in Cancun: The EU Offensive for WTO–Investment Negotiations*, InvestmentWatch, July, www.corporateeurope.org/mai/conquistadors.html

Corporate Europe Observatory (2005a) *And Not a Drop to Drink! World Water Forum Promotes Privatisation and Deregulation of World's Water*, Corporate Europe Observatory, www.corporateeurope.org/observer7/water/, accessed 3 January

Corporate Europe Observatory (2005b) *European Water TNCs: Towards Global Domination?*, Corporate Europe Observatory, www.corporateeurope.org/water/infobrief1.htm, accessed 3 January

Corporate Europe Observatory (2005c) *WTO and Water: The EU's Crusade for Corporate Expansion*, Corporate Europe Observatory, www.corporateeurope.org/water/infobrief3.htm, accessed 3 January

Corporate Watch (2005) 'Influence/Lobbying', *Corporate Watch*, www.corporatewatch.org/?lid=259, accessed 18 August 2005

CorpWatch (2001) 'Corporate Globalization Fact Sheet', *CorpWatch*, 22 March 2001, www.corpwatch.org/print_article.php?&id=378

Costigan, P. (2000) 'Why S11 Should Welcome the WEF', *The Age*, 30 August

Cowhey, P. F. and Aronson, J. D. (1993) *Managing the World Economy: The Consequences of Corporate Alliances*, Council on Foreign Relations Press, New York

Dallek, R. (2003) *An Unfinished Life: John F. Kennedy, 1917–1963*, Little, Brown & Co, New York

Davidson, J. O. C. (1994) 'Metamorphosis? Privatisation and the Restructuring of Management and Labour', in Jackson, P. M. and Price, C. M. (eds) *Privatisation and Regulation: A Review of the Issues*, Longman, London and New York

Davis, J., Ossowski, R., Richardson, T. and Barnett, S. (2000) 'Fiscal and Macroeconomic Impact of Privatization', *IMF Occasional Paper*, 22 June, www.IMF.org/external/pubs/nft/op/194/index.htm

de Jonquieres, G. (1998) 'Network Guerillas', *Financial Times*, 30 April

Deal, T. (1998) 'Investment E–paranoia', *Journal of Commerce*, 7 January, p7A

Dekker, W. (1984) 'Europe 1990: An Agenda for Action', N.V. Philips, Eindhoven, The Netherlands

Desai, R. (1994) 'Second–Hand Dealers in Ideas: Think–Tanks and Thatcherite Hegemony', *New Left Review*, vol 203, no Jan–Feb, pp27–64

Dickson, T. and Wolf, M. (1993) 'Sutherland Faces Toughest Brief', *Financial Times*, 28 May, p3

Doherty, A. and Hoedeman, O. (1994) 'Knights of the Road', *New Statesman and Society*, vol 7, no 327, pp27–29

Domhoff, G. W. (1983) *Who Rules America Now? A View for the 1980s*, Prentice-Hall, Englewood Cliffs, NJ

Domhoff, G. W. (2002) *Who Rules America? Power and Politics*, 4th edition, McGraw Hill, New York

Drahos, P. and Braithwaite, J. (2004) 'Who Owns the Knowledge Economy? Political Organising Behind TRIPS', *The Corner House Briefing*, no 32, September, www.thecornerhouse.org.uk/item.shtml?x=85821

Dryden, S. (1995) *Trade Warriors: USTR and the American Crusade for Free Trade*, Oxford University Press, New York

Dubash, N. K. (2002) 'The Changing Global Context for Electricity Reform', in Dubash, N. K. (ed) *Power Politics: Equity and Environment in Electricity Reform*, World Resources Institute, Washington, DC

Dunne, N. (1990a) 'Congress Urged to Suspend Judgement on Trade Talks', *Financial Times*, 24 October, p3

Dunne, N. (1990b) 'New Bid to Speed Trade Talks', *Financial Times*, 26 March, p5

Dunne, N. (1990c) 'US Business Forms Trade Pressure Group', *Financial Times*, 16 May, p4

Easton, B. (1993) 'From Rogernomics to Ruthanasia: New Right Economics in New Zealand', in Rees, S., Rodley, G. and Stilwell, F. (eds) *Beyond the Market: Alternatives to Economic Rationalism*, Pluto Press, Leichhardt, NSW

ECAT (Emergency Committee for American Trade) (2002) *About ECAT*, ECAT, www.ecattrade.com/about/

ECAT (2003a) *Trade Resources*, ECAT, www.ecattrade.com/resources/subsection.asp?id=17, accessed 8 June 2003

ECAT (2003b) *Summary of ECAT Positions on Issues*, ECAT, www.ecattrade.com/statements/content.asp?ID=127 accessed 8 June 2003

Economist (1991) 'Think-Tanks: The Carousels of Power', *Economist*, 25 May, pp23–26

Economist (1992) 'The Good Think-Tank Guide', *Economist*, 21 December, pp49–53

Economist (1998) 'The Sinking of the MAI', *Economist*, 14 March, pp85–86

Economist (1999) 'Energy, the New Convergence', *Economist*, 29 May, pp59–60

Edison, H. J. and Reinhart, C. M. (2000) 'Capital Controls During Financial Crises: The Case of Malaysia and Thailand', *International Finance Discussion Papers*, vol, no 662, http//ideas.repec.org/p/fip/fedgif/662.htm

Edwards, L. (2002) *How to Argue with an Economist: Reopening Political Debate in Australia*, Cambridge University Press, Cambridge, UK

Eichbaum, C. (1992) 'Market Liberalisation in New Zealand: Fightback! In Practice?' in Vintila, P., Phillimore, J. and Newman, P. (eds) *Markets, Morals and Manifestos: Fightback! and the Politics of Economic Rationalism in the 1990s*, Institute for Science and Technology Policy, Murdoch University, Murdoch, WA

Engineering News-Record (1985) 'Management and Labor Roundtable's Blough Dies', *Engineering News-Record*, 17 October, 1985, p78

Englander, E. and Kaufman, A. (2004) 'The End of Managerial Ideology: From Corporate Social Responsibility to Corporate Social Indifference', *Enterprise and Society*, vol 5, no 3, pp404–450

Engler, M. (2003) 'Globalization's Lost Decade', *Z Magazine*, 5 August, www.zmag.org/content/print_article.cfm?itemID=401&sectionID=13

ERT (European Round Table of Industrialists) (1993) *Beating the Crisis: A Charter for Europe's Industrial Future*, ERT, Brussels, December

ERT (2003a) *Achievements*, ERT, 23 June 2003, www.ert.be/pg/eng_frame.htm

ERT (2003b) *The European Round Table of Industrialists*, ERT, 8 June 2003, www.ert.be/

ERT (2003c) *ERT Highlights 1983–2003*, ERT, Brussels, June 2003, pp33, 46

ERT (2004) *The European Round Table of Industrialists*, ERT, 5 August 2004, www.ert.be/

ESF (European Services Forum) (2002) 'ESF Second Position Paper on Public Procurement in Services', ESF, 25 November, www.esf.be/pdf/ESF%202nd%20Position%20Paper%20on%20Public%20Procurement%20in%20Services%20.pdf

ESF (2003) *About ESF*, ESF Forum, www.esf.be/e_pages/about.htm, accessed 2 May
   2003
Esty, D. (2000) 'Trade Storms', *World Link*, May/June, pp12–13
Esty, D. (2002) 'The World Trade Organization's Legitimacy Crisis', *World Trade Review*,
   vol 1, no 1, pp7–22
European Commission (2003) *Opening World Markets for Services: Towards GATS 2000*,
   www.gats-info.eu.int/gats-info/g2000.pl?NEWS=bbb, accessed 10 May 2003
Farnsworth, C. H. (1990) 'Winners and Losers in Trade Talks', *New York Times*, 29 Nov-
   ember, pD1
Flecker, K. (2004) *Operation Water Rights Project – Lobby Groups*, Polaris Institute, May,
   www.polarisinstitute.org/polaris_project/water_lords/lobby_groups/wwc_gwp_
   PRINT.html
FLG (Financial Leaders Group) (2001) *Commentary on Proposals for Liberalisation in
   Financial Services*, FLG, 21 September, www.uscsi.org/publications/papers/FLG%20
   Commentary%20Sept%202001.pdf
Flowers, E. B. (1998) *US Utility Mergers and the Restructuring of the New Global Power
   Industry*, Quorum Books, Westport, Connecticut
FOE (Friends of the Earth) (1998) 'International Monetary Fund 101', *Multinational
   Monitor*, January/February, pp24–27
FOE (2001) *Dirty Water: The Environmental and Social Records of Four Multinational
   Water Companies*, FOE, London, December, www.foe.co.uk/resource/briefings/dirty_
   water.pdf
Forbes (1996) 'One of the Greatest Shows on Earth', *Forbes*, 2 December 1996, www.igc.
   org/ice/davos/english/greatest_show.htm
Foreman-Peck, J. (1994) *Public and Private Ownership of British Industry 1820–1990*,
   Clarendon Press, Oxford
Forero, J. (2002a) 'As Bolivians Vote, Populism is on the Rise', *New York Times*, 30 June,
   pA8
Forero, J. (2002b) 'Still Poor, Latin Americans Protest Push for Open Markets', *New York
   Times*, 19 July, pA1
Fox, B. (2005) 'Europe Fights Tide of Absurd Patents', *New Scientist*, 8 January, p22
Freeman, H. (2000) 'Comments and Discussion', *Brookings-Wharton Papers on Financial
   Services 2000*, pp453–463
Friedman, T. L. (1999) *The Lexus and the Olive Tree*, Farrar, Straus and Giroux, New
   York
Garnaut, R. (1994) 'Australia', in Williamson, J. (ed) *The Political Economy of Policy
   Reform*, Institute for International Economics, Washington, DC
Geller, A. (1994) 'But How's the Bubble Gum? GATT Lobbyists Paper the Capital in
   Trading Cards', *The Trenton Record*, 26 July
Gellner, W. (1995) 'The Politics of Policy "Political Think Tanks" and Their Markets
   in the US – Institutional Environment', *Presidential Studies Quarterly*, vol 25, no 3,
   pp497–510
Georges, C. (1995) 'Conservative Heritage Foundation Finds Recipe for Influence: Ideas
   Plus Marketing Equal Clout', *Wall Street Journal*, 10 August, p10
Gerritsen, R. (1994) 'Microeconomic Reform', in Bell, S. and Head, B. (eds) *State,
   Economy and Public Policy*, Oxford University Press, Melbourne

Gibbon, H. (2001) *Guide for Divesting Government-Owned Enterprises*, Reason Public Policy Institute, www.privatization.org/Collection/Publications/htg_15–divesting_assets.htm, accessed 20 July

Global Intelligence Update Weekly Analysis (1999) 'World Bank Reverses Position on Financial Controls and on Malaysia', *Global Intelligence Update Weekly Analysis*, 20 September 1999

Global Services Network (1998) *Global Services Network Formed; Services 2000 Issues Agreed*, Global Services Network, 26 April 1998, www.globalservicesnetwork.com/ditchley_park_declaration.htm

Global Services Network (2003) *European Services Industry Unites in Favour of Ambitious World-Wide Trade Liberalisation*, Global Services Network, www.globalservicesnetwork.com/esn_announcement.htm, accessed 2 May 2003

Godov, J. (2003) *Water and Power: The French Connection*, Center for Public Integrity, 4 February, www.icij.org/water/printer–friendly.aspx?aid=47

Gonzalez, G. (1999) 'Chilean Forestry Project a Symbol of Fight Against WTO', in *Who Owns the WTO? Corporations and Global Trade*, Corporate Watch, www.corpwatch.org/

Goodman, J. (2000a) 'Stopping a Juggernaut: The Anti-MAI Campaign', in Goodman, J. and Ranald, P. (eds) *Stopping the Juggernaut: Public Interest Versus the Multilateral Agreement on Investment*, Pluto Press, Sydney

Goodman, J. (2000b) *The WEF: Capital's First International?*, S11, http://www.s11.org/wef_1sti.html, accessed 5 September

Goozner, M. (2001) 'Free Market Shock', *The American Prospect*, 27 August, www.prospect.org/print-friendly/print/\/12/15/goozner-m.html

goTrade (1999) *The Go Trade Initiative*, Business Roundtable, www.gotrade.org/tradeducation.html, accessed 24 December 1999

Gould, E. (2004) 'Panel Strips WTO of Another Fig Leaf', *WTOWatch*, 16 July, www.polarisinstitute.org/polaris_project/public_service/news/july_2004.html

Graff, J. and Sancton, T. (2000) 'Davos Listens to the World', *Time International*, 14 February, p52

Gray, J. (2002) *False Dawn: The Delusions of Global Capitalism*, Granta Books, London

Gray, R. D. and Schuster, J. (1998) 'The East Asian Financial Crisis – Fallout for the Private Power Projects', *The World Bank Group – Public Policy for the Private Sector*, August, p1

Greenpeace International (1992) *UNCED Undermined: Why Free Trade Won't Save the Planet*, Greenpeace UNCED Report, Washington, DC, March

Greider, W. (1992) *Who Will Tell the People: The Betrayal of American Democracy*, Simon and Schuster, New York

Gross, J. A. (1995) *Broken Promise: The Subversion of US Labor Relations Policy, 1947–1994*, Temple University Press, Philadelphia

Haas, R. N. (2002) 'Think Tanks and US Foreign Policy: A Policy-Maker's Perspective', *US Foreign Policy Agenda*, vol 7, no 3, pp5–8

Hakim, Z. P. and Wahyuni, S. (2004) 'Government Committed to Liberalizing Education Sector', *The Jakarta Post*, 27 October, www.asia-pacific-action.org/southeastasia/indonesia/netnews/2004/ind_44v8.htm#Government%20committed%20to%20liberalizing%20education%20sector

Haley, M. A. (2001) *Freedom and Finance: Democratization and Institutional Investors in Developing Countries*, Palgrave, New York

Hall, D. and Lobina, E. (2004) 'Private and Public Interests in Water and Energy', *Natural Resources Forum*, vol, no 28, pp268–277

Harbrecht, D. (1994) 'Dealy Would Mean the Death of GATT', *Business Week*, 5 December, p34

Hawkins, W. R. (2002) 'Sanctions "Reform" Hits a Dead End', *Trade Alert*, 21 March 2002, www.tradealert.org/view_art.asp?Prod_ID=402

Hawley, S. (2000) 'Exporting Corruption: Privatisation, Multinationals and Bribery', *The Corner House Briefing*, www.cornerhouse.icaap.org/briefings/19.html

Healy, B. K. S. (2000) *Guide to the Seattle Meltdown*, Common Dreams News Center, 10 March, www.commondreams.org/headlines/031000–03.htm

Healy, S. (2000) *Corporate Club 'Shapes Global Agenda'*, S11 Resource Kit, Wollongong

Helleiner, E. (1996) 'Post-Globalization: Is the Financial Liberalization Trend Likely to be Reversed?' in Boyer, R. and Drache, D. (eds) *States Against Markets: The Limits of Globalization*, Routledge, New York

Heritage Foundation (2004) *Consolidated Financial Statements and Supplemental Schedules of Functional Expenses for the Years Ended December 31, 2003 and 2002, and Independent Auditors Report*, Heritage Foundation, Washington, DC, p12

Hersh, S. M. (1983) *The Price of Power: Kissinger in the Nixon White House*, Summit Books, New York

Higgins, W. (1991) 'Missing the Boat', in Galligan, B. and Singleton, G. (eds) *Business and Government under Labor*, Longman Cheshire, Melbourne

High Level LOTIS Group (1999) 'Minutes of Meeting, Monday 15 November', Barclays Bank PLC

Higley, C. (2000) 'Disastrous Deregulation', *Public Citizen*, December, www.citizen.org/documents/disastrousdereg.PDF

Hilary, J. (2004) *Divide and Rule: The EU and US Response to Developing Country Alliances at the WTO*, ActionAid International, July, www.actionaid.org.uk/wps/content/documents/divideandrule_0704_282004_93111.pdf

Hildyard, N. and Sexton, S. (1996) 'Cartels, "Low Balls", Backhanders and Hand-Outs', *The Ecologist*, vol 26, no 4, p148

Hill and Knowlton (2000) *'S11' Protest Brief*, Hill and Knowlton, Melbourne

Himmelstein, J. L. (1990) *To the Right: The Transformation of American Conservatism*, University of California Press, Berkeley, CA

Hirsh, R. F. (1999) *Power Loss: The Origins of Deregulation and Restructuring in the American Electric Utility System*, MIT Press, Cambridge, MA

Hirst, N. (2002) 'Consumer Protection in a Deregulated Market', Paper presented at the IEA Regulatory Forum: Competition in Energy Markets, Paris, 7–8 February

Hochuli, M. (2002) 'Investment Agreements as One-Sided Enforcement of Investor Rights I', in *Investment and Competition Negotiations in the WTO – What's Wrong with It and What Are the Alternatives*, Seattle to Brussels Network, Brussels/Berlin

Hoedeman, O. (2002) 'Corporate Lobbying for a "MAI" in the WTO', in *Investment and Competition Negotiations in the WTO – What's Wrong with It and What Are the Alternatives*, Seattle to Brussels Network, Brussels/Berlin

Hoedeman, O. and Doherty, A. (2002) 'Joining Forces: Big Business Rallies after Seattle', in Lubbers, E. (ed) *Battling Big Business: Countering Greenwash, Infiltration and Other Forms of Bullying*, Green Books, Devon, UK

Hoedeman, O., with Balanya, B., Doherty, A., Ma'anit, A. and Wesselius, E. H. (1998) 'MAIgalomania: The New Corporate Agenda', *The Ecologist*, vol 28, no 3, pp154–161

Hoffman, W. H. Jr (1985) 'Retired US Steel Executive, Roger M. Blough, Dies at Home', *PR Newswire*, 9 October 1985

Holland Walker, S. and Sklar, P. (1938) *Business Finds Its Voice: Management's Effort to Sell the Business Idea to the Public*, Harper and Brothers, New York and London, p53

Horne, D. (1992) 'It's Time for a Think', in Horne, D. (ed) *The Trouble with Economic Rationalism*, Vic, Scribe, Newham

Hornik, R. and Schwab, K. (1999) 'Economics and Social Cohesion', *Time*, international edition, 15 February, p46

Hudson, S. (1992) 'Lion Chief Criticises "Stalled" NZ Reform', *Australian Financial Reform*, 8 April, p9

Hughes, A. (1998) 'All Charged and Ready to Go', *Sydney Morning Herald*, 11 March, supplement

Hughes, T. (1983) *Networks of Power: Electrification in Western Society, 1880–1930*, John Hopkins University Press, Baltimore and London

Hurtado, M. E. (1999) *More Power to the World Trade Organisation? The International Trade Controversy*, Panos, London, November, www.panos.org.uk/PDF/reports/MorePowertotheWTO.pdf

ICC (International Chamber of Commerce) (1998) *Business States Its Views on OECD Investment Agreement*, ICC, 16 January 1998, www.iccwbo.org/home/news_archives/1998/business_states_its_views.asp

ICC (2002) *Business and the Global Economy*, ICC, 8 May 2002, www.iccwbo.org/home/statements_rules/statements/2002/G8kananskis.as

IFSL (International Financial Services, London) (2003a) *Trade Policy*, IFSL, www.ifsl.org.uk/tradepolicy/home_left.cfm, accessed 2 May 2003

IFSL (2003b) *What We Do*, IFSL, www.ifsl.org.uk/tradepolicy/whatwedo.cfm, accessed 2 May 2003

IIE (Institute for International Economics) (1998) *Financial Services Liberalized Little in Recent WTO Agreement*, IIE, 22 June, www.iie.com/publications/cases/dobsjqpr.htm

IIE (2001) *About the Institute for International Economics*, IIE, www.iie.com/ADMINIST/aboutiie.htm, accessed 6 January 2001

Industries Assistance Commission (1989) *International Initiatives to Liberalise Trade in Services*, Inquiry into International Trade in Services, Australian Government Publishing Service, Canberra,

International Commission of Jurists (1985) *Siracusa Principles on the Limitations and Derogation Provisions in the International Covenant on Civil and Political Rights*, American Association for the International Commission of Jurists, Washington, DC

International Forum on Globalization (1998) 'Should corporations govern the world?' *Third World Resurgence*, vol 90/91, pp9–10

International Trade Administration (2003) *Industry Consultation Program*, International Trade Administration, www.ita.doc.gov/td/icp/mission.html, accessed 30 June 2003

InvestmentWatch (2003a) 'Letter to WTO Delegates Warning of the High-Standard Agreement WTO–Investment Agreement Demanded by the ICC', Corporate Europe Observatory, 25 April, www.investmentwatch.org/articles/shefali25april.html

InvestmentWatch (2003b) *US Business Round Table (BRT)*, Corporate Europe Observatory, www.investmentwatch.org/tncdb/BRT.html, accessed 30 June

IPC, Keidanren and UNICE (1988) *Basic Framework of GATT Provisions on Intellectual Property: Statement of Views of the European, Japanese and United States Business Communities*, The Intellectual Property Committee, Keidanren and UNICE

Jackson, P. M. and Price, C. M. (1994) 'Privatisation and Regulation: A Review of the Issues', in Jackson, P. M. and Price, C. M. (eds) *Privatisation and Regulation: A Review of the Issues*, Longman, London and New York

Jacobs, D. (1998) 'Labor and Social Legislation in the United States: Business Obstructionism and Accommodation', *Labor Studies Journal*, vol 23, no 2, pp52–73

James, S. (1993) 'The Idea Brokers: The Impact of Think Tanks on British Government', *Public Administration*, vol 71, winter, pp491–506

Jeter, J. (2001) 'For South Africa's Poor, a New Power Struggle', *The Washington Post*, 6 November, pA01

Jones, D. (2005) *Transcript: British High Commission*, Foreign and Commonwealth Home Office, 10 January, www.fco.gov.uk/Files/kfile/TRANSCRIPT%20-%20Digby%20Jones.doc

Jones, E. (1993) 'Economic Language, Propaganda and Dissent', in Rees, S., Rodley, G. and Stilwell, F. (eds) *Beyond the Market: Alternatives to Economic Rationalism*, Pluto Press, Leichhardt, NSW

Judis, J. B. (2001) *The Paradox of American Democracy: Elites, Special Interests, and the Betrayal of Public Trust*, Pantheon, New York

Kahn, H. and Pepper, T. (1980) *Will She Be Right? The Future of Australia*, University of Queensland Press, St. Lucia, Queensland

Kangas, S. (2004) 'Chile: The Laboratory Test', *Liberalism Resurgent*, www.huppi.com/kangaroo/L–chichile.htm, accessed 15 August 2004

Kaplan, E. and Rodrik, D. (2001) *Did the Malaysian Capital Controls Work*, John F. Kennedy School of Government, Harvard University, February, www.ksghome.harvard.edu/~drorik/Malaysia%20controls.pdf

Kapstein, E. (2000) 'Directions to Democracy', *World Link*, May/June, pp42–45

Kasper, W., Blandy, R., Freebairn, J., Hocking, D. and O'Neill, R. (1980) *Australia at the Crossroads: Our Choices to the Year 2000*, Harcourt Brace Jovanovich, Sydney

Katz, A. (1998) *Remarks by Abraham Katz*, US Council for International Business, 8 December 1998, www.uscib.org/index.asp?documentID=2239

Kelly, P. (1992) *The End of Uncertainty: The Story of the 1980s*, Allen and Unwin, St Leonards, NSW

Kelsey, J. (1995) *Economic Fundamentalism*, Pluto Press, London

Kennedy, J. F. (1962) *News Conference No 30*, John F. Kennedy Library and Museum, 11 April 1962, www.jfklibrary.org/jfk_press_conference_620411.html

Kentor, J. and Jang, Y. S. (2004) 'Yes, There is a (Growing) Transnational Business Community: A Study of Global Interlocking Directorates 1983–1998', *International Sociology*, vol 19, no 3, pp355–368

Kerneis, P. (2000) 'The Perspective of the European Private Sector in the GATS Negotiations', Paper presented at the Regional Seminar on Services, ASEAN, Bangkok, Thailand, 27 June

Kerr, R. (1993) 'Keeping NZ Out of the Hands of the Chattering Class', *Independent Business Weekly*, 30 August, p9

Khor, M. (1998a) 'US and IMF Putting More Squeeze on the South?', *MAI Discussion List/Third World Network Features*, 14 April, http://lists.essential.org/1998/stop-imf/msg00058.html

Khor, M. (1998b) 'What is MAI?' *Third World Resurgence*, vol 90/91, no, pp5–8

Kohler, A. (1997) 'The Radical Right Wing Speeds the Kennett Revolution', *The Age*, 14 February, p15

Kolko, G. (1998) 'Ravaging the Poor: IMF Indicted by its Own Data', *Multinational Monitor*, June, pp20–23

Kornbluh, P. (1989) 'Washington's Secret Economic War on Nicaragua', *The San Francisco Chronicle*, 6 September, p1/Z

Korten, D. C. (2001) *When Corporations Rule the World*, 2nd edn, Kumarian Press, Bloomfield, CT and Berrett-Koehler, San Francisco, CA

Kwa, A. (2003) *Power Politics in the WTO*, Focus on the Global South, Bangkok, January, www.focusweb.org/publications/Books/power-politics-in-the-WTO.pdf

Lambrook, J. (1986) 'The CIA in Australia: Part 4', *Watching Brief, Public Radio News Services*, October/November, www.serendipity.li/cia/cia_oz/cia_oz4.htm

Landay, J. M. (2002) *The Powell Manifesto*, Mediatransparency.org, 20 August 2002, www.mediatransparency.org/stories/powell.htm

Langmore, J. (1991) 'The Labor Government in a De-regulatory Era', in Galligan, B. and Singleton, G. (eds) *Business and Government under Labor*, Longman Cheshire, Melbourne

Lapper, R. (2002) 'Piling on the Pressure', *Financial Times*, 5 October, p1

LBJ (2005) 'Charles E. Walker', LBJ School of Public Affairs, University of Texas, www.utexas.edu/lbj/faculty/view_faculty.php?fid=55, accessed 16 August 2005

Legal Times (1994) 'Pro-GATT Forces Play Their Face Cards', *Legal Times*, 1 August 1994, p5

Legge, J. M. (2003) 'Gordon Gecko's Economics', *Dissent*, autumn/winter, pp26–31

Lewis, P. (1977) 'Business Roundtable in Policy Statement.' *New York Times*, 10 February 1977, p57

Lindsay, G. (1997) 'Threats to Freedom Then and Now', *Policy*, autumn, pp18–20, www.cis.org.au/Policy/mps.html

Lipowicz, A. (1994a) 'Pols Join NY Business Crusading for GATT', *Crain's New York Business*, 18 July, p4

Lipowicz, A. (1994b) 'No Break for Trade Lobbyists', *Crain's New York Business*, 23 May, p4

Lloyd, V. and Weissman, R. (2001) 'Against the Workers: How IMF and World Bank Policies Undermine Labor Power and Rights', *Multinational Monitor*, September, www.essential.org/monitor/mm2001/01september/sep01corp1.html

Lobe, J. (1999) 'Rights Trade: Multinationals Win US Court Victory Over Activists', *Inter Press Service*, 24 June

LOTIS (Liberalisation of Trade in Services) Committee (1999a) 'Minutes of Meeting, 23 September 1999', LOTIS, Corporation of London's Marketing Suite, London

LOTIS Committee (1999b) 'Minutes of Meeting, Monday, 8 November 1999', Lloyd's, London

LOTIS Committee (2000a) 'Minutes of Meeting, Tuesday, 25 January 2000', HM Treasury, London

LOTIS Committee (2000b) 'Minutes of Meeting, Tuesday, 21 March 2000', Department of Trade and Industry, London

LOTIS Committee (2000c) 'Minutes of Meeting, Friday, 22 September 2000', Bank of England, London

LOTIS Committee (2000d) 'Minutes of Meeting, Friday, 8 December 2000', Institute of Chartered Accountants in England and Wales, London

LOTIS Committee (2001) 'Minutes of Meeting, Thursday, 22 February 2001', Lloyd's, London

Lowy, J. (1994) 'GATT Lobby Turns Effort to Pivotal Senate', *Pittsburgh Post-Gazette*, 28 November, ppA3

Machan, D. (1999) 'Power Broker', *Forbes*, 15 November, www.forbes.com/global/1999/1115/0223108a.html

Madeley, J. (2000) *Hungry for Trade: How the Poor Pay for Free Trade*, Global Issues Series, Zed Books, London and New York

Magnusson, P. and Baker, S. (1998) 'The Explosive Trade Deal You've Never Heard Of', *Business Week*, 9 February, p51

Mann, J. (2000) 'A Corporate Coup d'État', *Los Angeles Times*, 5 July, www.commondreams.org/headlines/070500-01.htm

Marsden, B. (2003) *Cholera and the Age of the Water Barons*, Center for Public Integrity, 4 February, www.icij.org/water/printer–friendly.aspx?aid=44

Martin, B. (1996) 'From the Many to the Few: Privatization and Globalization', *The Ecologist*, vol 26, no 4, pp145–155

Massey, P. (1995) *New Zealand: Market Liberalization in a Developed Economy*, St Martin's Press, New York

Matthews, T. (1994) 'Employers' Associations, Corporatism and the Accord: The Politics of Industrial Relations', in Bell, S. and Head, B. (eds) *State, Economy and Public Policy*, Oxford University Press, Melbourne

McEachern, D. (1991) *Business Mates: The Power and Politics of the Hawke Era*, Prentice Hall, Sydney

McGuire, P. and Granovetter, M. (1998) *Business and Bias in Public Policy Formation: The National Civic Federation and Social Construction of Electric Utility Regulation, 1905–1907*, Public Power Now, August, www.publicpowernow.org/story/2001/7/26/161517/294

McLaughlin, P. A. (1991) 'How Business Relates to the Hawke Government: The Captains of Industry', in Galligan, B. and Singleton, G. (eds) *Business and Government under Labor*, Longman Cheshire, Melbourne

McRae, S. (2005) *Hidden Voices: The CBI, Corporate Lobbying and Sustainability*, Friends of the Earth, London, June, www.foe.co.uk/resource/reports/hidden_voices.pdf&e=10342

Mead, W. (2000) 'The Case for Capitalism', *World Link*, September/October

Media Transparency (2005) *The Strategic Philanthropy of Conservative Foundations*, Media Transparency, www.mediatransparency.org/conservativephilanthropy.php

Merrills, J. G. (1996) 'Environmental Protection and Human Rights: Conceptual Aspects', in Boyle, A. E. and Anderson, M. R. (eds) *Human Rights Approaches to Environmental Protection*, Clarendon Press, Oxford

Miliband, R. (1982) *Capitalist Democracy in Britain*, Oxford University Press, Oxford

Mills, C. W. (1956) *The Power Elite*, Oxford University Press, Oxford

Mizuho Research (2001) *Credit Comment: National Power Corporation*, Mizuho Research, Tokyo, 28 September 2001

Mokhiber, R. and Weissman, R. (2001) 'The Wartime Opportunists', *Alternet*, 3 October, www.alternet.org/print.html?StoryID=11638

Monbiot, G. (2004) 'Exploitation on Tap', *The Guardian*, 20 October, www.guardian.co.uk/Columnists/Column/0,,1330422,00.html

Montagnon, P. (1990) 'World Trade System "in Danger" Says Brock', *Financial Times*, 10 April, p6

Montague, P. (1999) 'The WTO and Free Trade', *Rachel's Environment and Health Weekly*, 21 October, www.ratical.org/co-globalize/REHW673.html

Mooney, N. (1985) 'How Victoria Went Dry on Andrew', *The National Times*, 13–19 September, p8

Moore, B. and Carpenter, G. (1987) 'Main Players', in Coghill, K. (ed) *The New Right's Australian Fantasy*, McPhee Gribble and Penguin Books, Fitzroy, Victoria

Moran, A. (1999) 'The Great Victorian Sell Off', *Western Australian*, 23 November, www.ipa.org.au/Media/amwa231199.html

Morley, M. (1986) 'Behind the World Bank Loans', *Sydney Morning Herald*, 9 December, p17

Morton, T. (2003) 'The Global Water Business', *Background Briefing, ABC Radio National*, 20 April, www.abc.net.au/rn/talks/bbing/stories/s833698.htm

Murphy, C. N. (1999) 'Inequality, Turmoil and Democracy: Global Political–Economic Visions at the End of the Century', *New Political Economy*, vol 4, no 2, pp289–304

Murphy, J. (2001) 'Unions in South Africa Strike Over Selling of State Industries', *Baltimore Sun*, 30 August, p18A

Murphy, J. M. (2004) 'The Language of Liberal Consensus: John F. Kennedy, Technical Reason and the "New Economics" at Yale University', *Quarterly Journal of Speech*, vol 90, no 2, pp133–162

Murray, G. and Pacheco, D. (2001) *Think Tanks in the 1990s*, Australian National University, www.anu.edu.au/polsci/marx/interventions/thinktanks.htm accessed, 23 January 2001

Myer, R. (1999) 'Now It's Time for Stockdale Inc', *The Age*, 8 May, p1

National Security Archive (2004) *Chile and the United States: Declassified Documents Relating to the Military Coup, 1970–1976*, The National Security Archive, George Washington University, www2.gwu.edu/~nsarchiv/NSAEBB/NSAEBB8/nsaebb8.htm, accessed 28 December 2004

Newlin Carney, E. (1994) 'Washington Update', *National Journal*, 12 February, 1994, p373

NFTC (National Foreign Trade Council) (2003a) *Welcome to NFTC*, NFTC, www.nftc.org, accessed 8 June 2003

NFTC (2003b) *Membership Benefits*, NFTC, www.nftc.org/default.asp?Mode=Directory Display&id=121, accessed 8 June 2003

NFTC (2003c) *NFTC Policy Activities*, NFTC, www.nftc.org/default.asp?Mode=Directory ryDisplay&id=94, accessed 8 June 2003

NFTC (2003d) *NFTC's 2003 Goals*, NFTC, www.nftc.org/default.asp?Mode=Directory Display&id=117, accessed 8 June 2003

Niskanen, W. A. (1995) *Cato Institute*, Cato Institute, www.cato.org/people/niskanen. html

Norman, P. (1991) 'London Summit Headlines Mask Main Agenda', *Financial Times*, 8 July, p13

Norman, P. (1994) 'Survey of World Economy and Finance', *Financial Times*, 30 September, p24

OECD (Organisation for Economic Co-operation and Development) (1997a) 'MAI: The Multilateral Agreement on Investment', *Policy Brief*, vol 2, www.oecd.org/publications/ pol_brief/1997/9702_pol.htm

OECD (1997b) *Progress Report on Multilateral Agreement on Investment*, OECD MAI Negotiating Group, May, www.oecd.org//daf/investment/fdi/mai/mairap97.htm

OECD (1998a) *Communiqué: Ministerial Statement on the Multilateral Agreement on Investment (MAI)*, OECD, 27–28 April, www.oecd.org/media/release/nw98–50a.htm

OECD (1998b) *Informal Consultations on International Investment*, OECD, Paris, 3 December

OECD (1998c) 'Open Markets Matter: The Benefits of Trade and Investment Liberalisation', *Policy Brief*, vol 6, www.oecd.org/dataoecd/18/51/1948792.pdf.

OECD (2005) *About OECD*, OECD, www.oecd.org/about/0,2337,en_2649_201185_ 1_1_1_1_1,00.html, accessed 5 February 2005

O'Hare, D. R. (2001) 'The Future of the Global Trading System: Where to From Here?' Paper presented at the APEC CEO Summit 2001, Shanghai, 20 October 2001

O'Hare, D. R. (2002) 'Introductory Remarks', Paper presented at the Services 2002 Conference, Washington, DC, 5 February 2002

opensecrets.org (2003) *Business Associations*, Center for Responsive Politics, www. opensecrets.org/pubs/lobby00/topind08.asp and www.opensecrets.org/lobbyists/ indusclient.asp?code=N00&year=2000&txtSort=A, accessed 2 August 2003

Oppenheim, J. (2001) *US Electric Utilities: A Century of Successful Democratic Regulation of Private Monopolies; a Half-Decade of Failure of Experiments in Competition*, European Federation of Public Service Unions, Brussels, 12 December, www.psiru. org/epsuconference/OpenheimUSElecReg121201.doc

Overbeck, C. (1998) *Davos 98: The World Economic Forum Strikes Again*, ParaScope, www.parascope.com/mx/articles/davos98.htm, accessed 5 September

Oxfam International (2002) 'The Danger of an Investment Agreement Under the WTO', in *Investment and Competition Negotiations in the WTO – What's Wrong with It and What Are the Alternatives*, Seattle to Brussels Network, Brussels/Berlin

Palast, G. (1998) 'Pepsi Demands a US Coup: Goodbye Allende; Hello Pinochet', *Observer*, 8 November, p9

Palast, G. (2001a) 'IMF's Four Steps to Damnation', *Observer*, 29 April, p7

Palast, G. (2001b) 'Necessity Test is Mother of GATS Intervention', *Observer*, 15 April, http://observer.guardian.co.uk/business/story/0,6903,473205,00.html

Palast, G. (2001c) 'The WTO's Hidden Agenda', *CorpWatch*, 9 November, www. corpwatch.org/issues/PRT.jsp?articleid=722

Palast, G. (2002) *The Best Democracy Money Can Buy*, Pluto Press, London

Parenti, M. (1986) *Inventing Reality: The Politics of the Mass Media*, St Martin's Press, New York

Parenti, M. (1995) *Democracy for the Few*, St Martin's Press, New York

Parker, D. (1994) 'Nationalisation, Privatisation and Agency Status Within Government: Testing for the Importance of Ownership', in Jackson, P. M. and Price, C. M. (eds) *Privatisation and Regulation: A Review of the Issues*, Longman, London and New York

Patnaik, P. (1999) 'The Real Face of Financial Liberalisation', *Frontline: India's National Magazine*, vol 16, no 4, www.frontlineonnet.com/fl1604/16041010.htm

Patterson, W. (1999) *Transforming Electricity: The Coming Generation of Change*, Royal Institute of International Affairs and Earthscan, London

Paulson, M. (1999) 'Business Leaders Fight Back Against Anti-WTO Forces', in *Who Owns the WTO? Corporations and Global Trade*, www.corpwatch.org/

Pauw, J. (2003) *Metered to Death: How a Water Experiment Caused Riots and a Cholera Epidemic*, Center for Public Integrity, 4 February, www.icij.org/water/printer-friendly. aspx?aid=49

Peng, M. K. K. (1990) *The Uruguay Round and Third World Sovereignty*, Third World Network, Penang, Malaysia

People for the American Way (2002a) *Right Wing Organizations: Heritage Foundation*, People for the American Way, September 2002, www.pfaw.org/pfaw/general/default. aspx?oid=4287

People for the American Way (2002b) *Right Wing Organizations: American Enterprise Institute*, People for the American Way, September 2002, www.pfaw.org/pfaw/general/ default.aspx?oid=4456

People for the American Way (2003) *Right Wing Organizations: Cato Institute*, People for the American Way, March, www.pfaw.org/pfaw/general/default.aspx?oid=9261

Pike, A. (1990) 'Trade Round Failure "Could Lead to Chaos"', *Financial Times*, 17 April, p3

Polaris Institute (2003) *Global Water Grab: How Corporations Are Planning to Take Control of Local Water Services*, Polaris Institute, January, www.polarisinstitute.org/pubs/pubs_ pdfs/gwg_english.pdf

Pollitt, M. G. (1999) *A Survey of Liberalisation of Public Enterprises in the UK since 1979*, University of Cambridge, Cambridge, UK, January

PR Newswire (2005) 'Business Leaders See Coming Year as Pivotal for Enhancing America's Competitiveness', *PR Newswire*, 12 January 2005

Pratt, E. J. (1995) *Intellectual Property*, Pfizer, www.pfizer.com/are/about_public/mn_ about_intellectualpropfrm.html

Probert, B. (1992) 'Whose Economy is It?' in Horne, D. (ed) *The Trouble with Economic Rationalism*, Scribe, Newham, Vic

Probert, B. (1994) 'Globalisation, Economic Restructuring and the State', in Bell, S. and Head, B. (eds) *State, Economy and Public Policy*, Oxford University Press, Melbourne

Project Censored (1999) *Censored 1999: The Top 25 Censored Media Stories of 1998*, Project Censored, www.projectcensored.org/c1999.htm

Public Citizen (1998) 'OECD and Governments Launch "MAI Charm Offensive"', *Public Citizen*, May, www.citizen.org/print_article.cfm?ID=1095

Public Citizen (2003a) '"GATT–Zilla vs Flipper" Dolphin Case Demonstrates How Trade Agreements Undermine Domestic Environmental Public Interest Policies', *Public Citizen*, 11 April 2003, www.citizen.org/print_article.cfm?ID=9298

Public Citizen (2003b) 'MAI Shell Game – IMF', *Public Citizen*, www.citizen.org/print_article.cfm?ID=1098, accessed 3July 2003

Public Citizen (2003c) 'Multilateral Agreement on Investment (MAI)', *Public Citizen*, www.citizen.org/trade/issues/mai/, accessed 3 July

Public Services Privatization Research Unit (1996) *Public Services Privatization Research Unit*, The Privatization Network, January, www.psiru.org/reports/96–01–TPN.doc

Puscas, D. (2002) *A Guide to the Enron Collapse: A Few Points for a Clearer Understanding*, Polaris Institute, Ottawa, 12 February, www.polarisinstitute.org/corporateprofiles_files/enronguidefall.pdf

Puscas, D. (2003) *Enron-Style Corporate Crime and Privatization*, Polaris Institute, Ottawa, 19 June, www.polarisinstitute.org/pubs/pubs_pdfs/uscsi.pdf

Raghavan, C. (1990) *Recolonization: GATT, the Uruguay Round and the Third World*, Zed Books, London

Raghavan, C. (1997) 'Close Encounters at the WTO', *Third World Economics*, 16–31 December, www.twnside.org.sg/title/coun-cn.htm

Raghavan, C. (1999) 'FDI is No Panacea for South's Economic Woes', *Third World Resurgence*, October/November, www.twnside.org.sg/title/woe–-cn.htm

Raja, K. (2004) 'North Attempts to Split Developing-Country Alliances', *South–North Development Monitor*, 27 July, www.twnside.org.sg/title2/twninfo151.htm

Ranald, P. (2000a) 'Disciplining Governments: The MAI in the International and Australian Contexts', in Goodman, J. and Ranald, P. (eds) *Stopping the Juggernaut: Public Interest Versus the Multilateral Agreement on Investment*, Pluto Press, Sydney

Ranald, P. (2000b) *Global Institutions, Democracy and Accountability: The WTO After the MAI and Seattle*, The World in Context, www.context.co.nz:8080/stories/storyReader$601, accessed 3 July 2003

Rayner, M. (2005) *History of Universal Human Rights – Up to WW2*, Universal Rights Network, www.universalrights.net/main/histof.htm, accessed 25 April 2005

Reeves, R. (1993) *President Kennedy: Profile of Power*, Touchstone, New York

Regulatory Assistance Project (2000) *Best Practices Guide: Implementing Power Sector Reform*, Energy and Environment Training Program, Office of Energy, Environment and Technology and Global Bureau, Center for the Environment, United States Agency for International Development, Gardiner, ME and Montpelier, VT, p12

Reuters (1998) 'French government announces withdrawal from MAI negotiations', *Reuters*, 14 October 1998

Ricci, D. (1993) *The Transformation of American Politics: The New Washington and the Rise of Think Tanks*, Yale University Press, New Haven, CT

Ringe, A. and Rollings, N. (2000) 'Responding to Relative Decline: The Creation of the National Economic Development Council', *Economic History Review*, vol LIII, no 2, pp331–353

Roberts, C. (2002) *LOTIS Chairman Stresses Importance of Services Liberalisation*, International Financial Services, London, 24 October, www.ifsl.org.uk/pressreleases/detail.cfm?Id=79

Robins, B. (2002) 'Banks See Big Chance in Trading Electricity', *Sydney Morning Herald*, 5–6 October, p45

Rockefeller, D. (1999) 'New Rules of the Game: Looking for New Leadership', *Newsweek*, 1 February, p41

Rohter, L. (2002) 'In Free-Market Slump, Brazil's Voters Look for Change', *New York Times*, 5 October, www.nytimes.com/2002/10/05/international/americas/05BRAZ.html

Rohter, L. (2004) 'Argentina's Economic Rally Defies Forecasts', *New York Times*, 26 December, www.nytimes.com/2004/12/26/international/americas/26argent.html

Roth, Z. R. (2004) 'Those Loopy Conspiracy Theories', *Columbia Journalism Review Daily*, 7 February, www.campaigndesk.org/archives/000110.asp

Roxas, F. Y. (2001) 'The Importance and the Changing Role of the Independent Power Producers (IPPs) in the Proposed Competitive Power Market in the Philippines', Paper presented at the APEC 8th Technical Seminar and 7th Coal Flow Seminar, Bangkok, 30 October–1 November

Rudolph, R. and Ridley, S. (1986) *Power Struggle: The Hundred-Year War over Electricity*, Harper and Row, New York

Rusbridger, A. (1987) 'A Thought for Tomorrow', *The Guardian*, 22 December, http://politics.guardian.co.uk/thinktanks/comment/0,,527214,00.html

RWE (2004) *2003 Annual Report*, RWE, 2004, www.rwe.com/generator.aspx/investorrelations/financial-reports/id=2324/financial-reports-page.html

RWE (2005) *English Home Page*, RWE, www.rwe.com/generator.aspx/homepage/templateId=renderPage/id=496/home-en.html, accessed 5 January

RWE Thames Water (2004) *Financial Profile*, RWE Thames Water, www.rwethameswater.com/TW/division/en_gb/content/General/General_000192.jsp?SECT=General_000192

Ryan, M. P. (1998) *Knowledge Diplomacy: Global Competition and the Politics of Intellectual Property*, Brookings Institution Press, Washington, DC

Sale, K. (1993) *The Green Revolution: The American Environmental Movement, 1962–1992*, Hill and Wang, New York

Sally, R. (2000) 'Developing Country Trade Policy Reform and the WTO', *Cato Journal*, vol 19, no 3, pp403–423

Saloma, J. S. (1984) *Ominous Politics: The New Conservative Labyrinth*, Hill and Wang, New York

Sanger, D. E. (1995) 'How Washington Inc Makes a Sale', *New York Times*, 19 February, p3(1)

Santoro, M. A. and Paine, L. S. (1995) *Pfizer: Global Protection of Intellectual Property*, Harvard Business School, www.hbsp.harvard.edu

Saraswati, M. S. (2004) 'Court Annuls New Electricity Law', *Jakarta Post*, 16 December, www.thejakartapost.com/detailweekly.asp?fileid=20041216.@02

Sauvé, P. and Stern, R. M. (eds) (2000) *GATS 2000: New Directions in Services Trade Liberalization*, Brookings Institution Press, Washington, DC

Sawer, M. (1982) 'Political Manifestations of Australian Libertarianism', in Sawer, M. (ed) *Australia and the New Right*, George Allen and Unwin, North Sydney

Schott, J. J. and Watal, J. (2000) *Decision-Making in the WTO*, Institute for International Economics, March, www.iie.com/publications/pb/pb00-2.htm

Schultz, J. (1992) 'Where are the Alternative Views?' in Horne, D. (ed) *The Trouble with Economic Rationalism*, Scribe, Newham, Vic

SDI (Susan Davis International) (2003a) *Recent and Present Clients*, SDI, www.susandavis. com/newpage1.htm, accessed 8 June 2003

SDI (2003b) *About Us*, SDI, www.susandavis.com/aboutusdi.htm, accessed 8 June 2003

Select Committee to Study Governmental Operations with Respect to Intelligence Activities (1975) *Church Report: Covert Action in Chile 1963–1973*, Department of State, United States Senate, 18 December 1975

Self, P. (1993) *Government by the Market? The Politics of Public Choice*, Macmillan, Hampshire and London

Senate Committee on Education and Labor (1939) *Violations of Free Speech and Rights of Labor*, Senate Committee on Education and Labor, 14 August, pp208–209

Shesgreen, D. (1998) 'Can States Set Trade Policy?' *Legal Times*, 17 August, www.citizen. org/print_article.cfm?ID=1616

Silverstein, K. (1998) 'So You Want to Trade with a Dictator', *Mother Jones*, May/June, www.bsd.mojones.com/mother_jones/MJ98/silverstein.html

Sklair, L. (2002) *Globalization: Capitalism and Its Alternatives*, Oxford University Press, Oxford

Sklar, H. (ed) (1980) *Trilateralism: The Trilateral Commission and Elite Planning for World Management*, South End Press, Cambridge, MA

Slaughter, M. J. (2002) Technology, Trade and Investment: The Public Opinion Disconnect, Emergency Committee for American Trade, www.ecattrade.com/ publications/mainstay_study_IV.pdf

Smith, J. A. (1991) *The Idea Brokers: Think Tanks and the Rise of the New Policy Elite*, Free Press, New York

Spartacus Educational (2005) *John Connally*, Spartacus Educational, www.spartacus. schoolnet.co.uk/JFKconnally.htm, accessed 16 August 2005

Spicer, B., Emanuel, D. and Powell, M. (1996) *Transforming Government Enterprises: Managing Radical Organisational Change in Deregulated Environments*, Centre for Independent Studies, St Leonards, NSW

Sridhar, V. (1999) 'Big Business at Work', *Frontline*, 11–24 December, www.frontlineonnet. com/fl1626/1626180.htm

Startup, J. (1995) 'An Agenda for International Investment', in *OECD Documents: The New World Trading System: Readings*, OECD, Paris

Steinberg, R. H. (2002) 'In the Shadow of Law or Power? Consensus-Based Bargaining and Outcomes in the GATT/WTO', *International Organization*, vol 56, no 2, pp339–374

Stiglitz, J. E. (2002) *Globalization and Its Discontents*, W. W. Norton and Co, New York

Stilwell, F. (1993) 'Economic Rationalism: Sound Foundations for Policy?' in Rees, S., Rodley, G. and Stilwell, F. (eds) *Beyond the Market: Alternatives to Economic Rationalism*, Pluto Press, Leichhardt, NSW

Stoesz, D. (1987) 'Policy Gambit: Conservative Think Tanks Take on the Welfare State', *Journal of Sociology and Social Welfare*, vol 14, no 4, pp3–20

Stone, P. H. (1994a) 'Friends, After All', *The National Journal*, vol 26, no 43, p2440

Stone, P. H. (1994b) 'GATT-ling Guns', *The National Journal*, vol 26, no 27, p1571

Suez (2004) *2003 Annual Report*, Suez, www.suez.com/documents/english/ docderef2003en/SUEZ_RA2003_chap4_EN.pdf

Summers, L. (1997) 'America's Role in Global Economic Integration', Paper presented at the Integrating National Economies: The Next Step, The Brookings Institution, Washington, DC, 9 January 1997

Sustainable Energy and Economic Network (2002) *Enron's Pawns: How Public Institutions Bankrolled Enron's Globalization Game*, Institute for Policy Studies, Washington, DC, 22 March, www.seen.org/PDFs/pawns.pdf

TABD (TransAtlantic Business Dialogue) (2002a) *TABD History: 1995–2002*, TABD, www.tabd.com/history.html

TABD (2002b) *The TABD in 2002*, TABD, www.tabd.com/about/about.html

TABD (2004) *About the TABD*, TABD, www.tabd.com/about, accessed 6 November 2004

Taft, B. (1987) 'The New Right in Practice', in Coghill, K. (ed) *The New Right's Australian Fantasy*, McPhee Gribble and Penguin Books, Fitzroy, Victoria

Talbott, S. (2002) 'The Brookings Institution: How a Think Tank Works', *US Foreign Policy Agenda*, vol 7, no 3, http://usinfo.state.gov/journals/itps/1102/ijpe/pj73talbott.htm

Tasman Economics (2002) *Our Founders*, Tasman Economics, www.tasman.com.au/founders/founders.htm, accessed 26 June 2002

Tasman Institute (2001) *About Us/Projects*, Tasman Institute, www.tasman.com.au/main/a_nz.html, accessed 20 July 2001

Texas Instruments (1996) *Jerry R. Junkins*, Texas Instruments, www.ti.com/corp/docs/press/company/1996/jrjobit.shtml

The Ecologist (2000) 'Who Cares About Global Trade?' *The Ecologist*, May, pp16–19

The Ecologist (2003) 'Europe Forbids Sell-Off Debate', *The Ecologist*, March, 2003, p7

Third World Resurgence (1990) 'Titanic Battle for the World's Future', *Third World Resurgence*, November, pp24–26

Third World Resurgence (1998a) 'The Need to Regulate Foreign Investment', *Third World Resurgence*, vol 90/91, 1998, p17

Third World Resurgence (1998b) '565 Groups Say "No" to MAI', *Third World Resurgence*, vol 90/91, 1998, pp23–24

Thomas, S. (1996a) 'Strategic Government and Corporate Issues', in Surrey, J. (ed) *The British Electricity Experiment*, Earthscan Publications, London

Thomas, S. (1996b) 'The Privatization of the Electricity Supply Industry', in Surrey, J. (ed) *The British Electricity Experiment*, Earthscan Publications, London

Thompson, E. (1992) 'Where is the Economy?' in Horne, D. (ed) *The Trouble with Economic Rationalism*, Scribe, Newham, Victoria

Toussaint, E. (1998) *Your Money or Your Life! The Tyranny of Global Finance*, translated by R. Krishnan, Pluto Press, London

UN (United Nations) (1948) *Universal Declaration of Human Rights*, UN, www.un.org/Overview/rights.html

United Brotherhood (2005) *Labor History*, United Brotherhood of Carpenters and Joiners of America, www.local157.com/history.htm, accessed 16 August 2005

USA*Engage (2003) *About Us*, USA*Engage, www.usaengage.org/about_us/index.html, accessed 29 May 2003

USCIB (US Council for International Business) (1995) *USCIB Applauds Launch of OECD Negotiations on Multilateral Investment Agreement*, USCIB, 24 May, www.uscib.org/dboecdnego.asp

USCIB (1998a) *Civil Society and Trade Negotiations: A Business Perspective*, USCIB September, www.uscib.org/civsocst.asp

USCIB (1998b) *Summary of US Council Recommendations for the May WTO Ministerial*, USCIB, May, www.uscib.org/wtost.asp

USCIB (2002) 'Adoption of Trade Promotion Authority – A Big Step Forward', *USCIB E–Newsletter*, August/September, www.envoynews.com/uscib/e_article000092118. cfm

USCIB (2003a) *Policy Advocacy*, USCIB, www.uscib.org/index.asp?documentID=824, accessed 18 May 2003

USCIB (2003b) *About USCIB*, USCIB, www.uscib.org/index.asp?documentID=697, accessed 18 May 2003

USCSI (Coalition of Service Industries) (1999) *Services 2000 USTR Federal Register Submission*, Submission to Federal Register Notice, FR Doc. 98-22279: Solicitation of Public Comment Regarding US preparations for the World Trade Organization's Ministerial Meeting, www.uscsi.org/publications/papers/services_2000_ustr-federal. htm

USCSI (2003a) *About CSI*, USCSI, www.uscsi.org/about/, accessed 2 May 2003

USCSI (2003b) *Membership*, USCSI, www.uscsi.org/members/, accessed 2 May 2003

USCSI (2003c) *CSI Foundation*, USCSI, www.uscsi.org/csifoundation/, accessed 2 May 2003

USCSI (2003d) *Services 2000*, USCSI, www.uscsi.org/events/services2000conf.html, accessed 2 May 2003

USCSI (2004) *The Financial Leaders Group/Financial Leaders Working Group*, USCSI, www.uscsi.org/groups/finLeader.htm, accessed 30 October 2004

USDA (US Department of Agriculture) (2003) *US and Cooperating Countries File WTO Case Against EU Moratorium on Biotech Food and Crops*, USDA, 13 May, www.usda. gov/news/releases/2003/05/0156.htm

Useem, M. (1984) *The Inner Circle: Large Corporations and the Rise of Business Political Activity in the US and UK*, Oxford University Press, Oxford

US House Committee on Ways and Means Trade Subcommittee (2000) *Prepared Statement by Thomas M.T. Niles, President, United States Council for International Business*, US House Committee on Ways and Means Trade Subcommittee, 8 February 2000

US News and World Report (1977) 'Why Business Finds it Tough to Polish its Own Image', *US News and World Report*, 19 September 1977, p64

US Senate Finance Committee (1999) *Prepared Statement by Abraham Katz, President, United States Council for International Business*, US Senate Finance Committee, 28 January 1999

US Trade (US Alliance for Trade Expansion) (1999) *Unique Coalition Formed to Support Trade: Alliance to Promote Benefits of Trade, Importance of WTO Ministerial*, USCIB, 15 April 1999, www.uscib.org/index.asp?documentID=1376

US Trade (2002a) *US Trade*, IDFA, 10 May 2002, www.idfa.org/intl/ustrade.cfm

US Trade (2002b) *Unique Coalition Formed to Support Trade*, US Trade

Van Bennedom, S. and Van Brakel, M. (1992) *Will GATT Undermine UNCED? An Analysis of the Environmental Implications of GATT Policies*, Friends of the Earth Netherlands, Amsterdam

van der Pijl, K. (1998) *Transnational Classes and International Relations*, Routledge, London

Vastine, R. (1997) 'Hearing on World Trade Organization Singapore Ministerial Meeting', in *Subcommittee on Trade of the House Committee on Ways and Means*, House Committee on Ways and Means, waysandmeans.house.gov/legacy/trade/105cong/2-26-97/2-26vast.htm

Vastine, R. (1999) *Statement of Robert Vastine, President, Coalition of Service Industries*, Senate Finance Committee Subcommittee on International Trade, 21 October 1999

Vastine, R. (2002) 'Trade Remedy System Under the WTO Framework: Functions and Mechanism, the Role of Trade Associations', Paper presented at the 2002 Annual Conference of the Advisory Committee of the Shanghai WTO Affairs Consultation Center and 2002 WTO Forum, Shanghai, 5–7 November

Veolia Environnement (2004a) *Veolia Water*, Veolia Environnement, www. veoliaenvironnement.com/en/activities/water/, accessed 5 January 2004

Veolia Environnement (2004b) *Waste Management*, Veolia Environnement, www. veoliaenvironnement.com/en/activities/Waste, accessed 5 January 2004

Vintila, P. (1992) 'Markets, Morals and Manifestos', in Vintila, P., Phillimore, J. and Newman, P. (eds) *Markets, Morals and Manifestos: Fightback! and the Politics of Economic Rationalism in the 1990s*, Institute for Science and Technology Policy, Murdoch University, Murdoch, WA

Vogel, D. (1989) *Fluctuating Fortunes: The Political Power of Business in America*, Basic Books, New York

Wade, R. (2001) 'Showdown at the World Bank', *New Left Review*, January/February, www.globalpolicy.org/socecon/bwi–wto/wbank/2001/rwade.htm

Walker, S. H. and Sklar, P. (1938) *Business Finds Its Voice: Management's Effort to Sell the Business Idea to the Public*, Harper and Brothers, New York and London

Wallach, L. and Sforza, M. (1999) *The WTO: Five Years of Reasons to Resist Corporate Globalization*, G. Ruggiero (ed) The Open Media Pamphlet Series, Seven Stories Press, New York

Walsh, J. (2002) *The $10 Billion Jolt*, Silver Lake Publishing, Los Angeles

Wanna, J. (1992) 'Furthering Business Interests: Business Associations and Political Representation', in Bell, S. and Wanna, J. (eds) *Business–Government Relations in Australia*, Harcourt Brace Jovanovich, Sydney

Waste Management (2004) *Fact Sheet*, Waste Management, Inc, www.wm.com/WM/Press/MediaKit/facts.pdf

WDM (World Development Movement) (2001) *The Missing Link: Debt and Trade*, WDM, 3 February, www.wdm.org.uk/cambriefs/Debt/misslink.pdf

WDM (2004) *New Deal Exposes Flaws of Trade (Offs) System*, WDM, 1 August, www. wdm.org.uk/presrel/current/wtoframework_08.04.htm

Weaver, R. K. (1989) 'The Changing World of Think Tanks', *PS: Political Science and Politics*, vol 22, September, pp563–578

Weeks, J. (1994) 'Credit Where Discredit is Due', *Third World Resurgence*, April, pp32–34

WEF (World Economic Forum) (2000) *World Economic Forum*, WEF, www.weforum. org/ 2000

WEF (2005) *Global Competitiveness Report*, WEF, www.weforum.org/site/homepublic. nsf/Content/Global+Competitiveness+Programme%5CGlobal+Competitiveness+Report, accessed 6 February 2005

Weissman, R. (2002) 'The Anatomy of a Deal', *Multinational Monitor*, September, pp18–24

Wesselius, E. (2001) *Liberalisation of Trade in Services: Corporate Power at Work*, GATSwatch, www.gatswatch.org/LOTIS/LOTIS.html

Wesselius, E. (2002) *Behind GATS 2000: Corporate Power at Work*, Transnational Institute, Amsterdam, May, www.tni.org/reports/wto/wto4.pdf

Wexler and Walker Public Policy Associates (2003a) *International Trade*, Wexler and Walker Public Policy Associates, www.wexlergroup.com/trade_p.htm, accessed 8 June 2003

Wexler and Walker Public Policy Associates (2003b) *Coalitions and Grassroots*, Wexler and Walker Public Policy Associates, www.wexlergroup.com/coal_p.htm, accessed 8 June 2003

Wheat, A. (1994) 'A Year in the Life of the GATT Business Lobby', *Multinational Monitor*, October, www.multinationalmonitor.org/hyper/issues/1994/10//mm1094_05.html

Wheat, A. (2002) 'System Failure: Deregulation, Political Corruption, Corporate Fraud and the Enron Debacle', *Multinational Monitor*, January/February, pp34–44

Whitfield, D. (1983) *Making It Public: Evidence and Action Against Privatisation*, Pluto Press, London

Whitwell, G. (1993) 'Economic Ideas and Economic Policy: The Rise of Economic Rationalism in Australia', *Australian Economic History Review*, vol 33, no 2, pp8–28

Wikipedia: The Free Encyclopedia (2004) 'Koch Industries', in *Wikipedia: The Free Encyclopedia*, 16 November 2004, www.en.wikipedia.org/wiki/Koch_Industries

Williams, P. (1987) 'New Right Exerts its Power on Liberals', *Financial Review*, 17 December, p10

Williams, P. and Ellis, S. (1994) 'Dawkins Kisses and Tells on BCA', *The Australian Financial Review*, 15 July, pp1, 8

Williamson, J. (1994a) (ed) *The Political Economy of Policy Reform*, Institute for International Economics, Washington, DC

Williamson, J. (1994b) 'In Search of a Manual for Technopols', in Williamson, J. (ed) *The Political Economy of Policy Reform*, Institute for International Economics, Washington, DC, p20

Witherell, W. H. (1996) 'An Agreement on Investment', *The OECD Observer*, vol 202, pp6–9

Woodward, D. (2003) 'Financial Effects of Foreign Direct Investment in the Context of a Possible WTO Agreement on Investment', Paper presented at the NGO Workshop on WTO Negotiations on Investment and New Issues, Geneva, 18–19 March

WTO (World Trade Organization) (2003) *Mike More, WTO Director-General, 1999–2002*, WTO, www.wto.org/english/thewto_e/dg_e/mm_e.htm, accessed 4 June 2003

WTO Panel (2004a) *Mexico – Measures Affecting Telecommunications Services [Edited]*, WTO, 2 April 2004, www.internationaltraderelations.com/WTO.Mexico%20Telecom%20Case%20(Panel%202004).htm

WTO Panel (2004b) *United States – Measures Affecting the Cross-Border Supply of Gambling and Betting Services*, WTO, 10 November 2004, p135

WTOWatch (2004) 'Highlights of the US-Gambling Decision', *WTOWatch*, 2 December 2004

Yafie, R. C. (1999) 'Cerebral, Tough Exec Helped US Steel Grow', *American Metal Market*, 1 February, www.findarticles.com/p/articles/mi_m3MKT/is_18_107/ai_53691842

Zedillo, E. (2000) 'Unholy Alliance Against Development', *World Link*, March/April, www.josepinera.com/pag/pag_tex_unholy.htm

Zeller, S. (2003) 'Dutko's story: A testament to its founder', *The National Journal*, vol 35, no 10, pp748–749

Zumwalt, J. P. (1996) *Pressure Politics and Free Trade: Influence of the Services Industry on the Uruguay Round*, National Defense University, 16 December, www.ndu.edu/library/n1/97-E-32.pdf

Index